Panchayati Raj and Decentralised Planning

Dimensions and Development

Panchayati Raj and Decentralised Planning

Dimensions and Development

Dr. Parikshit Sahu

Kaveri Books
New Delhi-110002

First Published in 2021

ISBN: 978-81-7479-239-6

Published by

Kaveri Books

4832/24, Ansari Road
New Delhi - 110 002 (India)
Tel.: 011-2328 8140, 4707 2321
E-mail: info@kaveribooks.com
kaveribooks@gmail.com
Website: www.kaveribooks.com

Laser Typesetting by :
Tamalika Computers, Delhi

PRINTED IN INDIA

Acknowledgements

For publication of this book, I would like to give thanks to my well-wisher and guide Smt. Radhika Rastogi, IAS, Deputy Director General, NIRD & PR, Government of India, my teachers Prof. Kumar B. Das, Ex-VC, FM University and Prof. Padmaja Mishra, VC, Ramadevi Women University, Odisha and my elders Dr.Himanshu Sekhar Rout, Prof. A & A Economics, Utkal University, Sri. Pradeep Kumar Ray, Deputy Director, AIIMS, Bhubaneswar, my younger brother, Dr.Amarendra Das, Associate Professor, NISER, Bhubaneswar, Dr.Pratyushna Pattnayak, Asst. Prof, NIRD & PR. No words can adequately express my gratitude to Sri Manas Ranjan Debata, Additional Secretary to Government, PR & DW Department, Government of Odisha for generating a perennial interest in me for this publication. I must give thanks to Dr.Tapas Mishra, Professor and Head of Finance and Econometrics, Southampton Business School, Southampton University, UK for his inspiration for this publication. Moreover, I never forget the support of my dearest friend Mr. Akhil Kumar Mishra, IIS, Director, Regional Outreach Bureau, Bhubaneswar, Ministry of I&B, Govt. of India for this new creation. Similarly, I would like to give my sincere thanks to all my Utkal University friends for their moral support for this publication.

It would be a pride to appreciate the contribution of my wife Smt.Sasmita Sahoo, who inspired confidence in me to prosper in future against all trials and tribulations. Moreover, it would be injustice, if I will not give my sincere thanks to my beloved son MMP Shubhrakant (Bubu), who always takes pride in my achievements in all aspects of life and imbibes extraterrestrial effect on me. In addition to this, I would like to acknowledge the inspiration of my father-in-law Sri.Laxmidhar Sahoo, Sri. Dibakar Sahoo, Ex-Prof (History), my youngers Sri. Subash Chandra Sahoo, Ayashkant, Preetikrishna, PTS Kharabel, Luna, Duna, Liza, Pinki & Shreya for writing of this book.

Further, I would like to extend my heartiest thanks to my Principal Secretary, PR & DW Department, Government of Odisha, Director, Joint Director, Assistant Directors and all my colleagues of SIRD & PR for their support in this regard. I would like to acknowledge my hearty thanks to Mr. Abhishek Goel, the publisher of this book for his splendid works to bring this book for the readers in right time. Last but not the least; I would like to extend my debt to those friends and relatives who have rendered their altruistic support directly or indirectly for this new creation.

I shall welcome any suggestions from all quarters that may improve the utility and usefulness of this book. I will feel amply rewarded if this piece of book motivates a band of young development professionals, researchers, economists, government officials and the like on their way to work for the betterment and development of the people in particular and the nation or economy in general.

Dr. Parikshit Sahu

Foreword

Panchayats have always been an integral part of Indian local administration since ancient times. Inmacro perspective, efforts have been made to strengthen the Panchayati Raj system by promoting social harmony, foster farmers' welfare, support livelihoods of the poor and enhance rural development. The establishment of Panchayati Raj has planned towards the organized development that depends on the acceptance of change.This change can only be achieved with active participation of the people in the decision making process. Panchayati Raj can be a harbinger for such change. The local bodies serve as the best schools of citizenship and will increase the people's confidence in the working of democratic institutions by providing them the required training. These local bodies teach the people to take initiative to solve their problems without depending upon external agencies. It is, therefore, aptly said that good governance is no substitute for self-government.

The crucial objective of rural development will be achieved if the people are directly associated with the schemes or programmes. Planning of a scheme should be done at the local level by the PRIs keeping in view the veritable needs of the people. Identification ofbeneficiaries should be selected by them at the local level. Therefore, the philosophy of rural development, people's participation, Panchayati Raj and decentralized planning are closely interwoven. Healthy integration & bonding among these units would enrich the concept & prospect of a comprehensive development of the villages.

The government should make all out efforts to devolve funds, functions, and functionaries to panchayats, to prepare a holistic & pragmatic plan to ensure economic development and social justice. For accomplishment of the prime objectives of rural development, planning must be devised at the grassroots level associating the people. Hence, more the integration between grassroots planning agencies and the Panchayati Raj, greater is the prospect of the outcome of development. Participatory development plans attempted with a bottom-up approach has yielded better results in terms of reduction of social and gender disparities, judicious distribution and use of resources, equal development opportunities to all as against the top down approach of planning.

Dr. Parikshit Sahu is bringing out a very meditative book entitled "Panchayati Raj and Decentralised Planning: Dimensions and Development" with a clear manifestation of the area specific issues in the Panchayati Raj system in India. I am really very happy to see that the book has a number of chapters and is replete with the major critical areas. In this book Dr.Sahu has analyzed the concepts like73rd Amendment Act of Indian Constitution, the role of PRIs to achieve Sustainable Development Goals (SDGs), different developmental initiatives by government under the aegis of Panchayati Raj, process of capacity building of PRI members, system of community mobilization in PESA area, decentralized planning and importance of Gram Panchayat Development Plan (GPDP) in India and so on. I am sanguine that the readers will be amply benefited by reading these vigilantly drafted chapters by Dr. Sahu containing the fundamental knowledge as well as the recent developmental trends of Panchayati Raj system in India with an in-depth logical analysis and concerted practical support.

I wish the author for such endeavour and the readers, scholars to enrich the horizon of their knowledge.

Manas Ranjan Debata, OAS (SAG)
Additional Secretary to Government,
Panchayati Raj & Drinking Water Department,
Government of Odisha

Preface

Panchayati Raj system is an innovative mechanism to bridge the cavernous gap between the decision making centers and the centers of action. In real sense, the Panchayat Raj is a South Asian political system mainly operative in India, Pakistan, and Nepal. Traditionally, the Panchayats were meant to settled disputes between individuals and villages. Indian government has decentralized several administrative functions to the village level, empowering elected Gram Panchayats particularly after the enactment of 73rd Constitutional Amendment Act, 1992. The spirit of decentralization calls for preparation of plans and their implementation by involving people through a participatory bottom up approach. The 73rd and 74th Constitutional Amendment Acts have paved a way to evolve new system of governance in Panchayat Raj and Local self-government which has mandated local planning at the Gram Panchayat, Taluk Panchayat and District Panchayat levels as well as at urban local governments.

Since the Panchayati Raj Institutions fall under the state subject and each state is free to evolve its own system depending on local conditions, administrative convenience and so on. The local level governance varies from state to state as they are regulated mainly by the State Panchayati Raj Acts. As a result, there are varieties of Panchayati Raj Institutions in India with all kinds of permutations and combinations. Their success or failure mostly depends on their structures, powers, functions, leadership, finances and control. Panchayats have been mandated for ensuring economic development as well as social justice and for implementing Central and State Government Schemes including those 29 subjects listed in the Eleventh Schedule of the Constitution. In one hand, there is a commitment for decentralisation of power and suspicion or fear that such power would be misused by the local bodies in other hand and hence, a number of checks and balances have been envisaged by the states.

If we look into the deeper part of the subject, it can be seen that the basic purpose of Panchayati Raj Institutions has not yet been achieved. The problem would not end by making the Panchayati Raj Institution economically self-sufficient and structurally sound. The most important aspect is change at the attitudinal pattern, public behavior and ownership of public property. Otherwise, decentralization would remain only in papers.

The existing socio-economic structure of the Indian society is a major factor which is responsible for the limited success of Panchayati Raj Institutions. If we really want that the benefits of the Panchayati Raj Institutions have to reach the poor and if the poor are to be associated with the Panchayati Raj Institutions, it is necessary to strengthen their position by adopting certain need base and area specific measures. It is necessary to identify the areas of dependence of the poor and find measures to stop exploitation. Streamlining the public distribution system, social security measures, employment guarantee schemes, development in social sectors like education, health care, sanitation, rural infrastructure, housing, redistribution of assets in favour of the poor by implementing land reform laws and creation of assets to the poor through schemes like Mahatma Gandhi NREGA and so on.

Further, the expertise available to the Panchayati Raj Institutions is very limited particularly in the field of planning, implementation or monitoring of various developmental schemes. The most important problem faced by the Panchayati Raj Institutions is regarding finances. It is needless to mention that the quality and variety of activities which the Panchayati Raj Institutions are expected to perform will depend mostly on the resources at their command. The resource base would depend on the local economy and partly upon the allocations made by the state and central government. Moreover, the Panchayati Raj Institutions have a very limited scope to impose taxes in their jurisdiction. Similarly, the financial system and conditions of the states are also not symmetric. The Panchayati Raj Institutions have to look towards the higher authorities for necessary grants. The real danger lies in the discrepancy between resources and responsibilities as in the name of decentralization; more and more functions are transferred to the Panchayati Raj Institutions. The centre or the states should come forward with the same vigour to transferring resources proportionately.

Many vital issues like the ownership of minor forest produce, planning and management of minor water bodies, prevention of alienation of tribal lands etc., which have been duly recognized in PESA as the traditional rights of tribals living in the scheduled areas have still not received attention and the necessary correctives remain unapplied. PESA posed a totally new set of challenges before the members of PRIs. It creates the opportunities for enabling participation and capacity building of the elected representatives and the government functionaries, NGOs and the CSOs working in the Schedule-V areas. Central government should take appropriate action to eliminate the loopholes in the central legislation followed by a strong direction to abide by the constitutional mandate. State governments should follow the guidelines issued by the central government to incorporate changes in the state acts and take appropriate measures to amend state laws which are in conflict with the provisions of PESA. The essence of these initiatives of the government have been clearly analyzed in the book rightly through different chapters.

The book "Panchayati Raj and Decentralised Planning: Dimensions and Development" has enriched with seven chapters that tries to analyze the fundamental concepts and problems, genesis of Panchayati Raj system in India during pre and post independence era, 73rd Amendment Act of Indian Constitution, the role of PRIs to achieve Sustainable Development Goals (SDGs) have also been analyzed vividly. Moreover, different developmental initiatives by government under the aegis of Panchayati Raj, capacity building of PRI members, system of community mobilisation in PESA area and importance of Gram Panchayat Development Plan (GPDP) to ensure economic development and social justice have been clearly discussed in the book.

The Panchayati Raj Institutions are the real platforms for implementing the rural development programmes at the grass root level. Proper implementation of these programmes will improve the socio-economic conditions of the rural poor i.e. their per capita income will be increased, followed by increase in their purchasing power, demand for goods and services, level of production and employment in the economy. Ultimately it will boost up the national income and will make India as a developed nation in the global scenario.

Dr. Parikshit Sahu

Contents

Abbreviations

AAPs	-	Annual Action Plans
AAY	-	Antyodaya Anna Yojana
ACA	-	Additional Central Assistance
ANMs	-	Auxiliary Nurse Midwives
ARWSP	-	Accelerated Rural Water Supply Programme
BR	-	Block Resource Centres
BRGF	-	Backward Regions Grant Funds
BTCs	-	Block Training Centres
CAA	-	Constitutional Amendment Act
CB&T	-	Capacity Building and Training
CBOs	-	Community Based Organisations
CDP	-	Community Development Programmes
CRF	-	Calamity Relief Fund
CRPs	-	Community Resource Persons
CSR	-	Corporate Social Responsibility
CSSs	-	Centrally Sponsored Schemes
CVC	-	Customary Village Council
DAY-NRLM	-	Deen Dayal Antyodaya Yojana-National Rural Livelihood Mission
DDU-GJY	-	Deen Dayal Upadhyaya Gram Jyoti Yojana
DI	-	Devolution Index
DIET	-	District Institutes of Educational Training
DPCs	-	District Planning Committees
DPRC	-	District Panchayat Resource Centre
DRG	-	District Resource Group
EADs	-	Extremist Affected Districts

EO	-	Executive Officer
ETCs	-	Extension Training Centres
EVMs	-	Electronic Voting Machines
EWRs	-	Elected Women Representatives
FAQs	-	Frequently Asked Questions
FC	-	Finance Commission
FDI	-	Foreign Direct Investment
FIES	-	Food Insecurity Experience Scale
FRA	-	Forest Rights Act
FRC	-	Forest Rights Committee
GCC	-	Girijan Cooperative Corporation
GIS	-	Geographic Information System
GNI	-	Gross National Income
GPDP	-	Gram Panchayat Development Plan
GPPFT	-	Gram Panchayat Planning Facilitation Team
GSDA	-	Ground Surveyor and Development Authority
GSSK	-	Gram Sabha Sashaktikaran Karyakrama
GST	-	Goods and Services Tax
IAY	-	Indira Awaas Yojana
ICDS	-	Integrated Child Development Scheme
ICT	-	Information and Communication Technology
IEC	-	Information, Education and Communication
IGNOU	-	Indira Gandhi National Open University
IRRAD	-	Institute of Rural Research & Development
IWMP	-	Integrated Watershed Management Programme
JSY	-	Janani Suraksha Yojana
LSG	-	Local Self-Governance
MDGs	-	Millennium Development Goals
MLA	-	Members of Legislative Assembly
MMP	-	Mission Mode Project
MoPR	-	Ministry of Panchayati Raj
MOSPI	-	Ministry of Statistics & Programme Implementation
MP	-	Members of Parliament
MRPs	-	Master Resource Persons
MTFP	-	Medium Term Fiscal Plan

NCBF	-	National Capability Building Frame work
NCCD	-	National Calamity Contingent Duty
NCCF	-	National Calamity Contingency Fund
NDMA	-	National Disaster Management Authority
NDMF	-	National Disaster Mitigation Fund
NDRF	-	National Disaster Response Force
NeGP	-	National e-Governance Plan
NIELIT	-	National Institute of Electronics and Information Technology
NIRD&PR	-	National Institutes of Rural Development & Panchayati Raj
NITI Aayog	-	National Institute for Transforming India Aayog
NMEW	-	National Mission for Empowerment of Women
NMSA	-	National Mission for Soil and Agriculture
NPMU	-	National Programme Management Unit
NPTA	-	National Plan for Technical Assistance
NRLM	-	National Rural Livelihood Mission
NSDP	-	National Skill Development Programme
NSSK	-	Navjat Shisu Suraksha Karyakram
NWFPs	-	Non-Wood Forest Products
OECD	-	Organization for Economic Cooperation and Development
OSR	-	Own Source of Revenue
PAHELI	-	People's Assessment of Health and Livelihoods
PAL	-	Panchayat at Appropriate Level
PC	-	Planning Commission
PEAIS	-	Panchayat Empowerment and Accountability Incentive Scheme
PES	-	Panchayat Enterprise Suite
PESA	-	Panchayat (Extension to Scheduled Areas) Act
PL	-	Prospecting licence
PMEYSA	-	Panchayat Mahila Evam Yuva Shakti Abhiyan
PMKSY	-	Pradhan Mantri Krishi Sinchayee Yojana
PRA	-	Participatory Rural Appraisal
PRIs	-	Panchayati Raj Institutions
PTCs	-	Panchayat Training Centres

RADPFI	-	Rural Area Development and Plan Formulation and Implementation
RGGVY	-	Rajiv Gandhi Grameen Vidyutikaran Yojana
RGPSA	-	Rajiv Gandhi Panchayat Sashaktikaran Abhiyan
RGSA	-	Rashtriya Gram Swaraj Abhiyan
RGSY	-	Rashtriya Gram Swaraj Yojana
RKVY	-	Rashtriya Krishi Vikas Yojana
RSS	-	Resource Support to State
SAT	-	Systematic Approach to Training
SBA	-	Swachh Bharat Abhiyan
SCERT	-	State Council of Educational Research and Training
SCP	-	Sustainable Consumption and Production
SCs	-	Scheduled Castes
SDF	-	Sustainable Development Framework
SDGs	-	Sustainable Development Goals
SDMF	-	State Disaster Mitigation Fund
SEC	-	State Election Commission
SFC	-	State Finance Commission
SHGs	-	Self-Help Groups
SIRD	-	State Institutes of Rural Development
SITs	-	Satellite Interactive Terminals
SLMTT	-	State Level Master Trainers' Team
SLO	-	State Link Officer
SPMU	-	State Programme Management Unit
SPRC	-	State Panchayat Resource Centre
SSA	-	Sarva Shiksha Abhiyan
STs	-	Scheduled Tribes
TFR	-	Total Fertility Rate
TIA	-	Training Impact Assessment
TMD	-	Training Material Development
TNA	-	Training Needs Assessment
ToR	-	Terms of Reference
UEDs	-	Union Excise Duties
VSS	-	Van Suraksha Samiti

1

Panchayati Raj System in India

"When the Panchayat Raj is established, public opinion will do what violence can never do."

— ***Mahatma Gandhi***

Introduction

Political decentralization generally means strong and vibrant means of local government. Panchayat Raj, a synonym of democratic decentralization, was introduced in India in the late 1950s and early 1960s to restore to the earlier institution of Panchayat the immaculate glory that it enjoyed in ancient India. It was introduced by 73rd Amendment to the Constitution and formally recognized the three-tiers of government at the sub-state level, thereby creating the legal conditions for local self-rule or Panchayati Raj. India has a history starting from self-sufficient and self-governing village communities that survived the rise and fall of empires in the past to the modern institutions of governance with constitutional support. Though the basic structure of the Panchayat Raj Institutions is identical across the states of India, it is described via different nomenclatures in different states. Every panchayat has its own characteristic features and their working style also differs from one another.

The system of Panchayati Raj has been the hub of the Indian civilization since the early of Indian history. The ancient holy books like Rigveda, Manusamhita, Upanishads, Jatakas, Satapath Brahman etc. refer extensively to local self administration and in those days village was considered as the basic unit of government and it enjoyed complete autonomy. Records revealed that even a king did not dare to interfere in the local affairs of the villages. The importance of Panchayati Raj should be obvious in a country where four, out of every five citizens live in the villages and where the incidence of poverty is much higher than in towns. Thoughts on rural local governments or Panchayati Raj are thus an integral part of the concern for social and economic amelioration of the rural people. Panchayati Raj system is an innovative mechanism to bridge the vast gap between the decision-making centres and the centres of action.

The history of Panchayati Raj Institutions since 1959 could be conveniently divided into four phases: the phase of ascendancy (1959-64), the phase of stagnation (1965-69), the phase of decline (1969-83) and the phase of revival (1983-onwards). The overall attempts to revive the Panchayati Raj Institutions could be witnessed to the last phase when the Ashok Mehta Committee Report (1978) has evoked interest among the politicians and people alike in the year 1983. Panchayati Raj is a state subject. Hence, each state is free to evolve its own system depending on local conditions, administrative convenience etc. As a result, we have a variety of Panchayati Raj Institutions throughout the country with all kinds of permutations and combinations. Their success or failure mostly depends on their structures, powers, functions, leadership, finances, control etc. A general review of the working of Panchayati Raj Institutions would provide valuable insight into the different aspects of these institutions. Changes in different aspects of these bodies have been taking place as per the changing circumstances.

Evolution of Panchayati Raj in India

The term "Panchayat" literally means assembly (yat) of five (panch) wise and respected elders chosen and accepted by the village community. Traditionally, these assemblies settled disputes between individuals and villages. Modern Indian government has decentralized several administrative functions to the village level, empowering elected gram panchayats particularly after the enactment of 73rd Constitution Amendment Act, 1992. An elementary level of local self-government had long been operative in India since the Vedic times. However, with the passage of time, the nature, character and role of the local self-government have undergone a change. Mahatma Gandhi advocated Panchayati Raj as the foundation of India's political system, as a decentralized form of government in which each village would be responsible for its own affairs. Instead, India developed a highly centralized form of government. However, this has been moderated by the delegation of several administrative functions to the local level, empowering elected members of gram panchayat. There are significant differences between the traditional

Panchayati Raj system, that was envisioned by M K Gandhi and the system formalized in India in 1992.

The Panchayat Raj system was first adopted by the state of Rajasthan in Nagaur district on 2nd Oct 1959 but first started by Andhra Pradesh. During the 1950s and 60s, other state governments adopted this system as laws were passed to establish panchayats in various states. Maharashtra was the ninth state. It also founded backing in the Indian Constitution, with the 73rd amendment in 1992 to accommodate the idea.

In India, on 24th April 1993, the Constitutional (73rd amendment) Act 1992 came into force to provide constitutional status to the Panchayati Raj institutions. This amendment was extended to Panchayats in the tribal areas of eight states, namely: Andhra Pradesh, Gujarat, Himachal Pradesh, Maharashtra, Madhya Pradesh, Odisha and Rajasthan beginning on 24th December 1996. This amendment contains provision for devolution of powers and responsibilities to the panchayats, both for the preparation of economic development plans and social justice, as well as for implementation in relation to 29 subjects listed in the eleventh schedule of the constitution as well as the ability to levy and collect appropriate taxes, duties, tolls and fees. The act aims to provide a three-tier Panchayati Raj systems for all states having a population of over 2 million, to hold Panchayat elections regularly every five years, to provide seats reserved for scheduled castes, scheduled tribes and women; to appoint a State Finance Commission to make recommendations regarding the financial powers of the Panchayats and to constitute a District Planning Committee.

Evolution of Local Governance in India

Pre-British Local Governance

India's old sacred books and historical sources mentioned village communities (councils or assemblies) across the sub-continent, serving as the main interface between the predominantly agrarian village economies and the higher authorities. Custom and tradition elevated these earlier councils or assemblies called "Sabhas" to a position of considerable authority. Slowly, they assumed the form of the "Panchayat" (an assembly of five respected elders). These Panchayats became the pivot of administration, the focus of social solidarity and the principal forum for the dispensation of justice and resolution of local disputes. During the medieval and Mughal periods, these characteristics of the Village Panchayats remained unchanged.

Pre-Independence Panchayats

Several steps were taken during British rule in India towards setting up formal local bodies. In urban areas, a municipal corporation came to be formed in Madras-on the British model of a town council—as early as 1687.

In 1870, Lord Mayo (Governor General-in-Council) secured the passage of a resolution for the decentralization of power aimed at bringing about greater administrative efficiency in meeting the demands of the people but primarily designed to augment imperial finances. At the same time, a first significant step towards reviving the traditional village panchayat system in Bengal was taken through the Bengal Chowkidari Act, 1870 which empowered District Magistrates to set up Panchayats of nominated members in the villages.

The magna carta of local democracy in British India was the Ripon Resolution of 1882 providing for rural local boards with two-thirds of membership to be composed of elected, non-official representatives and presided over by a non-official Chairperson. Actual progress in implementation was slow but the role of rural local administration was elevated and the term "self-government" gained currency.

In 1906, the Indian National Congress, under the presidentship of Dadabhai Naoroji, affirmed "self-government" as the political goal for the country. In 1907, the government constituted a six-member Royal Commission on decentralization. The report of this commission released in 1909-elaborated the principles enunciated in the Ripon resolution and recognized the importance of Panchayats in the governance of India.

In the same year (1909), the 24th session of the congress at Lahore adopted a resolution urging the government to take early steps "to make all local bodies from village Panchayats upwards elective with elected non-official chairmen" and "to support them with adequate financial aid." At its 28th session in December 1913 in Karachi, the Congress adopted a resolution regretting that decentralization had remained largely on paper. In her presidential address at the congress session in Calcutta in 1917, Dr. Annie Besant blamed the "inefficient bureaucracy" for not doing even the little that was suggested in the Report of the Royal Commission on decentralization.

The Montagu-Chelmsford Reforms of 1919 made local self-government—under the proposed scheme of Dyarchy-a "transferred subject", is bringing self-government under the domain of Indian Ministers in the provinces. To make local self-government both fully representative and responsible, the Montagu-Chelmsford reforms suggested that there should be (as far as possible) complete popular control in local bodies and the largest possible independence for them from outside control.

The Government of India Act, 1935 and the inauguration of provincial autonomy is another crucial stage in the evolution of Panchayats. With popularly elected governments in the provinces, almost all provincial administrations enacted legislation for further democratization of local self-government institutions, including the Village Panchayats.

Panchayats during Ancient India

The Panchayati Raj system has been the pillar of rural social structure from the ancient period. In the early Vedic age, Aryans used to live in villages or grammas. The head of the village was called 'Gramini'. The affairs of the village were managed by an elected Panchayat. The Rajan or king was helped by several officers like priest (Purohit), Commander in chief (Senani) and the head of the village (Gramini) During the Gupta period, Indian society witnessed well developed system of village self administration. The lowest administrative units were the 'Kurram' (Union of villages) and 'Grama' (village) each under its own headman and his counterpart in the 'Nagarpati' of cities. In certain rural areas the village assembly consisted of the whole adult population and in other cases these were managed by Brahmins or a few great men who were selected by a king. During the Moughal administration, Akbar had inaugurated the policy of "India for Indians". During this period of socio-political turmoil there self governing institutions were relegated to a position of no-importance.

Development of Panchayats during British Period

It was the logic of events and of necessity which was mainly responsible for cropping up of a system of local administration in the early stage of British. The Act of 1858 strengthened the rule of British parliament which gave rise to certain welfare activities .The Government of India Resolution of 1870 gave a strong stimulus to the development of local self-government. This system which was introduced in 1871 was undoubtedly a remarkable improvement. This was the foundation on which the liberal regime of Lord Ripon built the superstructure of District Boards.

Ripon's Reforms

Lord Ripon's Reforms constitutes a landmark in the history of local self-government in India, for they attempted to put it for the first time on a popular or elected basis. The nominated district committees that then existed had not proved a success. Experiment proves says Ripon's Resolutions of 1882, that district committees are as a rule very badly attended by members not actually residing in the vicinity of head quarter station.

Ripon's Resolution (1881)

Lord Ripon's first scheme was elaborated in his resolution of 30th September 1881, on financial decentralization. It said that though considerable progress in the direction of local self-self government had been made since the days of Lord Mayo when the subject was first taken up it was very unequal in various provinces and that the time has now come for further practical developments.

Ripon's Resolution (1882)

Ripon's famous resolutions of 18th May 1882 have justly been regarded as the magma carta of local self-government in India. Besides, answering the objections raised to Ripon's first proposals, this resolution also contains his final and mature plan of local self-government reorganization in India (Government of India, 1882, Para-4).

The resolution recommended that the smallest administrative unit the sub-division, taluka or the tehsil-shall ordinarily to be placed under a local board (Government of India, 1882, para-10). The resolution desired the local boards to be as constituted as to have on them a predominant nonofficial majority ordinarily not less than 2/3rd of their entire membership. The term of the members was to be two years and compulsory retirement by rotation was to be provided for (Government of India, 1915, Para-12). Stimulate the candidature of men of standing courtesy titles of "Rai Bahadur" or "Rai Sahib" was allowed to the Indian members during their term of service on the local bodies.

Royal Commission on Decentralisation (1909)

The Royal Commission on Decentralization was constituted in 1909, after reviewing the marking of the local and the district boards in the various provinces of the country came to the conclusion that due chiefly to their unrepresentative character and adequate powers, these local bodies had not been success.

Government of India's Resolution (1915)

These recommendations received the attention of the Government of India in its resolution on local self-government of 1915. Referring to the liberalization of the boards constitutions, it said that the local government in general are in sympathy with the commission's proposals (Government of India Resolution-1915, para-27). The principle of elected majority on the boards was accordingly accepted, but the resolution gave no lead to the question of the reform of the board's electorates.

Montague-Chelmsford Report

This resolution on account of its extreme cautiousness was condemned on all hands as having cut down the proposals of the decentralization commission. Following the declaration of 1917 announcing substantial reforms in the direction of responsible government and the publication of Montague-Chelmsford Report(1918) containing the proposals for immediate political advance, a new significance came to be attached to the questions of local self-government

Government of India's Resolution (1918)

These proposals were ultimately embodied in Government of India's Resolution of 1918. It accepted fully and frankly the principle of substantial elective majorities on all the boards. The elective principle was to be reinforced by the democratization of the local electorate. The representation of minorities was to be secured by retaining the practice of nomination rather than by introducing some system of communal or proportional representation. Therefore, it is clear that a systematic effort was made during the British rule to build and strengthen the institutions of Local Self-Government. But it was designed to suit the colonial masters. In spite of these efforts the institutions did not emerge as the true centre of weakness.

Post-Independence Development of Panchayats

While outlining his vision of free India which instantly captivated Indian masses as well as sophisticated intellectuals-Mahatma Gandhi was careful to state that his concept of "Ramrajya of which Panchayat autonomy was an integral component was not derived from any specific historical period but was rather an "ideal construct" based on mixture of the best features of diverse periods of ancient history.

The constitutions of India provides for the village self-government under Articles-40. The state shall endeavour to endow village panchayats with sufficient powers and authority to enable them to function as units of self- government (Constitution of India, Article-40). The framers of the Constitution considered the inclusion of self-governing institutions as the most important in the democratic life of the country. They were inspired by the recurring prominence of Mahatma Gandhi on the establishment of panchayats all over India.

Mahatma Gandhi advocated Gram Swaraj. During the struggle for the independence, this constructive programme was evolved by him, making the villages as the epicentre of his entire programme of Gram Swaraj. Gandhi was in favour of a broad based pyramid structure of decentralized power with numerous village panchayats at the bottom as the vibrating source of power and a national panchayat at the apex elected by the intermediate level of districts and state panchayats with the ultimate control vesting in the hand of village based government.

Balwant Rai Mehta Committee

Community Development (CD) projects were inaugurated in 1952 and were modeled after the earlier experiments at Santiniketan, Baroda (Vadodara) and Nilokheri. However, the dynamic driving force behind the CD movement, Minister S. K. Dey, was of the reliable view that CD projects could not achieve their full potential in the absence of effective institutions for people's participation. In 1957, a historic breakthrough in establishing Panchayati Raj was elected through the report of the Balwantrai Mehta Committee which recommended: "Public participation in community works should be organized through statutory representative bodies." It was of the view that without an agency at the village level that could represent the entire community, assume responsibility and provide the necessary leadership for implementing development programmes, real progress in rural development could not come about at all. The study team on Community Development Panchayati Raj-popularly known as Balwantrai Mehta Committee (1957) recommended the establishment of a three-tier Panchayati Raj system with the middle tier, viz. Panchayat Samiti, being the key level in the scheme of decentralization (Balwantrai Mehta Committee Report, 1957, p-5). The samiti's jurisdiction was to be coterminous with that of a community development block, the members being directly elected. This system envisaged that the Pradhans of the Panchayat Samities would together constitute the Zilla Parishad with the collector/ Deputy Commissioner as the Chairman. The Parishad was visualized as an advisory body at the district level. The village panchayats would constitute the lowest level in the three-tier structure. Accordingly, most of the states had enacted their legislation on Panchayati Raj .While the Balwantrai Mehta committee pattern was generally followed in most states, there were some local variations in accordance with local needs and perceptions.

The committee suggested the following:

- An early establishment of elected local bodies and devolution to them of necessary resources, power and authority.
- Panchayats should have special powers to levy a special tax on land revenues and home taxes, etc.,
- Its function should cover the development of agriculture in all the aspects, promotion of cottage and local industries, etc.,
- The body must be constituted for five years by means of indirect elections from the village panchayats.
- Governance is a way that was large enough for efficiency and economy of administration and small enough for sustaining a sense of involvement in citizens.

Following were the landmark recommendations of the Balwant Rai Mehta Committee:

Panchayati Raj Institutions should be composed of elected representatives and should enjoy enough autonomy and freedom. The Balwant Rai Mehta Committee recommended a 3-tier Panchayati Raj System which includes;

- Zila Parishad at the District Level
- Panchayat Samiti at the Block/ Tehsil/Taluka Level
- Gram Panchayat at the Village Level

But the committee did not insisted on a rigid pattern. It recommended that the states should be given freedom to choose and develop their own patterns as per the local conditions. The committee recommended that the above 3-tiers should be organisationally linked together through an instrument of indirect election.

The Panchayats receive funds from three sources:

- Local body grants, as recommended by the Central Finance Commission
- Funds for implementation of Centrally Sponsored Schemes
- Funds released by the state governments on the recommendations of the State Finance Commissions

The committee recommended that the Gram Panchayats should be constituted with directly elected representatives, whereas the Panchayat Samiti and Zila Parishad should be the constituted with indirectly elected members.

- The status of the Panchayat samiti should be of that of an executive body, while the status of the Zila Parishad should be that of an advisory body.
- The Zila Parishad should be chaired by the District Collector.
- These democratic bodies must be given genuine powers.
- These bodies should be given adequate resources to carry out the functions and fulfill the responsibilities.

Subsequently, the National Development Council (NDC) endorsed the basic principles of democratic decentralization enunciated in the Balwantrai Mehta Report and laid on the states the duty of working out the structures suitable to each state. It was during this period that the term "Panchayati Raj" gained currency as a process of governance organically linking the will of the people from the Gram Sabha to the Lok Sabha. The then Prime Minister Nehru inaugurated the 3-tier Panchayati Raj in Nagaur, Rajasthan on 2nd October, 1959.

The committee's recommendation was implemented by NDC in January 1958 and this set the stage for the launching of Panchayati Raj Institutions throughout the country. The committee recommended the establishment of the scheme of 'democratic decentralization', which finally came to be known as Panchayati Raj. This led to the establishment of a three-tier Panchayati Raj system: Gram Panchayat at the village level, Panchayat Samiti at the block level and Zila Parishad at the district level.

Gram Panchayat Sabha

Sarpanch is its elected head. The members of the gram panchayat are elected from each for a period of five years by the members of Gram Sabha.

Sources of Income

Taxes collected locally such as on water, place of pilgrimage, local mandirs (temples), and markets

- A fixed grant from the state government in proportion to the land revenue and money for works and schemes assigned to the parishads
- Donations

Block level Panchayat or Panchayat Samiti

A Panchayat Samiti (block panchayat) is a local government body at the tehsil level. This body works for the villages of the tehsil that together are called a "development block". The Panchayat Samiti is the link between the Gram Panchayat and the district administration. Just as the tehsil goes by other names in various parts of India, notably mandal and taluka, there are a number of variations in nomenclature for the block panchayat. For example, it is known as Mandal Praja Parishad in Andhra Pradesh, Taluka Panchayat in Gujarat and Karnataka, and Panchayat Samiti in Maharashtra. In general, the block panchayat has the same form as the gram panchayat but at a higher level.

Composition

Membership in the block panchayat is mostly ex-official; it is composed of: all of the Sarpanchas (gram panchayat chairman) in the Panchayat Samiti area, the MPs and MLAs of the area, the Sub-District Officer (SDO) of the subdivision, co-opt members (representatives of the SC/ST and women), associate members (a farmer from the area, a representative of the cooperative societies and one from marketing services) and some elected members.

There is an officer for every department. A government-appointed Block Development Officer (BDO) is the executive officer to the Samiti and the chief of its administration and is responsible for his work to the CEO of ZP.

Functions

- Implementation of schemes for the development of agriculture and infrastructure
- Establishment of primary health centres and primary schools

- Supply of clean drinking water, drainage and construction/repair of roads
- Development of a cottage and small-scale industries and the opening of cooperative societies
- Establishment of youth organisations in India

Zila Parishad

The governing of the advance system at the district level in Panchayat Raj is also popularly known as Zila Parishad. The chief of administration is an officer of the IAS cadre and chief officer of the Panchayat Raj for the district level.

Composition

The membership varies from 40 to 60 and usually comprises:

- Deputy Commissioner of the district
- Presidents of all Panchayat Samitis in the district
- Heads of all government departments in the district
- Members of Parliament and Members of Legislative Assemblies in the district
- A representative of each cooperative society
- Some women and Scheduled Caste members, if not adequately represented
- Co-opted members having extraordinary experience and achievements in public service.

Functions

- Provide essential services and facilities to the rural population
- Supply improved seeds to farmers and inform them of new farming techniques
- Set up and run schools and libraries in rural areas
- Start primary health centres and hospitals in villages; start vaccination drives against epidemics
- Execute plans for the development of the scheduled castes and tribes; run ashram schools for adivasi children; set up free hostels for them.

- Encourage entrepreneurs to start small-scale industries and implement rural employment schemes.
- Construct bridges, roads and other public facilities and their maintenance
- Provide employment.
- Works on Sanitation related issues

The Jayaprakash Narayan Committee spoke of the contradictory positions developing within the government in respect of Panchayati Raj, pointing out that: "After having accepted Panchayati Raj as the agency responsible for planning and execution of plans...there is no longer any valid reason for continuing individual allocations subject-wise even to serve as a guide." The Ministry of Community Development was brought under the Ministry of Food and Agriculture and in 1971; the title 'Community Development' was dropped and replaced by 'Rural Development.'

K. Santhanam Committee (1963)

The committee was appointed to look society at the issue of PRI s finance. The committee was asked to determine issues related to sanctioning of grants to PRIs by the state government, evolving mutual financial relations between the three-tiers of PRIs, gifts and donations, handing over revenues in full or part to PRIs.

The committee recommended the following;

i) Panchayat should have special powers to levy special tax on land revenue and home taxes etc.

ii) People should not be burdened with too many demands.

iii) All grants and subventions at the state level should be mobilized and sent in a consolidated form to various PRIs.

iv) A Panchayati Raj Finance Corporation should be set up to look into the financial resources of PRIs at all levels, provide loans and financial assistance to those grassroots level governments and also non-financial requirements of village.

Ashok Mehta Committee

By the early seventies, however, the Panchayats had gone from a phase of early superiority to one of decline and stagnation. The Ashok Mehta Committee (formed in 1978) made far reaching recommendations to amend the situation and recommended that Panchayati Raj be included in the Constitution. In keeping with the spirit of the Ashok Mehta Committee recommendations, some states including West Bengal, Karnataka and Andhra Pradesh revisited their respective Panchayati Raj systems and undertook several new initiatives to endow local bodies with more powers which served as a prime inspiration and example for subsequent reform.

The West Bengal Panchayat Act, 1973 (West Bengal Act XLI of 1973) brought some fresh air in the Panchayat system. Direct elections in all three tiers (through universal adult franchise) had to be held at regular intervals. They were made mandatory without any discretionary power of any authority to postpone such elections indefinitely. Powers to collect tax and non-tax revenue were clearly defined. Functional domain of the Panchayats was more clearly delineated as compared to the earlier Panchayats. The new legislation empowered the Panchayats to spread their wings in various fields of activities encompassing rural life. Mandal Panchayats, in addition to the village panchayats, as envisaged in the Ashok Mehta Committee, exist only in Andhra Pradesh.

The committee was appointed to examine and suggest measures to strengthen PRIs. The committee had to evolve an effective decentralized system of development for PRIs .They made the following recommendations:

i) The district is viable administrative units for which planning coordination and resource allocation are feasible and technical expertise is available.

ii) PRIs as a two-tier system, with Mandal Panchayat at the base and Zilla Parishad at the top.

iii) The PRIs are capable of planning for themselves with the resources available to them.

iv) Representatives of SCs and STs In the election to PRIs on the basic of their population.

v) Participation of political parties in election.

G V K Rao Committee (1985)

The Ashok Mehta Committee was followed by GVK Rao Committee in 1985. This committee was appointed prior to the 7th Five Year Plan, to recommend on an integrated concept for growth and poverty alleviation. The committee had the following tasks:

- Examine the existing administration structure for rural development and detail out the functions and revenue resources of the PRIs
- Recommend the administrative arrangements for rural development and poverty alleviation programmes.
- Recommend on revitalizing the PRIs.

The essence of the recommendations of the GVK Rao Committee is as follows:

- The district level Zila Parishad should be the basic unit for policy planning and programme implementation.
- The Zila Parishad should be the pivotal body for the scheme of the democratic decentralization.
- The state level planning functions should be transferred to the Zila Parishad for effective decentralized planning.

So, in a nutshell, the GVK Rao Committee was of the view of making the district as the pole of democratic centralization. The committee also recommended that a post of District Development Commissioner should be created, who would work as the CEO of the Zila Parishad. The District Development Commissioner should be the in charge of all the developmental departments at the district level. This was a big deviation from the previous committees which recommended the lower bodies as bases and assigned the major role to the Panchayats and Mandal Panchayats in the development.

L M Singhvi Committee (1986)

A year after the GVK Rao committee, the Government of India set up Dr. L M Singhvi Committee. At that time the prime minister was Rajiv Gandhi. The LM Singhvi Committee was of the view that the Panchayati Raj Institutions declined in the country because of ;

- Absence of a clear concept
- Absence of political will
- Lack of research, evaluation and monitoring.

The committee was in favour of making ways for the PRIs to ensure the availability of the enough financial resources. The LM Singhvi Committee is best known for recommending the constitutional status for Panchayats. This was virtually the first committee after decades of India's experiments with the decentralization which found the "Gram Sabhas" as the "incarnation of the direct democracy".

Here are the notes from its recommendations:

- The PRIs should be recognized, protected and preserved constitutionally. A new chapter should be added in the Constitution of India which should enshrine the provisions to ensure free, regular and fair elections in the PRIs.
- For revenue procedures, the Singhvi Committee was of the view that there should be optional and compulsory levies which should be entrusted to the PRIs. For initial years, the state government may levy on behalf of the PRIs and disburse money to them. This disbursement should be based upon the recommendations of the State Finance Commissions.
- For Jurisdiction of the PRI's, Nyaya Panchayats should be established for a cluster of villages.
- Gram Sabha is the embodiment of the direct democracy and the village panchayats should be more organized. Gram Sabha should be given importance.
- The Singhvi Committee also recommended establishment of the Judicial Tribunals in the states which would tackle the controversies regarding the elections to the Panchayati Raj Institutions.

Singhvi Committee versus Sarkaria Commission

The recommendations of the Singhvi Committee, though revolutionary, were opposed by the Sarkaria Commission on Centre-State Relations, which submitted its report in 1988. This commission was of the view that enacting any law on the Panchayats is exclusive power vested in the states and rather than adding a new chapter in the Constitution, there should be a uniform law, applicable throughout India. A model bill can be drafted on the basis of consensus among all the state at the level of inter-state council.

64th Amendment Bill

Despite the contradictory view of the Sarkaria Commission, the government had focussed on giving constitutional protection to the PRIs. In this regard, the 64th amendment bill was introduced in the parliament by Rajiv Gandhi government on 15th May 1989. The bill got lapsed because it could not pass in Rajya Sabha. This was on 15th October 1989. On 27th November 1989, the tenure of the Rajiv Gandhi government ended and elections were held. Rajiv Gandhi lost the elections and the result was a minority government under V.P. Singh and the National Front. This was the first minority government, since 1947, with the help of the Left Parties and Bharatiya Janta Party, who supported the government from outside. The Government of India brought in the Constitution 64th Amendment bill which was passed by the Lok Sabha on 10th August 1989.This was a comprehensive bill covering vital aspects of the PRIs including the constitution of a uniform three-tier Panchayatiraj Raj system at the village , intermediate and district levels in all states and union territories having a population of not less than 2 lakhs; reservation of seats for SCs STs and women; guaranteed term of five years for the Panchayats at all levels and election within six months in case of dissolutions ahead of schedule; specific powers, authority and responsibility to the PRIs; addition of a new schedule (XI-schedule) to the constitution indicating an illustrative list of subject the functions on which could be entrusted to the Panchayats; conduct of election to the Panchayats, by the Election Commission, etc (Constitution Sixty Forth Amendment Bill,1989). Although the Lok Sabah passed the bill, it was not approved by the Rajya Sabah.

73rd Constitutional Amendment

The Constitution (73rd Amendment) Act, 1992 (or simply the Panchayati Raj Act) marks a new era in the federal democratic set up of the country. The Constitution (73rd Amendment) Bill, 1991 was introduced on 16th September, 1991 which was subsequently referred to a Joint Select Committee of Parliament in December 1991 for a detailed examination. The Joint Committee presented its report to Parliament in July, 1992. The Constitution (73rd Amendment) bill was finally passed by the Lok Sabha on 22nd December, 1992 and by the Rajya Sabha on 23rd December, 1992 which was notified by the central government through official gazette on 20th April,1993 as it got rectified by the state legislatures. Seventeen states ratified the act in a record time. The then Prime Minister P.V. Narasimha Rao of Congress government introduced a fresh bill on Panchayat Raj in September 1991. It provided the much needed constitutional sanction to the Panchayati Raj Institutions (PRIs) for functioning as an organic and integral part of the nation's democratic process. Panchayati Raj system does not apply to the Schedule-V areas of the nine states, Schedule-VI Areas of the North-East and the district of Darjeeling in West Bengal as

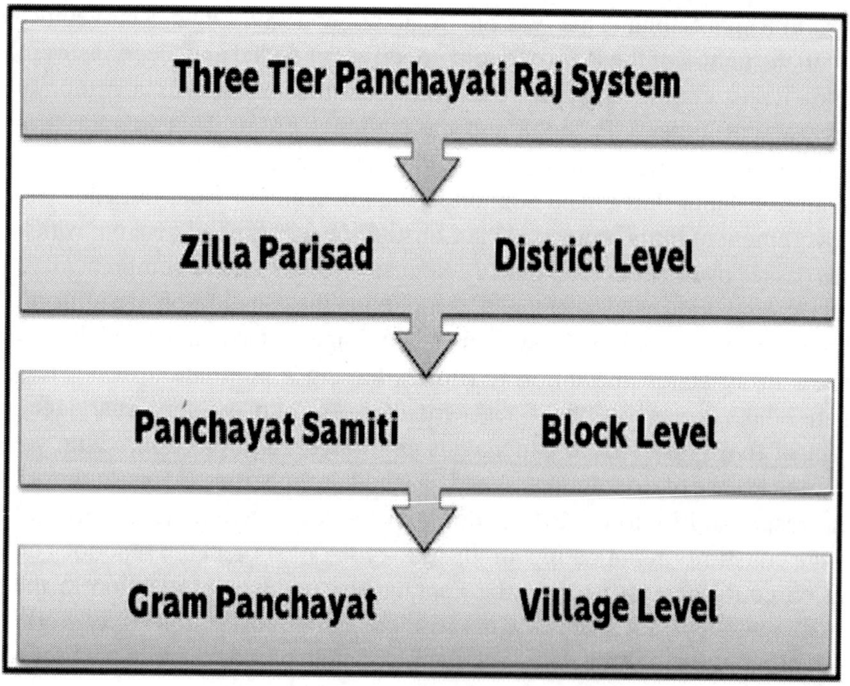

well as J&K. Currently, the Panchayati Raj system functions in all states except Nagaland, Meghalaya, and Mizoram and in all Union Territories except Delhi. The President of India accorded his assent on 20th April 1993 (Gazette of India, 1993, Part-II). After notification the Panchayati Raj institutions have now got constitutional legitimacy. Thus, after facing many storms PRIs got Constitutional status in April 1993 by way of 73rd Constitutional Amendment Act. The Constitution (73rd Amendment) Act, 1992 came into effect on 24th April, 1993 (Government of India, S.O., 267, 1993). After having a minute observation of Constitutional 64th Amendment Bill, 74th Amendment bill and 73rd Amendment Act, one may come to the conclusion that the act is just on amalgamation of the 64th and 74th Constitutional Amendment Bills. The Constitution Amendment Act has given a practical shape to Article-40 of the Constitution included in the directive principles of the state policy casting a heavy duty on the centre as well as the states to establish and nourish village panchayats so as to make them effective institutions of self-government. The new model is a unique arrangement by the centre which has made it mandatory on the part of the states to apply these principles in making laws without in any way jeopardizing the federal polity of the country.

The provisions of the amendment include Articles-243, 243A to 243-O which were added as parts of newly inserted Part-IX of the Constitution. It is the first formal democratic institution at the village level. The chairperson of this unit is called as Sarpanch.

The amendment introduced across the board three-tier system of the PRIs at village Panchayat, Block and District levels.

Salient Features of 73rd Amendment Act

The Constitution (73rd Amendment) Act provides for establishment of three-tiers of Panchayats as units of local self-government. It also contains provisions regarding regular elections to Panchayat bodies, setting up of a State Election Commission and a State Finance Commission, reservation for SCs, STs and women, enabling provisions for reservation for backward classes of citizens, etc. Adequate powers and responsibilities will have to be developed upon these institutions at appropriate levels to enable them to prepare and implement the schemes for economic development and social justice.

The salient features of the act are as follows:

Reservation of Seats

There shall be reservation of seats at every level for SCs/STs in proportion to their population in a given Panchayat area and for women to the extent of not less than one-third of the total number of seats. Similarly, office of the chairpersons in the Panchayats at each level shall be reserved for women, to the extent of not less than one-third of the total number of chairpersons in the Panchayats at each level and for SCs and STs in proportion to the total number of chairpersons of Panchayats at each level as the population of SCs/STs in the state bears to the total population of the state (Article-243D). In addition, the legislature of any state can make provision for reservation of seats in any Panchayats or office of chairpersons in the Panchayats at any level in favour of the backward classes.

❒ For SC/ST

Article-243D provides for reservation of seats at all levels for Scheduled Castes (SCs), Scheduled Tribes (STs) and women. While the reservation for the SCs/STs are as per their actual proportion in a population of the concerned area. Let's take, for example, the Scheduled Castes which constitute 30per cent of the total population and the Scheduled Tribes at

21 per cent, then 30 per cent and 21 per cent seats shall be reserved for them respectively.

Since the Panchayat Raj Act do not automatically cover the scheduled areas, the Panchayat (Extension to Scheduled Areas) Act (PESA) was enacted on 24th December 1996 to enable tribal self rule in these areas. The act has also been extended the provisions of Panchayats to the tribal areas of nine states that have Fifth Schedule Areas. It should also be noted that most of the North-Eastern states falling under Sixth Schedule Areas are not covered by PESA, the reason being, they have their own autonomous councils for governance. The nine states with Fifth Schedule Areas are Odisha, Gujarat, Jharkhand, Maharashtra, Rajasthan, Andhra Pradesh, Madhya Pradesh, Himachal Pradesh, Chattisgarh. However, it is a clear indication that sincere implementation of PESA has not been seriously attempted by the state governments.

In *Union of India* vs. *Rakesh Kumar*, it was held that Jharkhand Panchayat Raj Act 2001[sec- 21(B),40(B),55(B)] providing 100per cent reservation in favour of scheduled tribes for chairman's position in panchayats located in the scheduled area in Jharkhand is constitutionally permissible. The SC thus allows parliament to provide the 'modifications and exceptions' expressly in the application of part IX to scheduled areas.

❒ For Women

Article-243 D of the Constitution of India mandates that at least one-third of the total number of seats filled by direct elections in the Panchayats shall be reserved for women. However, the Constitution (One Hundred and Tenth Amendment) Bill, 2009 was introduced in the Lok Sabha on 26th November 2009 by the then Minister of Panchayati Raj, Shri C.P. Joshi in order to amend Article-243 D of the Constitution of India. The bill is aiming at increasing the proportion of women to be the part of panchayats from one third to one half. It is be noted that the states like Andhra Pradesh, Chhatisgarh, Jharkhand, Kerala, Maharashtra, Odisha, Rajasthan and Tripura have already a reservation for 50per cent of their posts for women.

❒ For Chairpersons

A state may by law make provision for similar reservation of the offices of Chairpersons in the Panchayats at the village and other levels. These reservations favouring the Scheduled Castes and Scheduled Tribes shall cease to be operative at the period specified in Article-334. A State may by law also reserve seats or offices of Chairpersons in the Panchayat at any level in favour of backward classes of citizens.

General Working

❒ Tenure

Article-243 E is a provision on the duration of members in Panchayat. A clear term for 5 years has been provided for the Panchayats and elections must take place before the expiry of the terms. However, the Panchayat may be dissolved earlier on specific grounds in accordance with the state legislation. In that case, the elections must take place before the expiry of 6 months of the dissolution.

❒ Disqualification

Article-243F makes provisions for disqualifications from the membership. As per this Article, any person who is qualified to become an MLA is qualified to become a member of the Panchayat, but for Panchayat the minimum age prescribed is 21 years. Further, the disqualification criteria are to be decided by the state legislature by law.

❒ State Legislature on Panchayats

- ❒ The state legislature can confer power upon panchayat systems (Article-243G to 243H) and the 11th schedule enshrines the distribution of powers between the state legislature and the panchayats.
- ❒ The state can authorize a panchayat by law to levy, collect and appropriate taxes, duties, etc
- ❒ To review the financial position and status of the panchayat the state legislatures are authorized to appoint a Finance Commission.
- ❒ The main source of income of the Panchayat Samiti is grants-in-aid and loans from the respective state governments.

❒ Ban on Interference by Courts

Referring to Article-329 of the Constitution, the courts cannot interfere in matters relating to allotment of seats, delimitation of Constituencies as under Article-243K. Any matters relating to the election of panchayats can be questioned only by means of election petition following certain procedures prescribed by the state legislature.

Benefits

Each village has its own set of issues, which only the locals can understand. Members of a Panchayat are far more cognizant of the region-specific problems and thus they are capable of taking a more informed decision in favour of the people of their village. Taking into consideration the specified needs of their inhabitants, the panchayats work accordingly. The panchayats undertake works of varied levels starting from creation of necessary establishments such as primary schools, to hygiene-related issues, to water requirements, to seek the central government's help towards generating jobs at the village level as well. They also have a major share of contribution towards mobilization of local resources, encouraging, large-scale community participation, planning at the lower levels and reduction of corruption as well as improvement in quality of work culture of nations.

Bottlenecks

- Few states have not yet rested and delegated the powers to the panchayats to the true meaning and spirit of the 73rd constitutional amendment. Even if, the functions have been delegated, the required powers to execute the said functions are not with the PRIs.
- There is a general lack of manpower in the PRIs, particularly at the village level. With a limited number of officials, even after the complete devolution of powers, it may become difficult for the PRIs to look after all the works assigned to them by the state government. The PRIs needs to equipped with adequate staff to discharge their functions.
- As per the Panchayat Act, the Gram Sabhas have not been efficient in ensuring and empowering the participation of people at the lower levels to the fullest sense possible.
- Powers given to the State Election Commissions also vary from state to state. No uniformity is ensured in this regard. Also, recommendations of State Finance Commissions (SFCs) are generally not taken seriously.
- While women got political representation, the real power was usurped by their husbands, "*The Sarpanch Pati*" depriving them of any meaningful gains. Caste and gender-based discrimination are still prevalent and despite earning a political position, women are denied their due respect. Widespread illiteracy and ignorance further inhibit their capacity to perform.

Gram Sabaha

The Gram Sabha has been envisaged as the foundation of the Panchayati Raj system (Eastern Book Company, 1993, p.2). It shall perform such functions and exercise such powers as may be entrusted to it by the State legislature (Constitution (73rd Amendment) Act, 1992: Government of India Article-243-A].

Three-tier PR System

There shall be three-tiers of Panchayats at the village, inter-mediate and district levels (Article-243-B) .Only states having population not exceeding 20 lakhs have the discretion not to constitute the Panchayats at the intermediate level. Under Article-243-L, the President can make special dispensation for Union Territories (Article-243-L)

Direct Elections

All seats in a Panchayat at every level are to be filled up by direct elections from territorial constituencies demarcated for this purpose, with the ratio between the population of such constituency and the number of seats allotted to it being the same throughout the Panchayat area.

Five-Year Term

The term of office of Panchayats at every level shall be five years (Article-243-AE) and if dissolved earlier or on expiry of the term, elections must be completed within six months from the date of dissolution or expiry.

Finance Commission

Within one year from 24th April, 1993 i.e. the coming into effect of the Constitution (73rd Amendment) Act, 1992 and thereafter, at the expiration of every fifth year, a Finance Commission shall be constituted in every state to go into the principles governing the distribution and devolution of financial resources between the state and the Panchayats at every level and the measures to improve the financial position of the Panchayats (Article-243-1).

State Election Commission

The direction and control of the preparation of electoral rolls and the conduct of all elections in the Panchayats shall be vested in a State Election Commission; to be constituted by the concerned state (Article-243-K).

Eleventh Schedule

Finally, the XI-Schedule comprising of 29 items has been added to the Constitution which ought to provide an effective role to the PRIs in the planning and implementation of works of local significance ranging from drinking water, agriculture, land and water conservation, communication, poverty alleviation programmes, family welfare, education, libraries and cultural activities, maintenance of community assets etc (Article-243-G).

List of committees constituted for recommendations regarding Panchayati Raj in India:

Balwant Rai Mehta	1957
V.T. Krishnammachari	1960
Takhatmal Jain Study Group	1966
Ashok Mehta Committee	1978
G.V.K. Rao Committee	1985
Dr. L.M. Singhvi Committee	1986
P.K. Thungon Committee	1989
S. Mohinder Singh	2013

Local Governance in the Tribal Areas

Article-244 of the Constitution envisages three categories of tribal areas, namely:

- Areas notified as 'Scheduled Areas' in the specified states (Fifth Schedule).
- Areas listed as 'Tribal Areas' in the Sixth Schedule in NER.
- Areas not covered in the above two categories.

While Fifth Schedule relates to 'Administration and Control of Scheduled Areas and Scheduled Tribes, Sixth Schedule concerns 'Administration of Tribal Areas'. There is no special schedule for the rest.

Fifth Schedule Areas and PESA

The Fifth Schedule to the Constitution (Article-244) relates to administration and control of the Scheduled Areas and Scheduled Tribes other than those in North-East states. The Panchayats (Extension to the Scheduled Areas) Act (PESA) was enacted in 1996 which extended Part-

IX of the Constitution to the Schedule-V Areas. PESA promotes people-centric governance and provides a central role to the Gram Sabha.

The legal framework of Local Self-Governance (LSG) in NER broadly comprises three typologies:

- Sixth Schedule Frame (Meghalaya, parts of Assam, Mizoram and Tripura)
- State Legislation Frame (Nagaland, Hill Areas of Manipur and non-council areas in Mizoram)
- National Frame (Arunachal Pradesh, Sikkim, Manipur excluding hill areas and non-Council areas in Assam and Tripura).

Each tribal area mentioned in Para-20 of the sixth schedule is designated as an 'autonomous district'. The area inhabited by each of the tribes in a district may be carved out as autonomous region. Each autonomous district is governed by a 'District Council' (Council, in brief) and autonomous region by a 'Regional Council'. These Councils endowed with legislative, judicial and executive powers, are constitutionally virtually function as 'state within state'.

However the most important aspect in strengthening of the Panchayats is the devolution of 3Fs (i.e. Funds, Functions and Functionaries) related to the matters listed in the Eleventh Schedule of the Constitution. Another is their enablement for preparing and implementing bottom-up participatory plans for economic development and social justice. The states vary a great deal in both these respects. While some states have forged new paths, others are still to catch up. Of course, many states are trying out new approaches and mechanisms, and making corrections/improvements along the way.

Devolution and PEAIS/DI

The Panchayat Empowerment and Accountability Incentive Scheme (PEAIS) aims at encouraging states to adequately empower the Panchayats and put in place systems for bringing about efficiency, transparency and accountability of the Panchayats. Performance of states in these respects is measured through a Devolution Index (DI). Token award is also given to the States which rank high on the DI.

The DI has been improved continuously over the years since the inception of the scheme in 2005-06. Since 2007-08, evaluation of states under PEAIS is based on a two-stage assessment. The first stage, called the Framework Criteria, was based on the following four fundamental constitutional requirements: (i) Establishment of State Election Commission; (ii) Holding of elections to the PRIs; (iii) Setting up State Finance Commission; (iv) Constitution of the District Planning Committees (DPCs). States that fulfilled each of these four fundamental requirements qualified for evaluation in terms of DI. The indicators for the DI aim at assessing the state of devolution in respect of the 3Fs. DIs developed for PEAIS so far do not specifically capture the degree of Panchayat accountability and performance.

Panchayati Raj; A Comparative analysis among the Indian States

Some states have taken measures towards meeting the basic requirements of devolution as specified in the Constitution, other states have taken off to the next level in terms of promoting good governance, efficient service delivery, decentralised democracy, transparency, accountability and connectivity. Some of the recent initiatives as visible from the efforts of the state governments are presented below for the benefit of other states

Karnataka

The Karnataka government has enacted the Karnataka Sakala Services Act 2011, which guarantees delivery of essential civic services to the citizens of Karnataka, within the stipulated time limit. Eleven services pertaining to gram panchayats are covered under Sakala, which includes maintenance of drinking water, street lights and village sanitation, issue of records such as cattle and crop census, BPL list, e-payment for work executed under developmental schemes, etc.

Rajasthan

Measures have been taken by the Rajasthan government, to strengthen the District Planning Committees and the standing committees' at all three tiers of the panchayats.

Maharashtra

Government of Maharashtra had launched the project called SANGRAM – Sanganakiya Grameen Maharashtra, a computerised programme for enabling rural Maharashtra to fight against corruption. This project is for effective implementation of development programmes, which is the convergent implementation of administrative reforms, on-line services, computerization, biometrics attendance, etc.

Madhya Pradesh

Panch Parameswar Yojana, was launched to consolidate the funds made available to panchayats in the Panchayati Raj account through Integrated Action Plan for Rural Development. As per this initiative, the Gram Panchayats would get consolidated funds on the basis of the population during the financial year.

Odisha

The Gram Sabha Sashaktikaran Karyakrama (GSSK) campaign was launched, which is a drive for social mobilization and enhancing the institutional capacity of panchayats through administrative and technical support.

Chattisgarh

Through a notification, a time limit has been stipulated for the delivery of nine public services to citizens by Gram Panchayat and Janpad Panchayats. Responsibilities have also been fixed on certain public authorities for – (a) The delivery of each public service (b) In the event of default and (c) Appellate authority. Every applicant who cannot obtain public services within the stipulated time shall be entitled to get the compensation.

Panchayat systems in all the states aim at effective decentralization and self-rule. But the means they adopt to achieve the same vary from states to states as mentioned above.

Women and Panchayats

On 27th August 2009, the Union Cabinet of the Government of India approved 50per cent reservation for women in Panchayati Raj Institutions (PRIs). The Indian states Andhra Pradesh, {Bihar, 1st state among all to reserve 50 per cent of seats for women}, Chhattisgarh, Himachal Pradesh, Jharkhand, Kerala, Karnataka, Madhya Pradesh, Maharashtra, Odisha , Rajasthan, Sikkim, Tamil Nadu, Tripura, West Bengal and Uttarakhand have implemented 50 per cent reservation for women in PRIs. The majority of candidates in these Panchayats are women. Currently 100 per cent of elected members' in Kodassery Panchayat in Kerala are women.

A number of steps are necessary for empowerment of women, such as:

- A provision of women component plans in PRI budgets.
- Linkages with SHGs in all levels of PRIs.
- Adequate training and capacity building of EWR.
- Leadership training programmes for EWRs
- Training of other functionaries on gender issues
- Peer-to-peer and horizontal learning from success stories
- Sharing good practices and exposure visits
- Political parties must put up women candidates.
- Women candidates are given opportunity to serve a full term.
- Mahila Sabhas are to be encouraged to facilitate women's concerns and be raised on priority basis in meetings of Gram/Ward Sabhas.
- Separate quorum for women's participation in Gram/Ward Sabhas.

MoPR will take up with the states for inclusion of provisions under the Panchayat laws for recognition of Mahila Sabha and separate quorum for women participation in Gram/Ward Sabhas.

The System in Practice

The Panchayats, throughout the years, have relied on federal and state grants to sustain themselves economically. The absence of mandatory elections for the Panchayat council and infrequent meetings of the Sarpanch have decreased the spread of information to villagers, leading to more state regulation. Many Panchayats have been successful in achieving their goals, through cooperation between different bodies and the political mobilization of previously underrepresented groups in India. There is an obstacle of literacy that many Panchayats face for engagement of villagers, with most development schemes being on paper. However, homes linked to the Panchayati Raj System have seen an increase in participation for local matters. The reservation policy for women on the Panchayat councils have also led to a substantial increase in female participation and have shaped the focus of development to include more domestic household issues.

Participation at Village Level: Gram Sabha and Ward Sabha

Article-243A gives constitutional recognition to the GS as 'a body consisting of persons registered in the electoral rolls relating to a village comprised within the area of the Panchayat at the village level.' The Constitution further stipulates that a GS may exercise such powers and perform such functions at the village level as the legislature of a state may, by law, provide. GS is the key to self- governance and to transparent and accountable functioning of the GP. The GS is the only forum that can ensure direct, participative democracy. It offers equal opportunity to all citizens of a village or cluster of villages to discuss and criticize, approve or reject proposals of the Panchayat executive and also to assess its performance. It is the platform for effective social audit, which lies at the core of ensuring transparency and accountability in the functioning of the system. To this end, there is a need to accord clearly enunciated statutory powers and authority to the GS. The first round table of State Panchayati Raj ministers at Kolkata on 24-25 July, 2004 recommended that the GSs should in fact be given power and functions in accordance with Article-243A of the Constitution to enable them to make the elected Panchayats answerable to the people.

Present Functioning of the Gram Sabha

It is generally seen that meetings of the GSs are not held regularly and are marked by thin attendance, particularly of women and marginalized groups. There is little discussion on the proposals put forward for approval by the Panchayat. Issues of common interest and of the marginalized sections are often not discussed. People do not perceive GS as empowered bodies that will effectively resolve issues placed before it in an inclusive manner. Another reason why GSs are seen as ineffective is the dysfunctional relationship between Panchayats and GSs.

The general perception is that the task before the GS is approval of the lists of beneficiaries, approval for issuance of utilization certificates and passing of the annual accounts. Panchayat heads bring their own supporters and potential beneficiaries to attend the meetings so that while the quorum is completed, most of the other electors keep away. Hence, a sense of pessimism has developed about the efficacy of GS meetings. In fact, the ineffectual nature of GSs in affected areas is stated to be one of the primary causes behind the rise of Left Wing Extremism in the Scheduled Areas and their vicinity.

For the rural local governance to be effective, energizing GSs is the real challenge. There is need to evolve mechanisms for regular and meaningful meeting of the GS, active participation of its members and monitoring of its functioning. Good practices that provide people's assemblies below the GS such as Ward Sabha, Mahila Sabha and Bal Sabha should be promoted. Since the area and population of a Ward Sabha is smaller and commonality of interest greater, people would discuss with close involvement matters that they wish taken up through the Ward Member to the GP and evolve a consensus.

Gram Sabha and Social Audit

Social audit is a close corollary of energetic GS functioning. It would inculcate respect for downward accountability amongst elected representatives and government officials. If GS keeps a close vigil on implementation and leakages, inefficiencies can be virtually eliminated. GS can monitor and discuss attendance of government functionaries, functioning of schools, dispensaries, Anganwadi Centres, ration shops and other local institutions. GS can discuss reports of the Standing Committees of the GP. GS can also go through the list of beneficiaries under schemes such as Indira Awaas Yojana (IAY), Antyodaya Anna Yojana (AAY) and National Old Age Pension Scheme. GS can be an effective forum for familiarizing the electors with the provisions of Right to Information (RTI) for eliciting information that they are unable to obtain in the normal course.

Energising the Gram Sabha

The scope of deliberations in the GS meetings can be enhanced to make these more interesting and meaningful, such as:

- GS can be an effective forum for information sharing on programmes, schemes, good practices and matters of common interest for which assistance from the state and centre is available through different policies and programmes.
- GS can discuss issues such as: (i) quality of life and Millennium Development Goals; (ii) social security, gender justice, female foeticides, substance abuse (alcohol, tobacco and drugs), hygiene and nutrition; (iii) sustainable development, diversification of agriculture, better cropping practices, opportunities for improving incomes, drought/flood management, soil and water conservation; and (iv) infrastructure development, etc.
- GS should fully participate in planning, implementation and performance review of various schemes viz. BRGF, MGNREGA, NRHM, SSA, ICDS, IWMP, RKVY etc. In

- Preparing plan and shelf of projects, realistic assessment of resources should be made. All state departments should clearly articulate the role of GS in their Policy/Programme/ Scheme.

Manpower for the PRIs

In the advisory issued by MoPR to the States/UTs vide letter dated 13.10.2009, the following transitional and permanent arrangements with a definite timeline were suggested:

(a) Gram Panchayat Cadre

GP should normally have four categories of staff:

- Core staff for its internal processes: PDO/ Secretary, Accountant, Technical Assistant and Computer Operator
- Scheme Specific Staff: for example, Rozgar Sahayak for MGNREGA
- Functional Staff: such as Teachers, ASHA, Anganwadi Workers
- Contractual skilled workers: such as Pump Operator, Motor Mechanic, Hand Pump Mechanic, Electrician, Sanitary workers

(b) District Panchayat Cadre

District Panchayat Cadre (DP Cadre) could comprise of officials who have jurisdiction over areas larger than a GP.

- The DP cadre could be constituted by a judicious mix of direct recruitments and promotion from GP cadre.
- Employees of DP cadre would supervise the work of the functionaries at the GP level. Examples of this would be: Extension Officers, Junior Engineers etc. Some employees listed above for GP cadre could also fall in this cadre.

(c) State Cadre

GP cadre could serve as a feeding cadre to DP cadre. Class I and II could be state cadre for which DP could be the feeding cadre.

The possible promotional channel could be illustrated as follows:

- Panchayat Secretary (GP Cadre)/Village Development Officer (DP Cadre)/Extension Officer (Panchayat) (DP Cadre)/BDO (State Cadre) – Further promotions as per State policy.

- Anganwadi Worker (GP Cadre)/Mukhya Sevika (DP Cadre)/ ACDPO (DP Cadre) CDPO (State Cadre)/State Directorate/ Commissionerate.
- Agriculture Asst. (GP Cadre)/Extension Officer (Agr.) (DP Cadre)
- Agriculture Officer (DP Cadre)/State Cadre

It is well recognised that the size of Panchayats varies widely from state to state and therefore, the core and other staff strength, mode of selection, appointment etc. may not be uniform. Reasonable norms based on the area/population/terrain of the Panchayat and functions devolved need to be laid down.

As regards the creation of a Panchayat cadre, the Maharashtra model is worth considering, which is broadly as follows:

- Class-I and II officers are state cadres and are posted from line departments to Zilla Parishads on deputation.
- However, Class-III and Class-IV employees are Parishad employees and not state govt. employees.
- There are separate service rules for each of these categories.
- In the state govt. cadre (Class-II), certain percentages of vacancies are always filled through promotion from the district cadre.

Resources for deploying core staff of Panchayats could be found out of the state resources, BRGF (not functional now), MGNREGA, Finance Commission Awards etc. as per a well considered phasing. Other staffs could be financed under the existing plan/non- plan arrangements.

Problems Faced by Panchayati Raj

There are a number of problems faced by the Panchayati Raj Institutions and can be discussed as follows:

(i) Conceptual Confusion

It is said, that basically, there is lack of clarity regarding the concept of Panchayati Raj and about the objectives for which the institutions have been established. Over the years, the concept has undergone some changes. In the first instance, the concept of Panchayati Raj is very narrow as it was not viewed as an institutional framework which could play an important role in the overall development of rural masses. The present concept does not envisage even a single unit of Panchayati Raj Institutions as an instrument of planning as well as implementation agency of different rural development programmes. There is also lack of clarity about Panchayati Raj Institutions as agencies that can manage routine administration, infrastructure and bring about socioeconomic welfare of the rural population. There are multiplicities of agencies in the rural scene charged with the responsibility of undertaking a plethora of developmental activities.

Secondly, there is no clarity about the relationship between Panchayati Raj Institutions and the administrative organisation of the government. It is also clear that the administration has a dual responsibility i.e. towards state departments and towards Panchayati Raj Institutions. This has resulted in a lot of confusion and complications.

Thirdly, there are a few who call the Panchayati Raj Institutions the "tools of democratic seed drilling in the Indlan soil." In the process, the Panchayati Raj Institutions are dominated by socially and economically privileged sections in rural India who continue to dominate the poor people. For instance, people belonging to so-called higher castes, continue to dominate the people belonging to so called lower castes and benefits do not reach the people who are in real need. There is thus widespread confusion about the role of Panchayati Raj Institutions in rural development programmes.

Finally, there is no clear trend emerging in regard to the concept of power. There is a strong feeling that decentralisation of power and authority exists at the district level and down the lines. But at the same time, a number of central schemes and agencies, both in number and size have been emerging, independent of these bodies. It is paradoxical that all these concepts co-exist side by side leading to increasing confusion and conflicts in-their working.

(ii) Structures

While establishing Panchayati Raj bodies, no uniform pattern is adopted for creating units and identifying the units of planning and development. This may not be a cause for failure but the structures that have been adopted by various state governments are just not capable of performing the role that is expected of them. The distribution of functions and powers are; a) among the Panchayati Raj Institutions, b) between the Panchayati Raj Institutions and State government and c) between the Panchayati Raj Institutions and the central government have not been made on the basis of any sound principle. There is a great deal of confusion, overlapping and sometimes duplication in the function. To some extent, Maharashtra, Karnataka and Gujarat have made some effort to demarcate the functions between Panchayati Raj Institutions and the state government. Rest of the states did not make any serious attempt in this direction.

Further, the expertise available to the Panchayati Raj Institutions is very limited particularly in the field of planning, implementation or monitoring of various developmental schemes. Thus the planning process suffered to a large extent. In fact, planning at the grass root level remains in paper while there is a strong tendency towards centralisation in the country. This is not a healthy sign. In many development programmes, the Panchayati Raj Institutions have not play their role to the fuller extent.

(iii) Financial Resources

The most important problem faced by the Panchayati Raj Institutions is regarding finances. The quality and variety of activities which the Panchayati Raj Institutions are expected to perform will depend mostly on the resources at their command. The resource base would depend on the local economy and partly upon the allocations made by the state and central governments. The Panchayati Raj Institutions have a very limited scope to impose taxes in their jurisdiction. In India, there is centralisation of revenue resources which is a bone of contention between the centre and the states. Similarly, the financial system in the state is also of the same nature. The Panchayati Raj Institutions have to look towards the higher authorities for necessary grant. There is thus a real danger of imbalance between resources and responsibilities, as in the name of decentralisation, more and more functions are to be transferred to the Panchayati Raj Institutions. To cope up these situations the transfer of financial resources should be done in true spirit proportionately. In this context the demand for some statutory arrangements should be viewed to strengthen the resource base of these bodies.

(iv) Socio-Economic and Political Conditions

The existing socio-economic structure of the Indian society is a major factor which is responsible for the limited success of Panchayati Raj Institutions. In fact, the leadership of the Panchayati Raj Institutions acts as a "gate-keeper" to prevent the flow of benefits to the weaker sections of the rural community. Although, reservation of seats at the different levels have been made in some states but the reservation concept has not been effectively adopted. For example, in Karnataka, there is no provision of reservation to the key elective posts such as Chairperson, Vice-Chairperson or Adhyaksha and Upadhyaksha etc. It means, there is no possibility of mass participation of the poor in the developmental process in our hierarchically stratified society where the weaker sections are almost completely unorganised. The concept of participation of people in the process of democratic decentralisation is highly difficult under such conditions. It is necessary to point out that there may be stray instances of poor and downtrodden taking part in the developmental activities. Thanks to reservation of certain elective posts in states like Andhra Pradesh.

(v) Position of Civil Service

An efficient, adequate, responsive and committed administration is the essential condition of success of Panchayati Raj. The functions of these bodies are too many and too complex. There is a need for technical personnel, proper orientation and above all commitment in the civil service. The aspirations of the citizens in the rural areas are getting stirred. There is a demand for improvement in the services. We find a different and a difficult situation as far as civil services in India are concerned. The bureaucracy is getting alienated and has begun to by-pass these institutions. Several programmes have been introduced without involving Panchayati Raj Institutions in them. These programmes have become close preserves of bureaucracy, under-mining and frustrating the Panchayati Raj Institutions as units of representative bodies and local self-government.

(vi) Lack of Political Support from the Top

The elite and the so-called higher levels generally do not provide political support to strengthen the democratic process at the grass root levels. The Members of Parliament, State Legislatures always felt that the Panchayati Raj leadership would emerge as a threat to their position in their respective constituencies. Therefore, every effort is made by the state and central leadership to weaken the powers and functions of the grass root functionaries and they always exhibit a negative attitude. The best example is the way in which the 64th Constitutional Amendment Bill on Panchayati Raj was introduced and defeated and finally shelved for the reasons extraneous to the development of local self-government institutions in the country.

Thus, the potential of Panchayati Raj Institutions as centres of peoples' power aroused doubts among a few and jealousy among many. Elected representatives in the Parliament and State Legislatures saw with dismay their inevitable dependence on the Panchayati Raj functionaries with whom they are not willing to share power.

(vii) State Control and Supervision

Since the Panchayati Raj Institutions fall under the state subject and are created by the state, there exists a superior-inferior relationship between the state and the Panchayati Raj Institutions. The state governments always tend to exhibit a high degree of paternalism. The control exercised by the state over Panchayati Raj Institutions is of a comprehensive character. There is practically no subject relating to the Panchayati Raj Institutions, over which the state cannot exercise powers of control. With the result, in several states the rulers at the state level discovered a number of problems, real or imaginary, like structural weaknesses, organisational shortcomings, functional insufficiency, incompetent performances, lack of adequate resources etc. On a number of occasions, an inconvenient office bearer is either suspended or dismissed by the state government under some pretext or the other. Thus, several short-comings have been highlighted and listed out by the states. It has become a regular feature in all the slates and it needs corrective measures.

(viii) Absence of Statutory Provision

The success or failure of an institution depends mostly on the status, on the basis of which an organisation is established. According to Article-40 of the Constitution, "The state shall take steps to organise village panchayats..." Since it is included in the Directive Principles of State Policy, it is not mandatory. Similarly, in a number of states, elections have not been held regularly. The superseded bodies have not been revived and they were kept under the charge of special officers drawn from the civil service. Thus, the Panchayati Raj Institutions have been undermined with several constraints, particularly, the constitutional constraint which is a very serious matter.

Prospects of Panchayati Raj Institutions

There is no substitute for democratic decentralisation in a developing country such as India. Panchayati Raj has come to stay as a part of democratisation of Indian polity in the wake of independence. The fact of the matter is that the Panchayati Raj Institutions have not been given a chance to serve as a forerunner of development in the rural areas of India. With necessary correctives, the basic objectives could be achieved without much of a difficulty. Let us try to list out some of the necessary conditions which appear to be necessary for the success of Panchayati Raj Institutions.

(i) Conceptual Clarity

The first and foremost important aspect that needs immediate attention is that of evolving a comprehensive concept of Panchayati Raj. Its goal, role etc., have to be clearly defined and there should not be any ambiguity, so that the people would have a clear perception of Panchayati Raj Institutions. The following important roles may be taken a serious note for this purpose. Firstly, the Panchayati Raj Institutions should be treated as the basic units of self-government. It implies that there is a need for decentralisation of administrative and political power. This would encourage self-governance and mass participation in its working. Secondly, the Panchayati Raj Institutions have to contribute towards strengthening of the planning process at micro-level as well as overall development. Finally, the Panchayati Raj Institutions have to improve the condition so that the down trodden can reach the highest level of decision-making bodies.

(ii) Protection of the Poor

In addition to conceptual clarity, it is necessary to strengthen the condition of the poor to protect them from the rural rich and their dominance. It is clear that the existing power structure in the rural areas is mostly in favour of rich who would exploit the poor. After all, the efforts made by all in the rural areas were directed mainly to improve the conditions of the weaker sections. If the benefits of the Panchayati Raj Institutions have to reach the poor and if the poor are to be associated with the Panchayati Raj Institutions, it is necessary to strengthen their position by adopting certain measures. It is necessary to identify the areas of dependence of the poor and find measures to stop exploitation. Streamlining the public distribution system, social security measures, employment guarantee schemes, organisation of the rural poor are some of the measures which would be mentioned in this context. In addition, redistribution of assets in favour of the poor by implementing land reform laws, and creation of assets to the poor could be another set of measures which would go a long way in reducing dependency of the poor on the rural rich.

(iii) Awareness among Panchayati Raj Functionaries

It has been realised that the Panchayati Raj functionaries do not have sufficient knowledge about their need based and area specific roles. They are ignorant of several aspects of Panchayati Raj system. It is, therefore, necessary to provide an opportunity to them to know about the Panchayati Raj Acts, the objectives and role of Panchayati Raj Institutions, the rural situation, possible areas of growth and minimum skills of planning for overall development of their respective areas. It is necessary to train them so that they could perform their functions effectively. This would also help them to minimise the citizen's apathy towards the Panchayati Raj activities.

(iv) Financial Support

There is a need for sound financial base for the Panchayati Raj Institutions. The establishment of a Panchayati Raj Finance Corporation could be the first step. This would enable the Panchayati Raj Institutions to establish remunerative enterprises. Enlarged tax jurisdiction, sharing of revenue from selected state taxes and grants are the other possible alternatives to achieve the long-term objective. However, there is a growing demand for an institutional arrangement through which the distribution of the finances among the Panchayati Raj Institutions have to be made without further delay. A rational redistribution is a must in this situation and a lesson learnt might be cited from Karnataka model. As per the 1985 Act, the State Governments in Karnataka has to organise a State Finance Commission to work out the distribution of finances between the state and the Panchayati Raj Institutions. This step would go a long way in solving the financial problems of the Panchayati Raj Institutions. It does not, however, mean that the Panchayati Raj Institutions need not bother about their own resource base. The notion that "no taxation, only representation" 'is not a wise policy. The Panchayati Raj Institutions have to make serious attempts to tap the local resources.

(v) Integrated Administrative Structures

There is a need for remodelling the administrative organisation of Panchayati Raj Institutions. It is necessary that all the officials whose functions have been shifted to Panchayati Raj Institutions have to be placed under the respective institutions. It calls for a separate service called Panchayati Raj service. It is also necessary to see to it that the bureaucracy is committed to Panchayati Raj. In fact the Panchayati Raj Institutions should be provided with necessary administrative help which has a primary loyalty towards them. The concept of specialisation should be introduced so that the technical needs of the Panchayati Raj Institutions could be met without any problem. The adequate safeguards have to be provided in this direction. An integrated administrative structure, thus, becomes very essential. The states like Karnataka. Maharashtra and to some extent Gujarat have made provision for such an arrangement. Almost all the committees which studied the problem have unanimously recommended that an administrative structure for planning and development and the same should be integrated with the Institutions of local self-government.

(vi) Provision for Constitutional Status

Finally, let us look at the attempts made in recent times to provide Constitutional status to the Panchayati Raj Institutions. It is observed that the states are not very keen to organise Panchayati Raj Institutions as they are not prepared to share power with so-called lower local bodies. In fact, some critics pointed out that some state governments have grabbed the power back from the Panchayati Raj Institutions gradually. Several committees and commissions, appointed by the state governments from time to time highlighted the deficiencies in the functioning of Panchayati Raj Institutions. It is also felt that the Panchayati Raj Institutions in the coming years should be well-equipped to manage democratic development under the changing conditions in all spheres of rural life. Realising the need to restructure and revitalise these bodies, the Government of India came forward with a proposal to amend the Constitution.

- All states will have three tier Panchayati Raj system;
- Elections will be held regularly, every five years, under the control and supervision of the Chief Election Commissioner. Elections to the dissolved or superseded bodies will have to be held within six months.
- All the seats will be filled through direct election and office bearers will be members directly elected.
- Reservation of seats to the extent of 30 per cent to women and seats for scheduled castes and scheduled tribes in proportion to their population will be made.
- The State governments will provide adequate finances. State Finance Commissions will review the finances of the Panchayati Raj bodies every five years.
- Panchayati Raj bodies will prepare plans for economic development, social justice and social welfare of their population

as per the guidelines. These plans will be incorporated later on in the state plans.

- Strict accounting procedures would be laid down to control corruption and misuse of funds by the Panchayati Raj Institutions. Comptroller and Auditor General will supervise the accounts.

Causes of under delivery of the Panchayats

Some reasons for their uninspiring performance are:

- **Lack of adequate devolution:** Many states have not taken adequate steps to devolve 3Fs to the PRIs to enable them to discharge their constitutionally stipulated functions. Further, it is imperative that the PRIs have resources to match the responsibilities entrusted to them. While SFCs have submitted their recommendations, not many states have implemented these or taken steps to ensure the PRI's fiscal viability.
- **Excessive control by bureaucracy:** In some states, the GPs have been placed in a position of subordination: GP Sarpanches have to be spared much time by visiting Block Offices for funds and/or technical approval. These interactions with the block office staffs distort the role of a Sarpanch as elected representative.
- **Tied nature of funds:** Some funds given by state or central governments through different schemes or grants that are designated as untied fund, but in real practice, those are tied in nature. So their utilization for the development purposes is remaining underutilized and the outcomes of the projects are not being achieved properly as per the project objectives. Therefore, with the preparation of participatory planning the the untied fund may be utilized in the real sense. In this context, the PRIs must be provided the need based handholding supports.
- **Overwhelming dependency on government funding:** Statistics show the overwhelming dependence of Panchayats on government funding. When Panchayats do not raise own resources and instead receive funds from outside, people are less likely to request a social audit and the Panchayats are becoming less responsive and less accountable.
- **Reluctance to use fiscal powers:** The Panchayats have the rights to levy tax on property, business, markets, fairs and also for services

provided, like street lighting or public toilets etc. Very few Panchayats use their fiscal power to levy and collect taxes. The argument pushed by Panchayat heads is that it is difficult to levy tax on your own constituency, especially when you live in the community.

- **Non-harmonization:** There is lack of harmony of State Acts and Rules, central legislations and programmes with the 73rd Amendment.
- **Status of the GS:** Empowerment of GSs can be a powerful weapon for transparency, accountability, inclusive growth and social audit.. In the guidelines of different ministries for central schemes, specific functions for GS are being proposed by MoPR. Some states have also provided for specific functions of the GS and Ward Sabha under their Panchayat Laws.

Defects in Panchayati Raj System in India

Some of the main defects found in Panchayati Raj System in India are as follows:

1. Unscientific distribution of functions

The prime defect in Panchayati Raj system lies in the distribution of functions between the structures at different levels, which has not been made along scientific lines. The blending of development and local self-government functions has significantly curtailed the autonomy of the local self government institutions. Again it has virtually converted them into governmental agencies. Even the functions assigned to the Panchayats and the Panchayat Samiti overlap, leading to confusion, duplication of efforts and shifting of responsibility.

2. Incompatible relation between the three-tiers

The three-tiers do not operate as functional authorities. The tendency on the part of the higher structure to treat the lower structure as its subordinate is markedly visible. M. P. Sharma rightly observes the hierarchical domination and predominance, "fitters down step by step from Zilla Parishad to Panchayat Samiti and from them to the Village Panchayats" Needless to state that this kind of mutual relationship is not in commensurate with the genuine spirit of democratic decentralisation.

3. Inadequate Finance

The inadequacy of funds has also stood in the way of successful working of the Panchayati Raj. The Panchayati Raj bodies have limited powers in respect of imposing cesses and taxes. They have received as much adequate funds from the state government. Further, they are generally reluctant to raise necessary funds due to the political fear of losing popularity with the masses.

4. Lack of cordial relation between officials and people

Introduction of the Panchayati Raj aimed at securing effective participation of the people. But in reality this hardly happens since the key administrative and technical positions are manned by the government officials. Generally there is lack of proper cooperation and coordination between the people and the officials like Block Development Officers, the District Officers etc. Again the officers fail to discharge the development duties more efficiently and sincerely.

5. Lack of conceptual clarity

There is lack of clarity in regard to the concept of Panchayati Raj itself and the objectives for which it stands. Some would treat it just as an administrative agency while some others look upon it as an extension of democracy at the grass roots level, and a few others consider it a charter of rural local government. Some also consider it as an agent between government and the people. Then these confusions must be wiped out by clearly the system.

6. Undemocratic composition of various Panchayati Raj Institutions

Various Panchayati Raj Institutions are constituted setting aside democratic norms and principles. The indirect election of most of the members to Panchayat Samiti only increases the possibility of corruption and bribery. Even the Zilla Parishad consists of mainly ex-officio members. They are, for the most part, government officials. This negates sound democratic principles.

7. Disillusionment on Structural-Functional Front

The performance of Panchayati Raj Institutions has been slow down by corruption, inefficiency, negligible regard for procedures, political interference in day to day administration, narrow-minded loyalties, motivated actions and power concentration instead of true service mentality- all these have stood in the way of the success of Panchayati Raj. Furthermore, the power to supersede the local bodies on the part of the State Government clearly violates the spirit of democratic decentralisation.

8. Administrative Problem

The Panchayati Raj bodies experience several administrative problems. They are the tendency towards politicization of the local administration, lack of co-ordination between the popular and bureaucratic elements, lack of proper incentives and promotion opportunities for administrative personnel and indifferent attitude of the government servants towards development programmes etc.

9. PRIs as Organisational Arms of Political Parties

It is being increasingly noticed that the Panchayati Raj Institutions are viewed only as organisational arms of political parties, especially of the ruling party in the state. The state government, in most states, allows the Panchayati Raj Institutions to function only upon expediency rather than any commitment to the philosophy of democratic decentralisation.

Panchayati Raj Institutions; an Evaluation

- PRIs have witnessed simultaneously a remarkable success and a staggering failure in the journey of 26 years depending on the goalposts against which they are evaluated.
- While the PRI has succeeded in creating another layer of government and political representation at the grass-roots level, it has failed to provide better governance.
- The 73rd and 74th Amendments provisioned that no less than one-third of the total seats in local bodies should be reserved for women. Many seats and sarpanch/pradhan positions were also reserved for SC/ST candidates.
- Research using PRIs has shown that having female political representation in local governments makes women more likely to come forward and in districts with female sarpanches, significantly greater investments are made in drinking water, public goods.
- Moreover, the states have also provided the statutory safeguards for many devolution provisions, which have considerably empowered local governments.

- Successive (central) Finance Commissions have substantially increased fund allocations for local bodies and also the grants have been increased. 15th Finance Commission is also considering to further increase the allocations for local governments to match the international standards.

Concerns

- The grey area is the lack of adequate funds. There is a need to enlarge the domain of panchayats to be able to raise their own funds.
- The interference of area MPs and MLAs in the functioning of panchayats also adversely affected their performance.
- The 73rd amendment only mandated the creation of local self-governing bodies and left the decision to delegate powers, functions, and finances to the state legislatures, therein lies the failure of PRIs.
- The transfer of various governance functions-like the provision of education, health, sanitation and water was not mandated. Instead the amendment listed the functions that could be transferred and left it to the state legislature to actually devolve functions.
- Because these functions were never devolved, state executive authorities have proliferated to carry out these functions. The most common example is the terrible state water boards.
- The major failure of the amendment is the lack of finances for PRIs. Local governments can either raise their own revenue through local taxes or receive inter-governmental transfers.
- The power to tax, even for subjects falling within the purview of PRIs, has to be specifically authorized by the state legislature. The 73rd Amendment let this be a choice open to the state legislatures-a choice that most states have not exercised.
- A second avenue of revenue generation is inter-governmental transfers, where state governments devolve a certain percentage of their revenue to PRIs. The constitutional amendment created provisions for State Finance Commissions to recommend the revenue share between state and local governments. However, these are merely recommendations and the state governments are not bound by them.

- Though finance commissions, at every level, have advocated for greater devolution of funds, there has been little action by states to devolve funds.
- PRIs are reluctant to take on projects that require any meaningful financial outlay and are often unable to solve even the most basic local governance needs.
- PRIs also suffer from structural deficiencies i.e. no secretarial support and lower levels of technical knowledge which restricted the aggregation of bottom up planning.
- There is a presence of adhocism i.e. lack of clear setting of agenda in Gram Sabha, Gram Samiti meetings and no proper structure.
- Though women and SC/STs has got representation in PRIs through reservation mandated by 73rd amendment but there is a presence of Panch-Pati and Proxy representation in case of women and SC/ STs representatives respectively.
- Accountability arrangements of PRIs remain very weak.
- The issue of ambiguity in the division of functions and funds has allowed concentration of powers with the states and thereby restraining the elective representatives who are more aware and sensitive to the ground level issues to take control.

Evocative Points

- Genuine fiscal federalism i.e. fiscal autonomy accompanied by fiscal responsibility can provide a long term solution without these PRIs will only be an expensive failure.
- Sixth report of 2nd ARC, 'Local Governance- An inspiring journey into the future', had recommended that there should be a clear-cut demarcation of functions of each tier of the government.
- States should adopt the concept of 'activity mapping', wherein each state clearly delineates the responsibilities and roles for the different tiers of the government in respect to the subjects listed in the Schedule-XI.
- The subjects should divide and assigned to the different tiers on the basis of accountability to the public.
- States like Karnataka and Kerala have taken some steps in this direction but overall progress has been highly uneven.

- There is the need for bottom up planning especially at district level, based on grassroots inputs received from Gram Sabha.
- Karnataka has created a separate bureaucratic cadre for Panchayats to get away from the practice of deputation of officials who often overpowered the elected representatives. Such practices need to be replicated in other states for strengthening the true character of local self governance.
- The centre also needs to financially incentivize states to encourage effective devolution to the panchayats in fund, functions and functionaries.
- Training should be provided to local representatives to develop expertise so that they contribute more in planning and implementation of policies and programmes.
- To solve the problem of proxy representation social empowerment must precede the political empowerment.
- The states like Rajasthan and Haryana have set certain minimum qualification standards for Panchayat elections. Such necessary eligibility can help in improving effectiveness of governance mechanism.
- These standards should apply for MLAs and MPs also and in this direction government should speed up efforts for universal education.
- There should be clear mechanisms to ensure that states comply with the constitutional provisions, particularly in the appointment and implementation of the recommendations of the State Finance Commissions (SFCs).

Way Forward

- The need of the hour is to bring about a holistic change in the lives of beneficiaries among the villagers by uplifting their socio-economic and health status through effective linkages through community, governmental and other developmental agencies.
- Government should take remedial action in the interest of democracy, social inclusion and cooperative federalism.
- People's demands for the sustainable decentralisation and advocacy should focus on a decentralisation agenda. The framework needs to be evolved to accommodate the demand for decentralisation.

- It is important to have clarity in the assignment of functions and the local governments should have clear and independent sources of finance

Conclusion

A comprehensive insight into Article-40 and Articles-43 to 243-O shows that the makers of our constitution want the village panchayats to be responsible for its own affairs as well as to act as a solid foundation for political democracy of the country. For encouraging development in the rural parts of the country, it is necessary to mobilize the resources in the hands of people and thus accelerate the participation of them in the decision making the process that has an effect on their daily living. The higher level policy makers are also well aware that the empowerment goals at Panchayat level have not been fully achieved but with some procedural, legislative and most importantly attitudinal changes, it is not far from being achieved.

The basic purpose of Panchayati Raj Institutions has not yet been achieved. The problem would not end by making the Panchayati Raj Institution economically self-sufficient and structurally sound. The most important aspect is change at the attitudinal pattern. Otherwise, decentralisation would remain only in paper. In real practice, there would be concentration of power in the hands of those people who have money and who want to use .the institution for making more money. It would take many more decades to reach a stage when people are at least aware of their own rights. There would be a healthy atmosphere where each would grow but not at the cost of others. Panchayati Raj Institutions have come to stay in India but to achieve success; we have a long way to go.

There is a conventional classification of fiscal, political and administrative decentralization using which the three-volume study conducted by the World Bank on Indian decentralisation ranks India the first in terms of political decentralisation and last in terms of administrative decentralization. Our Indian statutes and other union territories are willing to accept the panchayat system and give them recognition to hold elections. They also respect their stipulations with regard to reservations for Scheduled Castes (SCs), Scheduled Tribes (STs) and women. However, they are not ready to give them sufficient administrative control without which efficient functioning is at stake. Again, although most states have established SECs, whose primary responsibilities are to organise and oversee Panchayat elections and to prepare the electoral rolls, many have been unwilling to relinquish powers of delimitation i.e. the power to define electoral constituencies. There is a lack of proper demarcation and clarity of functions among the panchayats and the other levels of government and the states also have the rights to either assign o if necessary, to withdraw functions given to the panchayats. This again shows the supremacy of state upon the so-called autonomous panchayat governance. A strong, vibrant local government is a means of political decentralization. Decision-making being closer to the people, decentralization ensures decision-makers more effective accountability to the governed. This also ensures more realistic programming, for local problems are apt to receive urgent attention. Local vigilance also increases; thereby reducing the room for corruption. This certainly goes a long way towards maximising returns on every rupee spent on development.

2

Panchayati Raj and 73rd Constitutional Amendment

"True democracy cannot be worked by twenty men sitting at the centre. It has to be worked from below by the people of every village." — ***Mahatma Gandhi***

Introduction

Democracy as a form of political institution may be viewed as an opportunity to accommodate people's participation not only in the sovereign power of the state but also in the day-to-day functioning of the government. J.S. Mill argues that 'the only government which can fully satisfy all the requirements of the state is one in which all the people participate'. The formal legitimate system of local self-government was introduced by the British in the later part of the 19th century British India. However, panchayats are believed to be ancient, especially in places where the villages were not closely covered by state administration. The residents gathered under the leadership of village elders or religious leaders to discuss and sort out their problems.

In multi-layered governance, the Panchayati Raj comes closest to the people and hence there is prima facie little scope for negligence to the needy villagers as there is little social space between the electorate and the elected. Every individual can get opportunity to participate in the decision-making process and functioning of the panchayat concerned. The true spirit of participatory democracy gets reflected in the working of the panchayat system. That is why this system is also known as 'self-governance, self-management, mutual co-operation, sharing equality, freedom and brotherhood to all', more practicable is a 'where man lived in small communities'.

Sir Charles Metcalfe, the then governor general of India (1835–1836), called the villages 'The Little Republics'. The Mayo Resolution of 1870, no doubt, added strength to the local self-government. Thereafter, the Lord Rippon Resolution emerged as a landmark in the history and evolution of the local governments. This resolution is still considered to be the 'Magna Carta' of local democracy in India (Mathew, 2013). The 73rd Constitutional Amendment 1993 gave the local self-government a constitutional status, although it remains a state subject as the status of the XIth Schedule is similar to the Directive Principles of State Policy. Even before the proverbial 73rd CAA, the Jyoti Basu's communist government in West Bengal in 1977 and Ramakrishna Hegde's Janata government in Karnataka in 1987 had given greater importance to the Panchayati Raj Institutions (PRIs) in their respective states. Gandhian socialists like Jayaprakash Narayan (JP) also advocated 'direct democracy' at the village level and stated that the Gram Sabha signifies democracy at village level. He argued that let us have direct democracy at the village level and representative government upwards to Delhi. He further said that the relationship between the panchayat and Gram Sabha should be that of the cabinet and assembly. The principal focus of the panchayat has to be the special consideration of local issues and resolution of local disputes. There are several studies that have highlighted the importance, status and functions of the Panchayati Raj after the 73rd constitutional amendment. Among these, some of them try to understand the working of new PRI system. Ranbir Singh (2009) suggests that the Drafting Committee of the constitution had paid lip service to the local self-government institutions. Dr Ambedkar was critical of the village republics (panchayats of village communities) calling them the 'ruination of India'. They were nothing but 'sink of localism and of ignorance and communalism'. Whatever may be the approach of the Drafting Committee, the 73rd Constitutional Amendment Act of 1993 also failed to have a significant impact on the local administration as the political elites in most of the states were not willing to share political power with the PRIs. Medha Kotwal Lele (2001), has argued that the 73rd and 74th Constitutional Amendment Acts have introduced democratic process in these deliberative bodies. Moreover, Constitutional Amendment Acts have opened up a larger debate on democratisation where the marginalised groups get easy access to the decision-making process quite legitimately. However, in reality, even the participation in the decision-making process as well as the statutory provisions fails to provide guarantee to their empowerment. In majority of cases, the marginalised groups who get elected to these bodies are facing open confrontations with traditional bodies such as Gavki in Maharashtra, Khap Panchayat (KP) in Haryana and Customary Village Council (CVC) in Karnataka. M.K. Lele has highlighted that the 73rd Constitutional Amendment Act has forced the states to create the panchayat bodies. The inadequacy of the Panchayati Raj resources falls short of its needs for development expenditure. In 2002, the government of Andhra Pradesh had diverted most of the funds of Swarna Jayanti Gram Samriddhi Yojana under the gram panchayat to the construction of individual household latrines and school toilets. Had the PRIs functioned effectively, adequate and regular funds should have been provided. Mohinder Singh and Vijay Kumar (2005) observe that the state control always reduces the PRIs to subordinate status. The Article provides details of different types of state control, such as, administrative control and financial control over the PRIs. With the institutional control, the ruling party at the state level always tried to gain its own political interests. However, it could not succeed because of the stay order issued by the Punjab and Haryana High Court. The inadequate resource of the PRIs with the financial control in the hands of the state government has put the PRIs in dilemma between autonomy and dependency. Such a control of the state government does undermine the very purpose for which the PRIs have been idolised.

Panchayati Raj in Independent India

Immediately after Independence, many leaders thought of establishing the PRIs at the grassroots level for democratic decentralisation. Mahatma Gandhi argued for the Gram Swaraj and pleaded for the transfer of power to the rural masses. On the other hand, Dr. B.R. Ambedkar strongly opposed village panchayats because the villages represent regressive India, 'a source of oppression'. He further argued that the empowerment of village institutions would mean perpetual dominance of the upper castes, who would continue to exploit the lower castes and the poor. Dr. Ambedkar, the chairman of the Drafting Committee of the Constituent Assembly, was a powerful voice representing the Dalit community of the country. He himself had experienced caste discrimination and exploitative practices of the upper castes. In these circumstances, the village panchayats did not get much attention/promise as he argued them as nothing 'but a sink of localism, den of ignorance and narrow-mindedness'.

Gandhiji, however, severely criticised this attitude, because the village communities have been the basic units wherein individual happiness, freedom and independence had been realised since ancient times. With this experience, he suggested that the Indian polity should be based on communitarian principles where power does not flow from the top to the bottom, but travels from the village communities to the districts, and then upward to the provinces and then the Centre. Dr. Ambedkar, however, opposed the concept of communitarian principle because the deprived sections were not part of the 'community'. These circumstances prompted Dr. Ambedkar not to include village panchayats in the draft constitution in the beginning and later the idea was included as a limited measure in the Directive Principles of the State Policy. Article-40 of the Directive Principles of State Policy states that 'the state should take steps to organise village panchayats and endow them with such powers and authority as may be necessary to enable them to function as units of self-governments'.

At the beginning, most of the development plans were prepared without giving much importance to the village panchayats. When these programmes 'failed to generate popular interest and enthusiasm' in development work, the Planning Commission appointed a committee headed by Balwantrai Mehta in 1957. The committee viewed that 'only grassroots level agencies can establish a link between the local leadership who enjoy the confidence of local people and translate the policies of the government into action' and it recommended three-tier Panchayati Raj system in the country. While inaugurating the Panchayati Raj system at Nagaur in Rajasthan on the 2nd October 1959, Nehru hailed the system as 'the most revolutionary and historical step in the context of new India'. Democracy at the top would not be a success unless it was built from the below.

By the mid-1960s, the Panchayati Raj covered almost all parts of the country and the people experienced the presence of a system which could address the local issues of everyday life. Within two years of its accomplishments, it failed to keep on strengthening owing to a number of crises like food crisis and war with China. Achieving adequate food grain production was major cause of concern for the policymakers and in that direction; many agricultural schemes were launched by the government relying mostly on bureaucracy. In absence of the constitutional sanction and clarity, most of the panchayats functioned as government agents rather than self-governing institutions. According to Mathur, these institutions were not seen as institutions of peoples' participation that played a role in deepening democracy but rather as instruments to facilitate the implementation of national policies (Mathur, 2013, p. 25).

As soon as the Janata Party came to power at the centre in 1977, it showed interest in reviving the Panchayati Raj system and it urged the government that there should be full-time planning machinery at the block and district level so that people can take part in the planning and implementation at the local level. The Janata government appointed the Ashok Mehta Committee to review and suggest suitable measures for the strengthening of Panchayati Raj in 1978. The committee recommended a two-tier system of Panchayati Raj consisting of Zilla Parishad at the district level as the unit of administration and planning and Mandal Panchayat as the base. It also recommended that the PRI should have powers of taxation to generate their own financial resources. The development functions should be transferred to the Zilla Parishad and all development staff should work under its control and supervision. Another significant recommendation by this committee was to hold regular elections to these bodies and participation of political parties. With the fall of the Janata Party government, the Ashok Mehta Committee recommendations did not come into effect. However, states such as Andhra Pradesh, Karnataka and West Bengal formulated new legislations based on the Ashok Mehta Committee. The studies of several scholars suggest that after the Emergency (1975–1977), when the non-Congress and regional parties formed the governments in several states, they wanted to retain their power by building their cadres at the grassroots level, and they implemented the Ashok Mehta Committee recommendations. Among these states, Karnataka was the first state to implement the two-tier system of Panchayati Raj, which is also known as sub-state level governance structure. The Karnataka government has attempted to have genuine and autonomous panchayat bodies at the villages and in the districts.

During Rajiv Gandhi's tenure, two more committees (i.e., G.V.K. Rao Committee and L.M. Singhvi Committee) were appointed to study the existing administrative system at local level and also to regenerate PRI system. The G.V.K. Rao Committee recommended the activation of the 'Panchayati Raj bodies', while the L.M. Singhvi Committee recommended that the PRIs should be enshrined in the Constitution and the 'Gram Sabha' should be the base for decentralised democracy. It also recommended an Election Commission to conduct elections to local bodies and a Finance Commission to ensure the rural development programmes to the PR bodies by adding Schedule-VII to the Constitution.

Based on the recommendations of these two committees, Rajiv Gandhi, the then prime minister of India, introduced the 64th Constitutional

Amendment Bill on local self-government in 1989. The sole idea behind the 64th CA bill was to restructure the Panchayati Raj bodies and to bring uniformity, efficiency and responsiveness in public services. While introducing the Bill in the Lok Sabha, the prime minister said, this bill seeks to enshrine democracy at grassroots level' as it intends 'to give power to people', and it will 'end corruption, fight to finish power brokers and middlemen' in politics. The prime minister claimed this bill would be a 'historic and revolutionary bill'. However, the bill got defeated in the Rajya Sabha with a small margin, and subsequently during the Narasimha Rao's government, the bill was passed with near unanimity by the Lok Sabha on 22th December 1992 and by the Rajya Sabha on 23th December 1992. It became the 73rd CAA on 24th April 1993. The CAA has incorporated all the recommendations of L.M. Singhvi Committee and urged all the states to come up with legislations commensurate with the Act. However, the CAA has exempted the small states with a population less than 20 lakh (Arunachal Pradesh: 13 lakh; Goa: 14 lakh; Nagaland: 19 lakh; Sikkim: 6 lakh) from constituting the intermediate bodies.

73rd Constitutional Amendment

The system of Raj of Panchayat has always existed in India. The traditional Panchayats had been formed in various parts of India after the pastoral society was converted into an agrarian one following the emergence of agriculture as the major mode of production and the consequent settlement of the villages. Every village community formed a council for the system maintenance and conflict resolution. The British too admired the village 'Panchayat'. Sir Charles Metcalfe, a British governor in India in the 19th Century even called them "the little republics". But these so called little republics were not ideal centers with democratic participation of all the people, due to the caste ridden feudal system of those days.

During the British period, the working village assemblies were kept alive and wherever there was a demand for them they were revived, in fact, local self government in India, in the sense of a representative institution accountable to the electorate, was the creation of Lord Ripon in 1882. It provided for local board consisting of large majority of elected non-official members and presided over by a non-official chairman. By 1925, British India had passed acts for the establishment of village Panchayat Acts. However, those panchayats covered only a limited number of villages and had, generally, a limited number of functions.

Background

Gandhiji had spoken of Gram Swaraj (Village Republics) in which adult villagers would annually elect the government and which would have authority and jurisdiction in the fields of legislation, jurisdiction and executive decision-making without interference, from the state government. With independence, although the panchayat Raj found strong advocates in the Gandhian tradition and Sarvodaya movement but the reality which is often contradict to Gandhiji's vision of Gram Swaraj being traumatized, when panchayat Raj was include only as Article-40 of directive principle of state policy of our constitution.

India's development in the early fifties was planned without taking cognizance of the Gandhian vision of Gram Swaraj. After the Community Development project was inaugurated in 1952, it was realized that without an 'agency' at the village level which could represent the entire community, assume responsibility and provide the necessary leadership for implementing development programs, real progress in the area of rural development could not come about. In 1957, the Balwant Rai Mehta Committee's report recommended the establishment of statutory elective local bodies. On that basis a three-tier system of panchayat raj was established in 1959 and almost all the states passed legislations to establish panchayats. In the period 1959 to 1964 the Panchayat Raj Institutions (PRIs) were conceived as local bodies meant to ensure peoples' participation in development.

The three tier model was accepted by all states but sufficient powers were not given to them and neither were finances, thereby leaving the panchayats to suffer to their fate. In such a scenario the importance of ensuring the participation of women after the death of Jawaharlal Nehru, political leaders were determined to end the possible threat to their leadership from village, mandal, or district leadership and began to discredit the decentralization of power. In 1977 the Ashok Mehta Committee emphasized that, in practice, at no point of time during 1959 to 1993, PRIs in any part of the country were endowed with sufficient 'power and authority' to enable them to 'function as units of self-government'. It was nowhere defined in the constitution and its meaning and scope were never authoritatively interpreted by the judicial guardians of the Constitution viz., the High Court's and the Supreme Court. Therefore, there was apple growing realization that it was the lack of constitutional support.

Mathew points out those certain essential prerequisites are necessary to make PRIs function as local self-government institutions:

(a) A clear-cut demarcation should be drawn between the state and Panchayati Raj bodies and also among the three-level local bodies,

(b) Adequate financial power and authority commensurate with the development responsibility and (c) Functional autonomy within the federal structure.

The need was felt to set up the boundaries of the PRI bodies so that they can function without any criss-cross of responsibilities. Since the constitutional amendment opens possibilities for fulfilling these conditions, the new PRIs must be seen as the third tier of governance.

Article-243D of CAA made mandatory reservation for the Scheduled Castes (SCs) and Scheduled Tribes (STs) in proportion to their total population in that area, both for seats and posts of chairpersons at all levels of the PRI. The CAA also says that not less than one-third seats should be reserved for women, both at the membership and headship levels for women including SC and ST. Many people think that the Constitutional Amendments and their provided powers and functions would make the local bodies active. However, there has been a prolonged delay by the state governments in transferring these constitutionally desirable powers and functions to the local bodies by state legislation. There are a number of reasons that have been spelt out ahead for the delay:

1. The first lacuna with the 73rd CAA is that its delegated powers and functions to the PRIs are subject to the federal division of powers in the Seventh Schedule of the Constitution. Article- 243G of the CAA says that the legislature of a state may, by law, endow the panchayats with such powers and authority as may be necessary to enable them to function as institutions of self-government. The word 'may' implies that the sharing of power with panchayats depends on the political will and political alignment at the state level. Empirically, it becomes clear that not authority but duty has been delegated to the PRIs in the name of democratic decentralisation. Under the constitutional scheme of devolution, the state government enjoys the custody of the PRIs. Moreover, the party politics destabilize the constitutional scheme of democratic decentralisation of power. The party in power at the state level rules and the same party politics trickles down to the

panchayats at the grassroots level. Therefore, there is an interface of both the democratic decentralisation and democratic centralisation; the former is constitutional and the latter is political. Therefore, democratic centralisation prevails over decentralisation. In the context of West Bengal that inspired the panchayat system as a model across the country it suffered from the same syndrome.

2. There is a failure on part of state governments to prepare electoral rolls and conduct regular elections to these bodies. Bihar has not been conducting elections to the PRI bodies for twenty years until 2001. Even after the 73rd CAA, the government of Bihar did not conduct elections to the local bodies and kept delaying because of litigations pertaining to the reservation of top leadership positions (ekal offices) in panchayats. Finally, it conducted elections to these bodies in 2001 without reservations provided for leadership positions in panchayats. Based on these facts, the working group on Decentralised Planning and Panchayati Raj of the Tenth Plan observed:

   Most of the court cases, grievances of aggrieved parties related to reservation of seats for SCs/STs/OBCs/women, delimitation of constituencies, percentage of reservation for chairpersons of lower tier to higher tier, etc. and in most of the cases, the state governments have not pursued these pending court cases vigorously for their early hearing so that a final decision of the court becomes available as early as possible. This reflects that the political elites at the state level are not interested to incorporate women and marginalised groups into the rural governance and developmental processes.

3. Article-243D also spells out the mandatory rotation, that is, the structural constraints of reservation of seats among constituencies from one election to the next election in the three-tier Panchayati Raj system. As per this act, if a seat or a constituency is reserved for a particular category, he or she is eligible to contest for that particular term only and they cannot contest for second term from the same constituency. It implies that women and other marginalised groups cannot contest from the same constituency once their five-year term expires. This has denied them the right to contest from the same constituency. More or less, the same method is followed in all the states except Tamil Nadu where the

mandatory reservation is for every ten years. The states such as Andhra Pradesh, Haryana, Himachal Pradesh, Madhya Pradesh, Odisha, Chhattisgarh, Maharashtra and Rajasthan have also introduced the two-child norm as eligibility criteria for contesting elections. Though this norm goes against both men and women, it is more detrimental to women especially to the SC and ST communities because majority of the families follow the big and joint family norm. To assess the impact of this norm, a study was conducted by the Mahila Chetna Manch, a Bhopal-based NGO (2002–2003) and it observed that unless and until proper information of two-child norm is disseminated to the rural areas, it is impossible to empower the economically and socially vulnerable sections of the society.

4. With regard to the functional domain, it can be stated that the functions listed in the 11th schedule are merely illustrative and indicative and most of the states have delegated only traditional civic functions rather than developmental responsibilities. Moreover, the states also realised that the transfer of additional functions requires the transfer of concomitant funds and functionaries to panchayats. The new amendment act has devolved twenty-nine subjects as functions rather than activities or sub-activities of panchayats. The fund gets allocated to different varieties of activities within a function. For example, if a tank is allocated as a function to a particular village, the money required for all the aspects of the tank construction is not given to the panchayats. Instead, small portion of the task is assigned to the panchayat with very little resources. Bulk of the task is retained by the state itself and it does the work with the help of line departments concerned. Therefore, the core functions that traditionally belonged to panchayats-drinking water, rural roads, street lighting, sanitation, primary health and so forth-are being performed by the line departments of the state governments. As a result, the per capita total expenditure of panchayats remains abysmally low in all states except undivided Andhra Pradesh, Chhattisgarh, Goa, Gujarat, Karnataka, Kerala, Maharashtra and Tamil Nadu.

5. The CAA has mentioned the mandatory establishment of the Gram Sabha which is the vital decision-making body at the bottom of

the Panchayati Raj or in the hierarchy of multi-structured governance. Article-243B defines composition of Gram Sabha. However, it fails to stipulate the powers and functions of Gram Sabha. In fact, in many instances, the functions are seen to endorse, to suggest and recommend, to consider annual accounts and administrative reports, audit notes, etc. All the state governments have endorsed the 73rd CAA and created the Gram Sabha under Article-243A. However, there is no uniformity in the statutes and functions of the Gram Sabha across the country. In Andhra Pradesh and Karnataka, the Gram Sabha is defined as the revenue village, while in Kerala, it is a Ward Sabha . None of the state legislations on PRIs has empowered the Gram Sabha to have control over the gram panchayat, rather it has been made an advisory body. Only the Kerala Panchayati Raj Act has made it obligatory for the head of the gram panchayat to explain to Gram Sabha as to why a particular decision or a set of decisions could not be implemented. Under the Panchayats Extension to the Scheduled Areas (PESA), the Gram Sabha has the power to safeguard the community resources and to settle local disputes with customary methods. The acquisition of land for development projects and the subsequent rehabilitation or resettlement of displaced and affected persons need to be done in consultation with either the Gram Sabha or at the appropriate level of panchayat.

6. The awareness level among the rural masses of Karnataka, Kerala, Tamil Nadu, Rajasthan and Sikkim has brought significant changes in the functions of the Gram Sabha and its decisions, and they are successfully implementing the decisions of the Gram Sabha. However, in Assam, West Bengal and Uttar Pradesh, the functions of Gram Sabha are only confined to the ratification of the budget and audit reports. In this connection, an instance can be cited that the Tamil Nadu government has issued orders to conduct the Gram Sabha on 26th January, 15th August, 1st May and 2nd October every year without fail. The most significant feature of the Madhya Pradesh Panchayati Raj Act is that it conducts more than sixteen Gram Sabha meetings annually. This is a good way of self-governance at the grassroots level.

7. The experience of functioning of the Panchayati Raj bodies over last one-and-a-half decade suggests that stability-cum-continuity

is being achieved, including execution of civic functions. However, the development functions supposed to be performed by the PR bodies are still a distant dream. Many chairpersons and members of PR bodies feel deprived not because of their direct or indirect elections but lack of meaningful stake in local governance.

8. The traditional bodies like 'collectives' or 'Gavki' in Maharashtra and CVCs in Karnataka are functioning parallel to the village panchayats. In Maharashtra, Gavki is dominated by the upper castes and elite landlords. It does not have any legal sanctity in the state. Despite having no legal sanctity, these bodies are more powerful than elected representatives at village level. Gavki is very active in the Konkan region of Satara, Ahmad Nagar, Nandurbar, Raigad and several other districts. These Gavkis (Kangaroo courts) deliver illegal judgments such as social boycott, cleaning of public latrines, donating blood or arranging social functions. Even today, in many parts of India, the traditional bodies are part and parcel of the village culture, and the lawmakers should give a chance to these traditional bodies to play some sort of conciliatory role on local issues. This would certainly promote the cooperation between elected representatives and traditional bodies and avoid confrontation between them, which may again defeat the purpose of the CAA.

9. The Khap panchayat is another example of the traditional body that exercises powers parallel to the village panchayat especially in Jat-dominated areas of north India, that is, Haryana, Punjab and the Meerut region of Uttar Pradesh. In this region, the KP traditionally emerged as an extra-judicial body that pronounces harsh punishments as retribution based on the age-old customs and traditions. In Haryana, when a Dalit girl was gang-raped by four youths, instead of condemning the incident, the KP directed that girls should be married off early so that rapes can be avoided. Later, the same Dalit girl committed suicide. Even the former Chief Minister Bhupender Singh Hooda said that Khaps are social institutions and steps taken in a hurry to curb them would have dangerous impacts on the law and order situation in the state. The appeasement policy taken by the political leaders would certainly encourage the KP to act more vigorously.

10. One of the main objectives of the 73rd CAA is to empower the weaker sections by offering the constitutional halo to the PRI

bodies. However, in reality, certain state governments are passing more and more obstructive laws against these sections of the society. For example, the Rajasthan government has issued an ordinance stating that if a person wants to contest for the post of village sarpanch, then he/she has to have the minimum qualification of Std-VIII. In case of reserved constituency for SCs, one should have the qualification of Std-V. In states like Rajasthan where women literacy is 46 per cent, much below the national average, it severely affects the prospects of SC and ST women candidates who mostly fail to satisfy the educational criteria for contesting elections as their educational status is much lower than that of the general women. It is intended to create hurdles in the way of weaker sections. Another discriminatory law against the marginalised sections is the Haryana Panchayati Raj (Amendment) Act 2015. Recently, the government of Haryana has passed this Act fixing the educational qualifications for the contest of local body elections. In addition to this, the candidates have to provide proof of having household toilets. In a country where the educational qualification is not fixed for the Lok Sabha and State Assembly elections, how can one fix educational qualification as criteria for eligibility to local body elections. This kind of legislations will certainly hinder women, OBCs and Dalits who are forced to give up education because of their socio-economic backwardness and gender discrimination .

The 73rd Amendment Act; in Brief

The 73rd Amendment Act 1992 came into effect from the 24th April 1993. All states enacted legislation by 23rd April 1994. The Panchayats previously were a mere suggestion in the Directive Principles of State Policy whereas the 73rd Amendment resulted in the Panchayati Raj Institutions (PRIs) being conferred constitutional sanction. This means that all activities of PRIs as stipulated by the Act have now legal and constitutional status and any violation of this by anybody and at any time would be punishable by law. Constitutional status vide Article-243 of Part-IX of the Constitution which came into effect from 24th April 1993 made it mandatory for all states to promulgate their own new acts consequent to the 73rd Constitutional Amendment Act or amend their old ones by April 1994.

Keeping in view the provisions of 73rd Constitutional Amendment Act, state Panchayat Raj acts have been constituted which incorporate a three-tier system of Panchayat Raj, Consisting of Zilla Panchayats at the district level, Panchayat Samitis or Kshetra Panchayats at intermediate level & Gram Panchayats at the village level.

A. Short title and commencement.

- This Act may be called the Constitution (Seventy-Third Amendment) Act, 1992.
- It shall come into force on such date as the Central Government may, by notification in the official gazette, appoint.

B. Insertion of new Part IX. After Part-VIII of the Constitution, the following part shall be inserted, namely:

The Panchayats

243. Definitions. In this part, unless the context otherwise requires –

(a) "District' means a district in a State;

(b) "Gram Sabha" means a body consisting of persons registered in the electoral rolls relating to a village comprised within the area of Panchayat at the village level;

(c) "Intermediate level" means a level between the village and district levels specified by the Governor of a state by public notification to be the intermediate level for the purposes of this part;

(d) "Panchayat" means an institution (by whatever name called) of self-government constituted under Article-243B, for the rural areas;

(e) "Panchayat area" means the territorial area of a Panchayat;

(f) "Population" means the population as ascertained at the last preceding census of which the relevant figures have been published;

(g) "Village" means a village specified by the Governor by public notification to be a village for the purpose of this part and includes a group of villages so specified.

243A. Gram Sabha. A Gram Sabha may exercise such powers and perform such functions at the village level as the Legislature of a state may, by law, provide.

243B. Constitution of Panchayats

(1) There shall be constituted in every state, Panchayats at the village, intermediate and district levels in accordance with the provisions of this part.

(2) Notwithstanding anything in clause (1), Panchayats at the intermediate level may not be constituted in a state having a population not exceeding twenty lakhs.

243C. Composition of Panchayat: All the seats in a Panchayat shall be filled by persons chosen by direct election from territorial constituencies in the Panchayat area and, for this purpose, each Panchayat area shall be between the population of each constituency and the number of seats allotted to it shall, so far as practicable, be the same throughout the Panchayat area.

243D. Reservation of Seats. Seats shall be reserved for–

(a) the Scheduled Castes; and

(b) the Scheduled Tribes,

In every Panchayat and the number of seats so reserved shall bear, as nearly as may be, the same proportion to the total number of seats to be filled by direct election in that Panchayat as the population of the scheduled castes in that Panchayat area or of the scheduled tribes in that Panchayat area bears to the total population of that area and such seats may be allotted by rotation of different constituencies in a Panchayat.

243E. Duration of Panchayats, etc. Every Panchayat, unless sooner dissolved under any law for the time being in force, shall continue for five years from the date appointed for its first meeting and no longer.

243F. Disqualification for Membership. A person shall be disqualified for being chosen as, and for being, a member of a Panchayat, if he is so disqualified by or under any law for the time being in force for the purposes of elections to the legislature of the State concerned.

243G. Powers, Authority and Responsibilities of Panchayats. Subject to the provisions of the Constitution, the legislature of a state may, by law, endow the Panchayats with such powers and authority as may be necessary to enable them to function as institutions of self-government and such law may contain provisions for the devolution of powers and responsibilities upon Panchayats at the appropriate level.

243H. Powers to impose Taxes by and Funds of the Panchayats. The legislature of a state may, by law, -

(a) Authorize a Panchayat to levy, collect and appropriate such taxes, duties, tolls and fees in accordance with such procedure and subject to such limits;

(b) Assign to a Panchayat such taxes, duties, tolls and fees levied and collected by the state government for such purposes and subject to such conditions and limits;

243J. Audit of Accounts of Panchayats. The Legislature of a state may, by law, make provisions with respect to the maintenance of accounts by the Panchayats and the auditing of such accounts.

243K. Elections to the Panchayats. The superintendence, direction and control of the preparation of electoral rolls for, and the conduct of all elections to the Panchayats shall be vested in a state Election Commission consisting of a State Election Commissioner to be appointed by the Governor.

Major Challenges in Panchayati Raj System

Major challenges of Panchayati Raj in India are discussed in the following manner:

(a) Social Challenges:

- (i) Lack of literacy in the public especially in women
- (ii) Lack of political consciousness
- (iii) Passiveness of public in political activities.
- (iv) Undemocratic social structure in India
- (v) Caste and religious discrimination.

(b) Economic Challenges:

- (i) Lack of financial resources for panchayat
- (ii) Possession of MNCs on water, land and jungle
- (iii) Poor economic condition of SC, ST and OBCs member in rural areas.

73rd Amendment Act and Devolution of Power

This act has added Part-IX to the Constitution of India. It is entitled as 'The Panchayats' and consists of provisions from Articles-243 to 243-0. In addition, the Act has also added eleventh schedule to the Constitution. It contains 29 functional items of the Panchayats and deals with Article-243G.Moreover, the act has given a practical shape to Article-40 of the Constitution which says that, "The state shall take steps to organise village Panchayats and endow them with such powers and authority as may be necessary to enable them to function as units of self- government." This Article forms a part of the Directive Principles of State Policy.

The act gives a constitutional status to the Panchayati Raj institutions. The state governments are under con-stitutional obligation to adopt the new Panchayati Raj system in accordance with the provisions of the act. Consequently, neither the formation of Panchayats nor the holding of elections a regular interval de-pends on the will of the state government any more.

The provisions of the act can be grouped into two categories—compulsory and voluntary. The compulsory provisions of the act have to be included in the state laws creating the new Panchayati Raj system. The voluntary provisions, on the other hand, may be included at the discretion of the states. Thus the voluntary provisions of the act ensure the right of the states to take local factors like geographical, politico-administrative and others, into consideration while adopting the new Panchayati Raj system. In other words, the act does not disturb the constitutional balance between the centre and the states in the Indian federal system. Even if it is a central law on a state subject (i.e., local government is a subject included in the state list under the seventh schedule of the constitution), the act does not encroach upon the jurisdiction of the states which are given adequate discretionary powers with regard to the Panchayats. The act is a significant landmark in the evolution of grassroots democratic institutions in the country. It transfers the representative democracy into participatory democracy. It is a revolutionary concept to build democracy at the grassroots level in the country. Almost immediately after the 73rd and 74th Amendments, every state government began the process of creating the requisite layer of PRIs and urban local bodies. State Election Commissions were in charge of the infrastructure required to elect local representatives. On all other margins except representation, PRIs are either a failure or at best a series of missed opportunities.

Before 1993, India had only two levels of government. The 73rd Amendment introduced local governing bodies across India. This amendment, however, did not require the implementation of local self-governing bodies. It only mandated the creation of local self-governing bodies, and left the decision to delegate powers, functions, and finances to the state legislatures. The PRIs in Indian context not get its desired output due to the 73rd Amendment Act due to the following reasons;

- The first malfunction of the 73rd Amendment was that the transfer of various governance functions—like the provision of education, health, sanitation, and water was not mandated. Instead the amendment listed the functions that could be transferred, and left it to the state legislature to actually devolve functions. There has been very little devolution of authority and functions in practice. PRIs cannot govern unless they are given the authority to actually perform functions related to governance.
- The second malfunction of the 73rd Amendment is the lack of finances for PRIs. Local governments can either raise their own revenue through local taxes or receive inter-governmental transfers. The amendment recognized bxoth forms of public finance, but did not mandate either. Though finance commissions, at every level, have advocated for greater devolution of funds, there has been little action by states to devolve funds. As a result, PRIs are so starved for funds that they are often unable to meet even payroll obligations. They are reluctant to take on projects that require any meaningful financial outlay and are often unable to solve even the most basic local governance needs. The only long-term solution is to foster genuine fiscal federalism where PRIs raise a large portion of their own revenue and face hard budget constraints, i.e. fiscal autonomy accompanied by fiscal responsibility. Presently, in 14th and 15th the fund flows to the 3-tiers are became more and more freedom has been given to them to prepare their need based and area specific plan to ensure economic development and social justice for the people of their jurisdiction.

Devolution of Power to Rural Local Bodies

The devolution of powers to the rural local bodies can be discussed with respect to three dimensions i.e. political, functional and financial.

Political Devolution

As against the spirit of 73rd Amendment Act, most of the states have retained considerable powers over the rural local bodies with them and have acted as an 'aggrandiser government'. Though, some of the states have conducted elections to these PR bodies, it has not been at a regular interval of 5 years. Many a time, the Supreme Court and the High Courts had to assertively intervene to preserve the spirit of the Constitution, as in the cases of Odisha,

Andhra Pradesh and Uttar Pradesh. In most of the states, the state governments supported by the bureaucracy believes that they are and should be the only the main actors of the state. Also, most of the states had direct elections of the panchayat chairperson, which was perpetuating this position's status as 'first among equals'. The roles and functions of Gram Sabha were left to the discretion, whims and fancies of state legislatures and just remained developmental organisations and implementing agencies.

Functional and Financial Devolution

In preference to have an array of functions under the 11th Schedule, which was overlapping to a great extent with those mentioned under the 7th Schedule, the functioning of local governments has always remained confined to street lighting, sanitation, water supply and local roads. With respect to developmental activities, they have acted as implementing agencies for the state governments merely to identify beneficiaries. They could never oversee management and implementation of plethora of governmental schemes.

Even after the Constitutional Amendment, the legislations enacted or amended by the states to widen the domain of functioning of panchayats have been in a skeletal form and the 'flesh and blood' of it has been missing for the reason that the administrative rules and procedures have been controlled largely by the executives. Specific rules and responsibilities of the PR bodies have been substantially absent from these enactments.

Many states have not established the district planning committee mandated by Article-243ZD, and even where it is in place, they are being headed by state ministers, which again strikes severely at the decentralization of power. Further, even in some states, though the functions have been transferred, requisite amount of funds and personnel, through which these functions can be carried out, has remained under the control of state government and the state-level bureaucracy except in states of Karnataka, Kerala, West Bengal and Maharashtra.

Conclusion

The Panchayati Raj Institutions (PRIs) have brought significant change in the Indian system of governance. The most important development has been that the democratic base of the Indian polity has become very wide. By virtue of the constitutional status bestowed upon the PRIs, it now has the potential to revolutionize the way we have been seeing local self-governance. It is not only a system of participative self governance but it ensures political empowerment to the poor, marginalized, and the oppressed, which traditionally in our country have been the Scheduled Castes, the Scheduled Tribes, and the women. These features activate the Panchayat Raj institutions today, to contribute to the process of development.

The following things may be suggested for making the system of Panchayati Raj successful:

- There should be change in present social structure.
- The participation of NGOs should be there to eliminate social evils as untouchability, casteism, communalism, child marriage dowry system and veil system etc.
- Panchayati Raj Institutes should emphasize improvement in Health, education and roads.
- Transparent Audit Agency should be established to eliminate corruption and red tapism.
- Panchayat members should be trained by state govt. especially women.

Rajani Kothari highlights the importance of decentralization of Panchayati Raj. He said that national leadership established the Panchayati Raj system in India. Unity is strengthening in the country through uniformity of local bodies.

Panchayati Raj Institutes could not achieve their goals because there is a lot of difference between their saying and doing. Actually, there is no real democracy at grass root level. Voters are influenced by casteism, communalism, kinship, and money matters and drinking. These social evils create social conflicts. So, if we want success of PRIs, we should create a healthy society. A healthy society can make a healthy nation.

3

Panchayati Raj and Decentralised Planning in India

"Any lover of true democracy and village life can take up a village, treat it as his world and sole work, and he will find good results." — ***Mahatma Gandhi***

Introduction

The (73rd Amendment) Bill, 1991 of Indian Constitution was introduced on 16th September, 1991 which was subsequently referred to a Joint Select Committee of Parliament in December 1991 for a detailed examination. The Joint Committee presented its report to Parliament in July, 1992. The bill was finally passed by the Lok Sabha on 22nd December, 1992 and by the Rajya Sabha on 23rd December, 1992 which was notified by the Central Government through official gazette on 20th April 1993 as it got rectified by the state legislatures. The President of India accorded his assent on 20th April, 1993 (Gazette of India, 1993, Part-II). After notification the Panchayati Raj Institutions have got the constitutional legitimacy. Thus, after facing many storms PRIs got constitutional status in April 1993 by way of 73rd Constitutional Amendment Act. The Constitution (73rd Amendment) Act, 1992 came into effect on 24th April, 1993 by a minute observation of Constitutional 64th & 74th Amendment Bill and 73rd Amendment Act. This act is an amalgamation of the 64th and 74th Constitutional Amendment Bills.

Keeping in view the provisions of 73rd Constitutional Amendment Act, a three-tier Panchayat Raj system has introduced i.e Zilla Panchayats at the District level, Panchayat Samitis at intermediate level & Gram Panchayats at the village level. Previously the concept Panchayats was mere a suggestive one as per the Directive Principles of State Policy whereas the 73rd Amendment resulted in the Panchayati Raj Institutions (PRIs) being conferred constitutional sanction. This means that all activities of PRIs as stipulated by the act have now legal and constitutional status and any violation of this by anybody, by any means and at any time would be punishable by the court of law. The Constitution (73rd Amendment) Act also contains provisions regarding regular elections to Panchayat bodies, setting up of a State Election Commission and a State Finance Commission, reservation for SCs, STs and women, enabling provisions for reservation for Backward Classes of citizens, etc. Adequate powers and responsibilities will have to be developed upon these institutions at appropriate levels to enable them to prepare and implement the schemes for economic development and social justice.

Decentralization; Concept and Meaning

Decentralization refers to a process of assigning the public functions and responsibilities of planning and implementation from central government to sub-district level in order to carry out specific tasks at the local level. Moreover, the public affairs are to be managed at the local level and there are certainly specific objectives for the need to choose the path of decentralization. Firstly, to handle promptly the local specified development needs. Secondly, to improve the efficiency of programme implementation. For administrative efficiency, thre is a need to divide up and dispense the work load to the organization in the field to benefit from local knowledge for their efficient implementation. Decentralization of functions gives dividends in terms of speed and efficiency in service and performance. It helps in achieving better coordination of related functions assigned to a

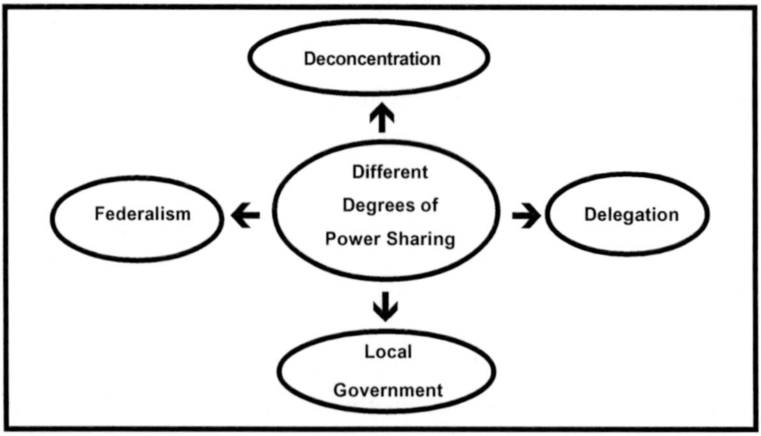

variety of local officers and it takes lesser time in taking decisions at the local level than the time taken in centralized planning system. Thirdly, to reach out the distant locations more effectively. Fourthly, to increase the responsiveness of local administration as per the people's needs.

Decentralization can be referred as the transfer of authority and responsibility for public functions from the central government to subordinate or quasi-independent government organizations and/or the private sector—is a complex multifaceted concept. Different types of decentralization should be distinguished because they have different characteristics, policy implications, and conditions for success.

Forms of Decentralization

There are some specific forms of decentralization that includes political, administrative, fiscal, and market decentralization. Drawing distinctions between these various concepts is useful for highlighting the many dimensions to successful decentralization and the need for coordination among them. Nevertheless, there is clearly overlap in defining any of these terms and the precise definitions are not as important as the need for a comprehensive approach. Political, administrative, fiscal and market decentralization can also appear in different forms and combinations across countries, within countries and even within sectors.

(a) Political Decentralization

Political decentralization aims to give citizens or their elected representatives more power in public decision-making. It is often associated with pluralistic politics and representative government, but it can also support democratization by giving citizens, or their representatives, more influence in the formulation and implementation of policies. Advocates of political decentralization assume that decisions made with greater participation will be better informed and more relevant to diverse interests in society than those made only by national political authorities. The concept implies that the selection of representatives from local electoral jurisdictions allows citizens to know better their political representatives and allows elected officials to know better the needs and desires of their constituents.

Political decentralization often requires constitutional or statutory reforms, the development of pluralistic political parties, the strengthening of legislatures, creation of local political units, and the encouragement of effective public interest groups.

(b) Administrative Decentralization

Administrative decentralization looks for to redistribute authority, responsibility and financial resources for providing public services among different levels of government. It is the transfer of responsibility for the planning, financing and management of certain public functions from the central government and its agencies to field units of government agencies, subordinate units or levels of government, semi-autonomous public authorities or corporations, or area-wide, regional or functional authorities.

The three major forms of administrative decentralization viz; deconcentration, delegation, and devolution and each have different characteristics.

(i) *Deconcentration*

Deconcentration; often considered to be the weakest form of decentralization and is used most frequently in unitary states- redistributes decision making authority and financial and management responsibilities among different levels of the central government. It can merely shift responsibilities from central government officials in the capital city to those working in regions, provinces or districts, or it can create strong field administration or local administrative capacity under the supervision of central government ministries. It refers to the introduction of administrative

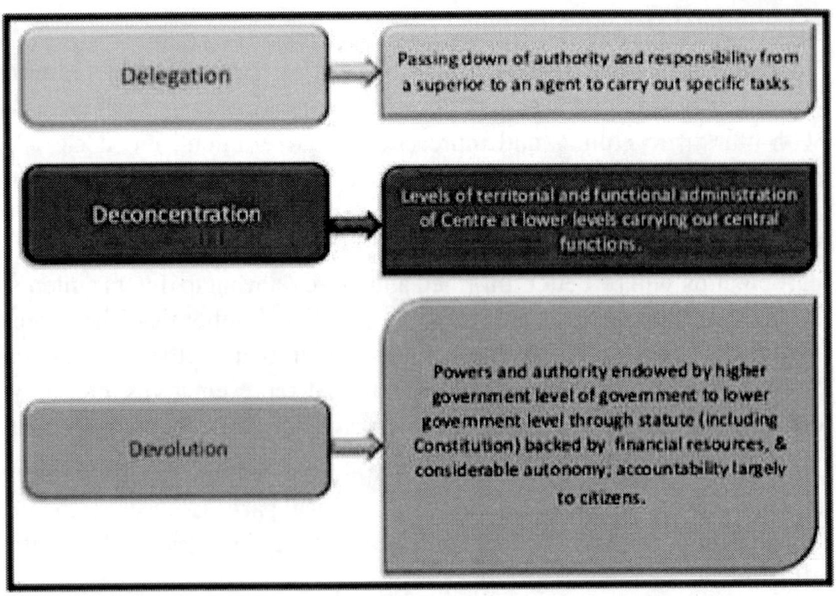

and cultural changes within the existing unitary structures, shifting responsibility, decision-making authority and resources for front-line operations only to the managers of local units. Public delivery and public financing coincide within a single administration. Deconcentration assigns specific functions and tasks performed by the staff of the headquarters of central administrations to staff posted in peripheral locations within the national territory. Staff, equipment, vehicles and budgetary resources are transferred to units such as regional and district offices. The managers of these units are given authority for autonomous decision making regarding the operations

(ii) *Delegation*

Delegation is a more extensive form of decentralization. Through delegation central governments transfer responsibility for decision-making and administration of public functions to semi-autonomous organizations not wholly controlled by the central government, but ultimately accountable to it. Governments delegate responsibilities when they create public enterprises or corporations, housing authorities, transportation authorities, special service districts, semi-autonomous school districts, regional development corporations, or special project implementation units. Usually these organizations have a great deal of discretion in decision-making. They may be exempt from constraints on regular civil service personnel and may be able to charge users directly for services. Responsibility and resources for implementing specific tasks and delivering certain services are transferred to a public agency, a state enterprise, a private enterprise, or an NGO under a contract that may provide some autonomy in interpreting the tasks assigned under the contract. In this case, decentralization takes the form of delegation.

(iii) *Devolution*

A third type of administrative decentralization is devolution. The primary objective needs that beneficiaries participate, normally through elected representatives of the local government in planning the delivery of services and in the evaluation of the services provided. In these cases, significant changes in the system of public administration are introduced and decentralization takes the form of devolution. Local governments are assigned the responsibility of deciding which services should be provided on a priority basis and to whom. Representation of and accountability to, beneficiaries are provided through the election mechanism. Public production or delivery and public financing coincide, but the lower levels of government normally receive only part of the funding required from the central government, the balance must be raised from local tax revenue and cost recovery.

When governments devolve functions, they transfer authority for decision-making, finance, and management to quasi-autonomous units of local government with corporate status. Devolution usually transfers responsibilities for services to municipalities that elect their own mayors and councils, raise their own revenues, and have independent authority to make investment decisions. In a devolved system, local governments have clear and legally recognized geographical boundaries over which they exercise authority and within which they perform public functions. It is this type of administrative decentralization that underlies most political decentralization.

Devolution implies changes in the political and fiscal dimensions of government. Local governments to which authority and resources are devolved acquire the power of autonomous initiative and decision making with respect to setting their own rules, goals and objectives. They also acquire the power of elaborating and implementing their own policies and strategies and of allocating resources to different activities within the domain assigned to them. In addition, they often are given authority to raise financial resources, through taxes, and in some cases, to borrow on the capital markets.

(c) Fiscal Decentralization

Financial responsibility is a core component of decentralization. If local governments and private organizations are to carry out decentralized functions effectively, they must have an adequate level of revenues –either raised locally or transferred from the central government as well as the authority to make decisions about expenditures. Fiscal decentralization can take many forms that include the following;

- Self-financing or cost recovery through user charges,
- Co-financing or co-production arrangements through which the users participate in providing services and infrastructure through monetary or labor contributions;
- Expansion of local revenues through property or sales taxes, or indirect charges;

- Intergovernmental transfers that shift general revenues from taxes collected by the central government to local governments for general or specific uses; and
- Authorization of municipal borrowing and the mobilization of either national or local government resources through loan guarantees.

In many developing countries local governments or administrative units possess the legal authority to impose taxes, but the tax base is so weak and the dependence on central government subsidies so ingrained that no attempt is made to exercise that authority.

(d) Economic or Market Decentralization

The most complete forms of decentralization from a government's perspective are privatization and deregulation because they shift responsibility for functions from the public to the private sector. Privatization and deregulation are usually, but not always, accompanied by economic liberalization and market development policies. They allow functions that had been primarily or exclusively the responsibility of government to be carried out by businesses, community groups, cooperatives, private voluntary associations, and other non-government organizations.

(i) *Privatization*

Privatization can range in scope from leaving the provision of goods and services entirely to the free operation of the market to "public-private partnerships" in which government and the private sector cooperate to provide services or infrastructure. Privatization can include:

- Allowing private enterprises to perform functions that had previously been monopolized by government;
- Contracting out the provision or management of public services or facilities to commercial enterprises indeed, there is a wide range of possible ways in which function can be organized and many examples of within public sector and public-private institutional forms, particularly in infrastructure;
- Financing public sector programs through the capital market (with adequate regulation or measures to prevent situations where the

central government bears the risk for this borrowing) and allowing private organizations to participate; and

- Transferring responsibility for providing services from the public to the private sector through the divestiture of state-owned enterprises.

(ii) *Deregulation*

Deregulation reduces the legal constraints on private participation in service provision or allows competition among private suppliers for services that in the past had been provided by the government or by regulated monopolies. In recent years privatization and deregulation have become more attractive alternatives to governments in developing countries. Local governments are also privatizing by contracting out service provision or administration.

Selection of a need based form of Decentralization

Centralization and decentralization are not "either-or" conditions. In most countries an appropriate balance of centralization and decentralization is essential to the effective and efficient functioning of government. Not all functions can or should be financed and managed in a decentralized fashion. Even when national governments decentralize responsibilities, they often retain important policy and supervisory roles. They must create or maintain the "enabling conditions" that allow local units of administration or non-government organizations to take on more responsibilities. Central ministries often have crucial roles in promoting and sustaining decentralization by developing appropriate and effective national policies and regulations for decentralization and strengthening local institutional capacity to assume responsibility for new functions. The success of decentralization frequently depends heavily on training for both national and local officials in decentralized administration. Technical assistance is often required for local governments, private enterprises and local non-governmental groups in the planning, financing, and management of decentralized functions

It may so happen that the decentralization may not always be efficient, especially for standardized, routine, network-based services. It can result in the loss of economies of scale and control over scarce financial resources by the central government. Weak administrative or technical capacity at local levels may result in services being delivered less efficiently and effectively in some areas of the country. Administrative responsibilities may be transferred to local levels without adequate financial resources and make equitable distribution or provision of services more difficult. Decentralization can sometimes make coordination of national policies more complex and may allow functions to be captured by local elites. Also, distrust between public and private sectors may undermine cooperation at the local level.

The planners must be able to assess the strengths and weaknesses of public and private sector organizations in performing different types of functions. Before developing elaborate plans for decentralization, they must assess the lowest organizational level of government at which functions can be carried out efficiently and effectively and — for functions that do not have to be provided by government - the most appropriate forms of privatization. Even a program planners who do not see 'decentralization' as their primary motive must carefully analyze the types of decentralization already present in a country in order to tailor policy plans to existing structures.

In many situations, all of these forms of decentralization can play important roles in broadening participation in political, economic and social activities in developing countries. Where it works effectively, decentralization helps alleviate the bottlenecks in decision making that are often caused by central government planning and control of important economic and social activities. Decentralization can help cut complex bureaucratic procedures and it can increase government officials' sensitivity to local conditions and needs. Moreover, decentralization can help national government ministries reach larger numbers of local areas with services; allow greater political representation for diverse political, ethnic, religious, and cultural groups in decision-making; and relieve top managers in central ministries of "routine" tasks to concentrate on policy. In some countries, decentralization may create a geographical focus at the local level for coordinating national, state, provincial, district, and local programs more effectively and can provide better opportunities for participation by local residents in decision making. Decentralization may lead to more creative, innovative and responsive programs by allowing local "experimentation." It can also increase political stability and national unity by allowing citizens to better control public programs at the local level.

Milestones in Indian Decentralisation

- 1882 - The Resolution on Local Self-Government.
- 1907 - The Royal Commission on Decentralization.
- 1948 - Constitutional debates between Gandhi and Ambedkar on Gram Swaraj, 'self-rule'.
- 1957- Balwantrai Mehta Commission; an early attempt to implement the Panchayat structure at district and block (Samiti) levels.
- 1963- K. Santhanam Committee – recommended limited revenue raising powers for Panchayats and the establishment of State Panchayati Raj Finance Corporations.
- 1978 - Asoka Mehta Committee – appointed to address the weaknesses of PRIs, concluded that a resistant bureaucracy, lack of political will, ambiguity about the role of PRIs, and élite capture had undermined previous attempts at decentralization, recommending that the district serve as the administrative unit in the PRI structure. Based on these recommendations, Karnataka, Andhra Pradesh and West Bengal passed new legislation to strengthen PRIs.
- 1985 - G.V.K. Rao Committee – appointed to address weaknesses of PRIs, recommended that the block development office should assume broad powers for planning, implementing a monitoring rural development programmes.
- 1986 - L.M. Singvhi Committee – recommended that local self-government should be constitutionally enshrined and that the Gram Sabha (the village assembly) should be the base of decentralized democracy in India.
- 1992 - The 73rd Amendment to the Indian Constitution-PRIs at district, block and village levels are granted constitutional status. The Gram Sabha is recognized as a formal democratic body at the village level. The 74th Amendment, granting constitutional status to municipal bodies, is passed soon after.
- 1996 -The Adivasi Act-Powers of self-government are extended to tribal communities living in fifth schedule areas.

Objectives of Decentralized Planning

The major objectives of decentralized planning can be divided into two categories, economic and social.

Economic Objective

- Employment opportunities must be provided to each and every able member of the community including the poorest of the poor to remove the incidence of poverty.
- The local resources and the means of production should be gradually brought under the control of the local community; so that the true equality may be achieved.
- Local resources (material and human) should be used in combination with external inputs if the necessity arises.
- The primary aim of the production process is to meet the basic needs of the people. Whenever, any surplus is generated in the process this should go towards capital formation leading to development.
- The state plan goals should be met.
- Sustainable development should be achieved.
- There should be no duplication of work and there should be an effective inter-departmental coordination.
- Infrastructural facilities should be set up.

Social Objectives

- The plan should try to do away with exploitation and injustice.
- It should be designed in such a way that people's participation is fostered so that they may develop a sense of belongingness and become self-reliant.
- Local needs and aspirations should be reflected in the plan.
- It should aim at removing disparities.
- Fellow felling and mutual help should be promoted through the plan and various groups should feel motivated to take up development tasks.

Advantages of Decentralization

- Bridging the gap between central and local levels.
- Decentralization of responsibilities to lower levels facilitating implementation of technical programmes.
- Enhancing the influence of decentralized bodies in national politics.
- Ensuring poor, remote regions of fairer representation in national politics.

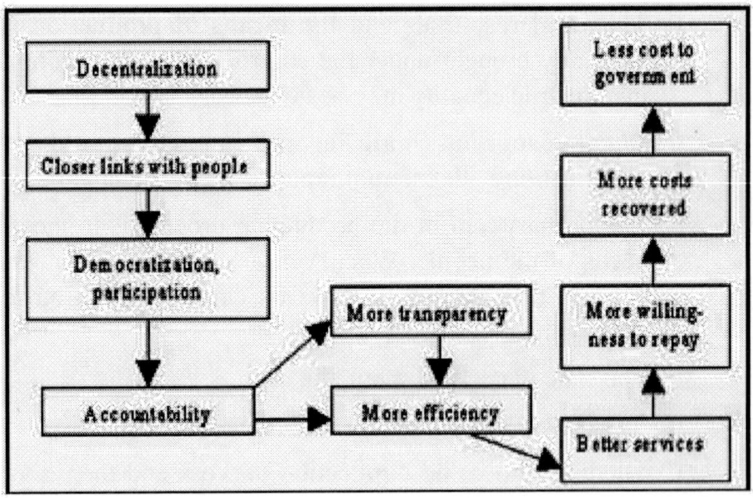

- Facilitating local authorities' access to administrative resources at the regional level.
- Enhancing coordination of development administration from different line ministries.
- Facilitating complex development projects.
- Facilitating scaling up from the local level.
- Facilitating the upward flow of information from the local level and the responsiveness of central government.
- Combating absenteeism and irresponsible behaviour by government employees.
- Enhancing the accountability and responsiveness of regional level bureaucrats.
- Facilitating poverty alleviation and fairness of minorities.

- Facilitating fairness to women.
- Earning the problem of the fore-shortened time perspective of local level politicians.
- Facilitating collaboration between NGOs and decentralized authorities.
- Integrating the efforts of local level voluntary associations.
- Overcoming authoritarian enclaves.
- Facilitating the integration of local level politicians into national politics.
- Facilitating the integration of competitive political parties in to decentralized institutions.

Democratic Decentralisation in India

Democratic decentralization is the process of devolving the functions and resources of the state from the centre to the elected representatives at the lower levels so as to facilitate greater direct participation of citizens in governance.73rd and 74th Constitutional Amendments, by constitutionally establishing Panchayati Raj Institutions (PRIs) in India, mandated the establishment of panchayats and municipalities as elected local governments. They devolved a range of powers and responsibilities to the local governments and made them accountable to the people for their implementation, but very little actual progress has been made in this direction even after more than 25 years.

Devolution, envisioned by the constitution, is not mere delegation.

It implies that precisely defined governance functions are formally assigned by law to local governments, backed by adequate transfer of a basket of financial grants and tax handles, and they are given staff so that they have the necessary wherewithal to carry out their responsibilities. Local government, including panchayats, is a state subject in the Constitution and consequently, the devolution of power and authority to panchayats has been left to the discretion of states. The Constitution mandates that panchayats and municipalities shall be elected every five years and empower states to devolve functions and responsibilities to them through law. A study for the Fourteenth Finance Commission by the Centre for Policy Research shows that all states have formally devolved powers with respect to five core functions of water supply, sanitation, roads and communication, streetlight provision and the management of community assets to the Gram Panchayats.

Introduction of Decentralised Planning in India

Decentralised planning is a kind of percolation of planning activities or process from the centre to the sub-state levels, i.e. district, sub-division, block and village level. Since the inception of First Plan, the importance of decentralised planning was emphasised in order to achieve active people's participation in the planning process.

Post-independence period in India is noted as the inception period of planning activities with the visions of the then Prime Minister Jawahar Lal Nehru. Planning at that time was more of an economic nature and resource allocations. Nehru appointed several notable economists like Dr. Mahalanobish and Dr. Ashok Mitra in forefronts in planning activities. Post-independence India was suffering from an acute shortage of resources, finance and employment. The vicious cycle of poverty and malnutrition was affecting the country's economy. Jawahar Lal Nehru adopted the economic planning approach, clearly a top-down effort which expected that inequality and poverty should be minimised by way of the 'trickle down' effect. The main focus was to rebuild the economic base of the country through strengthening agriculture and controlled industrial development. Planning at this time was more of axial development with focus on special regions.

The Indian economy took a new shape after the Liberalisation, Privatisation and Globalisation (LPG) era in the 1990s. The twentieth century was very vital in terms of planning aspects. After 1991, the economy began to change with emphasis on foreign investments, globalisation and free trade. The neoliberal economic policies had a direct impact upon the planning process. With the top-down approach it was observed that regional disparities were increasing, as were rural-urban differences. Urban areas were facing a large amount of migration as a part of the 'pull effect'. With an influx of population, the urban services were steadily degrading. Local authorities were unable to provide services to a majority of the population because they were not capable in terms of technical knowledge as well as financial resources. The top-down approach has shifted to a bottom-up approach with more community participation added to a dimension of social planning on account of 73rd and 74th constitutional amendments.

Until the enactment of the Constitution (73rd and 74th Amendments) Acts, 1992, the planning and decision-making functions in India remained centralised around the two political levels, namely the Union and the States, whose spheres of responsibility had been defined in the Constitution. Urban and rural local bodies such as municipalities and village Panchayats, by and large, functioned as agencies of civic functioning and rural development schemes and not as instruments of micro-level planning and development.

The Administrative Reforms Commission (1966-70), appointed during the third five year plan period, came out with its report that criticised the highly centralised character of Indian planning and advocated the strengthening of the machinery for planning at the state and district levels. It explained a methodology of preparing a state plan for rural development on the basis of the district and block plans. Attempts were also made to develop the three-tier Panchayati Raj system based on the recommendations of the Balwant Rai Mehta Committee and with it the idea of 'planning from below' gained some currency, but was not very effective. The Planning Commission made special efforts to promote district planning by issuing guidelines for the formulation of district plans in 1969.

The Planning Commission set up a working group on district planning under the Chairmanship of Dr. C. H. Hanumantha Rao, member of the Planning Commission, 1984, with the aim: (i) to define the precise scope and content of state planning; (ii) to delineate the procedure for decentralised planning at the state level to make the concept of district planning operational; (iii) to devise the various steps in district planning and indicate the methodology for each step; (iv) to suggest the methodology for integrating block level planning with district planning; and (v) to recommend the procedure for converting the district plans into the state plans.

The working group has set up various sub-groups to look into the various aspects of district planning in depth. The deliberation of these groups reflected in their reports formed the basis of the report of the working group, and was submitted to the Planning Commission in 1984. The concept of district planning adopted by the working group was akin to the concept of integrated area planning. This, however, was the ultimate goal. Since then the process of decentralisation in the planning and developmental activities was continued. In 1969, the Planning Commission issued some guidelines on the introduction of district planning. Again in 1977; M.L. Dantewala working group recommended specific guidelines for the introduction of block-level planning. After that Ashok Mehta Committee has also submitted his report on Panchayati Raj in 1978.

Moreover, the Economic Advisory Council finally presented its Report on Decentralisation of Development Planning and its implementation in the states in 1983. Finally, in 1984, the group on district planning submitted its report and this was considered as the basis of proposals on decentralised planning under the seventh plan. Accordingly, the Planning Commission of India introduced the decentralised planning in the country for the first time during the seventh plan. From the very beginning, India has adopted the system of centralised planning with little variation. But with the passage of time there has been radical departure in the planning process in India from a centralised to a decentralised one where the decision making in the planning process has been reversed from top-to-bottom type to a system of bottom-to-top type. Thus the decentralised planning is a kind of planning at the grass-root level or planning from below. Planning process in a country is having various tiers, viz., centre, state, district, sub-division, block and village. Under decentralised planning emphasis has been given on the introduction of district planning, sub-divisional planning and block-level planning so as to reach finally the village level planning successfully.

In India, governmental activities are being performed right from the central to states and then to local, i.e. to the districts level (Zilla Parishads), taluk level (Panchayat Samities) and also to the village level (Gram Panchayats). Thus in order to realise a better response, the Planning Commission of India introduced the decentralised planning since the seventh plan. Although in most of the states of India, the decentralised planning was extended to district level but in some states like Assam, West Bengal etc. the same plan was decentralised up to sub-division level. Accordingly, in order to conduct the planning activities at the sub-divisional level, the Sub-division Planning and Development Council was formed in every sub-division of some states with public representatives from different levels.

Decentralised planning is very much important in a country like India, where majority of our population live in rural areas. These types of plans raise the involvement of the people in implementing the plan. Moreover, decentralised planning is being prepared in the light of local problems and on the basis of local resources potential. Thus under the present economic scenario, the decentralised planning is considered as most important strategy in respect of planning for economic development

Decentralized Planning in India: Pre and Post Reform Phase

The Planning Commission era can be divided into two phase viz. Pre-1991 (Pre-reform Phase) and Post-1991 till 2015 (Post reform phase).

The Pre-reform phase was characterized by heavy reliance on public sector; regulated expansion of private sector, development of heavy industries, protection of small industries, inward looking trade strategy and highly centralized planning and fund allocation. In the post-reform period, Planning Commission gradually started losing relevance as India saw free play of market forces. The economic planning was to be based on competition instead of controls. While Liberalisation, Privatisation and Globalisation became three components of New Economic Policy; the role of government was expected to incline towards social balance and social justice. This is mainly because from 1991, while economy was driven by the market forces, government was expected to give maximum attention to the range of social sector (especially health, education and food security).

However, planning in India had not yet lost its relevance. India's rural infrastructure was still in mess. The government needed to focus more on rural roads, agriculture, rural land development and land reforms etc. As the economy opened up for private sector; the role of government in economy needed to be more as a partner with private sector instead of controller of private sector.

Thus, in post-reform period, following were key changes that came into India's planning:

- Despite of rise of private sector, the public investment, both at centre and in states would continue to have a major role in the development and thus, prioritisation of public investment would become important part of planning process.
- PPP got significant weightage in planning.
- More emphasis in planning would be on national objectives of poverty alleviation, population control, employment generation and balanced regional development.
- The way ahead was a shift from centralized planning to decentralize planning.

The concept of decentralized planning in India is not of recent origin. In fact its antecedents can be traced back to the pre-independence days and the philosophy of Mahatma Gandhi. He was an ardent advocate of small village-based communities which would be more or less self-sufficient. To make the Gandhiji's dream come true, the Directive Principle of State Policy had commented in detail on the importance of village panchayats which are one of the principal institutions of a decentralized system of governance. The Ripon Resolution of 1882 laid the foundation of local self-governments in the country. However, nominations in place of elections became the practice. The Royal Commission on Decentralization (1909) proposed setting up of taluk boards and village panchayats. The Directive Principles of State Policy commented in detail on the position of the village panchayats in the new situation. Furthermore, the division of powers and functions enshrined in Article-246 read with the seventh schedule of the Constitution (Directive Principles of State Policy) states that the state should take steps to organize village panchayats and endow them with such powers and authority as may be necessary to enable them to function as units of self-government.

The establishment of country-wide network of community development blocks on 2nd October 1952 was a major administrative innovation in the history of India. The idea of CDPs, the creation of NES and the establishment of institutional structure of command, control and co-ordination of developmental activities at the block level were, in one sense or the other, major innovations in the administrative history of India which went a long way towards giving birth to what is now being increasingly named as a development administration as a contrasted people, political elite and policy planners have been familiar for several millennia.

A study team under the leadership of Balwant Rai Mehta was set up in 1957 to review the working of the Community Development Programme and National Extension Service. Among other things, it recommended the setting up of a three-tier Panchayati Raj system at the village, block and district levels to ensure participatory rural development. The Panchayat Samiti at the block level and the Zila Parishad at the district level were organically linked through the device of indirect elections.

The committee made a distinction between delegation of power and devolution of power. The latter amounted to decentralisation whereby the government divests itself completely of certain duties and responsibilities and devolves them to local level bodies. Delegation on the other hands means engaging the local governments as agents of the higher level governments. Devolution was thus seen as an orderly transfer of authority, resources and institutional capabilities to local governments. Democratic decentralisation, to become a reality, must be backed by a political will.

Once again in 1986, another committee headed by L.M. Singhvi was appointed by late Prime Minister Rajiv Gandhi, to suggest approaches as to how Panchayati Raj Institutions could be given constitutional status. The committee recommended the reorganization of village to make village panchayat more viable. It also suggested that more financial resources should be made available to these institutions. It further recommended that Panchayati Raj Institutions should be viewed as institutions of self government which would naturally facilitate the participation of the people in the process of planning and development following from below as part of the concept of self-government and development planning should be democratic planning. While these activities were going on, in the meantime Sarkaria Commission was already enquiring in to the 'federal structure' particularly with regard to Centre-State relations, which also made a passing remark in its report on nature of rural and urban local self-government. The commission observed that many of the local self-governing bodies were being outdated on insubstantial grounds.

A sub-committee to the Parliamentary Consultative Committee attached to Ministry of Personnel, Public Grievances and Pensions was set up under the chairmanship of P.K. Thungon to consider the type of political and administrative structure needed in the district for district planning. The committee felt that the PRIs should be constitutionally recognized and recommended that a constitutional provision should be made to ensure timely and regular elections to these bodies with their terms lasting for five years. The Zila Parishad should be the only planning and development agency in the district according to the opinion of this sub-committee. It also suggested setting up of a planning and coordination committee at the state level under the chairmanship of the Planning Minister and Presidents of the Zila Parishads should be made members of the committee.

Decentralised Planning and NITI Aayog

Between 1950 and 2015, India's economic planning was centralized on the pattern of socialist and communist countries. The decentralization of the planning process was paid attention to right since beginning but was never materialized. For example, the establishment of National Development Council was one instrument of decentralized planning, but decentralization was never achieved. By the 1980s, it was almost clear that without decentralization and without making planning bottom-top, the goal of development would be difficult to achieve. Through the 73rd and 74th amendment acts of constitution, the local bodies were given constitutional status and for the first time, decentralization of planning was visible in India at local level. However, the fiscal status of local bodies never allowed it to be implemented in letter and spirit. It was only after 2014 general elections that a central government decided to redraw the contours of decentralized planning. The basic premise of the new planning landscape is that “development of India cannot happen without development of states” and “one size fits all is not a suitable idea for India”. Thus, the key change we notice since 2015 is the changed outlook of centre towards states. The states now get 42% of the share in central pool of taxes; they are getting liberal funding and grants from states; their grievances are being accommodated in GST; they have been allowed to go for higher market borrowings without permission from.

NITI Aayog

NITI Aayog (National Institution for Transforming India) on 1st January 2015, as replacement for the Planning Commission, which was established was on 15th March 1950 as an advisory institution to form five year plans in the country on the line of USSR (former Soviet Union).This change has been made after extensive consultation across the spectrum of stakeholders, including state governments, domain experts and relevant institutions. The functions of the Planning Commission are to estimate the physical, capital and human resources of the country, to prepare plan for making effective and balanced utilization of human resources and to determine various stages of planning and to propose the allocation of resources on priority basis.

NITI Aayog has been set up “to provide a critical directional and strategic input into the development process”. It will act as a “think-tank” and advise the Centre and states on policy matters. The Aayog seeks to end “slow and tardy implementation of policy, by fostering better Inter-Ministry coordination and better Centre-State coordination (co-operative federalism). Prime minister is it’s ex-officio chairman

Objectives

- To evolve a shared vision of national development priorities, sectors and strategies with the active involvement of States.

- To foster cooperative federalism through structured support initiatives and mechanisms with the States on a continuous basis, recognizing that strong States make a strong nation.
- To develop mechanisms to formulate credible plans at the village level and aggregate these progressively at higher levels of government.
- To ensure, on areas that are specifically referred to it, that the interests of national security are incorporated in economic strategy and policy.
- To pay special attention to the sections of our society that may be at risk of not benefiting adequately from economic progress.
- To design strategic and long term policy and programme frameworks and initiatives, and monitor their progress and their efficacy. The lessons learnt through monitoring and feedback will be used for making innovative improvements, including necessary mid-course corrections.
- To provide advice and encourage partnerships between key stakeholders and national and international like-minded Think tanks, as well as educational and policy research institutions.
- To create a knowledge, innovation and entrepreneurial support system through a collaborative community of national and international experts, practitioners and other partners.
- To offer a platform for resolution of inter-sectoral and inter-departmental issues in order to accelerate the implementation of the development agenda.
- To maintain a State-of-the-art Resource Centre, be a repository of research on good governance and best practices in sustainable and equitable development as well as help their dissemination to stake-holders.
- To actively monitor and evaluate the implementation of programmes and initiatives, including the identification of the needed resources so as to strengthen the probability of success and scope of delivery.
- To focus on technology upgradation and capacity building for implementation of programmes and initiatives.

- To undertake other activities as may be necessary in order to further the execution of the national development agenda, and the objectives mentioned above.

Characteristic Features

NITI Aayog is developing itself as a State-of-the-art Resource Centre, with the necessary resources, knowledge and skills, that will enable it to act with speed, promote research and innovation, provide strategic policy vision for the government, and deal with contingent issues. NITI Aayog's entire gamut of activities can be divided into four main heads:

- Design Policy & Programme Framework
- Foster Cooperative Federalism
- Monitoring & Evaluation
- Think Tank and Knowledge & Innovation Hub

There are some justifications for replacement of Planning Commission and formation of NITI Aayog ;

- The new National Institution for Transforming India (NITI) will act more like a think tank or forum, say its supporters, in contrast with the Commission which imposed five-year-plans and allocated resources to hit set economic targets.
- NITI will include leaders of India's 29 states and seven union territories. But its full-time staff - a deputy chairman, Chief Executive Officer and experts - will answer directly to the 64-year-old Prime Minister, who will be chairman. It is different from planning commission, which used to report National Development Council.
- The major difference in approach to planning, between NITI Aayog and Planning Commission, is that the former will invite greater involvement of the states, while the latter took a top-down approach with a one-size-fits-all plan.
- The Planning Commission's role was formulation of broad policy and its capacity was more advisory. NITI Aayog shall have powers for resource allocation to states, based on their respective needs.
- The states had little direct say in policy planning, which was the purview of the Planning Commission. Involvement of the states

was indirect through the National Development Council; it will not be repeated in the NITI Aayog.

The NITI Aayog aims to transform India through the following actions:

- Leveraging of India's demographic dividend, and realization of the potential of youth, men and women, through education, skill development, elimination of gender bias, and employment.
- Elimination of poverty, and the chance for every Indian to live a life of dignity and self-respect
- Reddressal of inequalities based on gender bias, caste and economic disparities
- Integrate villages institutionally into the development process
- Policy support to more than 50 million small businesses, which are a major source of employment creation
- Safeguarding of our environmental and ecological assets

Gains from Decentralised Planning in India

(i) Better Linkages between the Villages and Small Towns

Considering the huge size and proportion of rural population in India, it is felt that proper linkages must be established between scattered small villages and also between such villages and adjacent small towns by developing appropriate infrastructural facilities such as feeder roads, improved transport facilities, marketing and storage facilities, health and sanitation facilities and other welfare centres. Under decentralised planning better linkages between villages and small towns can be developed under local conditions, priorities and resources.

(ii) Planning becomes Realistic and Flexible

Decentralised planning is considered as more realistic as it maintains a close coordination between locally available resources, local skills, local manpower and local requirements. It is considered as a flexible one as it is easily adjustable and adaptable under the changing local conditions and requirements. Moreover, it is considered as the practical one as it can fulfil the normal requirements of the rural population. Adaptation and flexibility of planning largely depends upon the environment prevailing in each region and sub-region. Thus decentralised planning can achieve the best result in implementing plan projects at the local level.

(iii) Development of Agriculture

Decentralised planning is suitable for the development of agricultural and allied activities such as animal husbandry, horticulture, fisheries, forestry along with development of village and cottage industries.

(iv) Promote People's Participation

Decentralised planning can promote active participation of local people in implementing various local plans and programmes. Thus it can enhance the involvement of local communities in such development activities.

(v) Minimising Wastage of Resources

Under decentralised planning, wastage of resources can be reduced to a minimum level as the people participating in these developmental activities keep a close watch over the utilisation of fund as well also on the implementation of plan projects.

(vi) Trickle-Down Effects

Decentralised planning can show more trickle-down or percolation effects in respect of poverty alleviation programmes and employment generation in rural areas as in this type of planning; various projects are selected for generating huge productive employment opportunities in the rural areas. Moreover, this can help in building up of various types of community assets, viz., panchayat house, village roads, schools, tanks etc. which can supplement rural income and also can enhance the levels of living of the rural people.

(vii) Social Services

Decentralised planning is helpful in raising the level of social services by launching various programmes of health, nutrition, drinking water, education etc. in a more effective, quicker and sustainable manner.

(viii) Use of Non-conventional Energy Sources

Decentralised planning is more helpful in utilizing the various non-conventional energy sources such as solar power, wind, animal and plant wastes etc. in rural areas. Such utilisation of non-conventional energy sources requires various agencies which can work in close association with communities in villages and small towns and also can provide necessary technical and financial support from such agencies. Decentralised planning can pave the way for utilisation of such resources.

(ix) Simple Planning Process

Decentralised planning process is more simple and transparent and thus it has a close link with democracy, co-operation and development. It has a vast scope for the active involvement of political and social forces at the appropriate level.

Performance of Decentralised Planning in India

(i) Unsuccessful Land Reforms

The success of decentralised planning depends much on the implementation of land reform measures viz., imposition of land ceiling and the redistribution of surplus lands, tenancy reforms, consolidation of holdings etc. Under the semi-feudal conditions, land reforms in India could not be carried upon as per its true spirit. The Panchayati Raj Institutions are dominated by landed interests and naturally they failed to show much interest in the implementation of beneficiary oriented programmes in rural areas of the country.

(ii) Lack of Appropriate Administrative Bodies

In India, decentralised planning could not achieve much success due to lack of adequate administrative bodies at the local level for the implementation of its various programmes. Till today, various state governments failed to develop appropriate administrative bodies at the district and block level representing the local people having adequate norms.

(iii) Lack of Adequate Resource Transfer

The government machinery has also failed to develop adequate managerial structures for also to finalize the modalities of decentralised planning in detailed form.

(iv) Ad-Hocism

State governments are often following the path of ad-hocism as the regular elections of village panchayats and other local bodies are not being held. Thus, the decentralised planning has not become effective and thus failed to become a powerful instrument of social change in India.

(v) Absence of Effective Organizations

In the absence of effective organisations of marginal and small farmers, agricultural labourers, artisans, scheduled castes, scheduled tribes and other backward sections, there is no proper representation of these sections in the local bodies for serving their economic interests.

(vi) Regional Disparities

Various states of India adopting decentralised planning could not make much headway in reducing regional disparities in respect of development. Among various states, disparities have been accentuated in respect of Rayalaseema in Andhra Pradesh, Maratha Wada and Vidarbha in Maharashtra, Uttarakhand and Northern parts of West Bengal etc. District planning machineries have failed to stem the problem of regional backwardness in various states. This has raised a disincentive factor against the popularity of decentralised planning among the non-implementing states.

(vii) Use of Inferior Resources

In the rural area, superior resources are under the effective control of elite section of rural society and the productive resources like forests, minerals etc. are also under the control of rich urban located groups having adequate financial resources.

Thus under such circumstances, decentralised planning machinery has been dealing with inferior type of resources having low potential return factor. Thus due to its involvement with inferior resources only, the performance of decentralised planning as an instrument of development and change is not at all satisfactory.

Importance of Planning at Gram Panchayat Level

As stated by Mahatma Gandhi, "Swaraj" for the hungry and starving millions can effectively be achieved through participatory decentralized planning process, which is provided by Gram Panchayat Development Plan (GPDP). As local government, GPs are responsible for delivery of basic services to local citizens and address vulnerabilities of poor and marginalized ones. This can only be achieved through implementation of well thought plans through efficient and responsible utilization of available resources. Hence, an efficient and robust planning process as part of GP's core functioning becomes necessary. GPDPs are to be prepared in a fair, inclusive, transparent manner within the available resources or expanding the resources through people's participation, ownership and enlightened leadership. The focus should be on local development issues, local perceived needs and priorities, analysis of local problems and solutions, convergence of schemes etc. and resource management of G P with a collective vision and action.

Need for Comprehensive Decentralised Planning

The Constitution of India and the State Panchayati Raj Acts lay emphasis on decentralized planning for local economic development and social justice by Panchayats. The decentralized planning process may fulfill following important needs:

- Capturing local needs
- Tapping of local potential
- Operationalising methodology for convergence, at the ground level, based on local need and demand
- Accessing to reach the unreached/excluded within a panchayat area
- Responding to differential needs of different groups
- Enabling mobilisation of all sections and their participation in governance and development
- Providing space for integration of people's knowledge and wisdom into local development efforts
- Understanding development by citizens and elected representatives
- Accessing resources/entitlements/services
- Absorption and targeting of funds from different sources, especially Centrally Sponsored Schemes (CSSs)
- Helping forge better bond between the panchayats and local citizens
- Leading to Responsive Governance
- Facilitating enhanced local resource mobilization
- Promoting economy and efficiency
- Ensuring direct accountability of the local government to its citizens
- Activate Gram Sabha (GS), and other local institutions and structures as functional bodies

- Activating officials working at the cutting edge level
- Promoting democracy and local ownership

Planning by Gram Panchayat for Economic Development and Social Justice

Panchayat is a Sate Subject. Though 73rd Amendment of the Constitution has given a framework of Panchayati Raj Institutions, the actual devolution of funds, functions and functionaries have been by and large left to state government.Article-243G of the Constitution provides for: "Powers, authority and responsibilities of Panchayat.- subject to the provisions of this Constitution, the Legislature of a state may, by Law, endow Panchayats with such powers and authority and may be necessary to enable them to function as institutions of self government and such law may contain provisions for the devolution of powers and responsibilities upon Panchayats, at the appropriate level, subject to such conditions as may be specified therein, with respect to;

- The preparation of plans for economic development and social justice;
- The implementation of schemes for economic development and social justice as may be entrusted to them including those in relation to the matters listed in the eleventh schedule."

The above provision is intended to empower the GPs by enabling the state governments to devolve powers and authority including those matters listed in the eleventh schedule for planning and implementation of schemes for economic development and social justice. This will also cover the powers to impose taxes and provisions of funds to the Panchayats.

Thus, GPs have been mandated for the preparation of Gram Panchayat Development Plan (GPDP) for economic development and social justice utilizing the resources available to them. The GPDP planning process has to be comprehensive and based on participatory process, which inter alia involves the full convergence with schemes of all related Central Ministries / Line Departments related to 29 subjects enlisted in the eleventh schedule of the Constitution. Panchayats have a significant role to play in the effective and efficient implementation of flagship schemes on subjects of national importance for transformation of rural India. Thus, GPs are authorised to envision, plan and implement GPDP to achieve economic development and social justice

Gram Panchayat Development Plans (GPDPs), a Decentralized Participatory Planning

The GPDP is the development plan of the GP. It is prepared through a participatory process involving all stakeholders matching people's needs and priorities with available resources. The GPDP does three essential things: (i) It provides a vision of what the people would like their village to look like (ii) It sets out clear goals to achieve that vision, and (iii) Gives an action plan to reach those goals. The Planning at GP level enables the following actions:

- Activate the Panchayats to prepare development plans and thus establish their identity as local government
- Mobilize and motivate people to participate in decision making thereby bringing governance more close to the people
- Provide a platform for discussing local perceptions, local issues and analysis to decide priorities
- Assess the felt needs and aspiration of people
- Identify the magnitude of development gaps
- Prioritize the issues and problems existing in the village
- Bring all the available schemes and resources through effective convergence
- Provide for convergence and integration of different schemes / departments/ sectors.
- Optimize the utilization of resources in the larger interest of people of the area

Preparation of GPDP by Gram Panchayats

Preparation of GPDP is a time-bound process. GPDP should ideally match people's needs, basic services and their aspirations, prioritized in accordance with the available resources. It should be prepared through a participatory, inclusive and transparent process. The plan should be long-term (perspective plan) in nature (ideally five years plan), which is implementable on annual basis, based on priorities arrived at Gram Sabha. After implementation of annual plan, the perspective plan will be reviewed taking the performance/ feedback/impact of the annual plan implementation into account and make changes and reprioritize the activities/projects for the coming financial year. Thus, after the end of fifth year, a fresh five year perspective plan will be prepared. All these processes need to be taken up and completed within a stipulated time. Panchayat and its committee play very important role from initiating to completing of planning and then implementing and monitoring.

Components of GPDP Plan Cycle

The following are the components of GPDP "Plan Cycle":

i. Formation of Gram Panchayat Planning Facilitation Team (GPPFT) for every GP for shared understanding and facilitation of the entire planning process orienting and activating them to take up and carry forward the entire process of GPDP

ii. Environment creation and community mobilization

iii. Collection of primary and secondary data

iv. Situation analysis, need assessment and gap identification

v. Visioning exercise for goal setting

vi. Resources and identification/estimation of corresponding activities – Special Gram Sabha

vii. Plan development, prioritisation and projectisation

viii. Approval of GPDP by Gram Sabha

ix. Implementation, monitoring and impact analysis

Formation of a Gram Panchayat Planning Facilitation Team (GPPFT)

GP needs to prepare GPDP as part of enabling wider participation, optimal utilization of resources and getting maximum developmental benefits. Large number of well-meaning / philanthropic / voluntary human resources should be fastened in who can help the GP in coming up with holistic and visionary plan. For this, a group may be formed namely "Gram Panchayat Planning Facilitation Team (GPPFT)" in every GP under the chairmanship of Pradhan/Sarpanch/President of the GP. The size and composition of GPPFT may vary. The representatives of sectoral / line departments at GP level should invariably be the members of this team. Apart from this, the citizens of the GP who are working / living elsewhere either in the country or outside should also be invited to become members of the GPPFT. The known "Leaders of Beacon Panchayats" of other GPs of the district / nearby districts/states/other states can also be invited as special invitees of GPPFT. The instructions issued by the state government/district administration to all line departments should be leveraged to ensure whole-hearted participation of these members.

Indicative Composition of Gram Panchayat Planning Facilitation Team (GPPFT)

- Sarpanch - Chairperson
- GP secretary - Member Convenor
- Elected Ward members of GP
- Former Elected Representatives of GP
- Other employees of the GP
- Employees of the line departments operating at the GP level e.g. Krishi Prajukti Sahayak, AWWs, ASHA, Health Workers, Health Supervisors, AW Supervisors, MGNREGA Workers
- Serving and retired government functionaries of the GP
- Education Experts / Teachers
- Frontline workers of Swach Bharat and ASHA Health Workers
- Community leaders/community representatives
- Gram Rozgar Sahayak
- Elderly citizens of the GP.
- SHG/GP Level Federation office bearers
- Volunteers from youth/ students/ NSS/NCC
- NGOs working in local areas
- CSR representative
- Citizens of the Panchayats working/living in the country or outside (Special invitees)

In this respect, the GP has also the freedom to add more categories depending upon availability.

The GP may divide the members of the GPPFT into "Ward Planning Facilitation Team" (WPFT) with a minimum of 3-5 members headed by the respective GP ward members to facilitate community-based planning processes for GPDP. WPFT has to ensure that all members / residents of the ward participate in the planning exercise and freely express their felt needs and grievances. Every year the GPPFT may be reconstituted by the GP with need-based addition / alteration of members. The GPPFT will facilitate all the steps of planning exercise right from the stage of environment creation to the final stage of plan approval including implementation and monitoring. The entire planning process has to be taken up in a campaign mode with continuous involvement of all stakeholders.

Formation of Working Groups in GPPFT

The GPs already have the standing/functional committees for various thematic areas (the nomenclature may vary from state to state). The members of the GPPFT may be distributed into working groups on various thematic areas. Each working group will consist of members from the GPPFT having expertise in the relevant field or having inclination in the specific subjects. The chairperson of the standing / functional committee of the concerned thematic areas will chair the working group. The block level officer of the concerned line department or any local experts in the field may be the vice-chairperson of the respective working group. These groups will function under overall guidance and supervision of the GP. The following working groups may be constituted by the GP:

i. **Human Development Working Group:** To deal with health, nutrition, education and public health related issues including environment and sanitation

ii. **Women & Child Development Working Group:** To deal with gender issues and issues related to rights of women and children, women's empowerment, protection of women and children against atrocities / abuse and their skill development related issues

iii. **Livelihoods Development Working Group**: To deal with agriculture and allied sectors, small medium and cottage industries, entrepreneurship, natural resource management including soil and water conservation, green cover and bio-diversity related issues

iv. **Social Justice & Social Security Working Group**: To deal with development of SC/ST communities and other backward sections of the society including persons with disabilities (PwDs) and elderly aiming at equity, empowerment and well-being

v. **Infrastructure & Miscellaneous Working Group**: To deal with the local infrastructure and other issues as relevant to the GP

In addition, the GP may constitute more working groups depending upon the local needs such as working group on Environment Protection, Spatial Planning and Disaster Management Planning etc.

Focus Areas in GPDP

The GPs have the constitutional mandate of social justice and economic development. Every GP is responsible to provide basic public services and also take up development works relating to the functions devolved to them. Moreover, under Article-243G the intention of the Constitution regarding 29 subjects listed in Eleventh Schedule is quite clear and Panchayat need to address them in GPDP. Therefore, focus of GPDP should be on analyzing the development gaps in the socio-economic sectors, public service delivery and capturing needs and aspirations of the vulnerable and marginalized groups. One of the challenges for the GP will be to prioritize the socio-economic development issues and inclusive development of marginalized sections of the community over routine infrastructural developments as the experience had been bulk of the investment is flowing towards such infrastructure creation. Thus, GPDP must trigger interventions to address the issues of socio-economic development parameters so as to achieve holistic and inclusive development. With adequate resource envelope at the disposal of GPs, along with the tied and untied funds for panchayats have provided adequate financial resources for their holistic development. The GPs need to ensure a participatory planning process with special focus on the most excluded and marginalized sections to achieve social justice. GPDP provides an opportunity to not only work towards the realization of the constitutional mandate of social justice and economic development but also comprehensive development of rural areas and thereby progressively move towards the global agenda of SDGs. While developing GPDP, the state government should ensure that the GPs focus on the following thematic areas:

- Economic Development and Poverty reduction
- Human Development
- Social Development
- Sustainable Development Goals (SDGs)
- Ecological and Environment Development
- Public Service Delivery
- Good Governance

- Skill Building
- Gender Responsive Governance
- Child Protection and Development
- Inclusion of Vulnerable Groups such as SCs, STs, OBCs, NT-DNTs, elderly, people with disabilities, single headed women households, widow, destitute, homeless and others
- Spatial Planning
- E-enablement of Panchayats
- Infrastructure Development
- Renewable Energy

Basic Services

Under the Article-243G of the Constitution of India, Panchayats have been mandated to function as an institution of self-government. Therefore, GPs needs to cater basic services to the people of their area. The basic services includes water supply, sanitation including septic management, sewage and solid waste management, storm water drainage, maintenance of community assets, maintenance of roads, footpaths, street-lighting, burial, cremation grounds etc. These basic services are important for the good quality of life in rural areas. These services are also included in the 29 subjects listed in the Eleventh Schedule of the Constitution of India and Sustainable Development Goals to be achieved by 2030.

Economic Development and Poverty Reduction

Primary objective of preparation of GPDP is to identify and formulate ways of addressing real needs of local people. In this content, economic development stands for improving the economic well-being and quality of life of the community by supporting sources of income. GPDP should have a strong poverty reduction focus by identifying patterns of poverty in the village. Through GPDP, GP should increase economic activity in their area and enhanced the income of rural communities particularly marginalized and poor households. GPs should be encouraged to develop and use locally relevant indicators on issues of development, including aligning actions with localizing the SDGs and take up activities which would increase local production and productivity, increase employment and employability, improve market access and marketability of the local produce, promote value addition, create productive infrastructure like markets, ponds, fisheries, livestock development, horticulture development, land development, minor irrigation facilities, dug wells, irrigation tanks etc. The GP should be converged different programs for livelihood promotion through MGNREA, NRLM, PMAY, PMGSY, NSAP, PMASY, RKVY etc.

Human Development

GPDP should have components related to literacy, education, skill development, health, nutrition, livelihood promotion etc. The focus should be on improving quality of human development services through Anganwadis, schools, hospitals and enhancing access to them. The GPDP should aim to achieve clear outcomes in line with the targets set by State Governments. In human development, the deficiencies need to be assessed and addressed. For example, reasons for not achieving the minimum levels of learning, causes for dropout, reasons for malnutrition, etc. have to be identified and focused efforts to be made to address them.

Social Development

GPDP should be aimed at improving the wellbeing of vulnerable and marginalized groups like SCs, STs, Other Backward Classes including minorities, persons with disabilities, elderly people, women, children, bonded laborers, child laborers, distress migrants, manual scavengers, victims of trafficking etc. In social development, the main issues based on people's perception and expert opinion. For example, the issues faced by the community like lack of skills, employment opportunities, and access to public services can be listed, discussed and plan for addressing the issues.

GPDP and SDGs

Under SDGs, there are 17 goals with 169 targets. These are universal goals with local implications and intervention possibilities. Many SDG targets are within the purview of the GPs. Thus the GPs have a crucial role to play in achieving the SDGs. The GPDP presents an opportunity for the GPs to enable GPDP for ultimate achievement of the SDGs. In the planning process the Panchayats may set GP level targets with measurable indicators that will have vertical and horizontal linkages, convergence possibilities and feasible action plans. The localizing SDGs framework could be used as a consolidating tool for actions and impacts, on the ground, on a range of issues that promote and support GP level development in the long term.

Such localized SDGs framework to be developed with full and informed participation of all relevant local stakeholders.

Ecological and Environment Development

Conscious efforts should be made so that activities taken up under GPDP should be environment friendly and bio-diversity enhancing. The GP therefore should necessarily take up maintenance and upgradation of various ecosystems like water bodies, pastures, grass lands etc. The GP should plan towards conservation of biological resources. Considering the possible impact of climate change, the GP should strive to assess the impact and make ameliorative measures as part of GPDP. Additionally, actions related to environmental sustainability should capture the contributions of natural resources, including ecosystems and biodiversity to both economic and social security of local communities. Formal mainstreaming of economic benefits of conservation and management action will enhance the ability of GPs to achieve sustainable development that is economically and socially viable.

Public Service Delivery

GPDP should give greater emphasis on the quality of service delivery. Improvement of local public services like issuance of certificates, compulsory registration of birth/death, marriages, migration, issue of licenses /permits and social security pensions should be given special priority with emphasis on electronic delivery of services. The scheme of CSC of Ministry of MeitY should be utilized to provide public services to the people in rural areas. GPs should also ensure proper functioning of school, health centers, Anganwadis etc.

Skill Building

GPDP should also focus on how Panchayats can play a major role in skill building and ensure that the most vulnerable sections, including women participate in the programme. GPs have to plan for generating awareness about the skills related programme, facilitating the mobilization efforts, creating databases for skill demand and placement, assist in conducting the job mela and support the project implementing agencies in all stages of skill training. Skill building should focus not just on gaining employment and economic empowerment but also ensuring sustainable use of resources, ability to negotiate and retain development needs that are locally relevant and responsive as well as support development that is sustainable. In this regard, it is important for the GPs to come up with innovative ideas of skill development, apart from the mainstream ideas.

Women and Child Protection & Development

GPDP should keep gender mainstreaming as an important theme across all the activities/projects. The GP has to plan activities for attainment of rights of women and children in the village and take steps to operationalise the same. The GP should recognize that the services rendered to children are not welfare measures or favours given to them, rather the rights entitled to them. This approach offers an opportunity to have child friendly GP.

Spatial Planning

Spatial planning is a process for the planned development and regulation of growth of urban and rural areas to secure to their present and future. Spatial planning provides options for sustainable development of rural areas. Since all development projects have direct impact on the use of the land, they need to be coordinated and integrated within a desirable spatial frame. The Rural Area Development and Plan Formulation and Implementation (RADPFI) guidelines describe the process of spatial planning.

E-enablement of Panchayat

E-governance makes the governance more efficient and transparent through disclosure of information, efficient delivery of services and improving internal processes and management. The Panchayat Enterprise Suite (PES) deployed in the Panchayats addresses all the core functions of Panchayats such as decentralized planning, budgeting, accounting, implementation and monitoring of service delivery like issue of certificates, licenses etc.

Infrastructure Development

In the case of infrastructure, GP should identify the gaps in infrastructure and priorities their needs. For example, in respect of physical connectivity, list out habitations without roads; length of road required etc. This could also include repair, restoration, up gradation and new construction. In the case of civic amenities, the effort should be made to maintain the set standards of service provision and delivery. The maintenance of public assets should also be given due priorities.

Data Collection for Plan Preparation

The primary objective of preparation of GPDP is to identify and formulate ways of addressing the development needs of the GP. Hence, getting first-hand information about the, issues related to health, education, livelihoods, availability of amenities, services and fulfillment of rights and entitlements of marginalized sections, local infrastructure etc., are very important. Situation Analysis refers to assessment of existing development status in different sectors of the GP through analysis of data already collected and available in the GP or sourcing from various secondary sources such as Census, SECC data, Mission Antyodaya, published data by line departments and previous GPDP surveys etc. Secondary data based on analysis of Census, SECC, Mission Antyodaya data etc. will be pre-populated in the Plan Plus software. GP may use it for better plan preparation after verification. Over and above the secondary data, primary data collection will also be required to update/validate the secondary sources, fill the gaps and to have 360-degrees coverage of each household for enabling individual household development plan based on the potential of each member of the family, for which household surveys will be done. Data can be collected through citizen surveys, focused group discussions involving neighborhoods groups at hamlet level, semi structured interviews and through Participatory Rural Appraisal (PRA) methods. Format prescribed by the State Government should be used for data collection. If not, the format designed for data collections given below may be customized for the purpose.

Participatory Rural Appraisal

Participatory Rural Appraisal (PRA) is a set of techniques to assess the existing resources, services, infrastructures etc., in the GP through direct interaction and consultation with people of the locality. It is a process, which enables and empowers the local community to identify their problems, resources, potentials and priorities with respect to GP to develop agenda and plan of action. Several PRA tools are available for collection of primary data; however a few of these are discussed which will be used in rapport building as well data collection at the village level.

Participatory Rural Appraisal (PRA) Tools

Participatory Rural Appraisal (PRA) is a set of techniques to assess the existing resources, services, infrastructures etc., in the GP through direct interaction and consultation with people of the locality. It is a process, which enables and empowers the local community to identify their problems, resources, potentials and priorities with respect to GP to develop agenda and plan of action.

Some important tools are explained as follows;

(a) Social Mapping

Social mapping is a visual method of showing the relative location of households and the distribution of different people (such as male, female, adult, child, landed, landless, literate, and illiterate) together with the social structure, groups and organisations of an area.

The focus here is on the depiction of habitation patterns and the nature of housing and social infrastructure: roads, drainage systems, schools, drinking water facilities, etc.

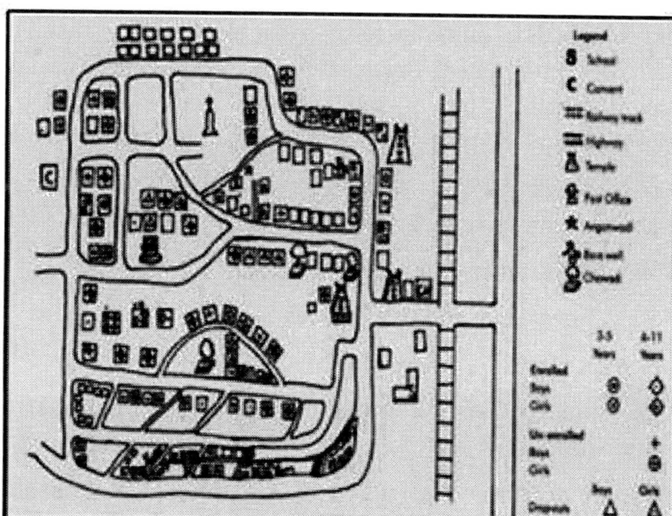

(b) Resource Mapping

Resource map is one of the most commonly used PRA methods next to social map. While the social mapping focuses on social infrastructures, the resource map focuses on the natural resources in the locality e.g. topography, land, forests, water bodies, fields, vegetation etc. A resource map in PRA is made by the local people. First of all, the local people are considered to have an in-depth knowledge for the surroundings and secondly, during data collection the emphasis is on the process of data

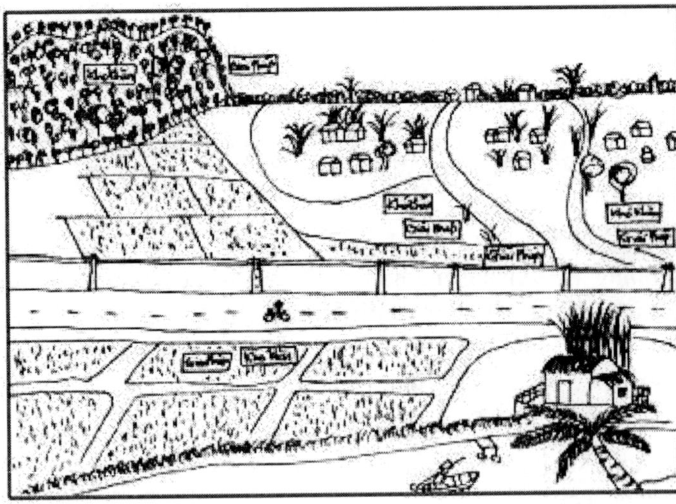

collection where people would contribute and share their knowledge about the area they reside. It is important to keep in mind, however, that it reflects the people's perception rather than precise measurements to scale. Thus, the resource map reflects how people view their own locality in terms of natural resources. Both Social and Natural Resource Map gives an overview of social, physical and natural resources of the GP area.

The natural resource management of a locality including:

- Topography, terrain and slopes
- Forest, vegetation and tree species
- Soil-type, fertility, erosion and depth
- Land and land use, command area, tenure, boundaries and ownership
- Water, water bodies, irrigation sources, rivers and drainage
- Watershed development, various soil and water conservation measures, etc.
- Agricultural developments, cropping pattern, productivity, etc

(c) Transect Walk

Transect is another PRA method used to explore the spatial dimensions of people's realities. It has been popularly used for natural resource management. It provides a cross sectional representation of the different agro- ecological zones and their comparison against certain parameters

including topography, land type, land usage, ownership, access, soil type, soil fertility, vegetation, crops, problems, opportunities and solutions. It helps to assess the condition of available infrastructure and identify the natural resources that can be used; it helps to identify availability of land for various public purposes and projects. It also helps in taking forward the process of problem identification and planning for the development of the natural resources in the area. It also helps to identify the extent of access of various communities to public services.

A transect walk in a habitation helps to identify the assets that need to be developed, the natural resources that can be used, land available for various public purposes, the extent of access to various public services etc. The GPPFT may discuss with the community and collect information on diverse scenarios within the village.

(d) Seasonal Mapping or Seasonal Calendar

An extended version of the crop calendar representing all the major changes within the rural year, such as rainfall patterns and other major climatic changes, cropping, livestock cycles, labour demand, etc. This helps in identifying lean periods for resources and in timing the supply of farm inputs and alternative employment initiatives. Many participatory approaches have been used in India for this purpose, either the locally known Hindu calendar months or festivals and fairs. People in the Indian countryside are more familiar, comfortable and accurate with these

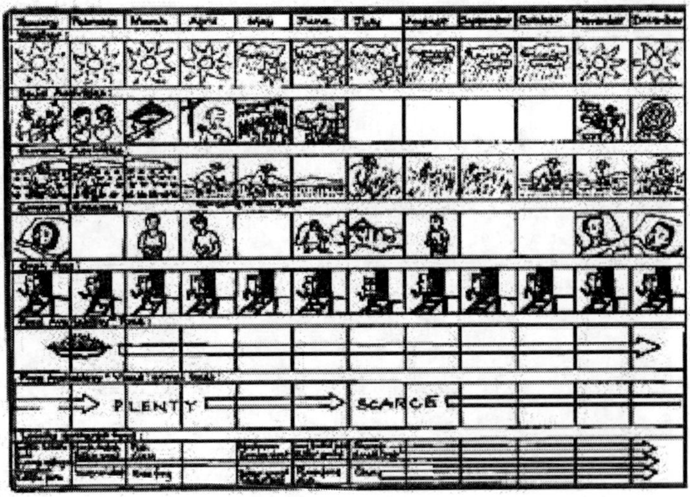

benchmarks. Seasons and months can be related to festivals that are known and generally celebrated by the large majority of the local population.

(e) Focus Group Discussion (FGD)

It is important to be able to understand people's perception on problems and issues. This can be effective if there is discussion on a specific issue and with key stakeholders as a group where matters are discussed openly and freely. It is also necessary to get an idea about what possible solutions people can suggest. This can be done through Focus Group Discussion

(FGD). FGD is a tool to gather people from similar backgrounds or experiences to discuss a specific topic of their interest. Separate FGDs can be organized for men, women, youth, aged, children, etc. In addition, as per requirement, FGDs can be conducted among SHGs, farmers club, landless people, aged, displaced community and so on.

(f) Venn Diagram

A Venn diagram shows the relationship between individuals, groups and institutions in a community as perceived by the people. It is made up of touching or overlapping circles of various sizes, with each circle representing an individual or institution. The size of the circle indicates their importance and the overlap indicates the degree of contact or inclusion in decision-making. This will help in the formulation and implementation of development initiatives at the local level, as well as in identifying marginalized individuals/groups in the community.

While a Venn diagram can be done on the ground, using natural markers such as stones and leaves, it is somewhat easier to use a large sheet of paper with shapes that are cut out of different colored card stock or paper. Alternatively, if the only paper available is white, markings can be made using different colored markers to distinguish between the different groups, associations, and individuals on the diagram.

Situation Analysis

People are well-versed with the situations that have been influencing their lives. Situation analysis is a process through which the issues and the needs of the community and the gaps where intervention is needed are identified. Situation Analysis refers to assessment of development status of the GP. It is primarily required to assess existing scenario of the GP on various development issues. It also provides basic information on the gaps in infrastructure, amenities and services that exist as well as the potential for future development. This analysis can serve as the basis for setting priorities for the issues to be incorporated in the GPDP.

Prioritization of Needs

Gram Sabha needs to discuss and develop a broad vision for improvement in identified key areas. Special focus may be given to economic development, poverty reduction, Water and Sanitation, Natural Resource Management, social justice etc. Identification of the most crucial issues is very important and it needs to be addressed on priority basis. The GPPFT shall guide the deliberations in Gram Sabha and GP meetings to identify the prioritized needs of the people to fill up the gaps in local development. This will be done based on the DSR. Prioritization of needs shall be done across the various identified thematic sectors covering all sections of the GP.

Resources for Planning

Resources are not confined to financial resources only. GPs should be aware about all kind of resources at its disposal to carry out activities through GPDP. Therefore, identification of these key resources is an essential part of the planning process. Broadly, these resources can be classified in following four categories:

1) **Social Resources**- Institutional strength, peace, social harmony/ unity within the community
2) **Natural Resources** – Land, forests, water, air and all naturally available resources
3) **Human Resources** – People living in the GP area, people associated with the area in any other capacity, GPPFT, women SHGs
4) **Financial Resources** – Funds available from Central and State Governments, OSR, Contribution by the Community etc. GP as local government should try to use these resources judiciously for sustainable development of the entire area.

Resources Identification/Estimation

Once data on all sectors are collected, the next important exercise is to take stock of available financial resources. The resource estimation has to take into account the diversity of sources that would be available at the command of GP. Therefore, GP Resources planning include the following:

- Estimating and mobilizing the own resource revenue through taxes, user charges and contributions etc.
- Innovative means of financing through community contributions including local philanthropists, NRIs, the Corporate Sector and NGOs etc.

- Getting information from line departments about the allocations made to GP under each scheme including devolutions and transfers etc.
- Direct fund flow to GP and also possible sources of convergence from flagship schemes of Centre and States

At least 10 to 20% of the resources should be locally mobilized. The GP funds can be divided into three categories: untied funds, partly untied funds (where there is some flexibility in use) and tied funds. The information on funding streams, besides own resources of GP, can be obtained from state and central budget documents and plan documents of district missions and other line departments. All funding streams coming to the GP from various sources can be listed using a simple form.

Resource Envelope

The effort of the state should be to expand the resource envelope for the GPs and to guide them to create additional resources at local level. It is also essential to monitor the timely flow of designated funds for the GPs. The resource envelope at a GP may be prescribed by the State; the indicative list is as follows:

i) Own Source Revenue (OSR)- to be projected based on actual of the last three years

ii) FFC grants

iii) SFC grants

iv) MGNREGS as per the Labour Budget

v) Other CSS and State Schemes entrusted to GPs

vi) Schemes for which the GP takes decision even if the fund is not transferred

vii) Voluntary contributions (cash, kind and labour)-States may fix a suggestive figure as appropriate

viii) CSR funds if assured and available to GPs

ix) Funds available through banking sector / leveraging bank finances

Resource envelope should also include all the resources received by the GPs. It may be clearly mentioned that the funds spent by the higher tiers like District Panchayat and Intermediate Panchayat in the Panchayat should be mandatorily part of the Resource Envelope of GP. After finalizing the elements of the resource envelope, the state should communicate in writing, well ahead of initiation of the planning process, the resources available to each GP.

GPDP as a Decentralised and Convergent Planning

Some government departments are implementing developmental programmes at GP level, but they are doing it in isolation. There is lack of synergy and also duplication of works and efforts. The guidelines of all the centrally sponsored schemes which are implemented at GP level such as MGNREGA, NRLM, SBM, ICDS etc., clearly insist on preparation of plans at the GP level. Since GPDP is an integrated and convergent plan document, it should encompass a holistic view of the Panchayat in all its facets. All plans of the line departments including labour budget shall derive from GPDP, though implementation of the approved activities may be done by the respective line departments. Such holistic and integrated plan helps to absorb more funds from different sectors and also through increased local resource mobilization thereby facilitating improvement of service delivery. The convergence of all plans and schemes of different line departments through GPDP will avoid duplication, reduce financial burden and accelerate achieving desired results. A list of various schemes implemented by Government of India that can be converged in GPDP is given in below;

List of Various Important Schemes

1 Fourteenth Finance Commission – Basic Grant and performance grants

2 Mahatma Gandhi National Rural Employment Guarantee Scheme (MGNREGS)

3 Pradhan Mantri AwaasYojana (Gramin)

4 National Social Assistance Programme (NSAP)

5 Deen Dayal Upadhyaya – Grameen Kaushalya Yojana (DDU-GKY)

6 National Rural Livelihood Mission (NRLM)

7 National Rurban Mission (NRuM)

8 Deen Dayal Antayodaya Yojana (DAY-NRLM)

9 Pradhan Mantri Gramin Sadak Yojana (PMGSY) or Rural Connectivity (RC)

10 National Rural Drinking Water Programme (NRDWP)

11 Swachh Bharat Mission - Gramin (SBM-Gramin)

12 Rashtriya Krishi VikasYojana (RKVY)

13 Prime Minister Krishi Sinchayee Yojana (PMKSY) - Integrated WatershedManagement Programme (IWMP)

14 Prime Minister Krishi Sinchayee Yojana (PMKSY) – Har Khet Ko Pani (HKKP)

15 Surface Minor Irrigation Scheme

16 Pradhan Mantri Fasal Bima Yojana (PMFBY)

17 Paramparagat Krishi Vikas Yojana (PKVY)

18 Soil Health Card (SHC)

19 National Food Security Mission (NFSM)

20 e-National Agriculture Markets (e-NAM)

21 National Rural Health Mission (NRHM/NHM)

22 Sarva Siksha Mission (SSM)

23 Mid-Day Meal Scheme (MDMS)

24 Beti Bachao, Beti Padhao (BBBP)

25 Integrated Child Development Scheme (ICDS)

26 Pradhan Mantri Ujjwala Yojana (PMUY)

27 Digital India: Common Service Centre (CSC)

28 Digital India Land Records Modernization Programme (DILRMP)

29 Deen Dayal Upadhyaya Gram JyotiYojana (DDUGJY)

30 Pradhan Mantri Kaushal Vikas Yojana

31 Pradhan Mantri Khanji Kshetra Kalyan Yojana (PMKKKY)

32 Integrated Power Development Scheme (IPDS)

33 Repair, Renovation and Restoration scheme

34 Prime Minister's Employment Generation programme (PMEGP)

35 Pradhan Mantri Adarsh Gram Yojana (PMAGY)

36. Smart City Mission
37. Atal Mission for Rejuvenation and Urban Transformation (AMRUT)
38. Heritage city Development and Augmentation Yojana (HRIDAY)
39. Programmes on infrastructure i.e telecom, railways, highways, waterways, mines, etc.
40. Pradhan Mantri AwaasYojana (Housing for All-Urban)
41. Swachh Bharat Mission (SBM)

Planning for Cost-less or Low Cost activities

Many activities to be undertaken up by GP may not be cost intensive or require any funds at all or it needs very less cost. In fact the Panchayat can take up lots of mobilization activities, which are mostly low cost or no cost during environment creation process. Community mobilization and community ownership are critical for low cost or no cost development process. An illustrative list of low cost or no cost activities is given below;

- Awareness generation at ward level through volunteers (SHG, youth groups etc.) for 100% immunization coverage.
- Awareness creation for zero-waste village through SHG collective, and other CBOs and NGOs
- Awareness creation and community monitoring for 100 % enrolment in schools
- 100 % enrolment in Anganwadis
- Mobilization of SHGs for collective farming and zero fallow land in the village
- Awareness creation and training for soak pit construction and management for household waste water
- Addressing malnutrition through Anganwadis and kitchen gardens
- Community action for elimination of child labour
- Formation of community care giving groups for bedridden patients through awareness creation and mobilization.
- Motivation and behaviour change for self- development
- Facilitating access and use of different services provided by higher levels of Government

- Dissemination of ideas and technologies in economic activities
- Encourage women's participation in economic activities under SHGs

Conclusion

The decentralised planning is to attain balanced development throughout the country with active participation of the people and to eradicate poverty. The two constitutional amendments have legally facilitated the changeover to a culture of decentralised planning. In practice, however, there is a strong pressure for centralised planning which is not a healthy feature for a vast country like ours and is against the interest of grass root planning. Several segregated attempts have been made, such as inclusion of social auditing in flagship schemes and programmes, evolution of PAHELI as a monitoring and evaluation method, gender inclusive plan of Udaipur district, entitlement-based planning approach in Bihar, etc. These success stories need to be followed and implemented. A rational choice between the two modes of planning i.e the decentralised and centralised is obvious. Forces of decentralised planning have to be encouraged, vigorously pursued and sustained to enable it to strike deep roots in the planning process.

In India, economists, social scientists and political thinkers consider the decentralised planning as the sole machinery for the control and solution of country's serious economic problems like poor growth rate, poverty, inequality, unemployment, unbalanced growth, regional inequalities etc. During the last forty years of centralised planning, the country has failed to tackle all these economic problems in appropriate manner. Thus, in order to tackle these problems effectively, the planning process in India should be decentralised at the grass root or local level in an appropriate manner. Although the seventh plan has introduced the decentralised planning process in a serious manner but the eighth plan (1992-97) has given special emphasis on the decentralised planning process for local area planning.

Some of important suggestive measures may be adopted for the improvement of workable performance of decentralised planning in India:

- Panchayati Raj Institutions of the country should be strengthened for the effective implementation of decentralised planning.
- Proper organisations of marginal and small farmers, landless agricultural labourers, artisans, scheduled castes and scheduled

tribe community and other backward classes should be developed for their proper representation in local bodies.

- Land reforms and other institutional reforms must be introduced for the successful implementation of decentralised planning in India.
- For wiping out regional disparities in respect of economic development, decentralised planning should be adopted simultaneously among all the states of the country. In order to have a proper shift from centralised planning process to decentralised planning process, the country should adopt a uniform policy throughout the country.
- State governments should make necessary arrangement for devolution of funds in adequate quantity for Panchayati Raj Institutions along with mobilisation of local private capital.
- In order to have successful implementation of decentralised planning at the district level, district planning bodies should be formed taking various experts from different discipline like economies, agriculture, statistics, banking, sociology, animal husbandry etc.
- In order to have successful implementation of decentralised planning, modalities of its implementation have to be sorted out systematically. Role of such agencies and functionaries needs to be clearly defined and demarcated.
- Moreover, government administrative machinery, elected people's representatives and banks should co-operate effectively for proper implementation of decentralised planning in India. Thus, in order to have proper implementation of economic planning, decentralisation of the planning process throughout the country is the need of the hour.
- Gram Sabhas and wards committees in urban areas have to be revitalised to achieve the objective of people's participation in real terms.
- The Standing Committee on Rural Development, that submitted its report in July 2018, recommended that state governments should put a quorum in Gram Sabha meetings for participation of panchayat representatives, including women.

- Local government organisational structures have to be strengthened with sufficient manpower. Sincere efforts should be made towards recruitment and appointment of support and technical staff to ensure the smooth functioning of panchayats.
- Devise a comprehensive mechanism for taxation at the local levels. It's a fact that we cannot have accountable GPs, without local taxation.
- There is a need for bottom up planning especially at the district level, based on grassroots inputs received from Gram Sabha.
- Strengthening of panchayats through capacity building and training should be given more encouragement from the centre and state governments. This would enable them to prepare better Gram Panchayat Development Plans, as well as become more responsive towards citizens' needs.
- India's efforts in decentralisation represent one of the largest experiments in deepening democracy.
- India has a robust democratic structure for local governance, what we need to practice is the robust democratic culture and giving life to our existing structure.
- Local bodies need to be seen as institutions of self-governance not as 'delivery mechanisms' to fulfill Gandhi's vision of Gram Swaraj.
- Ministry of Panchayati Raj should monitor the release and expenditure of Finance Commission grants to ensure that there is no delay in their release.
- It should also be ensured that grants are utilised in a proper and effective manner.
- Panchayats should also be encouraged to carry out local audits regularly so that Finance Commission grants are not delayed.

4

Developmental Initiatives Under Panchayati Raj

"The greater the power of the Panchayats the better for the people."

— ***Mahatma Gandhi***

Introduction

India has had a long tradition of panchayats in various forms. In the bygone days, the inhabitants of a village used to meet together under the leadership of village elders to discuss and resolve village problems. This system displayed the spirit of participatory democracy. Mahatma Gandhi, father of the nation, conceived village panchayats as a potential instrument for the socio-economic and political transformation of the rural society and promotion of democratic way of life at the grass-root level. Accordingly, the directive principles of state policy in our Indian Constitution enjoin the state to take steps to organize village panchayats and endow them with such powers and authority as may be necessary to enable them to function as units of self-government. Pursuant to this constitutional provisions, many states enacted suitable legislation for setting up village panchayats, while others amended the already existing law with a view to promote quicker development of panchayats and giving them a larger role than before. The community development projects, started by the Government of India on 2nd October 1952, conveyed an impetus to the movement of panchayats. In 1958, Balwant Rai Mehta Committee recommended a three-tier Panchayat system; Gram Panchayat at the lowest level, that is, the village; the Panchayat Samiti at the community development block level and the Zila Parishad at the district level. These recommendations were endorsed by the National Development Council and consequently the Government of India's policy was based on these recommendations.

It is to be noted that Panchayat Raj was not introduced all over the country on a particular day. Being a state subject it was introduced according to their own policy and convenience. Rajasthan state was the first state to introduce Panchayat Raj on 2nd October 1959 by giving effect to the Rajasthan Panchayat Samitis and Zila Parishad Act, 1959. It was followed by Andhra Pradesh which set up 235 Panchayat Samitis and 20 Zila Parishads in the same year i.e. 1959. The Mysore Village Panchayats and Local Board Act, 1959 envisages a three-tier system in the Panchayats at village level, Taluka-Board at Taluk level and Development Council at district level. In Assam, panchayats used to exist under the Assam Panchayat Act, 1958. Under the new "Assam Panchayat Act, 1959" the state has adopted a three-tier structure of local-governing institutions. In Madras, the Madras Panchayat Act, 1958, which came into force on 1st January 1960 provides for panchayats at village level and Panchayat Union Council at the Block level. In Odisha, the state has introduced a three-tier system of Panchayat Raj under the Odisha Zila Parishad Act, 1959. The Act has been given effect to by constituting Panchayat Samitis all over the state on 26th January 1962. In Punjab, the Punjab Panchayat Simitis and Zila Parishad Act, 1960 contemplates Panchayat Samitis at the block or Tehsil level and Zila Parishads at the district level. In the state of Maharashtra, a uniform system of Panchayat Raj has been introduced in the entire state under the Bombay Panchayat Act, 1958. In Bihar, panchayats exist under the Bihar Panchayat Raj Act, 1947, as amended by the Bihar Panchayat Raj (Amendment and Validating) Act, 1959. The state of Jammu & Kashmir has also introduced panchayat system on a two-tier level namely, Gram Panchayats at village level and Block Panchayats at Block Level. In Kerala, the Kerala Panchayat Act, 1960 has brought the whole state under a uniform legislation on panchayats. In Madhya Pradesh, the panchayat system was introduced from the year 1962. In other states as well as in the Union Territories, panchayats are functioning under their respective legislative enactments. The state of Haryana has adopted the Panchayat system under the Punjab Gram Panchayat (Haryana Amendment) Act, 1972. In Himachala Pradesh, the panchayats are functioning under the Himachal Pradesh Panchayat Raj Act, 1968.

Mahatma Gandhi advocated for 'Gram Swaraj' and argued for the handing over certain powers to the villagers. The 73rd Constitutional Amendment passed by the Parliament in the year 1993 was a pioneering step in decentralising political power in India. It required Indian states to enact laws for creation of the Panchayat Raj institutions. As a result, Gram Panchayats (GPs) get constituted after conducting elections more or less on regular basis in the states, though one or two instances can be found where elections have been delayed. The decision making process of the panchayats is such that the Gram Sabha (GS) discusses the development work plans of the GP called Gram Panchayat Development Plan (GPDP) and the elected representatives execute the plans. Formulation of GPDP improves efficiency of public services. Since all eligible voters of the village can participate in the Gram Sabha, it is a means to include the less privileged section of society and ensure their participation in the village level governance wherein they can advocate their developmental aspirations. This bottom-up approach is meant to reflect felt need of various stakeholders. GS is a vital as a decision-making body at the bottom. This process reflects practice of direct democracy at the village level while governance system at the state and union level is indirect or representative type. The relationship between the elected representatives of the panchayat and Gram Sabha is visualised to be similar to that of the cabinet and assembly.

Despite the constitutional empowerment, the local bodies faced problem of inadequate finance to carry out various activities assigned to them. There was a general demand from several quarters to make PRIs financially stronger to meet their needs. Transfer of fund (grants) made through the State Finance Commissions were insufficient in most states. Then central finance substantially increased the grants to the local bodies to bridge the financial gaps. The grants provided are intended to be used to support and strengthen the delivery of important basic public services.

For the development of rural people and empowering the PRIs, government of India has been taking a lot of developmental initiatives by implementing different various plans and programmes.

Centrally Sponsored Schemes routed through Panchayats

The role of panchayats varies across different Centrally Sponsored Schemes (CSSs), which are administered by different union ministries. Among the major CSSs, National Rural Employment Guarantee Programme, Indira Awas Yojana, Total Sanitation Campaign, Accelerated Rural Water Supply Programme, National Programme of Nutritional Support to Primary Education (Mid-Day Meals), National Horticulture Mission, Macro

Management of Agriculture, Micro Irrigation etc. are the schemes, which provide for roles and responsibilities for panchayats. Ministry of Panchayati Raj has issued detailed advisory in this regard to central ministries for defining the roles and responsibilities to Panchayati Raj Institutions in implementing CSSs.

The Backward Regions Grant Funds (BRGF) Programme was the main scheme administered by the Ministry of Panchayati Raj, as an Additional Central Assistance (ACA) scheme and not a CSS. The Panchayats, the Municipalities and other local bodies are the planning and implementing entities of this programme.

The role of the state government in operationalizing CSS is determined by the respective scheme guidelines and the extent to which states have devolved Funds, Functions and Functionaries (3Fs) to panchayats, as panchayat is a state subject and as per the Article-243G, states are to endow power and authority to panchayats to enable them to function as institutions of self-government and plan and implement schemes for socio-economic development and social justice, including matters listed in the eleventh schedule.

Rajiv Gandhi Panchayat Sashaktikaran Abhiyan (RGPSA)

The key role of panchayats in rural governance and socio-economic development has been recognized since the 1950s. In the current context, the need to strengthen panchayats has intensified with the rise in expenditure on programmes of social welfare and inclusion, as panchayats are vital to ensure that the benefits of these schemes reach the people, management of local institutions is improved and accountability is enhanced. There is a need to provide panchayats with adequate technical and administrative support, strengthen their infrastructure and e-enablement, promote devolution and to improve their functioning. The Centrally Sponsored Scheme of Rajiv Gandhi Panchayat Sashaktikaran Abhiyan (RGPSA) has been launched to strengthen Panchayati Raj. This scheme was approved on 07.03.2013.The erstwhile scheme of Ministry of Panchayati Raj-Panchayat Mahila Evam Yuva Shakti Abhiyan (PMEYSA), Rashtriya Gram Swaraj Yojana (RGSY), Panchayat (Extension to Scheduled Areas) Act (PESA), Panchayat Empowerment and Accountability Incentive Scheme (PEAIS), e-Panchayat and Resource Support to States (RSS) have been subsumed in the scheme of RGPSA with effect from 2013-14.

Objectives of RGPSA

RGPSA seeks to:

1. Enhance capacities and effectiveness of panchayats and the Gram Sabhas;
2. Enable democratic decision-making and accountability in panchayats and promote people's participation;
3. Strengthen the institutional structure for knowledge creation and capacity building of panchayats;
4. Promote devolution of powers and responsibilities to panchayats according to the spirit of the constitution and PESA Act;
5. Strengthen Gram Sabhas to function effectively as the basic forum of people's participation, transparency and accountability within the panchayat system;
6. Create and strengthen democratic local self-government in areas where panchayats do not exist;
7. Strengthen the constitutionally mandated framework on which panchayats are founded.

Components of the Scheme: There are two components of the scheme of RGPSA:

- Activities to be included in State Plans.
- Activities under the National Plan for Technical Assistance (NPTA)

A. Activities to be included in State Plans

States are expected to prepare plans under the scheme to undertake activities as per their requirement/priorities from a menu of activities permitted in the scheme. Each state is not expected to necessarily undertake all the activities. Activities in state plans under RGPSA are as follows:

(i) *Administrative and Technical Support*

Each state is expected to visualize the administrative and technical support needed at each tier of panchayats and ensure that the panchayats have appropriate staff or other administrative and technical support to discharge their functions. Funds will be provided for administrative and technical support at the Gram Panchayat (GP) as per the states visualization. For the block and district level panchayats, States will be expected to devolve appropriate functionaries to the panchayats. Expenses of existing technical and administrative support mechanism in panchayats cannot be transferred to RGPSA.

(ii) ***Gram Panchayat Buildings***

In general, states will be expected to obtain funds for Gram Panchayat buildings from various sources, especially through schemes of the Ministry of Rural Development. However, where funds cannot be accessed from other schemes, RGPSA will fund new Gram Panchayat buildings, repair of existing buildings, construction of barrier free access, construction of toilets (including separate toilets for women), electricity and water supply connections.

(iii) ***Capacity Building and Training of Elected Representatives & Functionaries***

The aim will be to ensure that all Elected Representatives (ERs) as well as functionaries of panchayats have appropriate knowledge and skills to discharge their functions. Capacity Building and Training (CB&T) activities will be funded as per the National Capability Building Framework (NCBF).

(iv) ***Institutional Structure for Training at State, District & Block level***

The Capacity Building and Training(CB&T) of Elected Representatives (ERs) and panchayat functionaries is a wide area, as it is necessary to address basic concepts, skills of ERs and Panchayat functionaries, including literacy as well as the domain knowledge of subjects handled by panchayats, such as drinking water, rural development, education, health, women's issues, social forestry, livelihoods etc. To address all these issues, a sound institutional structure and partnership with resource institutions are required. Under RGPSA, State Panchayat Resource Centres (SPRCs) may be established at State Institutes of Rural Development (SIRDs) or any other state level institution, District Panchayat Resource Centres (DPRCs) may be strengthened in existing institutions or new centres established, and block level satellite resource centres may be established at the Block Panchayat.

(v) ***E-enablement of Panchayats***

The Panchayat Enterprise Suite (PES) was formed the bedrock of e-enablement of panchayats to increase their effectiveness for governance and service delivery. States would be expected to make all efforts to ensure appropriate CB&T for e-enablement of panchayats.

(vi) ***Support to Panchayat Processes and Procedures with Inadequate Revenue Base***

Many Panchayats lack resources for basic activities such as Gram Sabha meetings, planning, social audit, public campaigns, forming federations etc. which hampers their functioning. These panchayats will be supported to carry out their basic processes/procedures.

(vii) ***Special Support for Gram Sabhas in PESA and N-E Areas***

Special activities may be undertaken to strengthen Gram Sabhas in PESA areas and in NE areas where Part-IX of the Constitution of India does not apply, in terms of organizing themselves and also knowledge and assertion of their rights.

(viii) ***Programme Management***

The present strength and capacity of state Panchayati Raj departments needs to be enhanced to enable them to undertake the task of preparing state plans and implementing RGPSA for the development of panchayats in the state. To support the Panchayati Raj departments of the states, Programme Managements Units at the state and district level may be set up for planning, implementation and monitoring of the scheme from within the 5% available in management costs.

(ix) ***Information, Education and Communication (IEC)***

States were expected to undertake IEC activities to raise the awareness level of panchayats. IEC activities to be funded would include Print Material, Newsletter, TV and Radio programmes including Community Radio etc. Further as a sequel to launching of Swachh Bharat Abhiyan (SBA) the states have been advised to ensure that some portion of funds provided under IEC activities are spent on generating awareness on sanitation.

(x) ***Strengthening of State Election Commission (SECs)***

Free and fair elections are the bedrock of Panchayati Raj. There is need to strengthen the State Election Commission (SECs) to ensure free and fair elections. The SECs may be provided financial assistance as per proposals made by the SECs. These proposals may include strengthening of infrastructure, purchase of Electronic Voting Machines (EVMs), process development etc.

(xi) *Innovative Activities in States*

Innovative activities, processes or projects to strengthen Panchayati Raj may be included in state plans for up to Rs.2 crores per annum. These may be undertaken through government or non-government agencies.

B. Activities under the National Plan for Technical Assistance (NPTA)

The aim of the National Plan for Technical Assistance is to provide technical and other support to states for implementing RGPSA and supervise and monitor the programme. The activities under National Plan for Technical Assistance are:

(i) *Institutional Support at National Level*

A suitable institutional mechanism at the national level was developed for overall academic and technical support including capacity building of SPRCs and DPRCs.

(ii) *Planning, Management and Supervision*

State plans were scrutinized and appraised before these are placed before the Central Executive Committee. There will be an annual assessment of the implementation of the goals of the scheme in states, which was provide the basis for disbursement of 20% funds on the basis of performance.

(iii) *Technical Support to States*

States were provided technical support for implementing RGPSA. The types of technical support activities would include *viz.* orientation of state teams on various issues such as planning, techniques of capacity building, women's issues, Gram Sabha mobilization, accounts, e-enablement etc.

(iv) *Performance Assessment and Incentivization of Panchayats and Gram Sabha*

An important focus of institutional development of panchayats would be feedback on their functioning and support to processes of democratic and accountable functioning. During the Eleventh Five Year Plan, Ministry of Panchayati Raj (MoPR) has developed processes for assessing panchayats and Gram Sabhas on their performance and linked these with small incentives. These assessment exercises will be continued and further refined. States were supported in creating a system whereby panchayats that are unable to perform their role adequately are also identified along with best performing panchayats. The former was supported in improving their performance while the latter was also be incentivized.

(v) ***Support for Innovation***

The improvement in panchayat capacities and processes can be achieved only if the government and non-government actors are encouraged to innovate with new forms of capacity building and accountability processes. Funds may be provided for innovative activities, such as developing processes of planning, strengthening of the Gram Sabhas, capacity building etc. to government as well as non-government agencies. Projects for innovative activities will be approved by the Central Executive Committee (RGPSA).

(vi) ***National Programme Management Unit***

A National Programme Management Unit (NPMU) was set up at the National level to provide technical support to states and MoPR. The NPMU have experts from relevant disciplines and was also hired short term consultants and consulting organizations.

Funding: States were required to fulfil some essential conditions for accessing any RGPSA funds which was include:

- ❐ Regular elections to panchayats or local bodies in non-Part IX areas under the superintendence and control of the State Election Commission (SEC).
- ❐ At least one third reservation for women in panchayats or other local bodies.
- ❐ Constitution of State Finance Commission (SFC) every five years and placement of Action Taken Report on the recommendations of the SFC in the state legislature.
- ❐ Constitution of District Planning Committees (DPCs) in all districts, and issuing of guidelines/rules to make these functional.

Funding Pattern under RGPSA

- The funding of RGPSA for state plans was 75:25 sharing basis by the central and state governments respectively. For North Eastern states (NE States), this ratio was 90:10.
- For the National Plan for Technical Assistance, up to 5 percent RGPSA funds may be used for supervision and technical assistance activities. In addition, upto Rs. 10 crores per annum may be utilized for support to innovation and up to Rs.50 crores per annum for incentivization of best performing Panchayats and Gram Sabhas. These national level activities were 100 percent centrally funded.
- The rest of the funds (called Central Share) were provided to states to implement their plans. A matching share of 10 percent by NE states and 25 by other states could have to be provided against the central share of 90 percent and 75 percent respectively. A minimum of 10 percent of state plan funds was available for North Eastern states.
- The eligibility of states to access the central share was as per their rural population, the area of the state under Schedule-V of the Constitution, the plan approved, utilization of funds provided and from 2014-15 onwards, performance as per set parameters. Ten percent of the central share was disbursed on the basis of the population and area of a state under Schedule-V. In 2012-13 and 2013-14 the eligibility of states to access funds available under RGPSA will be as per their share in the rural population, the area and population under Schedule-V in the state, the plan approved and the utilization of funds provided.
- From 2014-15 onwards, 80 percent of central share would be based on state's rural population, the area and population under Scheduled-V in the state, the plan approved and the utilization of funds provided, and 20 percent on the extent to which a state shows progress on goals stated in its action plans.
- Of the 20 percent funds to be allotted on the basis of performance, states that show greater progress will be entitled to a larger share of funds.
- The CEC. RGPSA is fully competent to decide the quantum of funds to be provided to each state.

- Each state is entitled to spend 5 percent of its approved funds on programme planning and management over the twelfth plan period. The percentage of funds to be spent on planning and management may exceed 5 percent and go up to 25 percent in the first two years, as it was take time for expenditure on activities to pick up and planning and management coasts in the initial years would be high.
- A state may spend up to 25 percent of its plan funds on construction and repair of GP buildings. Cost of land was not be funded under the scheme.
- A state may spend up to 1 percent of its plan funds on IEC activities.
- Salaries and other expenditures that are already funded by the state government on the date that the scheme is approved cannot be transferred to RGPSA.
- Activities already approved under any of the schemes of MoPR in the Eleventh Plan which have been subsumed in RGPSA continued to be funded during the Twelfth Plan under RGPSA

Rashtriya Gram Swaraj Abhiyan (RGSA)

The government on 24/04/2018 on the occasion of National Panchayati Raj Day launched the restructured Centrally Sponsored Scheme (CSS) of Rashtriya Gram Swaraj Abhiyan (RGSA) for implementation from 01.04.2018 to 31.03.2022 with the primary aim of strengthening Panchayati Raj Institutions (PRIs) for achieving Sustainable Development Goals (SDGs) with main thrust on convergence with Mission Antyodaya and emphasis on strengthening PRIs in the 117 Aspirational districts. The scheme has been approved with total budget outlay of Rs. 7255.50 crore out of which state share was Rs. 2755.50 crore and the Central share was Rs. 4500.00 crore. The scheme extends to all States and UTs including non-Part IX areas where panchayats do not exist.

The scheme consists of central and state components. The central component comprises (i) national level activities viz. National Plan for Technical Assistance (NPTA) including NPMU, collaboration with academic institutions/ institutions of excellence including NIRD&PR, Hyderabad for various activities of CB&T for PRIs (ii) Mission Mode Project (MMP) on e-Panchayat and (iii) Incentivization of Panchayats. The state component relates to activities to be undertaken by state governments for CB&T and other activities for strengthening of panchayats viz capacity building & training, training infrastructure and HR support for training, strengthening of Gram Sabhas in PESA areas, distance learning facility via SATCOM, support for innovations, technical support to PRIs, financial data and analysis cell, panchayat buildings, e-enablement of panchayats, project based funding for economic development and income enhancement, IEC and PMU. The sharing pattern for the state component is in the ratio of 60:40 except NE and hilly states where central and state sharing is in the ratio of 90:10. For all UTs, central share is 100%.

The scheme has programmatic focus for phased saturation mode on ensuring basic orientation training for the elected representatives of panchayats, within six months of their election and refresher trainings within 2 years. RGSA will have thrust for SHG-PRI convergence to ensure effective community mobilisation and greater public ownership of flagship programs of the government. Use of e-governance and technology driven solutions at panchayat level will be increased to attain administrative efficiency, improved service delivery and greater accountability.

For enabling the PRIs to implement the RGSA in a meaningful, concerted and result oriented manner, a framework for implementation of RGSA has been prepared and shared with the states.

During the year 2018-19, ministry has approved the Annual Action Plans (AAPs) of 32 States/UTs and Rs 598.21 crore has been released to states and implementing agencies etc under the scheme..

Further, with a view to expeditiously implement the scheme and for achieving the stipulated objectives in a progressive manner, this ministry has taken the initiative for approval of the Annual Action Plans for the year 2019-20 of all States / UTs by the Central Empowered Committee of RGSA, well in advance so that the States / UTs have full year for implementation of their approved activities. Towards this end, the 3rd meeting of the CEC of RGSA was held on 22nd and 23rd February, 2019 and the Annual Action Plans for 2019-20 of 33 States / UTs were approved. The minutes of the meeting have been accordingly communicated to the concerned States/UTs and participants.

E-Panchayat Project

Backdrop

As per the World Bank, "E-Government refers to the use by government agencies of information technologies (such as Wide Area Networks, the Internet, and mobile computing) that have the ability to transform relations with citizens, businesses and other arms of government." Government of India (GoI), with an intention to transform the governance landscape by ensuring participation of citizens in policy making and providing ease of access to information to the citizens, introduced the National e-Governance Plan (NeGP) in 2006. The vision of the NeGP was to "Make all government services accessible to the common man in his locality, through common service delivery outlets and ensure efficiency, transparency & reliability of such services at affordable costs to realise the basic needs of the common man." e- Panchayat is one of the Mission Mode Project (MMP), currently being implemented with a vision to empower and transform rural India.

As a first step towards formulating the project, the Ministry of Panchayati Raj constituted an Expert Group in June, 2007 under the Chairmanship of Dr. B.K. Gairola, Director General, NIC, Government of India. The Expert Group was entrusted with the task of assessing the IT Programmes of Ministry of Panchayati Raj and recommending cost effective solutions along with the cost implications. Adopting a consultative approach, the committee interacted with the States/UTs to assess the existing status of computerization up to the Gram Panchayat level, including the initiatives undertaken by the state governments. In order to understand the ground realities, the committee conducted field visits to some of the Gram Panchayats in the selected rural areas where some IT initiatives had been undertaken. Inputs from eminent experts in the public and private sector were also taken into account as part of the consultative process. In essence, it found that while some computerization efforts had already been made at panchayat level by states like Gujarat, West Bengal, Karnataka, Kerala, Andhra Pradesh and Goa, these attempts were limited as they were driven by short term goals and were unable to completely transform panchayats due to lack of a holistic perspective. It was felt that a more comprehensive approach was required to make a cognizable impact on the functioning of the panchayats for the benefit of the citizens. These recommendations formed the basis for the conceptualization of e-Panchayat Mission Mode Project.

The e-Panchayat project holds great promise for the rural masses as it aims to transform the Panchayati Raj Institutions (PRIs) into symbols of modernity, transparency and efficiency. This is a one of its kind nationwide IT initiative introduced by Ministry of Panchayati Raj that endeavours to ensure people's participation in programme decision making, implementation and delivery. The project aims to automate the functioning of the 2.45 lakh panchayats in the country.

Objectives of e-Panchayat Project

If the Panchayats are to perform efficiently and effectively all the mandated tasks, which are increasing day by day, extensive use of Information and Communication Technology (ICT) is needed. Moreover, there is a strong need to build a "Digital Inclusive Society" where large sections of rural population are able to benefit from new technologies; can access and share information and services freely and can participate in the development process more effectively.

The Panchayats being at the interface of rural citizens and governance structure are an effective vehicle to induce mass ICT culture at the grassroots level. It is with this broad vision that MoPR formulated a scheme for ICT enablement of all the panchayats in the country on a mission mode approach. The e-Panchayat Mission Mode Project (MMP) is intended to address all the aspects of panchayats' functioning from internal core functions such as decentralized planning, budgeting, accounting, implementation, monitoring, social audit and delivery of citizen services like issue of certificates, licenses etc.

Hence the key objectives of e-Panchayat Mission Mode Project are to use ICT for:

- Automation of internal workflow processes of panchayats
- Improving delivery of services to citizens
- Capacity building of panchayat representatives and officials
- Social Audit
- Transparency, Accountability, Efficiency and RTI compliance of panchayats
- Improving governance of local self-government

The panchayats being the basic unit for planning and implementation of a large number of schemes and services, this MMP would also go a long way in improving public service delivery through PRIs with better outcomes.

Project Conceptualization

E-Panchayat MMP is aimed at automating internal work flow processes of all the panchayats across the country. This will cover all the elected members and several lakhs PRIs functionaries. In 2009-10, in order to lay a strong foundation for e-Panchayat and to ensure that project evolved through an elaborate consultative process, Ministry of Panchayati Raj (MoPR) commissioned a comprehensive study covering all States and UTs to identify all the information and services needs of the stakeholders viz. central ministries, state departments, panchayats and citizens. Field studies were conducted in 135 Panchayats across 45 districts covering all 34 States/ UTs. 23 central schemes were studied and discussions were held with 11 central line ministries, their state departments, district and block administrations and several field level functionaries. Inputs were also taken from Gram Sabha meetings and through other focused group discussions with citizens.

Finance Commission Grants

As a federal nation, India suffers from both vertical and horizontal fiscal imbalances. Vertical imbalances between the central and state governments results from states incurring expenditures disproportionate to their sources of revenue, in the process of fulfilling their responsibilities. However, states are better able to measure the needs and concerns of their inhabitants and therefore more efficient at addressing them. Horizontal imbalances among state governments' results from differing historical backgrounds or resource endowments and can widen over time.

The Finance Commission was established by the President of India in 1951 under Article-280 of the Indian Constitution. It was formed to define the financial relations between the central government and the individual state governments. The Finance Commission (Miscellaneous Provisions) Act, 1951 furthermore defines the terms of qualification, appointment and disqualification, the term, eligibility and powers of the finance commission. As per the Constitution, the commission is appointed every five years and consists of a chairman and four other members. Several provisions to bridge the fiscal gap between the central and the states were already enshrined in the constitution of India, including Article-268, which facilitates levy of duties by the central but equips the states to collect and retain the same. Similarly, Articles-269, 270, 275, 282 and 293, among others, specify the ways and means of sharing resources between the Union and States. In addition to the above provisions, the finance commission serves as an institutional framework to facilitate centre-state transfers.

Since the institution of the first Finance Commission, desolate changes in the macroeconomic situation of the Indian economy have led to major changes in the finance commission's recommendations over the years. There have been fifteen commissions to date. The most recent was constituted in

2017 and is chaired by N.K.Singh, a former member of the Planning Commission.

Article-280 of the Indian Constitution defines the scope of the commission:

- The President will constitute a finance commission within two years from the commencement of the constitution and thereafter at the end of every fifth year or earlier, as the deemed necessary by him/her, which shall include a chairman and four other members.
- Parliament may by law determine the requisite qualifications for appointment as members of the commission and the procedure of selection.
- The commission is constituted to make recommendations to the president about the distribution of the net proceeds of taxes between the Union and States and also the allocation of the same among the states themselves. It is also under the scope of the finance commission to define the financial relations between the Union and the States. They also deal with the devolution of unplanned revenue resources.

Finance Commission and its Functions

The constitution makers were aware of the financial requirements of the centre and the states. They devised an elaborate method, clearly demarcating the duties and responsibilities of the units of the Union and of the Union itself while allocating resources to perform those duties. To meet these requirements, the Finance Commission came into being.

The Finance Commission has the following functions or duties:

- The Commission makes recommendations to the President of India on the distribution of tax proceeds between the Union and the States and the share of each state.
- The Commission also decides the principles that govern the payment of grants-in-aid to states from the Consolidated Fund of India.

The President of India can also refer any other matter to the finance commission in the interest of building a sound financial system. Under Article-280 of the constitution, the President of India is required to constitute a finance commission at an interval of five years or earlier.

Finance Commissions: A Critical Analysis

Vertical and horizontal imbalances are common features of most federations and India is no exception to this. The constitution assigned taxes with a nation-wide base to the Union to make the country one common economic space unhindered by internal barriers to the extent possible. States being closer to people and more sensitive to the local needs have been assigned functional responsibilities involving expenditure disproportionate to their assigned sources of revenue resulting in vertical imbalances. Horizontal imbalances across states are on account of factors, which include historical backgrounds, differential endowment of resources and capacity to raise resources. Unlike in most other federations, differences in the developmental levels in Indian states are very sharp. In an explicit recognition of vertical and horizontal imbalances, the Indian constitution embodies the following enabling and mandatory provisions to address them through the transfer of resources from the centre to the states:

- Levy of duties by the centre but collected and retained by the states (Article-268)
- Taxes and duties levied as well as collected by the centre but assigned in whole to the states (Article- 269).
- Sharing of the proceeds of all Union taxes between the centre and the states under Article-270. (effective from 1st April 1996, following the eightieth amendment to the constitution replacing the earlier provisions relating to mandatory sharing of income tax under Article-270 and permissive sharing of Union excise duties under Article-272).
- Statutory grants-in-aid of the revenues of states (Article-275)
- Grants for any public purpose (Article-282).
- Loans for any public purpose (Article-293).

The Finance Commission Grants are primarily divided into four sub-heads:-

1. Grants for Rural Local Bodies: The three-tier model of governance envisioned in the constitution assigns clear roles and responsibilities to Gram Panchayats. The Finance Commission recommendations ensure that these local bodies are adequately funded. In fact, nearly half of the Finance Commission Grants in union budget goes to village local bodies.

2. Grants for Urban Local Bodies: In addition to units of self-governance at the village level, the Constitution also envisages cities as units of self-governance. Urban local bodies like municipal councils receive the largest chunk of finance commission grants after rural local bodies and post devolution deficit grants to states.

3. Assistance to SDRF: The central government also provides funds to State Disaster Relief Funds in addition to funding the National Disaster Management Authority (NDMA). The assistance to state government's disaster relief authorities is provided as per the recommendations of the finance commission.

4. Post-devolution Revenue Deficit Grants: The finance commission also provides a mechanism for compensation of any loss incurred by states, which is called post-devolution revenue deficit grants. This finance commission grant forms the second largest chunk of finance commission transfers after the assistance to local rural bodies.

Devolution Criteria

The criteria used by the commission to determine each state's share in central taxes, and the weight assigned to each criterion.

Basic and Performance Grants to GPs

The 14th FC has recommended grants to the local rural bodies viz the Panchayats for planning and delivering of basic services smoothly and effectively within the functions assigned to them under the Act. As per the Fourteenth Finance Commission, the local bodies are required to spend the grants only to the basic services within the functions assigned to them under relevant legislations. The earmarked basic grants for Village Panchayats shall be distributed across the Panchayats using 2011 Census population with a weight of 90% and area with a weight of 10%. The said grants will be provided in two parts namely a Basic Grant and a Performance Grant.

i. Basic Grant: The grants will be released to Village Panchayats for the delivery of basic services such as including water supply, sanitation including septage management, sewerage and solid waste management, storm water drainage, maintenance of community assets, maintenance of roads, footpaths and street-lighting, and burial and cremation grounds.

ii. Performance Grant: The Performance Grant will be provided based on receipts and expenditure received through audited accounts and increase in own revenues. The Performance grants shall be released the next year based on the following criteria:

- The Village Panchayats shall utilize 80% of the Basic grants and shall submit the Utilization Certificates along with the list of activities performed and such other reliable data as may be required.
- In case 80% of the Basic grants are not utilized, then 80% of the physical activities shall be completed.
- The Gram Panchayat shall enhance the revenue collection at least by 5% every year.
- Every Gram Panchayat shall update data in the IT enabled software.
- The Gram Panchayat shall submit audited annual accounts of preceding year in which they seek to claim performance grant.

Criteria for Devolution (2020-21)

Criteria	14th FC(2015-20)	15th FC (2020-21)
Income Distance	50.0	45.0
Population (1971)	17.5	-
Population (2011)	10.0	15.0
Area	15.0	15.0
Forest Cover	7.5	-
Forest and Ecology	-	10.0
Demographic Performance	-	12.5
Tax Effort	-	2.5
Total	**100**	**100**

Sources: Report of 15th Finance Commission; 2020-21

- **Income Distance:** Income distance is the distance of the state's income from the state with the highest income. The income of a state has been computed as average per capita GSDP during the three-year period between 2015-16 and 2017-18. States with lower per capita income would be given a higher share to maintain equity among states.
- **Demographic Performance:** The Terms of Reference (ToR) of the commission required it to use the population data of 2011 while

making recommendations. Accordingly, the commission used only 2011 population data for its recommendations. The demographic performance criterion has been introduced to reward efforts made by states in controlling their population. It will be computed by using the reciprocal of the total fertility ratio of each state, scaled by 1971 population data. States with a lower fertility ratio will be scored higher on this criterion. The total fertility ratio in a specific year is defined as the total number of children that would be born to each woman if she were to live to the end of her child-bearing years and give birth to children in alignment with the prevailing age-specific fertility rates.

- **Forest and Ecology:** This criterion has been arrived at by calculating the share of dense forest of each state in the aggregate dense forest of all the states.

- **Tax Effort:** This criterion has been used to reward states with higher tax collection efficiency. It has been computed as the ratio of the average per capita own tax revenue and the average per capita state GDP during the three-year period between 2014-15 and 2016-17.

Grants-in-Aid

In 2020-21, the following grants will be provided to states: (i) revenue deficit grants, (ii) grants to local bodies, and (iii) disaster management grants. The commission has also proposed a framework for sector-specific and performance-based grants. State-specific grants will be provided in the final report.

- **Revenue Deficit Grants:** In 2020-21, 14 states are estimated to have an aggregate revenue deficit of Rs 74,340 crore post-devolution. The commission recommended revenue deficit grants for these states.

- **Special Grants:** In case of three states, the sum of devolution and revenue deficit grants is estimated to decline in 2020-21 as compared to 2019-20. These states are Karnataka, Mizoram, and Telangana. The commission has recommended special grants to these states aggregating to Rs 6,764 crore.

- **Sector-specific Grants:** The commission has recommended a grant of Rs 7,375 crore for nutrition in 2020-21. Sector-specific grants for the following sectors will be provided in the final report: (i) nutrition (ii) health (iii) pre-primary education (iv) judiciary (v) rural connectivity (vi) railways (vii) police training, and (viii) housing.

- **Performance-based Grants**: Guidelines for performance-based grants include: (i) implementation of agricultural reforms (ii) development of aspirational districts and blocks (iii) power sector reforms (iv) enhancing trade including exports (v) incentives for education and (vi) promotion of domestic and international tourism. The grant amount will be provided in the final report.
- **Grants to Local Bodies:** The total grants to local bodies for 2020-21 has been fixed at Rs 90,000 crore, of which Rs 60,750 crore is recommended for rural local bodies (67.5%) and Rs 29,250 crore for urban local bodies (32.5%). This allocation is 4.31% of the divisible pool. This is an increase over the grants for local bodies in 2019-20, which amounted to 3.54% of the divisible pool (Rs 87,352 crore). The grants will be divided between states based on population and area in the ratio 90:10. The grants will be made available to all three tiers of Panchayat- village, block and district.
- **Disaster Risk Management:** The commission recommended setting up National and State Disaster Management Funds (NDMF and SDMF) for the promotion of local-level mitigation activities. The commission has recommended retaining the existing cost-sharing patterns between the centre and states to fund the SDMF (new) and the SDRF (existing). The cost-sharing pattern between centre and states is (i) 75:25 for all states, and (ii) 90:10 for north-eastern and Himalayan states.

For 2020-21, State Disaster Risk Management Funds have been allocated Rs 28,983 crore, out of which the share of the union is Rs 22,184 crore. The National Disaster Risk Management Funds has been allocated Rs 12,390 crore

Major Finance Commission's Recommendations

The recommendations of the finance commission can be grouped under the following three heads-

(1) Division and distribution of taxes and duties of which the main have been Union Income Tax (other than agricultural income-tax

and corporate taxes), Central Excise Duties, Additional Excise Duties and Estate Duty.

(2) Grants-in-aid to States.

(3) Union loan to States.

Recommendations of 14th Finance Commission

Major Recommendations of 14th Finance Commission headed by Prof. Y V Reddy:

- The share of states in the net proceeds of the shareable central taxes should be 42%. This is 10 percentage points higher than the recommendation of 13th Finance Commission.
- Revenue deficit to be progressively reduced and eliminated.
- Fiscal deficit to be reduced to 3% of the GDP by 2017-18.
- A target of 62% of GDP for the combined debt of centre and states.
- The Medium Term Fiscal Plan (MTFP) should be reformed and made the statement of commitment rather than a statement of intent.
- FRBM Act needs to be amended to mention the nature of shocks which shall require targets relaxation.
- Both centre and states should conclude 'Grand Bargain' to implement the model Goods and Services Act (GST).
- Initiatives to reduce the number of Central Sponsored Schemes (CSS) and to restore the predominance of formula-based plan grants.
- States need to address the problem of losses in the power sector in time bound manner.

Recommendations of 15th Finance Commission

The Fifteenth Finance Commission was constituted by the President of India under Article-280 of the Constitution on 27th November 2017 to make recommendations for a period of five years commencing 1st April 2020. Mr. Nand Kishore Singh was appointed as the commission's chairman, with its full-time members being Shaktikanta Das and Anoop Singh and its part-time members being Ramesh Chand and Ashok Lahiri. However Ajay Narayan Jha was appointed replacing Shaktikanta Das who resigned from the commission to serve as the governor of the Reserve

Bank of India. The main tasks of the commission were to "strengthen cooperative federalism, improve the quality of public spending and help protect fiscal stability".

The major recommendations are as follows;

- Keeping in view the fact that there has to be a certain degree of predictability and stability in federal finances, our approach to vertical devolution mirrors that of our predecessor Commissions with modifications due to the change in the status of Jammu and Kashmir. The significant points of departure are:
  - (i) The ToR clearly stipulates that the commission use the population data of 2011 for our recommendations. As population is a major factor in the determination of the devolution formula, and it is also used for scaling other criteria, our recommendations are appropriately calibrated to address the parameters of equity and efficiency in the devolution of resources to the States.
  - (ii) The ToR enjoining us to use the census data 2011 created apprehensions that in the process those states that have achieved greater progress in reducing population growth since 1971 would be adversely affected. The commission have attempted to dispel these doubts by introducing a new criterion of Total Fertility Rate (TFR) as a measure of demographic performance.
  - (iii) During the interactions with the states and the union government, it was argued that issues relating to environment and climate change need to be given greater thrust and attention. The commission have continued with the approach of the FC-XIV in this regard, with a higher weightage to forest and ecology not only because of their impact on the revenue disabilities and expenditure needs of States, but also for the huge ecological benefits to the nation and for meeting our international commitments.
  - (iv) Incentivising tax effort had received the attention of several commissions, though the FC-XIV did not use it as a criterion. At a time when fiscal consolidation is a matter of concern, the commission have chosen to address it in our devolution mechanism.

(v) The commission have provided grants-in-aid for local bodies, disaster relief and for states with a post devolution revenue deficit. As the recommendations of this report are only for one year, the commission have refrained from giving any state-specific grants but have provided a road-map for sector-specific grants and performance-based incentives that the commission expect to address in greater detail in the final report.

- Based on the aforesaid architecture, the commission has made the following key macro assumptions. The union budget of 2019-20 implied a nominal GDP growth of 11 per cent in 2019-20, but the nominal growth observed in the first quarter (Q1) of 2019-20 was only 8 per cent. The economic data released subsequently do not show any perceptible improvement in economic activity. Nonetheless, since the GDP growth rates of Q2 to Q4 of 2018-19 were low, there is a base advantage in the subsequent quarters of the current year. The supply side measures announced by the union government may also have a positive impact on economic activity. Taking a full view of the possible growth rates during Q2 to Q4 of the current year, the commission have assessed that nominal GDP growth in 2019-20 would be 10 per cent with a downward bias. With some pick-up in economic activity and a mild increase in inflation rate, the nominal GDP can be expected to grow at 11 per cent in 2020-21.
- The gross tax revenue of the union government for 2019-20 and 2020-21 is based on the provisional accounts for 2018-19. Based on recent trends and tax policy changes, our assessment is that gross tax revenue for 2019-20 will be about Rs. 22.55 lakh crore, against the budget estimate of Rs. 24.61 lakh crore. The commission's projection of gross tax revenue for 2020-21 is based on the reassessed level of this revenue for 2019-20. The commission expect overall tax buoyancy to improve to 1.14 in 2020-21, translating into gross tax revenue of Rs. 25.38 lakh crore. The expenditure projections spelt out by the Union Budget 2019-20 were adopted by the commission, with a modest downward adjustment.
- The approach followed in the projection of Gross State Domestic Product (GSDP) has been to progressively reduce the variability in growth observed across states in the previous years. For making

an assessment of the revenue and expenditure of states, the commission broadly followed the approach of previous finance commissions. The commission applied norms for projections from the base year after making adjustments to the latest available actuals (2017-18). The tax buoyancy for states was projected uniformly at 1.16 during the period 2018-19 to 2020-21. For assessing the revenue expenditure of states, the commission took a disaggregated view on the committed and other revenue expenditure to arrive at the state-wise projections for 2020-21. The aggregate revenue expenditure of all the states taken together shows an average growth of 9.4 per cent in 2020-21.

- The commission sought to balance the principles of fiscal needs, equity and performance for determining the criteria for horizontal sharing. Another important principle followed is the broad need for stability and predictability in transfers.
- The commission recommend revenue deficit grants and special grants, besides laying out the broad contours of the sectoral grants and performance-based incentives that the commission intend to provide in the final report. This should enable governments to undertake the necessary preparatory work during 2020-21 to optimise the utilisation of resources in the remaining period of the award. Based upon our assessment of the post-devolution revenue surplus/deficit of the States for 2020-21, the commission have estimated that fourteen states will need revenue deficit grants amounting to Rs. 74,340 crore. The commission have also provided special grants of Rs. 6,764 crore for three States in which the sum of tax devolution and revenue deficit grants is projected to decline in 2020-21 over 2019-20. Malnutrition of infants is a human capital issue that cannot wait to be addressed. Hence, an exception have made in the case of the nutrition sector by giving it a grant of Rs. 7,735 crore in 2020-21.
- The commission has received a large number of proposals for state-specific grants. However, given the financial constraints in 2020-21, the commission propose to make appropriate recommendations on such grants in our final report.
- Recommendation made for an amount of Rs. 90,000 crore as grants to local bodies for 2020-21, which is 4.31 per cent of the estimated divisible pool. The commission have also identified the need to

increase the inter se share of local bodies' grants for urban areas from the 30 per cent given by FC-XIV, as the commission regard cities as engines of growth. Furthermore, unlike the FC-XIV, the commission have now provided grants to all the three tiers of panchayats, as also to areas under the fifth and sixth schedule of the constitution and cantonment boards in urban areas. While 50 per cent grants to rural local bodies are untied, the remaining 50 per cent would be tied as grants for sanitation and water supply which is identified national priorities. For rural local bodies, no conditions have been prescribed for getting the grants in 2020-21. However, from 2021-22 onwards, the entry level conditions for rural local bodies getting these grants is the timely submission of audited accounts.

- In the case of urban local bodies, the commission differentiated between cities by dividing them into two categories: (a) Million-Plus urban agglomerations/cities and (b) all other cities and towns with less than one million populations. Larger cities will have a tendency to grow faster, and grants are provided to fifty million-plus cities on agglomeration basis, with special emphasis on meeting the challenges of poor air quality, ground water depletion and sanitation. For non million-plus towns, 50 per cent of the funds are untied and the remaining 50 per cent tied, with an equal share for drinking water and sanitation. Though the commission have not recommended any conditions for urban local bodies in 2020-21, the commission recommend two entry level conditions in the subsequent years; notifying the floor or minimum rates of property tax to improve own revenues and timely submission of audited accounts.
- For determining state-wise allocations for disaster risk management, the commission recommend a new methodology which combines capacity (as reflected through past expenditure), risk exposure (area and population) and proneness to hazard and vulnerability (disaster risk index). The total amount recommended for the states is Rs. 28,983 crore in 2020-21, of which Rs. 22,184 crore is the Union share. In line with the provisions of the Disaster Management Act, 2005, the commission recommend the setting up of mitigation funds at both national and state levels in the form of a National Disaster Mitigation Fund (NDMF) and State Disaster

Mitigation Funds (SDMF). The commission also recommended funds for the National Disaster Response Fund (NDRF) since the levy of National Calamity Contingent Duty (NCCD) utilised to fund it has now largely been subsumed under the GST.

List of Finance Commissions

So far 15 Finance Commissions have been appointed which are as follows:

Finance Commission	Year of establishment	Chairman	Operational duration
First	1951	K. C. Neogy	1952–57
Second	1956	K. Santhanam	1957–62
Third	1960	A. K. Chanda	1962–66
Fourth	1964	P. V. Rajamannar	1966–69
Fifth	1968	Mahaveer Tyagi	1969–74
Sixth	1972	K. Brahmananda Reddy	1974–79
Seventh	1977	J. M. Shelat	1979–84
Eighth	1983	Y. B. Chavan	1984–89
Ninth	1987	N. K. P. Salve	1989–95
Tenth	1992	K. C. Pant	1995–00
Eleventh	1998	A. M. Khusro	2000–05
Twelfth	2002	C. Rangarajan	2005–10
Thirteenth	2007	Dr. Vijay L. Kelkar	2010–15
Fourteenth	2013	Dr. Y. V Reddy	2015–20
Fifteenth	2017	N. K. Singh	2020–25

State Finance Commissions (SFCs)

The 73rd Constitutional Amendment Act of 1992 created the Panchayati Raj Institutions as the third level of a three-tier democratic governance system at the village level, intermediate level and district level. It also mandated the constitution of a finance commission every five years by state governments to decide the division of resources (tax proceeds) between a state government and Panchayati Raj Institutions at all levels.

Distribution of Revenues between the Union and States

Duties levied by the Union but collected and appropriated by the states;

(1) Such stamp duties and such duties of excise on medicinal and toilet preparations as are mentioned in the union list shall be levied by the Government of India but shall be collected-

(a) In the case, where such duties are leviable within any Union Territory, by Government of India, and

(b) In other cases, by the states within which such duties are respectively leviable.

(2) The proceeds in any financial year of any such duty leviable within any state shall not form part of the Consolidated Fund of India, but shall be assigned to that State.

Taxes levied and collected by the Union but assigned to the States

Article-226A (1) Taxes on the sale or purchase of goods and taxes on the consignment of goods shall be levied and collected by the Government of India but shall be assigned and shall be deemed to have been assigned to the states on or after the 1st day of April, 1996 in the manner provided in clause-(2). Explanation-For the purposes of this clause;

(a) The expression "taxes on the sale or purchase of goods" shall mean taxes on sale or purchase of goods other than newspapers, where such sale or purchase takes place in the course of inter-state trade or commerce;

(b) The expression "taxes on the consignment of goods" shall mean taxes on the consignment of goods (whether the consignment is to the person making it or to any other person), where such consignment takes place in the course of inter-state trade or commerce;

(2) The net proceeds in any financial year of any such tax, except in so far as those proceeds represent proceeds attributable to UTs shall not form part of the Consolidated Fund of India, but shall be assigned to the state within which that tax is leviable in that year, and shall be distributed among those states in accordance with such principles of distribution as may be formulated by Parliament by law.

Article-227(3) Parliament may by law formulate principles for determining when a sale or purchase of, or consignment of, goods takes place in the course of inter-state trade or commerce.

Taxes levied and distributed between the Union and the States

Article-227A (1) All taxes and duties referred to in the Union List, except the duties and taxes referred to in Articles-268 and 269, respectively, surcharge on taxes and duties referred to in Article-271 and any cess levied for specific purposes under any law made by Parliament shall be levied and collected by the Government of India and shall be distributed between the Union and the States in the manner provided in clause-(2).

(2) Such percentage, as may be prescribed, of the net proceeds of any such tax or duty in any financial year shall not form part of the Consolidated Fund of India, but shall be assigned to the states within which that tax or duty is leviable in that year and shall be distributed among those states in such manner and from such time as may be prescribed in the manner provided in clause-(3).

(3) In this Article, "Prescribed" means -

(i) Until a finance commission has been constituted, prescribed by the President by order, and

(ii) After a finance commission has been constituted, prescribed by the President by order after considering the recommendations of the finance commission.'

Surcharge on certain duties and taxes for purposes of the Union

Notwithstanding anything in Articles-269 and 270, Parliament may at any time increase any of the duties or taxes referred to in those Articles by a surcharge for purposes of the Union and the whole proceeds of any such surcharge shall form part of the Consolidated Fund of India.

Grants from the Union to certain States

(1) Such sums as Parliament may by law provide shall be charged on the Consolidated Fund of India in each year as grants-in-aid of the revenues of such states as Parliament may determine to be in need of assistance, and different sums may be fixed for different states:

Provided that there shall be paid out of the Consolidated Fund of India as grants-in-aid of the revenues of a state such capital and recurring sums as may be necessary to enable that state to meet the costs of such schemes of development as may be undertaken by the state with the approval of the Government of India for the purpose of promoting the welfare of the scheduled tribes in that state or raising the level of administration of the scheduled areas therein to that of the administration of the rest of the areas of that state:

Provided further that there shall be paid out of the Consolidated Fund of India as grants-in-aid of the revenues of the state of Assam sums, capital and recurring, equivalent to-

(a) The average excess of expenditure over the revenues during the two years immediately preceding the commencement of this constitution in respect of the administration of the tribal areas; and

(b) The costs of such schemes of development as may be undertaken by that state with the approval of the Government of India for the purpose of raising the level of administration of the said areas to that of the administration of the rest of the areas of that state.

On and from the formation of the autonomous state under Article-244A -

(i) Any sums payable under clause (a) of the second provision to clause (1) shall, if the autonomous state comprises all the tribal areas referred to therein, be paid to the autonomous state, and, if the autonomous state comprises only some of those tribal areas, be apportioned between the state of Assam and the autonomous state as the President may, by order, specify;

(ii) There shall be paid out of the Consolidated Fund of India as grants-in-aid of the revenues of the autonomous state sums, capital and recurring, equivalent to the costs of such schemes of development as may be undertaken by the autonomous state with the approval of the Government of India for the purpose of raising the level of administration of that state to that of the administration of the rest of the state of Assam.

(2) Until provision is made by Parliament under clause (1), the powers conferred on Parliament under that clause shall be exercisable by the President by order and any order made by the President under this clause shall have effect subject to any provision so made by Parliament:

Provided that after finance commission has been constituted no order shall be made under this clause by the President except after considering the recommendations of the finance commission.

The Finance Commission (Miscellaneous Provisions) Act, 1951

1. *Short Title*

This Act may be called the Finance Commission (Miscellaneous Provisions) Act, 1951.

2. *Definition*

In this Act, "the Commission" means the finance commission constituted by the President pursuant to clause (1) of Article-280 of the Constitution.

3. *Qualifications for appointment as, and the manner of selection of, members of the commission*

The Chairman of the commission shall be selected from among persons who have had experience in public affairs, and the four other members shall be selected from among persons who-

(a) are, or have been, or are qualified to be appointed as Judges of a High Court; or

(b) have special knowledge of the finances and accounts of government; or

(c) have had wide experience in financial matters and in administration; or

(d) have special knowledge of economics.

4. *Personal interest to disqualify members*

Before appointing a person to be a member of the Commission, the President shall satisfy himself that that person will have no such financial or other interest as is likely to affect prejudicially his functions as a member of the commission; and the President shall also satisfy himself from time to time with respect to every member of the Commission that he has no such interest and any person who is, or whom the President proposes to appoint to be, a member of the commission shall, whenever required by the President so to do, furnish to him such information as the President considers necessary for the performance by him of his duties under this section.

5. *Disqualifications for being a member of the Commission*

A person shall be disqualified for being appointed as, or for being, a member of the Commission;

(a) If he is of unsound mind;

(b) If he is an undischarged insolvent;

(c) If he has been convicted of an offence involving moral turpitude;

(d) If he has such financial or other interest as is likely to affect prejudicially his functions as a member of the Commission.

6. *Term of office of members and Eligibility for Re-appointment*

Every member of the Commission shall hold office for such period as may be specified in the order of the President appointing him, but shall be eligible for reappointment: Provided that he may, by letter addressed to the President, resign his office.

7. *Conditions of Service and Salaries and Allowances of members*

- 1[(1)]-The members of the commission shall render whole-time or part-time service to the commission as the President may in each case specify, and there shall be paid to the members of the commission such fees or salaries and such allowances as the central government may, by rules made 2[by notification in the Official Gazette,] in this behalf determine.
- 2[(2)]- Every rule made under this section shall be laid, as soon as may be after it is made, before each house of Parliament, while it is in session, for a total period of thirty days which may be comprised in one session or in two or more successive sessions, and if, before the expiry of the session immediately following the session or the successive sessions aforesaid, both houses agree in making any modification in the rule or both houses agree that the rule should not be made, the rule shall thereafter have effect only in such modified form or be of no effect, as the case may be; so, however, that any such modification or annulment shall be without prejudice to the validity of anything previously done under that rule.

8. *Procedure and powers of the Commission*

(1) The commission shall determine their procedure and in the performance of their functions shall have all the powers of a civil court under the Code of Civil Procedure, 1908 (5 of 1908), while trying a suit in respect of the following matters, namely:

(a) Summoning and enforcing the attendance of witnesses;

(b) Requiring the production of any document;

(c) Requisitioning any public record from any court or office.

(2) The commission shall have power to require any person to furnish information on such points or matters as in the opinion of the commission may be useful for, or relevant to, any matter under the consideration of the

commission 3[and any person so required shall, notwithstanding anything contained in sub-section-(2) of section-54 of the Indian Income Tax Act, 1922 (11 of 1922), or in any other law for the time being in force, be deemed to be legally bound to furnish such information within the meaning of section-176 of the Indian Penal Code (45 of 1860)].

(3) The commission shall be deemed to be a civil court for the purposes of sections 480 and 482 of the Code of Criminal Procedure, 1898 (5 of 1898).

Explanation.—For the purposes of enforcing the attendance of witnesses, the local limits of the commission's jurisdiction shall be the limits of the territory of India

The Finance Commission (Salaries & Allowances) Rules, 1951

The Finance Commission (Salaries & Allowances) Rules, 1951 (issued under Government of India Notification No.10003-811/51 dated the 3rd November, 1951) as amended by the Finance Commission (Salaries & Allowances) Amendment Rules, 1960, 1964, 1968, 1972, 1977, 1983 and 1989 (vide Government of India Notifications No. S.O. 2915 dated the 3rd December 1960, S.O. No.1788 dated the 20th May, 1964, S.O. No.2349 dated the 1st July, 1964, S.O. No.809 dated the 28th February 1968, S.O. No.480 (E) dated 11th July 1972, S.O. No.580 (E) dated the 22nd July, 1977, S.O. No.349 (E) dated 6.5.1983, S.O. No.779 (E) dated 3.10.1989 and S.O. No. 310 (E) dated 24th March, 2003.

In exercise of the powers conferred by Section-7 of the Finance Commission (Miscellaneous provisions) Act, 1951 (XXXII of 1951), the Central Government hereby makes the following files namely:-

1. *Short Title*

These rules may be called the Finance Commission (Salaries and Allowances) Rules, 1951.

2. *Salary and Allowances of the Chairman*

(1) A Person appointed to render whole time service as the Chairman of the Commission shall be entitled:-

a) To draw a salary of Rs 3,500/- per mensem, less the pension, if any, including the pensionary equivalent of any other form of retirement benefit drawn by him; and to draw dearness allowance and additional dearness allowances at such rates as are admissible to an employee of the Central Government drawing a pay of Rs 3,500 per mensem.

b) To draw travelling allowance, including daily allowance, for any journey performed by him as Chairman, at such rates as are admissible to a Government servant of the first grade;

c) To the sue of a fully furnished residence in Delhi, throughout his term of office and for a further period of 15 days immediately thereafter, without payment of any rent for such use, and

d) To no amount by way of any compensatory allowance.

Provided that where any person who had been a judge of the Supreme Court is appointed as the Chairman of the commission, he shall be entitled:-

(i) To a monthly salary at the same rate as was admissible to him as a judge of the Supreme Court immediately before relinquishing office as such judge reduced by pension and pension equivalent of other forms of retirement benefits drawn by him:

(ii) (a) in respect of journeys undertaken for assuming charge as chairman of the commission, to the actual railway fare not exceeding the fare for the highest class including the air-conditioned class, for self and members of the family from the ordinary place of his residence to New Delhi, plus, the actual cost on transport, by passenger train, at owner's risk, of one motor car plus actual cost on transport of other personal effects not exceeding the expenditure which would be incurred on the transport of a full wagon of goods and the expenditure incurred on loading and unloading of

(b) in respect of travelling on duty as Chairman of the Commission, to the allowances as are admissible to Judge of the Supreme Court in accordance with rule, 5, excluding item (1) of the third provision to clause(f) thereof, of the Supreme Court Judges (Travelling Allowances) Rules, 1959, as in force for the time being; and

(c) on relinquishing charge as Chairman of the Commission, to the facilities as are admissible to a judge of the Supreme Court on retirement from service, in accordance with sub-rule (30 of Rule 6 of the Supreme Court Judges (Travelling Allowance) Rules, 1959, as in force for the time being; and

(iii) to the use of a fully furnished residence in lieu Delhi throughout his term of office and for a further period of 15 days immediately thereafter, without payment of any rent for such use; Provided further/that where any person, other than a person who had been a judge of the Supreme Court, so appointed is given the rank of a cabinet minister he shall, in lieu of the salary, allowances and other facilities provided for in the sub-rule, be entitled to such salary, allowances and other facilities as are admissible to a minister (not being a Deputy Minister) under the Salaries and Allowances of Minister Act, 1952 (58 of 1952).

(2) A person appointed to render part-time service as the chairman of the commission shall draw a daily allowance of Rs 75 per day for the period spent by him on duty as chairman and he shall further be entitled to draw traveling allowance (but not daily allowance) for journeys performed by him as such chairman at the rates admissible to a government servant of the first grade.

Provided that where the person so appointed is a Member of Parliament he shall in lieu of the allowances provided for in this sub-rule, draw a daily allowance for each day spent by him on duty as chairman of the commission at the same rate as in admissible to him under Section-3 of the Salaries and Allowances of Members of Parliament act, 1954 (30 of 1954) and he shall further be entitled to draw traveling allowance for any journey performed by him as such Chairman at the same rate as is admissible to him under Section-4 of the said Act and the rules made there under.

3. *Salaries & Allowances of other Members*

(1) A person in service under the Government of India, the State Govt. or the Reserve Bank of India, appointed to render whole-time or part-time service as a member of the commission shall draw such pay and allowances as in central drawn by him as a government having regard to the pay and allowances drawn by him as a government servant on, as the case may be, a servant of the Reserve Bank, may in each case, determine.

(2) A person (not being a retired high court judge or a government servant or a servant of the Reserve Bank or a retired government servant or a retired servant of the Reserve Bank) appointed to render whole time service as a member of the commission shall be entitled:-

a) To draw a salary of Rs 3,000/- per mensem;

b) To draw travelling allowance, including daily allowance, for any journey performed by him as a member of the Commission at such rates as are admissible to a government servant of the first grade;

c) To draw compensatory allowance at the rate of Rs 75/- per mensem; and

d) To draw no amount by way of house rent allowance.

(3) A person, being a retired Government servant or a retired servant of the Reserve Bank (other than a retired High Court Judge) appointed to render whole-time service as a member of the commission shall be entitled :-

a) To a monthly salary at the same rate as was admissible to him immediately before retirement from service of the government or, as the case may be, from service of the government or, as the case may be, from service of the Reserve Bank, reduced by pension and pension equivalent of other forms of retirement benefits drawn by him;

b) To draw traveling allowance, including daily allowance, for any journey performed by him as the member of the Commission at such rates as are admissible to a government servant of the first grade;

c) To draw compensatory allowance at the rate of Rs 75/- per mensem; and

d) when not in occupation of a residence provided by the central government, to house rent allowance at the same rate and subject to such terms and conditions as are applicable, from time to time, to a serving government servant of equivalent status.

(4) A person being a retired High Court Judge appointed as render whole-time service as a member of the commission shall be entitled :-

(a) To draw a salary of Rs 8,000/- per mensem less the pension and the pensionary equivalent of any other form of retirement benefit but excluding pension equivalent of gratuity drawn by him;

(b) To draw dearness allowance at such rates as are admissible to an employee of the Central Government drawing a pay of Rs 6,700 per mensem;

(c) To draw compensatory (city) allowance as admissible to a serving judge of high court at the headquarters station of the commission;

(d) To draw travelling allowance and daily allowance according to his entitlement on the rates at the time of his re-employment. He shall also be entitled to facility of temporary government accommodation in guest houses inspection bungalows run by the central government, wherever available on payment of formal rent at out-stations, of the class to which a government servant of the highest class is eligible;

(e) To draw travelling allowance in respect of journeys undertaken for assuming charge at headquarter of commission from the place of his ordinary residence at a rate admissible to an employee of the central government drawing pay of Rs 5,100/- and above per mensem;

(f) To draw travelling allowance in respect of journeys, undertaken on relinquishing of charge as member of a Commission from the headquarters of commission to the place of his ordinary residence at a rate admissible to an employee of the central government drawing pay of Rs 5,100/- and above per mensem;

(g) To rent free furnished accommodation or house rent allowance at the rate of 121% of pay in lieu thereof;

(h) To medical treatment and hospital facilities as provided in the Central Government Health Scheme and in place where the Central Government Health Scheme is not available the medical facilities available to a Cabinet Minister under the Salaries and Allowances of Ministers Act 1952 (58 of 1952) and the rules made there under;

(i) To all kinds of leave, as admissible to a person re-employed after retirement in accordance with rule-34 of the Central Civil Services (Leave) Rules, 1972;

(j) To avail leave travel concession for self and his family as admissible to re-employed pensioners at the rate admissible to an employee of the central government drawing pay of Rs 5100/- and above per mensem; and

(k) Conveyance facilities, "as admissible to a serving judge at the time of his re-employment".

(5) A person, not being a government servant or a servant of the Reserve Bank, appointed to render part-time service as a member of the commission shall be entitled:

(a) To draw a Daily Allowance of:

(i) Rs 60/- per day for the period spent by him on duty as a member of the commission at Bombay, Calcutta and Delhi;

(ii) Rs 50/- per day for the period spent by him on such duty elsewhere, and

(b) To draw travelling allowance (but not daily allowance) for any journey performed by him as such a part time member at such rates as are admissible to a government servant of the first grade;

(c) provided that where the person so appointed is a Member of Parliament, he shall, in lieu of the allowance provided for in this sub-rule, draw a daily allowance for each day spent by him on duty as a member of the Commission at the same rate as is admissible to him under Section-3 of the Salaries and Allowances of Members of Parliament Act, 1954, (30 of 1954) and he shall further be entitled to draw travelling allowance for any journey performed by him as such member at the same rate as is admissible to him under Section-4 of the said act and the rules made there under.

(6) Where the Central Government provides:-

(a) A member appointed to render whole time service, with a residence or

(b) A chairman or a member appointed to render part-time service, with temporary accommodation, in a government hostel or such like accommodation, such member or chairman shall pay rent for that residence or accommodation as the case may be in accordance with rule-45A of the Fundamental Rules.

Leave Salary admissible to Chairman

Whether a person, not being a government servant or of the Reserve Bank, is appointed to render whole-time as the chairman or any other member of the commission and person after such appointment is temporarily incapacitated, by or otherwise from rendering such service, then, he shall be entitled to leave salary at the same rate as when rendering whole-time service, for an aggregate period not exceeding one-eleventh period of whole-time service actually rendered by him as a chairman or other however, as the case may be.

The Functions of Finance Commission of India

The Finance Commission of India came into existence in 1951. It was established under Article-280 of the Indian Constitution by the President of India. It was formed to define the financial relations between the centre and the state. Finance Commission is a statuary, independent, semi judicious non-political body to be set up by President of India for every five years (or earlier) under Article-280 of the commission.

The Finance Commission consists of a chairman and four other members to be appointed by the President of India. The Constitution has not mentioned the qualifications of either the chairman or its member; they are to be determined by the Parliament.

The Parliament can also lay down the manner in which they shall be selected. That is the reason why the Chairmen of the Finance Commissions have been reputed politicians, former justices, economists, technocrats and reputed public personalities.

The commission makes recommendations to the president with regard to:

(a) The distribution of the proceeds of taxes between the union and the states.

(b) The principles which should govern the grants-in-aid to be given to the states.

(c) Any other matter referred to the Commission by the President in the interest of sound finance.

The recommendations of the commission are generally accepted by the Union Government as well as by the parliament.

Article-280 (3) speaks about the functions of the Finance Commission. The Article states that it shall be the duty of the Commission to make the recommendations to the President as to:

i) The distribution between the Union and the States of the net proceeds of taxes, which are to be, or may be, divided between them and the allocation among the states of the respective shares of such proceeds;

ii) To determine the quantum of grants-in-aid to be given by the Centre to states [Article-275 (1)] and to evolve the principles to govern the eligibility of the state for such grant-in-aid;

iii) Any other matter referred to the Commission by the President of India in the interest of sound finance. Several issues like debt relief, financing of calamity relief of states, additional excise duties, etc. have been referred to the Commission invoking this clause.

The commission shall determine its procedure and shall exercise such powers in the performance of its functions, as the Parliament may, confer on it by law. The President shall place the Report of the commission together with an explanatory memorandum before each house of Parliament. In practice, the recommendations of Finance Commission are accepted by the Government of India for the distribution of shared tax revenue, as well as for grant-in-aid

Difference between Finance Commission and Planning Commission of India

Planning Commission (PC) which is neither a constitutional nor a statutory body has usurped the role of Finance Commission (FC) PC has restricted FC's role to mere recommend grants to states on revenue account only under Article-275 of Indian constitution. However, after the formation of NITI Aayog (National Institute for Transforming India), which comes to replace the Planning Commission seeks to empower FC with the originally envisaged task of distribution of revenue to the states.

The Finance Commission is a constitutionally mandated body that is at the centre of fiscal federalism. Set up under Article-280 of the Constitution, its core responsibility is to evaluate the state of finances of the Union and State Governments, recommend the sharing of taxes between them, lay down the principles determining the distribution of these taxes among states. Its working is characterised by extensive and intensive consultations with all levels of governments, thus strengthening the principle of cooperative federalism. Its recommendations are also geared towards improving the quality of public spending and promoting fiscal stability. The first Finance Commission was set up in 1951 and there have been fifteen so far. Each of them has faced its own unique set of challenges.

There has been serious debate in the country regarding the role of the Finance Commission vis-a-vis the Planning Commission. Finance Commission is a constitutional body whereas the Planning Commission is a non-statutory institution.

Over a period of time, the working of both the institutions led to friction among them due to lack of clear-cut guidelines demarcating their areas of work. Scrutiny of plan expenditure and transfer of capital to the states have been left to the Planning Commission.

This has led to a number of practical problems. The relative roles of the Planning Commission and Finance Commission have come to be demarcated in the terms of reference of the Finance Commission. The finance commission assesses the non-plan requirements of the state governments and recommends a share in the net yield from the central and grants-in-aid. The divisible sum of central taxes is distributed among the states based on independent criteria.

This lead to a situation where many states experience non-plan revenue surplus after receiving the devolution and that surplus is supposed to be used by them for plan purpose. But that is not the job of the finance commission. It is left to the planning commission to take it into account while assessing the states resources for state plans.

The Planning Commission finds it very difficult to fill the shortfall in the states financial resources for plan purpose because of the limited budgetary support provided by the central government for the total public sector plan. Consequently, the plan expenditure becomes a casualty.

The various Finance Commissions have generally adhered to the criteria, for grants-in-aid to the states, that this popularly come to be known as the Gadgil formula (after the name of former Deputy Chairman of the Planning Commission), that takes into account in variable proportions the population of the state, developmental performance, budgetary deficit, etc.

Difference between Finance and Planning Commission:

Finance Commission	**Planning Commission**
It is temporary and appointed for every five years or even less.	It is a permanent body.
Chairman is appointed for a term.	Prime Minister is the chairman.
Makes devolution and grants-in-aid for non-plan purposes.	Provides resources for Plan purposes only.
A non-political semi-judicious and independent agency.	A political body and an arm of the government.
Provides non-plan or statutory grants under Article-275(1)	Provides plan or non-statutory grants under Article-282

Fiscal Transfers by Finance Commission of India among States

One of the first terms of reference of a Finance Commission is to recommend a percentage share of the shareable taxes and the principles or criteria of its distribution among the states. The two types of taxes, whose net proceeds are to be divided between the Union and the States according to Article-270 and 272 of the Constitution are, the Income Tax (IT) and the Union Excise Duties (UEDs).

(1) Trends in Percentage Share

The First Finance Commission increased the states' share from 50 per cent to 55 per cent and over the period, the share reached 85 per cent. Sharing of Union Excise Duty revenue is possible only through an Act of Parliament. The First Finance Commission recommended that 40 per cent of the net proceeds of the duties on tobacco, matches and vegetable products be given to the states.

(2) Criteria of Distribution

The other important aspect is the criteria adopted by the successive Finance Commissions for the inter-state distribution of the revenue from Income Tax (IT) and Union Excise Duties (UEDs). For a long period, the 'population' factor was used for the distribution of the net revenue from Income Tax while a criteria of 'backwardness' was adopted for the distribution of net revenue from Union Excise Duties.

The two different criteria adopted for the distribution of these two sources of revenue have been subjected to a lot of criticism. The main argument was that while the objective of transferring revenues to states by the centre through shared tax revenue is the same, there is no rationale for adopting two different criteria in case of IT and UEDs.

(3) Alternative Scheme of Devolution

The Tenth Finance Commission made a significant departure from the then existing criteria by recommending 29 per cent of gross tax revenue of all taxes of the central government instead of a share from the two taxes of Income Tax and Union Excise Duties.

This recommendation of devolution, known as global sharing (meaning sharing of all taxes), was accepted by the Government of India in 2000 with a modification. The modification relates to the word 'net revenue' instead of 'gross revenue' as recommended by the 10th Finance Commission. The XI Finance Commission increased this share to 29.5 per cent while the XII Finance Commission further raised it to 30.5 per cent.

(4) Grants-in-Aid

Article-275(1) deal with grants-in-aid. According to this Article, grant-in-aid are to be given to the states in need of assistance and the amount of grand-in-aid the principles for judging the eligibility of states for these grants-in-aid are to be determined by the finance commission. These grants recommended by the finance commission are generally known as 'statutory grants' or non-plan grants'.

Though the First Finance Commission stated a number of principles like;

i) Budgetary needs,

ii) Tax effort,

iii) Economy in expenditure,

iv) Standards of special – services, and

v) Broad purposes of national importance, almost all the successive finance commissions followed a single criterion of 'budgetary needs' of the states.

The grants given on the basis of budgetary needs are known as revenue-gap grants (or deficit grants). Besides the revenue-gap grants, several Finance Commissions have, give grants for upgradation the essential social and administrative services.

(5) Other Important Recommendations

Besides shared tax revenue and grants-in-aid, the successive Finance Commissions have been recommending various fiscal matters like calamity relief, debt relief and grants to local governments, etc. Some of them are:

(a) *Assistance for Calamity Relief*

When States experience natural calamities they need to undertake relief operations incurring huge expenditure. The successive Finance Commissions have been extending financial assistance in the form of loans and grants. For instance, the Ninth Finance Commission adopted an innovative scheme in which a Calamity Relief Fund (CRF) was to be established in each state to contribute the centre and states in the ratio of 75:25. The Eleventh Finance Commission suggested establishment of a National Calamity Contingency Fund (NCCF) with a corpus of Rs 500 crores.

(b) ***Debt Relief***

Several finance commissions recommended debt relief to states in various forms like rescheduling, moratorium, etc. The tenth finance commission recommended a scheme of debt relief linking it to fiscal performance in terms of reduction of revenue expenditure. The eleventh and twelfth finance commissions continued the debt relief scheme with some modifications, the main theme being reduction of revenue expenditure by the states.

(c) ***Assistance to Local Bodies***

The 73rd and 74th Constitution Amendment Acts envisage the Panchayats and Municipal bodies as institutions of self-government. Considering the need to transfer some resources to enable them to function more effectively, the tenth finance commission, for the first time, recommended an amount of Rs 1000 Crores, and Rs 4000 crores to Panchayats and municipalities, respectively. This grant amount was increased to Rs 2000 crores to Panchayats and Rs. 5000 crores to municipal bodies by the twelfth finance commission. These grants have contributed to improving the financial position of the local governments in India.

(6) Ceiling on Aggregate Resources

For the first time, the Eleventh Finance Commission felt the need to put a cap on the total resources transferred to the states from the centre on the ground that such a measure would help in encouraging the states to augment their own revenue. Suggesting that all transfers must be taken in their totality, it suggested a ceiling of 37.5 per cent on total resource transfer from the centre to the states. The twelfth finance commission slightly enhanced the ceiling to 38 per cent. The states were, however, critical of such a ceiling on the ground that it would inject fiscal inflexibility into the state finances.

(7) Equalisation

It is important to know about the impact of Finance Commission transfers on equalisation.

Equalisation here refers to both:

(i) Vertical equalisation and

(ii) Horizontal equalisation.

There are indications that the implementation of the Alternative Scheme of Resource Transfer, as recommended first by the X-Finance Commission, and subsequently also by the XI and the XII Finance Commissions, has reduced the vertical fiscal imbalance considerably. However, the expected reduction in regard to horizontal fiscal equalisation has not been achieved

Conclusion

Local level governance is still in the evolution process in India. There is the need to encourage the process to play a more effective role. Already visible signs of change can be seen in most of the villages in terms of village roads, water supply, sanitation, storm water drainage, and street-lighting. While connectivity of one village with another is beyond the jurisdiction of a GP, construction and maintenance of roads within the village is the responsibility of the GP. One can now walk without touching mud at least in some parts within a village and GPs are under pressure to construct roads in the left out parts as well. This is exactly as it should be in a functional democracy.

A potentially viable and useful structure of the Panchayat Raj, thus, exists in form, but its effectiveness has been limited in practice. There has been considerable erosion in the powers and functions of these institutions in many states. They suffer from inadequacy of financial resources. The external sources in the form of aid or assistance from the state governments have been found inadequate to meet the rural requirements. For raising internal sources in the form of "local taxes, fees etc. the Panchayats have shown little inclination. Thus, starved of financial resources, the Panchayats cannot deliver appropriate results, as required.

There are many areas that needed further attention for enhancing efficiency and effective delivery of services. Overall, close to 80% of the FFC grants from year 2015-16 to 2018-19 had been utilized in the selected GPs. Road construction and drinking water were top two priority activities. Most of the GPs are found reluctant to raise Own Source of Revenue (OSR) in the selected sample. However, some of the GPs are able to generate OSR in the form of tax or non-tax revenue by renting shops, house tax and clean water fee. GPs in Assam, Kerala, and West Bengal have more varied sources of own revenue. But, the unwillingness by local bodies to collect potential tax revenue in most of the GPs needs a change in the mind set and some amount of persuasion.

While convergence of various development programmes has been a priority for the government, it is mostly conspicuous by its absence in the programmes undertaken by the GPs. While roads in two different patches are being constructed utilising two different sources of funding (e.g. FFC and MPLAD), it is difficult to find one large activity with funding from multiple sources. Different guidelines by different departments were cited as a major constraint for lack of convergence of activities. Separate accountability to different departments is also a problem and provision of accountability to a consortium of funding agencies can overcome this.

The line departments cannot by themselves carry out all village level development programmes in the absence of local level initiative and participation. The local people must have a sense of belonging in the schemes. Involvement of GPs in a coordinating role in various projects of line departments would be a way forward for convergence. Some GPs do not have their own building and they share space with schools, anganwadi centre and other places. There are also GPs which have own building but without basic facilities like toilets, drinking water, and electricity connection. Several GPs are having internet connections through broadband and some under e-mitra scheme, but they are not functioning in many cases. For data entry purposes, panchayat official need to visit Block Development offices. The planning should be done for these developmental works with the participatory methods.

Solid waste management and waste disposal as well as overall cleanliness, still need considerable improvements. It is heartening that there is greater thrust on providing an effective and sustainable solid and liquid waste management system in Swacch Bharat (Grameen) Phase-II. Likewise, it is also gratifying that the integrated portal for planning, monitoring, accounting and auditing function of the Panchayat called e-Gram Swaraj, which is being launched, includes a user friendly mobile app that readily provides all information on income and expenditure of GPs. It is suggested that Ministry of Panchayati Raj could design a system of comparative ranking of different GPs in a state as this could help in building a competitive ecosystem at the grass root level. GPs are third tier in the democratic participation process by the citizens. The system should be strengthened for active participation by the rural community in Gram Sabha so that people can directly take part in the decision making process and governance of the village.

Despite the changing fiscal environment and considerable expansion in its functions, the institution of the Finance Commission has ensured smooth functioning of centre-state fiscal relations. If there has been no breakdown in the centre-state relations, the credit for this entirely goes to the Finance Commissions. It also goes to the credit of the framers of the Indian Constitution that the provisions relating to central-state fiscal relations have stood the test of time. They proved adequate even in meeting the changing environment. Fiscal federalism will always remain a work in progress and the institution of the Finance Commission, as in the past, will continue to deal with the changing environment and emerging challenges. The recent improvement in the fiscal situation can also be partly attributed to the focus that the recent Finance Commissions laid on fiscal restructuring. The global developments unfolding since September 2008, have cast shadow on the fiscal correction path undertaken by the centre and the states. The Thirteenth Finance Commission has a major task ahead in coping with the challenges posed by the global meltdown and in ushering in a new era in fiscal federalism with the proposed introduction of GST from April 2010.

A clear definition of the term 'Self Government' used in the Constitution, is necessary before any exercise for devolution of 'powers, authority and responsibilities' could be meaningful. Any assessment of their requirement of funds and functionaries is possible only when there is a clear understanding of this term, accompanied by delineation of responsibilities between the various tiers of Panchayats in rural areas and levels of municipalities in urban areas. This will help to avoid duplication of efforts between the two levels of governance at the state and local level and will remove the confusion that prevails at the district and sub-district level. People would know where to look for the performance of specific public duties and organize themselves to ensure that these are available.

5

Panchayati Raj Institutions and Sustainable Development Goals

"Economic equality must never be supposed to mean possession of an equal amount of worldly goods by everyone. It does mean, however, that everyone will have a proper house to live in, sufficient and balanced food to eat and sufficient Khadi with which to cover himself."

— ***Mahatma Gandhi***

Introduction

India is the sixth largest economy and remains a global engine of growth; halving the incidence of multidimensional poverty between 2005-06 and 2015-16. The poorest groups across states, social categories, religions and ages had the biggest reductions in multidimensional poverty, showing that they have been catching up, though they still experience high rates of poverty. In recognition of these and other challenges to further improve the policy ecosystem, the Government of India has unfurled the strategy for a new India that aligned to SDGs and aims to boost India towards a US$ 5 trillion economy by 2024. The Government of India is fully committed to the 2030 Agenda, including the Sustainable Development Goals (SDGs). There is a convergence of India's national development goals and agenda of, 'Sabka Saath, Sabka Vikas' or 'Collective Efforts, Inclusive Growth,' with the SDGs.

India is a democratic republic and the Constitution places faith in a three-tier system of governance through people's representative at the Centre, State & Local Levels. The local level governance framework was enshrined in the Constitution through the 73rd & 74th Amendments respectively. The 73rd Constitutional Amendment, 1992 introduced a new Part-IX titled "The Panchayats" with several provisions, which provided for decentralized local self-governments for village clusters at the grass-roots level called Panchayats with the Sarpanch as the elected head.

Sustainable development is one of the common phenomenon for which most of the countries are striving at present. The increase in the level of awareness among people of the world and their concern for continuous development along with the protection of natural resources for upcoming generations are very much inevitable to achieve Sustainable Development Goals (SDG's). The SDG's were adopted by members of United Nations (U.N.) as new global goals for sustainable development during 25-27, September 2015 as the successors of the MDG is for "Transforming our World: the 2030 Agenda for sustainable development" includes 17 universal, transformative goals, 169 targets, and 305 indicators.

The purpose behind these SDG's is to achieve a sustainable world in which 'no one is left behind' without compromising sustainability of the planet. These set of SDG's are supposed to be used by member countries of United Nations to develop the developmental plans, policies, agenda and action plan for low carbon pathways in coming 15 years. Sustainable development goals in India have been considered as a matter of national priorities for attaining development at grassroots level. The Ministry of Rural Development and Panchayati Raj considered these SDGs mandate and now is committed to poverty eradication and creating appropriate infrastructure to increase the pace of socioeconomic growth of rural regions in the country. Their aim is to promote strategies for attaining SDGs at the panchayat level by encouraging different states for capacity building and strengthening all local government by 2030.

Panchayati Raj Institutions in India are the means of decentralization in India; aimed for local governance at grassroots level. Indian economy is based on agriculture and it is being done primarily in the villages of the country and the development of the villages depend upon the democratic set up and it's execution at village level.

Panchayati Raj System at different periods in India

The historical backdrop of Panchayat Raj in India can be categorised into the following periods;

Vedic Era: In the old Sanskrit scriptures, word 'Panchayatan' has been mentioned which means a group of five persons, including a spiritual man.

- Gradually the concept of the inclusion of a spiritual man in such groups vanished.

- In the Rigveda, there is a mention of Sabha, Samiti and Vidatha as local self-units.

These were the democratic bodies at the local level. The king used to get the approval of these bodies regarding certain functions and decisions.

Epic Era: indicates the two great epic periods of India, that is, the Ramayana and the Mahabharata. The study of Ramayana indicates that the administration was divided into two parts -Pur and Janpad or city and village. In the whole of the state, there was also a Caste Panchayat and one person elected by the Caste Panchayat was a member of the king's Council of Ministers.

- Self-government of a village finds ample expression in the 'Shanti Parva' of the Mahabharata; in the Manu Smriti as well as in Kautilya's Arthashastra.
- As per the Mahabharata, over and above the village, there were units of 10, 20, 100, and 1,000 village groups. 'Gramik' was the chief official of the village, 'Dashap' was the chief of ten villages, Vinshya Adhipati, Shat Gram Adhyaksha and Shat Gram Pati were the chiefs of 20, 100, and 1,000 villages, respectively. They collected the local taxes and were responsible for the defence of their villages.

Ancient Period: There is a description of village panchayats in Kautilya's Arthashastra.

The town was referred to as Pur and its chief was the Nagarik.

- Local bodies were free from any royal interference.
- During the Mauryan and Post-Mauryan periods too, the headman, assisted by a council of elders, continued to play a prominent role in the village life.
- The system continued through the Gupta period, though there were certain changes in the nomenclature, as the district official was known as the Vishya Pati and the village headman was referred to as the Gram Pati.
- Thus, in ancient India, there existed a well established system of local government which was run on a set pattern of traditions and customs.

- However, it is significant to note that there is no reference of women heading the panchayat or even participating as a member in the panchayat.

Medieval Period: During the Sultanate period, the Sultans of Delhi divided their kingdom into provinces called 'Vilayat'.

- For the governance of a village, there were three important officials - Mukkaddam for administration, Patwari for collection of revenues and Choudhrie for settling disputes with the help of the Panch.
- The villages had sufficient powers as regards self governance in their territory.
- The casteism and feudalistic system of governance under the Mughal rule in the medieval period slowly eroded the self-government in villages.
- It is again noteworthy to mention that even in the medieval period there is no mention of women participation in the local village administration.

British Period: Under the British regime, village panchayats lost their autonomy and became weak.

- It is only from the year 1870 that India saw the dawn of representative local institutions.
- The famous Mayo's resolution of 1870 gave impetus to the development of local institutions by enlarging their powers and responsibilities.
- The year 1870, introduced the concept of elected representatives in urban municipalities.
- The revolt of 1857 had put the imperial finances under considerable strain and it was found necessary to finance local service out of local taxation. Therefore, it was out of fiscal compulsion that Lord Mayo's resolution on decentralization came to be adopted.
- Following the footsteps of Mayo, Lord Rippon in 1882 provided the much needed democratic framework to these institutions.
    - All boards were mandated to have a two-thirds majority of non-officials who had to be elected and the chairman of these bodies had to be from among the elected non-officials.

- This is considered to be the Magna Carta of local democracy in India.

❐ Local self-government institutions received a boost with the appointment of the Royal Commission on centralisation in 1907 under the Chairmanship of Sir Charles Edward Henry Hobhouse. The commission recognized the importance of panchayats at the village level.

❐ It is in this backdrop that the Montagu Chelmsford Reforms of 1919 transferred the subject of local government to the domain of the provinces.

  - The reform also recommended that as far as possible there should be a complete control in local bodies and complete possible independence for them from external control.
  - These panchayats covered only a limited number of villages with limited functions and due to organisational and fiscal constraints they did not become democratic and vibrant institutions of local self government at the village level.

❐ However, by 1925, eight provinces had passed the Panchayat Acts and by 1926, six native states had also passed panchayat laws. Local bodies were given more powers and functions to impose taxes were reduced. But, the position of the local self-government institutions remained unaffected.

Post–Independence Period: After the Constitution came into force, Article-40 made a mention of panchayats and Article-246 empowers the state legislature to legislate with respect to any subject relating to local self-government. However, this inclusion of panchayats into the Constitution was not unanimously agreed upon by the then decision-makers, with the major opposition having come from the framer of the Constitution himself i.e. B.R.Ambedkar. It was after much discussion among the supporters and opponents of the village panchayat that the panchayats finally got a place for themselves in the Constitution as Article-40 of the Directive Principles of State Policy.

❐ Since the Directive Principles are not binding principles, the result was the absence of a uniform structure of these bodies throughout the country.

- After independence, as a development initiative, India had implemented the Community Development Programmes (CDP) on the eve of Gandhi Jayanti, the 2nd October, 1952 under the major influence of the Etawah Project undertaken by the American expert, Albert Mayer. It encompassed almost all activities of rural development, which were to be implemented with the help of village panchayats along with the participation of people.
- In 1953, the National Extension Service was also introduced as a prologue to CDP. But the programme did not yield much result.
- There were various reasons for the failure of CDP like bureaucracy and excessive politics, lack of people participation, lack of trained and qualified staff, and lack of local bodies' interest in implementing the CDP especially the village panchayats.
- In 1957, the National Development Council constituted a committee headed by Balwant Rai Mehta to look into the working of community development programme. The team observed that the major reason for the failure of the CDP was the lack of people's participation. The committee suggested a three-tier PRIs, namely, Grama Panchayats (GPs) at the village level, Panchayat Samiti (PSs) at the block level, and Zilla Parishad (ZPs) at the district level.
- Because of this scheme of democratic decentralization was launched in Rajasthan on 2nd October 1959.
- In Andhra Pradesh, the scheme was introduced on 1st November 1959. The necessary legislation had also been passed and implemented in Assam, Gujarat, Karnataka, Madhya Pradesh, Maharashtra, Odisha, and Punjab etc.
- The appointment of the Ashok Mehta Committee in 1977 did bring new thinking in the concepts and practice of the Panchayat Raj. The committee recommended a two-tier Panchayat Raj institutional structure consisting of Zilla Parishad and Mandal Panchayat.
- In order to use planning expertise and to secure administrative support, the district was suggested as the first point of decentralization below the state level.
- Based on its recommendation, some of the states like Karnataka incorporated them effectively.

- In subsequent years in order to revive and give a new lease of life to the panchayats, the Government of India had appointed various committees.
- The most important among them are the Hanumantha Rao Committee (1983), G.V.K. Rao Committee (1985), L.M.Singhvi Committee (1986) and the Sarkaria Commission on Centre-State relations (1988), P.K. Thungan Committee (1989) and Harlal Singh Kharra Committee (1990).
- The G.V.K. Rao Committee (1985) recommended making the "district" as the basic unit of planning and holding regular elections while the L.M. Singhvi committee recommended providing more financial resources and constitutional status to the panchayats to strengthen them.
- The amendment phase began with the 64th Amendment Bill (1989) which was introduced by Rajiv Gandhi seeking to strengthen the PRIs but the Bill was not passed in the Rajya Sabha.
- The Constitution (74th Amendment) bill (a combined bill for the PRIs and municipalities) was introduced in 1990, but was never taken up for discussion.
- It was during the prime ministership of P.V.Narasimha Rao that a comprehensive amendment was introduced in the form of the Constitution 72nd Amendment bill in September 1991.
- 73rd and 74th Constitutional Amendments were passed by Parliament in December, 1992. Through these amendments, local self-governance was introduced in rural and urban India.
- The acts came into force as the Constitution (73rd Amendment) Act, 1992 on 24th April 1993 and the Constitution (74th Amendment) Act, 1992 on 1st June 1993.

Salient Features of the Constitution 73rd and 74th Amendments

- These amendments added two new parts to the Constitution, namely, added Part-IX titled "The Panchayats" (added by 73rd Amendment) and Part-IXA titled "The Municipalities" (added by 74th Amendment).
- Basic units of democratic system-Gram Sabhas (villages) and Ward Committees (Municipalities) comprising all the adult members registered as voters.

- Three-tier system of panchayats at village, intermediate block/ taluk/mandal and district levels except in states with population is below 20 lakhs (Article-243B).
- Seats at all levels to be filled by direct elections [Article-243C (2)].
- Seats reserved for Scheduled Castes (SCs) and Scheduled Tribes (STs) and the chairpersons of the Panchayats at all levels also shall be reserved for SCs and STs in proportion to their population.
- One-third of the total number of seats to be reserved for women.
- One third of the seats reserved for SCs and STs also reserved for women.
- One-third offices of chairpersons at all levels reserved for women (Article-243D).
- Uniform five year term and elections to constitute new bodies to be completed before the expiry of the term.
- In the event of dissolution, elections compulsorily within six months (Article-243E).
- Independent Election Commission in each state for superintendence, direction and control of the electoral rolls (Article-243K).
- Panchayats to prepare plans for economic development and social justice in respect of subjects as devolved by law to the various levels of Panchayats including the subjects as illustrated in Eleventh Schedule (Article-243G).
- 74th Amendment provides for a District Planning Committee to consolidate the plans prepared by Panchayats and Municipalities (Article-243ZD).
- Budgetary allocation from state governments, share of revenue of certain taxes, collection and retention of the revenue it raises, central government programmes and grants, union finance commission grants (Article-243H).
- Establish a Finance Commission in each state to determine the principles on the basis of which adequate financial resources would be ensured for panchayats and municipalities (Article-243I).

- The eleventh scheduled of the constitution places as many as 29 functions within the purview of the Panchayati Raj bodies.
- The following areas have been exempted from the operation of the Act because of the socio-cultural and administrative considerations:
  - Scheduled areas listed under the Schedule-V in the states of Andhra Pradesh, Bihar, Gujarat, Himachal Pradesh, Madhya Pradesh, Maharashtra, Odisha and Rajasthan.
  - The states of Nagaland, Meghalaya and Mizoram.
  - The hill areas of district of Darjeeling in the state of West Bengal for which Darjeeling Gorkha Hill Council exists.
- In conformity with provisions in the Constitution Amendment Act, an act called the Provisions of Panchayats (Extension to the Scheduled Areas) Act, 1996 passed by the Government of India.

About Panchayat

Panchayati Raj is the oldest system of local government in the Indian subcontinent. Panchayati Raj Institutions as units of local government have been in existence in India for a long time, in different permutations and combinations. However, it was only in 1992 that it was officially established by the Indian Constitution as the third level of India's federal democracy through the 73rd Amendment Act.

The Panchayati Raj Institutions (PRIs) consists of three levels:

- Gram Panchayat at the village level
- Block Panchayat or Panchayat Samiti at the intermediate level
- Zilla Panchayat at the district level

The word "Panchayat" means assembly (ayat) of five (panch) and raj means "rule". Traditionally Panchayats consisted of elderly and wise people chosen by the local community, who used to settle disputes between individuals and villages. The leader of the panchayat used to be called as Mukhya or Sarpanch. Generally the elder-most or most senior person would be elected to this position. The Panchayati Raj system is also recognised as a form of direct democracy (i.e they exercise all powers of a government at a village level), as opposed to the popular notion that it is a type of representative democracy.

In modern India, Mahatma Gandhi was one of the leading advocates of Gram Swaraj i.e village self-governance where the village would be responsible for its own affairs. The Panchayati Raj system of governance can be found all over South Asia in countries such as Pakistan, Bangladesh and Nepal, where it goes by the same name.

Key Features of Panchayat Raj System

- The Gram Sabha is a body consisting of all the people registered in the electoral rolls who belong to a village comprised within the area of the Panchayat at the village level. Gram Sabha is the smallest and the only permanent unit in the Panchayati Raj system. The powers and functions of Gram Sabha are fixed by state legislature according to the law on the subject.
- Seats are reserved for Scheduled Castes (SCs) and Scheduled Tribes (STs) and chairpersons of the Panchayats at all levels are reserved for SCs and STs in proportion to their population.
- One-third of the total number of seats is to be reserved for women. One-third of the seats reserved for SCs and STs are also reserved for women. This policy extends to the office of the chairperson at all levels as well (Article-243D). The reserved seats may be allotted by rotation to different constituencies in the Panchayat.
- There is a uniform policy with each term being five years. Fresh elections must be conducted before the expiry of the term. In the event of dissolution, elections compulsorily within six months (Article-243E).
- Panchayats have the responsibility to prepare plans for economic development and social justice with respect to the subjects as per the law put in place, which also extends to the various levels of Panchayat including the subjects as illustrated in the Eleventh Schedule (Article-243G).

Qualification for Election to Local Bodies

i) He must be an Indian citizen and not be less than 21 years of age.

ii) He must be a registered voter, in the case of Panchayats, member of the Gram Sabha, in the constituency.

iii) He should not be a convict or have been disqualified by a Law of the Parliament or an undischarged insolvent.

iv) He should not hold any office of profit under the Government.

(a) Gram Panchayat (Village Level)

Gram Panchayat is basically a village level institute. It is a formal and democratic structure at grass root level in the country. It acts as a cabinet of the village. The members of the Gram Panchayat are elected by the Gram Sabha. The Gram Sabha functions as the general body of the Gram Panchayat. Gram Panchayat consists of a village or a group of villages divided into smaller units called "Wards". Each ward selects or elects a representative who is known as the Panch or ward member. The members of the Gram Sabha elect the ward members through a direct election. The Sarpanch or the president of the Gram Panchayat is elected through a direct election or by the ward members as per the State Act. The Sarpanch and the Panch are elected for a period of five years. Gram Panchayat is governed by the elected body and administration. The secretary is normally in charge of the administrative duties of the Gram Panchayat.

Composition of Gram Panchayat

Sarpanch: She / He is the head of the Gram Panchayat. She/He is elected directly and in some cases indirectly by members of the Gram Panchayat.

Members: The membership of a Village Panchayat is between 5 to 31. One-third of seats of the Panchayat are reserved for women. Seats are also reserved for Scheduled Castes/ Tribes.

Office-bearers: The Sarpanch and Vice-Sarpanch are honorary members. They are not paid a salary. A paid Secretary to the Panchayat and a Treasurer, if the Panchayat is large, are also appointed by the state government.

Functions of Gram Panchayat

(i) *Administrative Functions*

1. Public works and welfare functions like construction, repair and maintenance of village roads, bridges, drains and wells.
2. Registration of births and deaths.
3. Providing primary education, etc.

Social and Economic Functions: These are not obligatory.

1. Construction of guest houses, libraries, marriage halls, etc;

2. Planting of trees, parks, gardens and playgrounds for recreation;
3. Establishing fair price shops, Cooperative Credit Societies.

(b) Panchayat Samiti (Block Level)

This is the second tier above the Gram Panchayat and below the Zilla Parishad. This intermediate body at the block level is known by different names in different states, like Panchayat Samiti, Kshetra Samiti, Janapada Panchayat and Panchayat Union Council. Panchayat Samiti (also called Taluka Panchayats or Block Panchayats) is the intermediate level in Panchayati Raj Institutions. The Panchayat Samiti acts as the link between Gram Panchayat (Village) and District Panchayat (Zilla). These blocks do not hold elections for the Panchayat Samiti council seats. Rather, the block council consists of all of the Sarpanchas and the Upa Sarpanchas from each Gram Panchayat along with Members of the Legislative Assembly (MLA), Members of Parliament (MPs), associate members (like a representative from a cooperative society) and members from the Zilla Parishad who are a part of the block. The Gram Panchayat members nominate their Sarpanch and Upa Sarpanch amongst their ranks, which extend to the selection of the chairperson and vice-chairperson as well. The Executive Officer (EO) is the head of the administration section of the Panchayat Samiti.

Composition of Panchayat Samiti

It has representatives of Panchayats and some others as its members as given below:

i) Sarpanchs of all Panchayats concerned.
ii) Members of Legislative Assembly of the state from the area.
iii) Members of Parliament belonging to the area.
iv) Block Development Officers of the block.
v) Co-opted members representing women, Scheduled Castes/Tribes.
vi) Representatives of Cooperative Societies.

Functions of Panchayat Samiti

- Panchayat Samitis are at the hub of developmental activities.
- To supervise and co-ordinate the working of Gram Panchayats.
- To scrutinise the developmental plans prepared by GPs

- To identify and prioritize the area specific issues that should be addressed at the block level.
- To evaluate the programme implementation from the angles of financial constraints, social welfare, and area development
- To frame rules and regulations for the markets
- To promote cottage industries such as handlooms, handicrafts, traditional art, and artisans
- To provide hospitals and health services at community block level.
- Develop agriculture by undertaking minor irrigation schemes, distribution of quality seeds, etc.
- To act as a link between the Gram Panchayat and Zilla Parishad.

(c) Zilla Parishad (District Level)

It is a local self-government unit at district level. Panchayat Samiti forms a link between the Gram Panchayat and Zilla Parishad. The Zilla Parishad is a link between the state government and the Gram Panchayats. The Zilla Parishad is also known by different names in different states, like District Develeopment Council, Zilla Parishad and Mohkuma Parishad. The District Panchayat also known as the District Council or Zilla Parishad is the third tier of the Panchayati Raj system. Like the Gram Panchayat, the District Panchayat is also an elected body. Chairpersons of Block Samitis also represent the District Panchayat. Like the Block Panchayat, the MP and MLA are also members of the district panchayat. The government appoints the Chief Executive Officer to carry out the administration of the district Panchayat along with the Chief Accounts Officer, the Chief Planning Officer and one or more Deputy Secretaries who work directly under the Chief Executive Officer and assist him/her. The Zilla Parishad chairperson is the political head of the district panchayat.

The primary objective of establishing the third tier of the government is to increase democratic participation, better articulate local needs and priorities and to ensure a more efficient use of local resources along with greater accountability and transparency. Accordingly, 29 functions have been transferred to local governments in the rural area. These institutions have been playing an important role in several flagship programmes of the central and state governments, perhaps more role in implementation and monitoring.

Composition of Zilla Parishad

It comprises of Deputy Commissioner of the district, Presidents of all Panchayat Samitis in the district and heads of all government departments in the district; Members of Parliament and Legislative Assembly in the district; a representative of each cooperative society; some women and scheduled caste members; and co-opted members having extraordinary experience and achievements in public service. Besides, there are some office bearers such as a Chairperson, Deputy Chairperson and Secretary.

Functions of Zillla Parishad

- Zila Parishad links Panchayat Samitis within the district.
- It coordinates their activities and supervises their functioning.
- It prepares district plans and integrates Samiti plans into district plans for submission to the State Government.
- Zila Parishad looks after development works in the entire district.
- It undertakes schemes to improve agricultural production, exploit ground water resources, extend rural electrification and distribution and initiate employment generating activities, construct roads and other public works.
- It also performs welfare functions like relief during natural calamities and scarcity, the establishment of orphanages and poor homes, night shelters, the welfare of women and children, etc.
- Supervision of working of Gram Panchayats.
- Advise the State Government on all matters relating to the Gram Panchayats and Panchayat Samitis under their own jurisdiction.

Sustainable Developmental Goals (SDG's) and Panchayati Raj System

Development at a village level can be reflected by the facilities that a village has to enrich a human life and sustain the environment around it. Water, sanitation, housing, no poverty, energy, health, environment, education, employment etc. reflect how developed a village is. While we think about village development, do think about justice for all, conserving our eco systems and gender equality. Human Development Index considers Health (Life expectancy at birth), Education (Mean of years of schooling for adults aged 25 years and more and expected years of schooling for children of school entering age) and Standard of living (Gross national income per capita) to measure human development. This is only for global comparisons. More dimensions can be considered. There are other similar indices also i.e inequality, gender disparity, human poverty and so on to measure human development.

Subjects Transferred to Local Governments

As per the Eleventh Schedule of Article 243 G of 73rd Amendment to the Indian Constitution, following subjects fall within the responsibilities of local governments

1. Agriculture including agricultural extension
2. Land improvement, implementation of land reforms, land consolidation and soil conservation
3. Minor irrigation, water management and watershed development
4. Animal husbandry, dairying and poultry
5. Fisheries
6. Social forestry and farm forestry
7. Minor forest production
8. Small-scale industries, including food-processing industries
9. Khadi, village and cottage industries
10. Rural housing
11. Drinking water
12. Fuel and fodder
13. Roads, culverts, bridges, ferries, waterways and other means of communication
14. Rural electrification, including distribution of electricity
15. Non-conventional energy sources
16. Poverty alleviation programmes
17. Education including primary and secondary school
18. Technical training and vocational education
19. Adult and non-formal education
20. Libraries
21. Cultural activities

22. Market and fairs
23. Health and sanitation
24. Family welfare
25. Women and child development
26. Social welfare, including welfare of the handicapped and mentally retarded
27. Welfare of the weaker sections and in particular, of the Scheduled Caste and Scheduled Tribes
28. Public distribution system
29. Maintenance of community assets

Almost all the determinants of human development are covered under these subjects.

United Nations adopted the millennium declaration comprising the Millennium Development Goals (MDGs) as an outcome of deliberations in the United Nations Millennium Summit on 8th September 2000. It gave a new vision to the global efforts on development over the next 15 years. The report of the United Nations Conference on sustainable development held in Rio-de-Janeiro, Brazil in June 2012 (also known as Rio+20) called "The Future We Want" paved the way for formal consultations on post-2015 development agenda in the form of Sustainable Development Goals (SDGs) based on three dimensions of development, namely, economic, social and environmental. SDGs are viewed as extensions of MDGs with sustainability parameter added to each MDG to be implemented in the post-2015 era along with a set of all new goals which were ignored in the MDGs. The Special Session of the UN General Assembly in September 2015 endorsed the 2030 agenda for sustainable development, widely regarded as the post 2015 development agenda. World leaders have already pledged their commitments to this agenda. India is a serious partner and as owned up to this agenda. This agenda comprise the Sustainable Development Goals (SDGs) which is a set of 17 goals and 169 targets integrated and indivisible in the universal sense. The SDGs are slated to be built upon the Millennium Development Goals (MDGs) which were adopted in 2000 as a set of eight goals on diverse dimensions with most direct relevance to welfare, development and sustainable use of resources globally. The SDGs are also known as "Transforming our World: the 2030 Agenda for Sustainable Development" or the 2030 Agenda. They aim to provide a uniform set of targets for human, social & economic development to be adopted by member countries based on their own priorities and positions, in order to move toward a prosperous and sustainable world where no one is left behind. "The Sustainable Development Goals (SDGs), otherwise known as the Global Goals, are a universal call to action to end poverty, protect the planet and ensure that all people enjoy peace and prosperity."

SDGs are expected to supplement the positive outcomes of the MDGs. The idea behind up-gradation of MDG 1 to SDG 1 lies in the evolution of various approaches to measure poverty. The most ancient approach to poverty was the "Subsistence Approach" and the new concept of "Basic-needs Approach" came later, which along with food requirement also included aspects of non-monetary elements required for human subsistence. The concept of poverty was further broadened when Amartya Sen gave the concept of "Entitlements or Capabilities Approach" which proposed that "the income-centered view of poverty, based on specifying an interpersonally invariant 'poverty line' income, may be very misleading in the identification and evaluation of poverty. Since income is not desired for its own sake, any income-based notion of poverty must refer directly or indirectly to those basic ends which are promoted by income as means".

Movement from MDGs to SDGs

The MDGs summarized eight globally agreed goals in the areas of poverty alleviation, education, gender equality and empowerment of women, child and maternal health, environmental sustainability, reducing HIV/AIDS and communicable diseases and building a global partnership for development. The MDGs were to exhaust its time period in 2015 and hence the relevance of a new agenda and a new set of goals. The MDGs were meant to eliminate extreme poverty and deprivation and ensure sustainable use of energy and water under a fruitful global partnership that could facilitate this process. The UN system was at the forefront for initiating the MDG process and ensuring adoption of the MDGs in the developing world and in the relatively poorer countries. However, SDGs has been an outcome of an intensely negotiated process at the UN by all member states since 2012, since world leaders pledged to a new development round post-2015 at the Rio+20 conference.

The SDGs are much expanded compared to the MDGs and covers all three dimensions – social sector development, economy and sustainability across 17 goals. This has lead to views suggesting SDGs to be overly ambitious. The 2030 Agenda for Sustainable Development promises to connect ***5 Ps – People, Planet, Prosperity, Peace and Partnership***. This cornerstone of this agenda is known as transforming our world: the 2030 agenda for Sustainable Development. India is one of the signatories to the resolution on SDGs. It has moved ahead on the nationalising of the implementation of the SDGs and initiated preparation of the Vision Document 2030 with NITI Aayog in the lead. Based on the guidance from NITI Aayog, State governments have begun the process of SDGs implementation. In addition to the State level, there is a critical need to take SDGs to the local level. Here lies the importance of local governments, especially the Gram Panchayats.

The SDGs are universal, integrated and interlinked, and pledges to leave no one behind. While, the first set of the SDGs (1-7) may be an extension of the MDGs with a more comprehensive mandate of mitigating developmental challenges in key sectors in all their forms, the later goals could be referred to an extension of the agenda itself. These in turn have two distinct characters. Those immediately following the first 7 goals (8, 9 and 10) are referred to as enablers of development covering areas like inclusiveness and jobs, infrastructure and industrialization and distribution. The final set of goals under the SDGs (11-17) lays down the framework for sustainability covering areas like urbanization; consumption and production; climate change; resources and environment; peace and justice and means of implementation and global partnership. However, the two final goals are sometimes referred to as meta-goals as they set the preconditions for every other goal.

While implementation of the SDGs rests with individual countries, the developing world must have access to adequate resources. Fulfillment of objectives under this agenda may be critically hinged on successful North-South Partnership and South-South Cooperation. For obvious reasons, SDGs are unique for having accommodated much larger spectrum of views and concerns of the developing world and is mandated to be a universal agenda with obligations for both the developed and the developing countries. The process per force necessitates national ownership of this agenda towards its fulfillment in the next 15 years. G-77, China, India and some of the other emerging counties have taken an active part in the negotiations around the post 2015 development agenda and have vehemently highlighted the importance of finance and technology for successful delivery of a global development agenda.

Seventeen Sustainable Development Goals (SDGs)

1. **No Poverty:** End poverty in all its forms everywhere
2. **Zero Hunger:** End hunger, achieve food security and improved nutrition and promote sustainable agriculture
3. **Good Health & Well Being:** Ensure healthy lives and promote well-being for all at all ages
4. **Quality Education:** Ensure inclusive and equitable quality education and promote lifelong learning opportunities for all
5. **Gender Equality:** Achieve gender equality and empower all women and girls
6. **Clean Water & Sanitation:** Ensure availability and sustainable management of water and sanitation for all
7. **Affordable and Clean Energy:** Ensure access to affordable, reliable, sustainable and modern energy for all
8. **Decent Work and Economic Growth:** Promote sustained, inclusive and sustainable economic growth, full and productive employment and decent work for all
9. **Industry, Innovation and Infrastructure:** Build resilient infrastructure, promote inclusive and sustainable industrialization and foster innovation
10. **Reduced Inequalities:** Reduce income inequality within and among countries
11. **Sustainable Cities and Communities:** Make cities and human settlements inclusive, safe, resilient and sustainable
12. **Responsible Consumption and Production:** Ensure sustainable consumption and production patterns
13. **Climate Action:** Take urgent action to combat climate change and its impacts by regulating emissions and promoting developments in renewable energy
14. **Life Below Water:** Conserve and sustainably use the oceans, seas and marine resources for sustainable development
15. **Life on Land:** Protect, restore and promote sustainable use of terrestrial ecosystems, sustainably manage forests, combat

desertification, and halt and reverse land degradation and halt biodiversity loss

16. **Peace, Justice and Strong Institutions:** Promote peaceful and inclusive societies for sustainable development, provide access to justice for all and build effective, accountable and inclusive institutions at all levels

17. **Partnerships for the Goals:** Strengthen the means of implementation and revitalize the global partnership for sustainable development

Localizing the SDGs in India

The NITI Aayog is taking the lead in co-ordinating India's efforts towards achieving the SDGs. The Aayog is attempting to mainstream the SDGs into national & sub- national development plans, to bolster progress towards their achievement. In the same way, the Ministry of Statistics & Programme Implementation (MOSPI) has undertaken an initiative of consultation with various ministries and drafted a set of national level indicators, which are reflective of the SDG goals & targets. State governments have begun to enter the process of SDGs implementation; however, effective translation of the 2030 agenda into reality requires the local governments to participate as well.

The SDGs are a framework of targets for localized action to achieve. The aim of the GPDP initiative is to promote participatory local planning & implementation for better rural development outcomes. This presents a natural synergy between the two initiatives. The location of the SDGs within the GPDP can provide GPs with a vision for development that is aligned with national & global priorities, providing the local thrust that is required for the SDGs to be a reality.

While the SDGs are primarily a collection of global & national targets, local level action is at the heart of them, just as in the case of the MDGs. Local community action is essential to the achievement of the SDGs, for the simple reason that as the step of administration that is nearest to the people, it is best placed to design & implement locally relevant policies aligned to local priorities. This is particularly crucial in a country like India, where several diverse contexts exist even within a state. In a heterogeneous context, achievement of the SDGs hinges on localized action with GPs playing a significant role.

Implementation of the SDGs in India

The key to the success of the SDGs is often highlighted in terms of maximum decentralisation for policy planning and implementation. This could be the only viable route for a country of India's size and proportions. India has always supported decentralisation and empowerment of grassroots institutions. State governments have a paramount role in implementing development projects undertaken by the centre as well as the states themselves. At this juncture, there is need to sensitize individual states on the forthcoming global development agenda and its implications for India. They should be legitimate partners in drawing up the most appropriate implementation roadmap. While overall economic policy direction is framed at the union level and national programmes on development are designed at the centre, states implement significant social sector infrastructure development projects and design policies to some extent on resource mobilisation. Increasingly, more powers in these areas are being transferred to the states in order to expedite programme implementation and ensure greater grassroots participation.

The Planning Commission (presently NITI Aayog) which has been considering an important institution in post independence and functioned as a central ministry was mainly in charge of annual disbursal of central funds to the states and determined the state specific shares. Needless to mention, this mechanism was heavily centralized with disproportionate say of government at the centre. The five year plans formulated by the planning commission continued to direct the central departments in terms of the objectives and expenditures.

Sustainable Development Goals; It's Targets and Indicators

Goal 1: End poverty in all its forms everywhere: Targets and Indicators

1.1 By 2030, eradicate extreme poverty for all people everywhere, currently measured as people living on less than $1.25 a day	**1.1.1** Proportion of the population below the international poverty line, by sex, age, employment status and geographical location (urban/rural)
1.2 By 2030, reduce at least by half the proportion of men, women and children of all ages living in poverty in all its dimensions according to national definitions	**1.2.1** Proportion of population living below the national poverty line, by sex and age **1.2.2** Proportion of men, women and children of all ages living in poverty in

	all its dimensions according to national definitions
1.3 Implement nationally appropriate social protection systems and measures for all, including floors, and by 2030 achieve substantial coverage of the poor and the vulnerable	**1.3.1** Proportion of population covered by social protection floors/systems, by sex, distinguishing children, unemployed persons, older persons, persons with disabilities, pregnant women, newborns, work- injury victims and the poor and the vulnerable
1.4 By 2030, ensure that all men and women, in particular the poor and the vulnerable, have equal rights to economic resources, as well as access to basic services, ownership and control over land and other forms of property, inheritance, natural resources, appropriate new technology and financial services, including microfinance	**1.4.1** Proportion of population living in households with access to basic services **1.4.2** Proportion of total adult population with secure tenure rights to land, with legally recognized documentation and who perceive their rights to land as secure, by sex and by type of tenure
1.5 By 2030, build the resilience of the poor and those in vulnerable situations and reduce their exposure and vulnerability to climate-related extreme events and other economic, social and environmental shocks and disasters	**1.5.1** Number of deaths, missing persons and personsaffected by disaster per 100,000 people **1.5.2** Direct disaster economic loss in relation to global Gross Domestic Product (GDP) **1.5.3** Number of countries with national and localdisaster risk reduction strategies
1.a Ensure significant mobilization of resources from a variety of sources, including through enhanced development cooperation, in order to provide adequate and predictable means for developing countries, in particular least developed countries, to implement programmes and policies to end poverty in all its dimensions	**1.a.1** Proportion of resources allocated by the government directly to poverty reduction programmes **1.a.2** Proportion of total government spending on essential services (education, health and social protection)
1.b Create sound policy frameworks at the national,regional and	**1.b.1** Proportion of government recurrent and capital spending to

international levels, based on pro-poor and gender-sensitive development strategies, to support accelerated investment in poverty eradication actions	sectors that disproportionately benefit women, the poor and vulnerable groups

Goal 2: End hunger, achieve food security and improved nutrition and promote sustainable agriculture: Indicators and Targets

2.1 By 2030, end hunger and ensure access by all people, in particular the poor and people in vulnerable situations, including infants, to safe, nutritious and sufficient food all year round	Prevalence of under-nourishment Prevalence of moderate or severe food insecurity in the population, based on the Food Insecurity Experience Scale (FIES)
2.2 By 2030, end all forms of malnutrition, including achieving, by 2025, the internationally agreed targets on stunting and wasting in children under 5 years of age, and address the nutritional needs of adolescent girls, pregnant and lactating women and older persons	Prevalence of stunting (height for age <-2 standard deviation from the median of the World Health Organization (WHO) Child Growth Standards) among children under 5 years of age Prevalence of malnutrition (weight for height >+2 or <-2 standard deviation from the median of the WHO Child Growth Standards) among children under 5 years of age, by type (wasting and overweight)
2.3 By 2030, double the agricultural productivity and incomes of small-scale food producers, in particular women, indigenous peoples, family farmers, pastoralists and fishers, including through secure and equal access to land, other productive resources and inputs, knowledge, financial services, markets and opportunities for value addition and non-farm employment	Volume of production per labour unit by classes of farming/pastoral/forestry enterprise size Average income of small-scale food producers, by sex and indigenous status
2.4 By 2030, ensure sustainable food production systems and implement	**2.4.1** Proportion of agricultural area under productive and sustainable

resilient agricultural practices that increase productivity and production, that help maintain ecosystems, that strengthen capacity for adaptation to climate change, extreme weather, drought, flooding and other disasters and that progressively improve land and soil quality	agriculture
2.5 By 2020, maintain the genetic diversity of seeds, cultivated plants and farmed and domesticated animals and their related wild species, including through soundly managed and diversified seed and plant banks at the national, regional and international levels, and promote access to and fair and equitable sharing of benefits arising from the utilization of genetic resources and associated traditional knowledge, as internationally agreed	Number of plant and animal genetic resources for food and agriculture secured in either medium or long-term conservation facilitiesProportion of local breeds classified as being at risk, not-at-risk or at unknown level of risk of extinction
2.a Increase investment, including through enhanced international cooperation, in rural infrastructure, agricultural research and extension services, technology development and plant and livestock gene banks in order to enhance agricultural productive capacity in developing countries, in particular least developed countries	The agriculture orientation index for government expenditures Total official flows (official development assistance plus other official flows) to the agriculture sector
2.b Correct and prevent trade restrictions and distortions in world agricultural markets, including through the parallel elimination of all forms of agricultural export subsidies and all export measures with equivalent effect, in accordance with the mandate of the Doha Development Round	Producer Support EstimateAgricultural export subsidies

2.c Adopt measures to ensure the proper functioning of food commodity markets and their derivatives and facilitate timely access to market information, including on food reserves, in order to help limit extreme food price volatility	2.c.1 Indicator of food price anomalies

Goal 3: Ensure healthy lives and promote well-being for all at all ages: Targets and Indicators	
3.1 By 2030, reduce the global maternal mortality ratio to less than 70 per 100,000 live births	Maternal Mortality Ratio Proportion of births attended by skilled health personnel
3.2 By 2030, end preventable deaths of newborns and children under 5 years of age, with all countries aiming to reduce neonatal mortality to at least as low as 12 per 1,000 live births and under-5 mortality to at least as low as 25 per 1,000 live-births	Under-five mortality rateNeo-natal mortality rate
3.3 By 2030, end the epidemics of AIDS, tuberculosis, malaria and neglected tropical diseases and combat hepatitis, water-borne diseases and other communicable diseases	Number of new HIV infections per 1,000 uninfected population, by sex, age and key populations Tuberculosis incidence per 1,000 population Malaria incidence per 1,000 population Hepatitis B incidence per 100,000 population Number of people requiring interventions against neglected tropical diseases
3.4 By 2030, reduce by one third premature mortality from non-communicable diseases through prevention and treatment and promote mental health and well-being	Mortality rate attributed to cardiovascular disease, cancer, diabetes or chronic respiratory disease Suicide mortality rate
3.5 Strengthen the prevention and treatment of substance abuse,	Coverage of treatment interventions (pharmacological, psychosocial and

including narcotic drug abuse and harmful use of alcohol	rehabilitation and aftercare services) for substance use disorders Harmful use of alcohol, defined according to the national context as alcohol per capita consumption (aged 15 years and older) within a calendar year in litres of pure alcohol
3.6 By 2020, halve the number of global deaths andinjuries from road traffic accidents	**3.6.1** Death rate due to road traffic injuries
3.7 By 2030, ensure universal access to sexual and reproductive health-care services, including for family planning, information and education, and the integration of reproductive health into national strategies and programmes	Proportion of women of reproductive age (aged 15-49 years) who have their need for family planning satisfied with modern methods Adolescent birth rate (aged 10-14 years; aged 15-19 years) per 1,000 women in that age group
3.8 Achieve universal health coverage, including financial risk protection, access to quality essential health-care services and access to safe, effective, quality and affordable essential medicines and vaccines for all	Coverage of essential health services (defined as the average coverage of essential services based on tracer interventions that include reproductive, maternal, newborn and child health, infectious diseases, non-communicable diseases and service capacity and access, among the general and the most disadvantaged population) Number of people covered by health insurance or a public health system per 1,000 population

Goal 4: Ensure inclusive and equitable quality education and promote lifelong learning opportunities for all: Targets and Indicators

4.1 By 2030, ensure that all girls and boys complete free, equitable and quality primary and secondary education leading to relevant and effective learning outcomes	**4.1.1** Proportion of children and young people: (a) in grades 2/3; (b) at the end of primary; and (c) at the end of lower secondary achieving at least a minimum proficiency level in (i) reading and (ii) mathematics, by sex

4.2 By 2030, ensure that all girls and boys have access to quality early childhood development, care and pre-primary education so that they are ready for primary education	**4.2.1** Proportion of children under 5 years of age who are developmentally on track in health, learning and psychosocial well-being, by sex **4.2.2** Participation rate in organized learning (one year before the official primary entry age), by sex
4.3 By 2030, ensure equal access for all women and men to affordable and quality technical, vocational and tertiary education, including university	**4.3.1** Participation rate of youth and adults in formal and non- formal education and training in the previous 12 months, by sex
4.4 By 2030, substantially increase the number of youthand adults who have relevant skills, including technical and vocational skills, for employment, decent jobs and entrepreneurship	**4.4.1** Proportion of youth and adults with Information and Communications Technology (ICT) skills, by type of skill
4.5 By 2030, eliminate gender disparities in education and ensure equal access to all levels of education and vocational training for the vulnerable, including persons with disabilities, indigenous peoples and children in vulnerable situations	**4.5.1** Parity indices (female/male, rural/urban, bottom/top wealth quintile and others such as disability status, indigenous peoples and conflict-affected, as data become available) for all education indicators on this list that can be disaggregated
4.6 By 2030, ensure that all youth and a substantial proportion of adults, both men and women, achieve literacy and numeracy	**4.6.1** Percentage of population in a given age group achieving at least a fixed level of proficiency in functional (a) literacy and (b) numeracy skills, by sex
4.7 By 2030, ensure that all learners acquire the knowledge and skills needed to promote sustainable development, including, among others, through education for sustainable development and sustainable lifestyles, human rights, gender equality, promotion of a culture of peace and non-violence, global citizenship and appreciation of	**4.7.1** Extent to which (i) global citizenship education and(ii) education for sustainable development, including gender equality and human rights, are mainstreamed at all levels in: (a) national education policies, (b) curricula, (c) teacher education and (d) student assessment

cultural diversity and of culture's contribution to sustainable development	
4.a Build and upgrade education facilities that are child, disability and gender sensitive and provide safe, non-violent, inclusive and effective learning environments for all	**4.a.1** Proportion of schools with access to: (a) electricity; (b) the Internet for pedagogical purposes; (c) computers for pedagogical purposes; (d) adapted infrastructure and materials for students with disabilities; (e) basic drinking water; (f) single-sex basic sanitation facilities; and (g) basic hand washing facilities (as per the WASH indicator definitions)
4.b By 2020, substantially expand globally the number ofscholarships available to developing countries, in particular least developed countries, small island developing States and African countries, for enrolment in higher education, including vocational training and information and communications technology, technical, engineering and scientific programmes, in developed countries and other developing countries	**4.b.1** Volume of official development assistance flows for scholarships by sector and type of study
4.c By 2030, substantially increase the supply of qualified teachers, including through international cooperation for teacher training in developing countries, especially least developed countries and small island developing States	**4.c.1** Proportion of teachers in: (a) pre-primary; (b) primary;(c) lower secondary; and (d) upper secondary education who have received at least the minimum organized teacher training (e.g. pedagogical training) pre-service or in-service required for teaching at the relevant level in a given country

Goal 5 : Achieve gender equality and empower all women and girls ; Targets and Indicators

Targets	Proposed Indicators	Comments
Target: 5.1 end all forms of discrimination against	**5.1.1** Whether or not legal frameworks are in	The gender dimension will have to be separately

women and girls everywhere.	place to promote, enforce and monitor equality and non- discrimination on the basis of sex.	seen even among different groups and communities. These will need to be supplemented by documentation of implementation/ impact across geographical areas.
Target: 5.2 eliminate all forms of violence against all women and girls in public and private spheres, including trafficking and sexual and other types of exploitation	**5.2.1** Proportion of ever-partnered women and girls aged 15 years and older subjected to physical, sexual or psychological violence by a current or former intimate partner in the previous 12 months, by form of violence and by age **5.2.2** Proportion of women and girls aged 15 years and older subjected to sexual violence by persons other than an intimate partner in the previous 12 months, by age and place of occurrence	Will have to address the problem of non reporting. Need of more inclusive programme support for encouraging them to break silence in this issue.
Target: 5.3 eliminate all harmful practices, such as child, early and forced marriage and female genital mutilations.	**5.3.1** Proportion of women aged 20-24 years who were married or in a union before age 15 and before age 18 **5.3.2** Proportion of girls and women aged 15-49 years who have undergone female genital mutilation/cutting, by age	The issue relevant here is child marriage on which legal and social initiatives have been initiated. This has not been a major issue in India but there are recent reports of the practice in some populations and areas and hence the action need.

Target: 5.4 recognize and value unpaid care and domestic work through the provision of public services, infrastructure and social protection policies, and the promotion of shared responsibility within the household and the family as nationally appropriate.	**5.4.1** Proportion of time spent on unpaid domestic and care work, by sex, age and location	This is valuable target and indicators may be inadequate and therefore will need to be evolved with further discussion of experience. However the paid and unpaid care has to be separate not combined.
Target: 5.5 ensure women's full and effective participation and equal opportunities for leadership at all levels of decision making in political, economic and public life.	**5.5.1** Proportion of seats held by women in national parliaments and local governments **5.5.2** Proportion of women in managerial positions	Includes, welcome addition of sub-national level elected offices. It does not of course take care of how much capacity they will have to stand for gender issues. In party based representation and with use of whips and anti-defection law, it will have limitation in effectiveness in pursuing gender related issues.

Goal 6: Ensure availability and sustainable management of water and sanitation for all: Targets and Indicators

6.1 By 2030, achieve universal and equitable access to safe and affordable drinking water for all.	**6.1.1** Proportion of population using safely managed drinking water services
6.2 By 2030, achieve access to adequate and equitable sanitation and hygiene for all and end open defecation, paying special attention to the needs of women and girls and those in vulnerable situations.	**6.2.1** Proportion of population using safely managed sanitation services, including a hand-washing facility with soap and water

6.3 By 2030, improve water quality by reducing pollution, eliminating dumping and minimizing release of hazardous chemicals and materials, halving the proportion of untreated wastewater and substantially increasing recycling and safe reuse globally.	Proportion of wastewater safely treated Proportion of bodies of water with good ambient water quality
6.4 By 2030, substantially increase water-use efficiency across all sectors and ensure sustainable withdrawals and supply of freshwater to address water scarcity and substantially reduce the number of people suffering from water scarcity.	Change in water-use efficiency over time Level of water stress: freshwater withdrawal as a proportion of available freshwater resources
6.5 By 2030, implement integrated water resources management at all levels, including through transboundary cooperation as appropriate.	Degree of integrated water resources management implementation (0-100) Proportion of transboundary basin area with an operational arrangement for water cooperation
6.6 By 2020, protect and restore water-related ecosystems, including mountains, forests, wetlands, rivers, aquifers and lakes.	**6.6.1** Change in the extent of water-related ecosystems over time
6.a By 2030, expand international cooperation and capacity-building support to developing countries in water-and sanitation-related activities and programmes, including water harvesting, desalination, water efficiency, wastewater treatment, recycling and reuse technologies.	**6.a.1** Amount of water-and sanitation-related official development assistance that is part of a government-coordinated spending plan
6.b Support and strengthen the participation of local communities in improving water and sanitation management.	**6.b.1** Proportion of local administrative units with established and operational policies and procedures for participation of local communities in water and sanitation management

Goal 7: Ensure access to affordable, reliable, sustainable and modern energy for all: Targets and Indicators

Targets	Indicators
7.1 By 2030, ensure universal access to affordable,reliable and modern energy services	Proportion of population with access to electricityProportion of population with primary reliance on clean fuels and technology
7.2 By 2030, increase substantially the share of renewable energy in the global energy mix	**7.2.1** Renewable energy share in the total final energyconsumption
7.3 By 2030, double the global rate of improvement inenergy efficiency	**7.3.1** Energy intensity measured in terms of primary energy and GDP
7.a By 2030, enhance international cooperation to facilitate access to clean energy research and technology, including renewable energy, energy efficiency and advanced and cleaner fossil-fuel technology, and promote investment in energy infrastructure and clean energy technology	**7.a.1** Mobilized amount of United States dollars per year starting in 2020 accountable towards the $100 billion commitment
7.b By 2030, expand infrastructure and upgrade technology for supplying modern and sustainable energy services for all in developing countries, in particular least developed countries, small island developing States and landlocked developing countries, in accordance with their respective programmes of support	**7.b.1** Investments in energy efficiency as a percentage of GDP and the amount of foreign direct investment in financial transfer for infrastructure and technology to sustainable development services

Goal 8: Promote sustained, inclusive and sustainable economic growth, full and productive employment and decent work for all: Targets and Indicators

Targets	Indicators
8.1 Sustain per capita economic growth in accordance with national circumstances and, in particular, at least 7 per cent gross domestic	**8.1.1** Annual growth rate of real GDP per capita

product growth per annum in the least developed countries	
8.2 Achieve higher levels of economic productivity through diversification, technological upgrading and innovation, including through a focus on high-value added and labour-intensive sectors	**8.2.1** Annual growth rate of real GDP per employed person
8.3 Promote development-oriented policies that support productive activities, decent job creation, entrepreneurship, creativity and innovation, and encourage the formalization and growth of micro-, small-and medium-sized enterprises, including through access to financial services	**8.3.1** Proportion of informal employment in non- agriculture employment, by sex
8.4 Improve progressively, through 2030, global resource efficiency in consumption and production and endeavour to decouple economic growth from environmental degradation, in accordance with the 10-Year Framework of Programmes on Sustainable Consumption and Production, with developed countries taking the lead	Material footprint, material footprint per capita, and material footprint per GDP Domestic material consumption, domestic material consumption per capita, and domestic material consumption per GDP
8.5 By 2030, achieve full and productive employment and decent work for all women and men, including for young people and persons with disabilities, and equal pay for work of equal value	Average hourly earnings of female and male employees, by occupation, age and persons with disabilities Unemployment rate, by sex, age and persons with disabilities
8.6 By 2020, substantially reduce the proportion of youth not in employment, education or training	**8.6.1** Proportion of youth (aged 15-24 years) not in education, employment or training
8.7 Take immediate and effective measures to eradicate forced labour, end modern slavery and human	**8.7.1** Proportion and number of children aged 5-17 years engaged in child labour, by sex and age

trafficking and secure the prohibition and elimination of the worst forms of child labour, including recruitment and use of child soldiers, and by 2025 end child labour in all its forms	
8.8 Protect labour rights and promote safe and secure working environments for all workers, including migrant workers, in particular women migrants, and those in precarious employment	Frequency rates of fatal and non-fatal occupational injuries, by sex and migrant statusIncrease in national compliance of labour rights (freedom of association and collective bargaining) based on International Labour Organization (ILO) textual sources and national legislation, by sex and migrant status
8.9 By 2030, devise and implement policies to promote sustainable tourism that creates jobs and promotes local culture and products	Tourism direct GDP as a proportion of total GDP and in growth rateNumber of jobs in tourism industries as a proportion of total jobs and growth rate of jobs, by sex
8.10 Strengthen the capacity of domestic financial institutions to encourage and expand access to banking, insurance and financial services for all	Number of commercial bank branches and automated teller machines (ATMs) per 100,000 adultsProportion of adults (15 years and older) with an account at a bank or other financial institution or with a mobile-money-service provider
8.a Increase Aid for Trade support for developing countries, in particular least developed countries, including through the Enhanced Integrated Framework for Trade-related Technical Assistance to Least Developed Countries	**8.a.1** Aid for Trade commitments and disbursements
8.b By 2020, develop and operationalize a global strategy for youth employment and implement the Global Jobs Pact of the International Labour Organization	**8.b.1** Total government spending in social protection and employment programmes as a proportion of the national budgets and GDP

Goal 9. Build resilient infrastructure, promote inclusive and sustainable industrialization and foster innovation: Targets and Indicators

9.1 Develop quality, reliable, sustainable and resilient infrastructure, including regional and trans-border infrastructure, to support economic development and human well-being, with a focus on affordable and equitable access for all	Proportion of the rural population who live within 2 km of an all-season road Passenger and freight volumes, by mode of transport
9.2 Promote inclusive and sustainable industrialization and, by 2030, significantly raise industry's share of employment and gross domestic product, in line with national circumstances, and double its share in least developed countries	Manufacturing value added as a proportion of GDP and per capita Manufacturing employment as a proportion of total employment
9.3 Increase the access of small-scale industrial and other enterprises, in particular in developing countries, to financial services, including affordable credit, and their integration into value chains and markets	Proportion of small-scale industries in total industry value addedProportion of small-scale industries with a loan or line of credit
9.4 By 2030, upgrade infrastructure and retrofit industries to make them sustainable, with increased resource-use efficiency and greater adoption of clean and environmentally sound technologies and industrial processes, with all countries taking action in accordance with their respective capabilities	**9.4.1** CO2 emission per unit of value added
9.5 Enhance scientific research, upgrade the technological capabilities of industrial sectors in all countries, in particular developing countries, including, by 2030, encouraging innovation and substantially increasing the number of research and development workers per 1	Research and development expenditure as a proportion of GDP Researchers (in full-time equivalent) per million inhabitants

million people and public and private research and development spending	
9.a Facilitate sustainable and resilient infrastructure development in developing countries through enhanced financial, technological and technical support to African countries, least developed countries, landlocked developing countries and small island developing States	**9.a.1** Total official international support (official development assistance plus other official flows) to infrastructure
9.b Support domestic technology development, research and innovation in developing countries, including by ensuring a conducive policy environment for, inter alia, industrial diversification and value addition to commodities	**9.b.1** Proportion of medium and high-tech industry value added in total value added
9.c Significantly increase access to information and communications technology and strive to provide universal and affordable access to the Internet in least developed countries by 2020	**9.c.1** Proportion of population covered by a mobile network, by technology

Goal 10: Reduce inequality within and among countries: Targets and Indicators

10.1 By 2030, progressively achieve and sustain income growth of the bottom 40 per cent of the population at a rate higher than the national average	**10.1.1** Growth rates of household expenditure or income per capita among the bottom 40 per cent of the population and the total population
10.2 By 2030, empower and promote the social, economic and political inclusion of all, irrespective of age, sex, disability, race, ethnicity, origin, religion or economic or other status	**10.2.1** Proportion of people living below 50 per cent of median income, by age, sex and persons with disabilities
10.3 Ensure equal opportunity and reduce inequalities of outcome,	**10.3.1** Proportion of the population reporting having personally felt

including by eliminating discriminatory laws, policies and practices and promoting appropriate legislation, policies and action in this regard	discriminated against or harassed within the previous 12 months on the basis of a ground of discrimination prohibited under international human rights law
10.4 Adopt policies, especially fiscal, wage and social protection policies, and progressively achieve greater equality	**10.4.1** Labour share of GDP, comprising wages and social protection transfers
10.5 Improve the regulation and monitoring of global financial markets and institutions and strengthen the implementation of such regulations	**10.5.1** Financial Soundness Indicators
10.6 Ensure enhanced representation and voice for developing countries in decision-making in global international economic and financial institutions in order to deliver more effective, credible, accountable and legitimate institutions	**10.6.1** Proportion of members and voting rights of developing countries in international organizations
10.7 Facilitate orderly, safe, regular and responsible migration and mobility of people, including through the implementation of planned and well-managed migration policies	Recruitment cost borne by employee as a proportion of yearly income earned in country of destination Number of countries that have implemented well-managed migration policies
10.a Implement the principle of special and differential treatment for developing countries, in particular least developed countries, in accordance with World Trade Organization agreements	**10.a.1** Proportion of tariff lines applied to imports from least developed countries and developing countries with zero-tariff
10.b Encourage official development assistance and financial flows, including foreign direct investment, to States where the need is greatest, in particular least developed countries, African countries, small island developing States and landlocked	**10.b.1** Total resource flows for development, by recipient and donor countries and type of flow (e.g. official development assistance, foreign direct investment and other flows)

developing countries, in accordance with their national plans and programmes	
10.c By 2030, reduce to less than 3 per cent the transaction costs of migrant remittances and eliminate remittance corridors with costs higher than 5 per cent	**10.c.1** Remittance costs as a proportion of the amount remitted

Goal 11. Make cities and human settlements inclusive, safe, resilient and sustainable: Targets and Indicators

11.1 By 2030, ensure access for all to adequate, safe andaffordable housing and basic services and upgrade slums	**11.1.1** Proportion of urban population living in slums, informal settlements or inadequate housing
11.2 By 2030, provide access to safe, affordable, accessible and sustainable transport systems for all, improving road safety, notably by expanding public transport, with special attention to the needs of those in vulnerable situations, women, children, persons with disabilities and older persons	**11.2.1** Proportion of population that has convenient access to public transport, by sex, age and persons with disabilities
11.3 By 2030, enhance inclusive and sustainable urbanization and capacity for participatory, integrated and sustainable human settlement planning and management in all countries	Ratio of land consumption rate to population growth rate Proportion of cities with a direct participation structure of civil society in urban planning and management that operate regularly and democratically
11.4 Strengthen efforts to protect and safeguard the world's cultural and natural heritage	**11.4.1** Total expenditure (public and private) per capita spent on the preservation, protection and conservation of all cultural and natural heritage, by type of heritage (cultural, natural, mixed and World Heritage Centre designation), level of government (national, regional and local/municipal), type of expenditure

	(operating expenditure/investment) and type of private funding (donations in kind, private non-profit sector and sponsorship)
11.5 By 2030, significantly reduce the number of deaths and the number of people affected and substantially decrease the direct economic losses relative to global gross domestic product caused by disasters, including water-related disasters, with a focus on protecting the poor and people in vulnerable situations	Number of deaths, missing persons and persons affectedby disaster per 100,000 people Direct disaster economic loss in relation to global GDP, including disaster damage to critical infrastructure and disruption of basic services
11.6 By 2030, reduce the adverse per capita environmental impact of cities, including by paying special attention to air quality and municipal and other waste management	Proportion of urban solid waste regularly collected and with adequate final discharge out of total urban solid waste generated by cities. Annual mean levels of fine particulate matter (e.g. PM 2.5 and PM10) in cities (population weighted)
11.7 By 2030, provide universal access to safe, inclusive and accessible, green and public spaces, in particular for women and children, older persons and persons with disabilities	Average share of the built-up area of cities that is open space for public use for all, by sex, age and persons with disabilities Proportion of persons victim of physical or sexual harassment, by sex, age, disability status and place of occurrence, in the previous 12 months
11.a Support positive economic, social and environmental links between urban, peri-urban and rural areas by strengthening national and regional development planning	**11.a.1** Proportion of population living in cities that implement urban and regional development plans integrating population projections and resource needs, by size of city
11.b By 2020, substantially increase the number of cities and human settlements adopting and implementing integrated policies and plans towards inclusion, resource efficiency, mitigation and adaptation to climate change, resilience to	Proportion of local governments that adopt and implement local disaster risk reduction strategies in line with the Sendai Framework for Disaster Risk Reduction 2015-2030 Number of countries with national and local disaster risk reduction strategies

disasters, and develop and implement, in line with the Sendai Framework for Disaster Risk Reduction 2015-2030, holistic disaster risk management at all levels	
11.c Support least developed countries, including through financial and technical assistance, in building sustainable and resilient buildings utilizing local materials	**11.c.1** Proportion of financial support to the least developed countries that is allocated to the construction and retrofitting of sustainable, resilient and resource-efficient buildings utilizing local materials

Goal 12. Ensure Sustainable Consumption and Production Patterns: Targets and Indicators

12.1 Implement the 10-Year Framework of Programmes on Sustainable Consumption and Production Patterns, all countries taking action, with developed countries taking the lead, taking into account the development and capabilities of developing countries	**12.1.1** Number of countries with Sustainable Consumption and Production (SCP) national action plans or SCP mainstreamed as a priority or a target into national policies
12.2 By 2030, achieve the sustainable management and efficient use of natural resources	**12.2.1** Material footprint, material footprint per capita, and material footprint per GDP **12.2.2** Domestic material consumption, domestic material consumption per capita, and domestic material consumption per GDP
12.3 By 2030, halve per capita global food waste at the retail and consumer levels and reduce food losses along production and supply chains, including post-harvest losses	**12.3.1** Global food loss index
12.4 By 2020, achieve the environmentally sound management of chemicals and all wastes throughout their life cycle, in	**12.4.1** Number of parties to international multilateral environmental agreements on hazardous waste, and other chemicals that meet their

accordance with agreed international frameworks, and significantly reduce their release to air, water and soil in order to minimize their adverse impacts on human health and the environment	commitments and obligations in transmitting information as required by each relevant agreement **12.4.2** Hazardous waste generated per capita and proportion of hazardous waste treated, by type of treatment
12.5 By 2030, substantially reduce waste generation through prevention, reduction, recycling and reuse	**12.5.1** National recycling rate, tons of material recycled
12.6 Encourage companies, especially large and transnational companies, to adopt sustainable practices and to integrate sustainability information into their reporting cycle	**12.6.1** Number of companies publishing sustainability reports
12.7 Promote public procurement practices that are sustainable, in accordance with national policies and priorities	**12.7.1** Number of countries implementing sustainable public procurement policies and action plans
12.8 By 2030, ensure that people everywhere have the relevant information and awareness for sustainable development and lifestyles in harmony with nature	**12.8.1** Extent to which (i) global citizenship education and (ii) education for sustainable development (including climate change education) are mainstreamed in (a) national education policies; (b) curricula; (c) teacher education; and (d) student assessment
12.a Support developing countries to strengthen their scientific and technological capacity to move towards more sustainable patterns of consumption and production	**12.a.1** Amount of support to developing countries on research and development for sustainable consumption and production and environmentally sound technologies
12.b Develop and implement tools to monitor sustainable development impacts for sustainable tourism that creates jobs and promotes local culture and products	**12.b.1** Number of sustainable tourism strategies or policies and implemented action plans with agreed monitoring and evaluation tools
12.c Rationalize inefficient fossil-fuel subsidies that encourage wasteful consumption by removing market	**12.c.1** Amount of fossil-fuel subsidies per unit of GDP (production and consumption) and as a proportion of

distortions, in accordance with national circumstances, including by restructuring taxation and phasing out those harmful subsidies, where they exist, to reflect their environmental impacts, taking fully into account the specific needs and conditions of developing countries and minimizing the possible adverse impacts on their development in a manner that protects the poor and the affected communities	total national expenditure on fossil fuels

Goal 13. Take urgent action to combat climate change and its impacts: Targets and Indicators

13.1 Strengthen resilience and adaptive capacity to climate-related hazards and natural disasters in all countries	Number of countries with national and local disaster risk reduction strategies Number of deaths, missing persons and persons affected by disaster per 100,000 people
13.2 Integrate climate change measures into national policies, strategies and planning	**13.2.1** Number of countries that have communicated the establishment or operationalization of an integrated policy/strategy/plan which increases their ability to adapt to the adverse impacts of climate change, and foster climate resilience and low greenhouse gas emissions development in a manner that does not threaten food production (including a national adaptation plan, nationally determined contribution, national communication, biennial update report or other)
13.3 Improve education, awareness-raising and human and institutional capacity on climate change mitigation, adaptation, impact reduction and early warning	Number of countries that have integrated mitigation, adaptation, impact reduction and early warning into primary, secondary and tertiary curricula Number of countries that have communicated the strengthening of

	institutional, systemic and individual capacity-building to implement adaptation, mitigation and technology transfer, and development actions
13.a Implement the commitment undertaken by developed-country parties to the United Nations Framework Convention on Climate Change to a goal of mobilizing jointly $100 billion annually by 2020 from all sources to address the needs of developing countries in the context of meaningful mitigation actions and transparency on implementation and fully operationalize the Green Climate Fund through its capitalization as soon as possible	**13.a.1** Mobilized amount of United States dollars per year starting in 2020 accountable towards the $100 billion commitment
13.b Promote mechanisms for raising capacity for effective climate change-related planning and management in least developed countries and small island developing States, including focusing on women, youth and local and marginalized communities	**13.b.1** Number of least developed countries and small island developing States that are receiving specialized support, and amount of support, including finance, technology and capacity-building, for mechanisms for raising capacities for effective climate change-related planning and management, including focusing on women, youth and local and marginalized communities

Goal: 14 Conserve and sustainably use the oceans, seas and marine resources for sustainable development-Targets and Indicators

Targets	Indicators	Relevant National Indicator
Target 14.1: By 2025, prevent and significantly reduce marine pollution of all kinds, in particular from land-based activities, including	14.1.1 Index of coastal eutrophication and floating plastic debris density.	• Run off into rivers, seas and oceans. • Amount of waste water flows directly into the seas and oceans. • Level of eutrophication

marine debris and nutrient pollution.		of estuaries. • Number of initiatives by state governments on protection of coastal and marine resources.
Target 14.2: By 2020, sustainably manage and protect marine and coastal ecosystems to avoid significant adverse impacts, including by strengthening their resilience, and take action for their restoration in order to achieve healthy and productive oceans.	**14.2.1** Proportion of national exclusive economic zones managed using ecosystem-based approaches.	• Number of Marine Protected Areas designated and managed. • Extent of restored mangroves and estuaries. • Spatial planning strategies for coastal and marine areas.
Target 14.3: Minimise and address the impacts of ocean acidification, including through enhanced scientific cooperation at all levels.	**14.3.1** Average marine acidity (pH) measured at agreed suite of representative sampling stations.	• National climate policy that considers a measurable de-carbonization strategy. • Reduction in the amount of CHC emissions in the AFOLU sector. • Ocean acidity measurements. • National Climate Change Action Index.
Target 14.4: By 2020, effectively regulate harvesting, and end overfishing, illegal, unreported and unregulated fishing and destructive fishing practices and implement science-based management plans, to restore fish stocks in the shortest time feasible at least to levels that can	**14.4.1** Proportion of fish stocks within biologically sustainable level.	• Sustainable harvesting practices indices for fisheries and coastal resources. • Certification schemes for sustainable fishery catch and management. • Synergies between state and national level organizations and institutions on developing and implementing sustainable

produce maximum sustainable yield as determined by their biological characteristics.		bio- resource management plans and actions.
Target 14.5: By 2020, conserve at least 10 per cent of coastal and marine areas, consistent with national and international law and based on best available scientific information.	**14.5.1** Coverage of protected areas in relation to marine areas.	National and state level marine and ocean resource conservation plans developed and used.
Target 14.6: By 2020, prohibit certain forms of fisheries subsidies which contribute to overcapacity and overfishing, and eliminate subsidies that contribute to illegal, unreported and unregulated fishing and refrain from introducing new such subsidies, recognizing that appropriate and effective special and differential treatment for developing and least developed countries should be an integral part of the World Trade Organization fisheries subsidies negotiation.	**14.6.1** Progress by countries in the degree of implementation of international instruments aiming to combat illegal, unreported and unregulated fishing.	Reduction and subsequent elimination of subsidies at national and state levels that is not consistent with regional and global practice and standards.
Target 14.7: By 2030, increase the economic benefits to small island developing States and least developed countries from the sustainable use of marine resources,	**14.7.1** Sustainable fisheries as a percentage of GDP in small island developing States, least developed countries and all countries.	• Social and economic benefits of fishing and resource management assessed for artisanal, sustenance and commercial fisheries and marine resources.

including through sustainable management of fisheries, aquaculture and tourism.		• Reduction and subsequent ban on use of destructive fishing practices. • Extent of coastal area restoration promoting enhanced biodiversity.
Target 14.a: Increase scientific knowledge, develop research capacity and transfer marine technology, taking into account the Intergovernmental Oceanographic Commission Criteria and Guidelines on the Transfer of Marine Technology, in order to improve ocean health and to enhance the contribution of marine biodiversity to the development of developing countries, in particular small island developing States and least developed countries.	**14. a.1** Proportion of total research budget allocated to research in the field of marine technology.	• Nature and impact of collaboration between public and private institutions on resource management and use • Measures to enhance the impact of investments into institutions – public sector that results in collective impacts on resource use and enhancement.
Target 14.b: Provide access for small-scale artisanal fishers to marine resources and markets.	**14.b.1** Progress by countries in the degree of application of a legal/ regulatory/policy/ institutional framework which recognizes and protects access rights for small-scale fisheries.	• Nature and type of access to marine resources for small-scale artisanal fishers and subsistence fisheries.
Target 14.c: Enhance the conservation and sustainable use of oceans and their	**14.c.1** Number of countries making progress in ratifying, accepting and	• Active participation in regional and international negotiations (eg. the ongoing UN led

resources by implementing international law as reflected in the United Nations Convention on the Law of the Sea, which provides the legal framework for the conservation and sustainable use of oceans and their resources, as recalled in paragraph 158 of "The future we want".	implementing through legal, policy and institutional frameworks, ocean related instruments that implement international law, as reflected in the United Nation Convention on the Law of the Sea, for the conservation and sustainable use of the oceans and their resources.	negotiations for a legally binding agreement on management of resources in areas beyond national jurisdiction. • National actions on synergies between Conventions and processes at global and regional levels. • Number of action programmes that respond to the international governance schemes.

Goal 15: Protect, restore and promote sustainable use of terrestrial ecosystems, sustainably manage forests, combat desertification, and halt and reverse land degradation and halt biodiversity loss: Targets and Indicators

15.1 By 2020, ensure the conservation, restoration and sustainable use of terrestrial and inland freshwater ecosystems and their services, in particular forests, wetlands, mountains and dry lands, in line with obligations under international agreements	Forest area as a proportion of total land area Proportion of important sites for terrestrial and freshwater biodiversity that are covered by protected areas, by ecosystem type
15.2 By 2020, promote the implementation of sustainable management of all types of forests, halt deforestation, restore degraded forests and substantially increase afforestation and reforestation globally.	**15.2.1** Progress towards sustainable forest management
15.3 By 2030, combat desertification, restore degraded land and soil, including land affected by desertification, drought and floods, and strive to achieve a land degradation-neutral world.	**15.3.1** Proportion of land that is degraded over total land area

15.4 By 2030, ensure the conservation of mountain ecosystems, including their biodiversity, in order to enhance their capacity to provide benefits that are essential for sustainable development.	Coverage by protected areas of important sites for mountain biodiversity Mountain Green Cover Index
15.5 Take urgent and significant action to reduce the degradation of natural habitats, halt the loss of biodiversity and, by 2020, protect and prevent the extinction of threatened species.	**15.5.1** Red List Index
15.6 Promote fair and equitable sharing of the benefits arising from the utilisation of genetic resources and promote appropriate access to such resources, as internationally agreed.	**15.6.1** Number of countries that have adopted legislative, administrative and policy frameworks to ensure fair and equitable sharing of benefits
15.7 Take urgent action to end poaching and trafficking of protected species of flora and fauna and address both demand and supply of illegal wildlife products.	**15.7.1** Proportion of traded wildlife that was poached orillicitly trafficked
15.8 By 2020, introduce measures to prevent the introduction and significantly reduce the impact of invasive alien species on land and water ecosystems and control or eradicate the priority species.	**15.8.1** Proportion of countries adopting relevant national legislation and adequately resourcing the prevention or control of invasive alien species
15.9 By 2020, integrate ecosystem and biodiversity values into national and local planning, development processes, poverty reduction strategies and accounts.	**15.9.1** Progress towards national targets established in accordance with Aichi Biodiversity Target 2 of the Strategic Plan for Biodiversity 2011-2020
15.a Mobilize and significantly increase financial resources from all sources to conserve and sustainably use biodiversity and ecosystems.	**15.a.1** Official development assistance and public expenditure on conservation and sustainable use of biodiversity and ecosystems

15.b Mobilize significant resources from all sources and at all levels to finance sustainable forest management and provide adequate incentives to developing countries to advance such management, including for conservation and reforestation.	**15.b.1** Official development assistance and public expenditure on conservation and sustainable use of biodiversity and ecosystems
15.c Enhance global support for efforts to combat poaching and trafficking of protected species, including by increasing the capacity of local communities to pursue sustainable livelihood opportunities	**15.c.1** Proportion of traded wildlife that was poached orillicitly trafficked

Goal 16: Promote peaceful and inclusive societies for sustainable development, provide access to justice for all and build effective, accountable and inclusive institutions at all levels : Targets and Indicators

16.1 Significantly reduce all forms of violence and related death rates everywhere	**16.1.1** Number of victims of intentional homicide per 100,000 population, by sex and age **16.1.2** Conflict-related deaths per 100,000 population, by sex, age and cause **16.1.3** Proportion of population subjected to physical, psychological or sexual violence in the previous 12 months **16.1.4** Proportion of population that feel safe walking alone around the area they live
16.2 End abuse, exploitation, trafficking and all forms of violence against and torture of children	**16.2.1** Proportion of children aged 1-17 years who experienced any physical punishment and/or psychological aggression by caregivers in the past month **16.2.2** Number of victims of human trafficking per 100,000 population, by sex, age and form of exploitation **16.2.3** Proportion of young women and

	men aged 18- 29 years who experienced sexual violence by age 18
16.3 Promote the rule of law at the national and international levels and ensure equal access to justice for all	**16.3.1** Proportion of victims of violence in the previous 12 months who reported their victimization to competent authorities or other officially recognized conflict resolution mechanisms **16.3.2** Unsentenced detainees as a proportion of overall prison population
16.4 By 2030, significantly reduce illicit financial and arms flows, strengthen the recovery and return of stolen assets and combat all forms of organized crime	**16.4.1** Total value of inward and outward illicit financial flows (in current United States dollars) **16.4.2** Proportion of seized small arms and light weapons that are recorded and traced, in accordance with international standards and legal instruments
16.5 Substantially reduce corruption and bribery in all their forms	**16.5.1** Proportion of persons who had at least one contact with a public official and who paid a bribe to a public official, or were asked for a bribe by those public officials, during the previous 12 months **16.5.2** Proportion of businesses that had at least one contact with a public official and that paid a bribe to a public official, or were asked for a bribe by those public officials during the previous 12 months
16.6 Develop effective, accountable and transparentinstitutions at all levels	**16.6.1** Primary government expenditures as a proportion of original approved budget, by sector (or by budget codes or similar) **16.6.2** Proportion of the population satisfied with their last experience of public services
16.7 Ensure responsive, inclusive, participatory and representative decision-making at all levels	**16.7.1** Proportions of positions (by sex, age, persons with disabilities and population groups) in public institutions (national and local legislatures, public

	service, and judiciary) compared to national distributions **16.7.2** Proportion of population who believe decision-making is inclusive and responsive, by sex, age, disability and population group
16.8 Broaden and strengthen the participation of developing countries in the institutions of global governance	**16.8.1** Proportion of members and voting rights of developing countries in international organizations

Goal 17: Strengthen the means of implementation and revitalize the Global Partnership for Sustainable Development : Targets and Indicators

Finance

17.1 Strengthen domestic resource mobilization, including through international support to developing countries, to improve domestic capacity for tax and other revenue collection	**17.1.1** Total government revenue as a proportion of GDP, by source **17.1.2** Proportion of domestic budget funded by domestic taxes
17.2 Developed countries to implement fully their official development assistance commitments, including the commitment by many developed countries to achieve the target of 0.7 per cent of gross national income for official development assistance (ODA/GNI) to developing countries and 0.15 to 0.20 per cent of ODA/GNI to least developed countries; ODA providers are encouraged to consider setting a target to provide at least 0.20 per cent of ODA/GNI to least developed countries	**17.2.1** Net official development assistance, total and to least developed countries, as a proportion of the Organization for Economic Cooperation and Development (OECD) Development Assistance Committee donors' gross national income (GNI)
17.3 Mobilize additional financial resources for developing countries from multiple sources	**17.3.1** Foreign direct investments (FDI), official development assistance and South-South Cooperation as a

	proportion of total domestic budget **17.3.2** Volume of remittances (in United States dollars) as a proportion of total GDP
17.4 Assist developing countries in attaining long- term debt sustainability through coordinated policies aimed at fostering debt financing, debt relief and debt restructuring, as appropriate, and address the external debt of highly indebted poor countries to reduce debt distress	**17.4.1** Debt service as a proportion of exports of goods and services
17.5 Adopt and implement investment promotion regimes for least developed countries	**17.5.1** Number of countries that adopt and implement investment promotion regimes for least developed countries
Technology	
17.6 Enhance North-South, South-South and triangular regional and international cooperation on and access to science, technology and innovation and enhance knowledge-sharing on mutually agreed terms, including through improved coordination among existing mechanisms, in particular at the United Nations level, and through a global technology facilitation mechanism	**17.6.1** Number of science and/or technology cooperation agreements and programmes between countries, by type of cooperation **17.6.2** Fixed Internet broadband subscriptions per 100 inhabitants, by speed
17.7 Promote the development, transfer, dissemination and diffusion of environmentally sound technologies to developing countries on favorable terms, including on concessional and preferential terms, as mutually agreed	**17.7.1** Total amount of approved funding for developing countries to promote the development, transfer, dissemination and diffusion of environmentally sound technologies
17.8 Fully operationalize the technology bank and science, technology and innovation capacity-	**17.8.1** Proportion of individuals using the Internet

building mechanism for least developed countries by 2017 and enhance the use of enabling technology, in particular information and communications technology	
Capacity-Building	
17.9 Enhance international support for implementing effective and targeted capacity-building in developing countries to support national plans to implement all the Sustainable Development Goals, including through North-South, South-South and triangular cooperation	**17.9.1** Dollar value of financial and technical assistance (including through North-South, South-South and triangular cooperation) committed to developing countries
Trade	
17.10 Promote a universal, rules-based, open, non- discriminatory and equitable multilateral trading system under the World Trade Organization, including through the conclusion of negotiations under its Doha Development Agenda	**17.10.1** Worldwide weighted tariff-average
17.11 Significantly increase the exports of developing countries, in particular with a view to doubling the least developed countries' share of global exports by 2020	**17.11.1** Developing countries' and least developed countries' share of global exports
17.12 Realize timely implementation of duty-free and quota-free market access on a lasting basis for all least developed countries, consistent with World Trade Organization decisions, including by ensuring that preferential rules of origin applicable to imports from least developed countries are transparent and simple, and contribute to facilitating market access	**17.12.1** Average tariffs faced by developing countries, least developed countries and small island developing States

Systemic Issues

Policy and Institutional Coherence	
17.13 Enhance global macroeconomic stability, including through policy coordination and policy coherence	**17.13.1** Macroeconomic Dashboard
17.14 Enhance policy coherence for sustainable development	**17.14.1** Number of countries with mechanisms in place to enhance policy coherence of sustainable development
17.15 Respect each country's policy space and leadership to establish and implement policies for poverty eradication and sustainable development	**17.15.1** Extent of use of country-owned results frameworks and planning tools by providers of development cooperation
Multi-stakeholder Partnerships	
17.16 Enhance the Global Partnership for Sustainable Development, complemented by multi-stakeholder partnerships that mobilize and share knowledge, expertise, technology and financial resources, to support the achievement of the Sustainable Development Goals in all countries, in particular developing countries	**17.16.1** Number of countries reporting progress in multi-stakeholder development effectiveness monitoring frameworks that support the achievement of the sustainable development goals
17.17 Encourage and promote effective public, public- private and civil society partnerships, building on the experience and resourcing strategies of partnerships	**17.17.1** Amount of United States dollars committed to public-private and civil society partnerships
Data, Monitoring and Accountability	
17.18 By 2020, enhance capacity-building support to developing countries, including for least developed countries and small island developing States, to increase significantly the availability of high-quality, timely and reliable data disaggregated by income, gender,	**17.18.1** Proportion of sustainable development indicators produced at the national level with full disaggregation when relevant to the target, in accordance with the Fundamental Principles of Official Statistics **17.18.2** Number of countries that have national statistical legislation that

age, race, ethnicity, migratory status, disability, geographic location and other characteristics relevant in national contexts	complies with the Fundamental Principles of Official Statistics **17.18.2** Number of countries with a national statistical plan that is fully funded and under implementation, by source of funding
17.19 By 2030, build on existing initiatives to develop measurements of progress on sustainable development that complement gross domestic product, and support statistical capacity-building in developing countries	**17.19.1** Dollar value of all resources made available to strengthen statistical capacity in developing countries **17.19.2** Proportion of countries that (a) have conducted at least one population and housing census in the last 10 years; and (b) have achieved 100 per cent birth registration and 80 per cent death registration

Localized SDGs and Role of Gram Panchayats

Goal 1: No Poverty (End poverty in all its forms everywhere)

Role of Gram Panchayats

Facilitate access to: Social protection, Housing, Water, Sanitation and electricity and Implementation of MGNREGS

- Income generation through: Skills training, Entrepreneurship development, Employment
- Building of institutions like self-help groups
- Access to financial services, including Microfinance

Identify

- Poor, destitute and critically vulnerable to shocks and disasters
- Appropriate new technologies to improve productivity

Plan

- Operational guidelines for care and protection of destitute and vulnerable
- Convergence of GPDP funds and programmes

People to support - Self-Help Groups (SHGs) and their federations, literacy workers, ASHAs, Teachers, National Rural Livelihood Mission (NRLM) Community Resource Persons (CRPs), Anganwadi Workers, Rozgar Sevaks

Resources for this- Deen Dayal Antyodaya Yojana (DAY-NRLM), MGNREGS, DDU-GKY, State Poverty Eradication Missions, National Social Assistance Programme (NSAP), PMAY, PDS, RSBY, SBM, Deen Dayal Upadhyaya Gram Jyoti Yojana, Other state and central schemes

Goal 2: Zero Hunger (End hunger, achieve food security and improved nutrition and promote sustainable agriculture)

Role of Gram Panchayats

Enroll

- ❐ Families under PDS
- Children, pregnant women and adolescent girls under the Integrated Child Development Scheme (ICDS)
- Elderly people
- Farmers, pastoralists and fishers, in particular women

Ensure

- Growth monitoring of children under 6 years
- Coverage of pregnant and lactating women, adolescent girls under ICDS supplementary nutrition programme
- Take home rations for children below 3 years age, pregnant and lactating mothers
- Quality mid-day meals
- Issues are addressed in GPDP

Build

- Information, education and communication (IEC) strategy for nutrition education
- System of community support for nutrition for destitute & elderly
- Comprehensive production plan for small-scale producers
- Capacity for adaptation to climate change

Promote

- Breastfeeding
- Locally available nutritious food
- Resilient agricultural practices by sensitizing farmers and small-scale food producers

People to support - ASHAs, SHGs, Anganwadi workers, literacy workers, Teachers, NRLM CRPs, social activists, PTA/ school management committee (SMC), health workers, doctors, local experts, agriculture-related functionaries, departments and agencies

Resources to look for - PDS, ICDS, NHM, National Mission for Soil and Agriculture (NMSA), Rashtriya Krishi Vikas Yojana (RKVY), Integrated Watershed Management Programme (IWMP), Pradhan Mantri Krishi Sinchayee Yojana (PMKSY), state sponsored schemes and programmes on health, nutrition, agriculture, animal husbandry, horticulture and livelihoods

Goal 3: Good Health and Well-being (Ensuring healthy lives and promoting well-being for all persons with disabilities)

Role of Gram Panchayats

Maintain and Monitor

- Quality of health care services
- Overall cleanliness to combat malaria, waterborne diseases and other communicable diseases

Ensure

- Effective functioning of village health sanitation and nutrition committees and Rogi Kalyan Samiti
- Linkage to referral centre and 24x7 availability of emergency services delivery infrastructure
- Addressing of local public health issues through GPDP
- Access to family planning services
- Collaboration with health department for mental health care

Facilitate

- Social audits of maternal deaths
- Enrolment of vulnerable in health insurance schemes
- Awareness of non-communicable diseases
- Home-based palliative care with health workers
- Prevention of vector-borne diseases

Promote

- Early diagnosis and timely treatment of diseases
- Hygiene and sanitation through seasonal campaigns
- Smokeless chulhas,/LPG,improved cooking stoves, adequate ventilation
- Awareness of healthy life practices

Use IEC Strategies to

- Help families care for newborns, pregnant women
- Promote immunization and breastfeeding
- Address substance abuse, including narcotic drug abuse and harmful use of alcohol

People to support - Auxiliary Nurse Midwives (ANMs), Doctors, ASHAs, Anganwadi workers

Resources to look for - NHM, Janani Suraksha Yojana (JSY), Navjat Shisu Suraksha Karyakram (NSSK), ICDS, RSBY

Goal 4: Quality Education (Ensure inclusive and equitable quality education and promote lifelong learning opportunities for all)

Role of Gram Panchayats

Facilitate

- Transport and hostels for children in isolated areas
- Access to entitlements like scholarships, uniforms, textbooks, mid-day meals etc.
- Access for special needs children to schools
- Building of girls' toilets to ensure retention of girls
- Evening and mobile schools, learning centres and residential camps to provide bridge courses for dropouts/out-of-school children
- Collaboration with line departments for Teacher Rationalization

Promote

- Awareness on rights of children under the Right to Education (RTE) Act
- Environment for 100 percent enrolment and retention of students in schools

- Education standing committee to oversee operationalization of RTE
- Comprehensive participatory education plan to improve basic physical school facilities/social environment/child assessment
- Plan to improve infrastructure for Anganwadis

Strengthen

- Preschool Anganwadi
- Libraries to support literacy programme and so on

Monitor

- Quality of Education
- Rates of and reasons for school dropouts for girls and boys
- Rates of and reasons for irregular attendance for girls and boys

People to support - Teachers, SMCs, Anganwadi workers, ASHAs, literacy workers, other department officials, ICDS supervisors

Resources to look for - ICDS, Sarva Shiksha Abhiyan (SSA), National Skill Development Programme (NSDP), National Digital Literacy Mission, DDU-GKY, DAY-NRLM

Goal 5: Gender Equality (Achieve gender equality and empower all women and girls)

Role of Gram Panchayats

Promote

- Universal birth registration
- Philosophy of Beti Bachao Beti Padhao
- Awareness against gender discrimination
- School enrolment and retention of girls
- Programmes for school children against cybercrimes and substance abuse

Facilitate

- Formation of Gram Samanvaya Samitis, comprising grassroots-level functionaries, and women's representatives from the community
- Gender status studies and dissemination of findings in Gram Sabha

- Enrolment and attendance of all girl children in Anganwadis
- Women's participation in economic activities under SHGs
- Poorna Shakti Kendras, the GP-level one-stop centre for services for women

Campaign

- To prevent child marriage
- Against sex-selective abortions
- Against trafficking

Ensure

- Active inclusion and engagement of adolescent girls in livelihood and skill development programmes
- Access to basic facilities for women and children
- Registration and tracking of women and girls who are migrating
- Discriminatory and illegal practices like child marriage, female foeticide, etc. do not take place
- Women's membership and participation in local development and governance

Empower

- Girls to acquire higher education and technical skills
- Girl to enter the labour market

People to support - ICDS supervisors, Anganwadi workers, school teachers, health workers, ASHAs, NGOs, local police, lawyers, SHGs

Resources to look for - National Mission for Empowerment of Women (NMEW), Beti Bachao Beti Padhao, JSY, Rashtriya Bala Swasthya Karyakram, ICDS, Sukanya Samridhi Yojana (Girl Child Prosperity Scheme), DAY-NRLM, Rajiv Gandhi Scheme for Empowerment of Adolescent Girls (SABLA), Swachh Bharat Mission, NHM, SSA

Goal 6: Clean Water and Sanitation (Ensure availability and sustainable management of water and sanitation for all)

Role of Gram Panchayats

Ensure

- Identification of households without toilets

- Toilet use and maintenance
- Facilities for solid and liquid waste management
- Water-use efficiency by rationalizing water use
- Inclusion of water and sanitation issues in GPDP
- Compliance with environmental safeguards of all GPDP activities

Promote

- Hygiene education
- Toilets for all households and institutions
- Modern agriculture and water-use technologies
- Water-use rationalization by selecting appropriate cropping patterns

Facilitate

- Appropriate irrigation methods
- Regulation of water extraction based on demand yield match
- Participation of local communities in improving water and sanitation management

People to support - Water supply scheme operators, masons, registrants of MGNREGS, swachhta doots, health workers, teachers, NGOs

Resources to look for - Accelerated Rural Water Supply Programme (ARWSP), Swachh Bharat Mission, Integrated Watershed Management Programme (IWMP), other relevant centrally and state sponsored programmes and schemes

Goal 7: Affordable and Clean Energy (Ensure access to affordable, reliable, sustainable and modern energy for all)

Role of Gram Panchayats

- Facilitate electricity connections through appropriate authority/ agency
- To households
- To public buildings like schools, health centres, Anganwadis etc.
- To commercial establishments
- To small-scale industries
- For irrigation

Popularize

- Construction and use of biogas systems in households, schools and Anganwadis
- Energy efficient building designs
- Energy efficient cooking devices and habits
- Adoption of energy conservation measures (LED lamps, star-rated appliances)
- Energy efficient pumps for irrigation and drip Systems

Facilitate

- Solar energy augmentation in households and public institutions
- Installation of energy efficient chulhas

People to support -Traditional masons and helpers, department officials, technical and academic institutions, NGOs

Resources to look for - Deen Dayal Upadhyaya Gram Jyoti Yojana (DDU-GJY) Previously known- Rajiv Gandhi Grameen Vidyutikaran Yojana (RGGVY)

Goal 8: Decent Work and Economic Growth (Promote sustained, inclusive and sustainable economic growth, full and productive employment and decent work for all)

Role of Gram Panchayats

- Micro, small and medium enterprises within the panchayat area
- Enterprise opportunities in the village
- Employment opportunities for different categories and degrees of disabilities
- Potential candidates to set up enterprises
- Skills of interested candidates
- Children at-risk by demographic data (dropouts /children of migrants /manual scavengers / orphans /women-and-child-headed households)

Facilitate

- Prevention of child labour and create awareness on prevention of child labour

- Jobs under MGNREGS
- Availability of facilities at MGNREGS worksite
- Prevention of manual scavenging
- Rehabilitation of and cash assistance for manual scavengers through the social welfare department
- Entrepreneurial development training
- Handholding support for new enterprises
- Job creation through convergence of ongoing schemes and sponsorships

Maintain

- Database on labour and employment
- Categorization of disabled based on nature and degree of disability

Create

- Awareness on equal wages for men and women for equal work
- IEC material on labour legislations, rights and entitlements
- Village-level child protection committees and promote child protection services

People to support - SHGs, local professionals, social workers, successful local entrepreneurs, AWW, literacy activists, teachers, NRLM CRPs, MGNREGS mates, youth organizations, rural development department, Department of Social Justice

Resources to look for - DAY-NRLM and other government schemes for enterprise development, MGNREGS, DDU-GKY, The Prohibition of Employment as Manual Scavengers and their Rehabilitation Act, 2013, state-sponsored schemes, other department schemes, youth welfare schemes

Goal 13: Climate Action (Take urgent action to combat climate change and its impacts)

Role of Gram Panchayats

Integrate- Sectoral climate change considerations into local Planning

Facilitate

- Awareness building on scale of climate change impact
- Conducting of vulnerability assessments

Build- Strategies to mitigate climate change risks with communities and Gram Sabha

Strengthen

- Local-level resilience to climate events
- Ability of communities to anticipate and effectively respond to climate change

Plan

- To reduce dependence on climate sensitive sectors
- To address spread of vector- and water-borne diseases due to extreme events

People to support - NGOs, relevant government department officials, academic and research institutions

Resources to look for- National Action Plan on Climate Change, Green India Mission, relevant state schemes and programmes,

Goal 15: Life on Land (Protect, restore and promote sustainable use of terrestrial ecosystems, sustainably manage forests, combat desertification, and halt and reverse land degradation and halt biodiversity loss)

Role of Gram Panchayats

Promote

- Conservation of micro watersheds and/or identifiable natural units
- Community-based management of sacred groves
- Planting of natural vegetation in high-slope areas, barren lands and other common lands
- Green belt development and catchment conservation
- Conservation of wetlands
- Nursery raising of local species of flora through MGNREGS

Initiate

- Afforestation drives,
- Steps to make wetland cultivation chemical-free and Sustainable Development
- Bio-diversity Register

- Community monitoring system on poaching

Facilitate

- Renovation of existing ponds
- Construction of check-dams and contour bunds in catchments
- Cropping patterns linked to landscape
- Preparation of list of threatened species of flora and fauna
- Estimates of sustainable levels of resources (sand and water)
- Irrigation, procurement, finance and labour to make wetland cultivation economical
- Identification of public lands, common grazing grounds and landslide prone areas

Plan

- Pollution monitoring and alleviation steps
- Resource-sharing (sand and water) arrangements with scientific water-use pattern
- Alternate livelihoods for labour engaged in resource extraction
- Coordination and convergence of eco-restoration Programmes

People to support - Registrants of MGNREGS, traditional farmers and labourers, NGOs, relevant government department officials, academic and research institutions

Resources to look for - MGNREGS, Rashtriya Krishi Vikas Yojana (RKVY), IWMP, PMKSY, Green India Mission, social forestry, relevant state sponsored schemes and programmes

Conclusion

Development of villages through local governance is impossible without strengthening the functional role of PRIs. There are many plans and policies made at the central government level to achieve sustainable development in coming years. However, it can't be achieved without understanding the issues and challenges in the process of execution of government's plans and policies at grass root level. The twin objectives of the Panchayati Raj system as envisaged by the Constitution of India are to ensure local economic development and social justice. The eleventh schedule of the Constitution expects the Panchayats to play key roles in various thematic domains enlisted as 29 functions, though the specific mandates and capacities of these local governments vary from state to state. Many of the SDGs targets are within the purview of these functions listed in the eleventh schedule. There are also the various flagship programmes such as Swachh Bharat Mission, Make in India, Digital India, Skill India, Jan Dhan Yojana and so on, which are based on the core principles of SDGs and local governance.

The Gram Panchayat Development Plans (GPDP) initiated after the historical recommendation of the Fourteenth Finance Commission paves the way for the Panchayats to link planning with the SDGs. For localisation of SDGs, the Ministry of Panchayati Raj (MoPR) has prepared a 'Draft Vision Document for Achieving SDGs', where the role of Panchayats in terms of SDGs and Centrally Sponsored Schemes (CSS) has been mapped by keeping the area specific needs of the local people. The challenge related to Panchayats is to capacitate them for planning, fund absorption and improving service delivery towards achieving sustainable development goals. It is important that the SDGs and it's targets are deconstructed with the perspective of local governments and presented to them in a way in which they can be used in local planning and implementation. By localising the SDGs along with the preparation of proper need based participatory and convergent planning the ultimate aim of Panchayati Raj approach to ensure economic development and social justice can be achieved.

6

Panchayati Raj and Community Mobilisation in PESA Area

"Unless I am satisfied that every self-governing institution has provisions in it which give the depressed classes special representation in order to protect their rights, and until that is done, I am afraid it will not be possible for me to assent to the first part of the Bill."
— ***Dr. B R Ambedkar***

Introduction

The tribal communities are traditionally self-governed in respect of regulation, control and conduct of their domestic, religious, socio-economic, political and judicial affairs through the age-old, collective wisdom of their traditional leaders and village councils. Moreover, having lived in a setting of exclusion or partial exclusion, they were not familiarized to a rigid, statutory 3-tier Panchayati Raj system which was institutionalized through the 73rd Constitution Amendment Act, 1992 along with its incorporation as Part-IX (Panchayats) into the Constitution. This amendment, really bring path-breaking provisions for an effective system of local self-government for mainstream, non-scheduled areas of the country. But keeping in view the unique characteristics and special needs of the Scheduled Tribes, the 73rd Amendment was not automatically extended to the Scheduled Areas or Tribal Areas. However, pressure on natural resources in these areas continued due to the large projects being set up therein and deceitful elements indulging in illegal mining and forest felling. Land alienation and exploitation also continued and that led to dislocation of the communities and loss of major sources of livelihood. It was, therefore, critical that customs, rights and livelihoods of these people are protected through their empowerment. Accordingly, PESA was enacted in 1996 which extended Part-IX of the Constitution to the Schedule-V Areas and provided for people-centric governance and people's control over community resources and their life, with a central role to the Gram Sabhas.

Different treatments have received by the tribals mainly due to two reasons. First, the tribes in Fifth Schedule areas were considered incapable of self-government. Secondly, unlike the Sixth Schedule areas, some tribal communities in peninsular India coexisted with a minority non-tribal population, and autonomy for the tribes in such a case seemed impractical. These were considerations that had been settled well before independence, so that by voting on the inclusion of the Fifth Schedule in the Constitution the founding architects were, in a sense, continuing the colonial typecast that the tribes' contentment depended not so much on "rapid political advance as on experienced and sympathetic handling and on protection from economic subjugation by the [non-tribal] neighbors". Even the Supreme Court of India later endorsed this paternalist justification when it said that "the tribals … need to be taken care of by the protective arm of the law, so that they may prosper and by an evolutionary process join the mainstream of the society."

Constitutional Provisions for Tribals

The socio-economic gap between the status of tribal communities and that of other communities is wide enough to necessitate special concern. The Constitution had laid the responsibility on the shoulders of both the state governments and the central government for the socio-economic and political development of the STs.

The Indian Constitution provides safeguards for the tribal people. Though the prohibition of discrimination on grounds of religion, race, caste, sex or place of birth (Article-15), equality of opportunity in matters of public employment (Article-16), abolition of untouchability (Article-17), prohibition of traffic in human beings and forced labour (Article-23), to secure a social order for the promotion of welfare of the people (Article-38) and protection of interests of minorities (Article-29), are of general nature, they still incorporate the interests of the tribal people.

The Articles of the Constitution which are directly related to safeguarding tribal interests are those which promote their educational and economic interests (Article-46), special provisions for the appointment of a minister to look after the tribal interest exclusively (Article-164), special administration of Scheduled Areas and Tribal Areas (Article-244), grants from the Union to certain States (Article-235), reservation of seats for Scheduled Tribes in the House of the People (Article-330), and in the Legislative Assemblies of the state (Article-332), reservation of seats and special representation (Article-332), special claims to service and posts

(Article-335), special officers for them (Article-338), control of the centre over the administration of Scheduled Areas and the welfare of Scheduled Tribes (Article-339) and special provision for Nagaland (Article-371A). Moreover, Article-342 of the Constitution is concerned exclusively with the Scheduled Tribes.

Panchayats (Extension to Scheduled Areas) Act, 1996

India had created history in fiscal federalism by means of the landmark 73rd and 74th amendments to the constitution in 1992. These amendments introduced a three-tier local self government to the federal structure, giving constitutional recognition to rural local self-government institutions and enabling decentralised governance through Panchayati Raj Institutions. Nevertheless, there was not much interest in strengthening participatory democracy by way of making the Gram Sabha the corner stone of the Panchayati Raj system. While the constitution of Gram Sabhas was made mandatory in states, the powers and functions of the Gram Sabhas have been left to the discretion of the state legislatures. As a result, different states have developed powers and functions for this body differently.

Following the amendment, a high-level committee was constituted under the chairmanship of Dileep Singh Bhuria, charged with recommending how scheduled areas should be incorporated under the 73rd Amendment Act. As recommended by this committee, a bill was introduced in parliament and passed on 19th December 1996. Subsequently, after getting the president's assent on 24th December 1996, the 73rd Amendment Act was extended the Scheduled Areas mentioned under Clause (2) of Article-244 of the constitution. It became mandatory for the states to amend their existing Panchayat Acts to conform to the Extension Act within a year.

The Panchayati Raj Extension to Scheduled Areas Act, 1996 (PESA) has made it mandatory for states having scheduled areas to make specific provisions for giving wide-ranging powers to tribals on matters relating to decision making and development of their community. Technically, when the act refers to extending the provisions of Part-IX of the constitution to the Schedule-V areas, politically, it gives radical governance powers to the tribal communities and recognises its traditional community rights over local natural resources. It not only accepts the validity of "customary law, social and religious practices, and traditional management practices of community resources", but also directs the state government not to make any law which is inconsistent with these. Accepting a clear-cut role for the community, it gives wide-ranging powers to Gram Sabhas, which had hitherto been denied to them by the law makers of the country.

Backdrop of PESA, 1996

The Constitution (73rd Amendment) Act, 1992, which came into force w.e.f. 24th April, 1993, inserted in Part-IX of the constitution of India and accorded panchayats a constitutional status as institutions of local self-governance for rural India. Article-243M (1) of the constitution exempts scheduled areas and tribal areas referred to in Clause (1) and (2) of Article-244 from application of the provisions of Part-IX of the constitution. However, Article-243M (4) (b) empowers the Parliament to legislate and extend the provisions of Part-IX to scheduled areas and tribal areas referred to in clause (1), subject to such exceptions and modifications as may be specified in such law and no such law shall be deemed to be an amendment of the constitution for the purpose of Article-368.

Scheduled Areas in India are predominantly inhabited by the tribal population who have been managing their natural resources and governing social, economic and political life in their habitat through a well-knit system of ancient customs and practices. In the era of this unprecedented social change, the imperative need was felt to usher the tribals in the mainstream of development efforts without disturbing or destroying their cultural identity and socio-economic milieu to meet this challenge. The Fifth Schedule of the Constitution deals with the administration and control of scheduled areas as well as of scheduled tribes residing in any State other than the States of Assam, Meghalaya, Tripura and Mizoram.

Bhuria Committee

To achieve this objective, the Government of India constituted a committee under the chairmanship of Shri Dilip Singh Bhuria in 1994, popularly called "Bhuria Committee" to examine various dimensions of self-rule for tribals, the constitutional requirements and to make recommendations for extending the provisions of Part IX of the constitution to the scheduled areas. Important recommendations of Bhuria Committee, *inter alia*, included:

- The Gram Sabha at the hamlet/village level should exercise traditional functions such as management of land, forest, water and air.

- States should consider reorganisation of the boundaries based on ethnic, demographic and geographic considerations.
- Tribal aspirations can be satisfied if tribal regions are conferred sub-state status. Grant of autonomous district council status for districts in central Indian tribal tracts will be in the nature of sub-federalism.
- The schemes should pre-eminently be related to participative democracy, particularly at the grassroots and district levels.
- The basic lacunae in the Land Acquisition Act have to be removed. The consent of the local village community should be obligatory. The rehabilitation package should be operated with the consent of the local village community. Viable and acceptable package of livelihood should be offered as a means of rehabilitation to the affected families.
- The lower functionaries of departments/government servants posted in the autonomous districts should be under the control of the district councils.
- The economic resources should be in command of the tribal community. The districts and other councils should make appropriate laws for regulation of land and other resources for industries.

On the basis of report of Bhuria Committee submitted in 1995, the Parliament enacted the Provisions of the Panchayats (Extension to the Scheduled Areas) (PESA) Act, 1996 for its applicability to Fifth Schedule Areas as per Article 243M of the Constitution.

Salient Features of the PESA Act

- Every village shall have its own Gram Sabha. A village may consist of one or more habitations or hamlets comprising a community and managing its affairs in accordance with traditions and customs [Sec-4 (b) and Sec- 4(c)].
- Gram Sabha is "competent" to safeguard and preserve the
    - traditions and customs of the people, and their cultural identity,
    - community resources, and
    - customary mode of dispute resolution [Sec- 4(d)]

- Gram Sabha has mandatory executive functions to:
    - Approve plans, programmes and projects for social and economic development [Sec-4(e)(i)]
    - Identify persons as beneficiaries under the poverty alleviation and other Programmes [Sec- 4(e) (ii)]
    - Issue a certificate of utilisation of funds by the Panchayat for the plans; programmes and projects referred to in clause (e) above; [Sec- 4(f)]
- Powers exclusive to Gram Sabha/Panchayat at appropriate level
    - Right to mandatory consultation in land acquisition, resettlement and rehabilitation of displaced persons [Sec- 4(i)]
    - Panchayat at an appropriate level is entrusted with planning and management of minor water bodies [Sec- 4(j)]
    - Mandatory recommendations by Gram Sabha or Panchayat at appropriate level for prospective licenses/lease, concessions for mines and minerals [Sec- 4(k), (l)]
- Powers endowed to Gram Sabha and Panchayat at appropriate level to
    - Regulate sale/consumption of intoxicants [Sec- 4 (m) (i)]
    - Ownership of minor forest produce [Sec-4 (m)(v)]
    - Prevent land alienation and restore alienated land [Sec- 4(m) (iii)]
    - Manage village markets [Sec-4 (m)(iv)]
    - Control over money lending to STs [Sec-4 (m)(v)]
    - Control over institutions and functionaries in social sector, local plans including Tribal sub plans and resources [Sec- 4(m)(vi)(vii)]

This Act seeks to extend the provisions of Part-IX of the Constitution as referred to in Clause (1) of Article- 244 and calls for the Legislature of a State not to make any law under that Part (i.e. Part- IX) which is inconsistent with any of the features given under Section-4 of the act, some of the important features of which are:-

- The state legislation should be in tune with the customary law, social and religious practices and traditional management practices of community resources.

- Every Gram Sabha should be competent to safeguard and preserve the traditions and customs of the people, their cultural identity, community resources and customary mode of disputes resolution.
- Every Gram Sabha should be responsible for identification or selection of persons as beneficiaries under the poverty alleviation and other programmes.
- Every Gram Sabha should have the authority to approve the plans, programmes and projects for social and economic development before such plans, programmes and projects are taken up for implementation by the Panchayats at the village level.
- The reservation of seats in the Scheduled Areas at every Panchayat shall be in proportion to the population of the communities in that Panchayat area for whom reservation is sought to be given under Part-IX of the Constitution; Provided that the reservation for the Scheduled Tribes shall not be less than a one half of the total number of seats; Provided further that all seats of Chairpersons of Panchayats at all levels shall be reserved for the Scheduled Tribes
- The state government may nominate persons belonging to such Scheduled Tribes as have no representation in the Panchayat at the intermediate level or the Panchayat at the district level: Provided that such nomination shall not exceed one-tenth of the total members to be elected in that Panchayat.
- The Gram Sabha or the Panchayat at the appropriate level should be consulted before making acquisition of land in the Scheduled Areas and before resettling or rehabilitating persons affected by such projects in the Scheduled Areas.
- The recommendations of the Gram Sabha and the Panchayats at the appropriate level should be mandatory prior to grant of prospecting license or mining lease for minor minerals in the Scheduled Areas.
- The Gram Sabha and the Panchayats should (a) have the power to enforce prohibition or regulate or restrict the sale and consumption of any intoxicant (b) be endowed with the ownership of the minor forest produce (c) be conferred the power to prevent alienation of land in the Scheduled Areas and to take appropriate action to restore any unlawfully alienated land of the Scheduled Tribes have the power to manage village markets and exercise control over money

lending to the Scheduled Tribes have the power to exercise control over institutions and functionaries in all social sectors (d) have the power of control over local plans and resources for such plans including the Tribal sub-Plan.

It is obvious from the specific provisions of PESA Act, 1996 that the Gram Sabhas and the Panchayats have been intended to assume total responsibilities for planning and implementation of plans, programmes and projects aimed at the two objectives contained in Article-243G of the Constitution namely- (a) The preparation of plans for socio-economic development and social justice, and (b) The implementation of schemes for economic development and social justice as may be entrusted to them including those in relation to the matters listed in the Eleventh Schedule to the Constitution. However, notwithstanding the almost plenary role assigned to the Panchayats by 73rd Amendment Act and a wide range of powers given in the PESA Act, Article-243G of the Constitution and Section-4(n) of the PESA Act, Panchayats rely on the state legislatures to "endow the Panchayats with such powers and authority as may be necessary to enable them to function as institution of self- government" and "such law may contain provisions for the devolution of powers and responsibilities upon Panchayats at appropriate level". Thus, by and large, the empowerment of Panchayats rests with the state governments. Although the PESA Act, 1996 prohibits the state governments to make any law inconsistent with the provisions given in Section-4, it has been noticed that the enactments made by the state governments vary from state to state and do not strictly correspond with the provisions of PESA Act. The state governments are required to take necessary action in terms of Section-4(n) of the PESA Act to equip Panchayats with requisite powers and authority to enable them to function as institution of self-government.

In terms of the PESA Act, 1996, the Gram Sabha or the panchayats at the appropriate level are required to be consulted before making any acquisition of land and before making any arrangements for resettlement and rehabilitation of displaced persons. No such provision exists in the Land Acquisition Act, 1894, which is a colonial hangover. This is a provision, which necessitates suitable amendments in the Land Acquisition Act, 1894. On similar lines, suitable amendments are also required to be made in Indian Forest Act, 1927 to make it consistent with the provisions of PESA Act. For instance, the PESA Act confers ownership of minor forest produce on Gram Sabha and Panchayats. On the contrary, the Indian Forest Act, 1927 does not make any distinction between major and minor forest produce and vests the ownership of the entire range of forest produce in the state, meaning thereby the forest department. In view of this, there is an urgent need to bring about necessary amendments in the Land Acquisition Act, 1894 and the Indian Forest Act, 1927 to bring them in conformity with the provisions of the PESA Act to enable the effective functioning of the Gram Sabhas and Panchayats in terms of the PESA Act.

Section-4(d) of the PESA Act, 1996 provides that the legislature of a state shall not make any law on Panchayats in Scheduled Areas which is inconsistent with the traditional management practices of community resources. This implies that the natural and physical resources vest in the community and hence these resources should be managed by it as per its traditions. Some states have created legal frameworks to regulate natural resources like water, forest etc. through their regulatory authorities which are at variance with the provisions of the PESA Act. There are numerous instances where traditionally villagers have been cultivating the land which has been subsequently brought under the joint forestry management programme leading, as a consequence, to virtually converting it into forest land in the books of the forest department and as a result necessitating the demand for 'Pattas'. This has also had the effect in some Scheduled Areas of wiping away the traditional forest village systems. It is necessary that the state legislation on panchayats should conform to the customary law, social and religious practices and traditional management practices of community resources.

Fifth and Sixth Schedules of the Constitution

The Constitutional and legal history of the formation of scheduled areas in India can be traced back to the colonial period. While the policy of the British government was solely directed and dominated by the colonial interests, it was based on isolation and exploitation of the tribals. Since the policy favoured the vested interests, i.e. non-tribal landlords, contractors and moneylenders, they not only took possession of tribal's land, but also brought the tribals in uninterrupted bondage. Such encroachments on tribals' right in land and forest led to the expression of anger in the form of tribal uprising in many places. While British used force to contain the unrest among the tribal population, to deal with the tribal unrest on a long-term basis, they evolved special laws for administering the tribal areas and to protect their interests, as they were culturally and economically different from the neighbouring peasant communities.

Accordingly, a number of acts such as Scheduled Tracts Act 1870, Scheduled Districts Act 1874 and the Government of India Act 1919 were enacted by the British Parliament wherein areas with large concentration of tribals were segregated and isolated for separately dealing with the problems of the tribal people. While the 'backward tracts' declared under the Government of India Act 1919 were nothing but the same as those of 'scheduled tracts' and 'scheduled districts' with certain additions and omissions, in the name of helping the tribals with special protections, the Government of India Act 1935 was brought in providing for the creation of 'excluded' and 'partially excluded' areas with separate political representation for the tribes.

Under the Government of India Act 1935, while the popularly elected governments took charge of the administration of the provinces, in the 'excluded' area the Governor functioned in his own discretion. In the case of 'partially excluded' areas, the governor functioned with the advice of his ministry. Since the North-Eastern tribal region was considered very backward, they were wholly excluded from the scope of the normal laws and the central or provincial legislature had no power to make laws. Only the Governor-in-Council had powers to legislate for the administration of these areas. In the second category of backward areas, which were classified as 'partially excluded' areas, the governor was vested with power to enforce or refrain from enforcing any provincial enactments.

These provisions were continued even after independence by incorporating them in the Constitution, of course with some modifications. While the wholly excluded areas were incorporated into the sixth schedule covering states of Assam, Meghalaya, Tripura and Mizoram in the North East, the fifth schedule of the Constitution covered the tribal areas of the rest of the country. Currently, the fifth schedule covers tribal areas in nine states of India namely Andhra Pradesh, Odisha, Jharkhand, Chhatishgarh, Madhya Pradesh, Maharashtra, Gujarat, Rajasthan and Himachal Pradesh.

Article-244 of the Constitution envisage two categories of Tribal Areas, namely:

i. Fifth Schedule: for the administration and control of the Scheduled Areas and Scheduled Tribes in any State other than the (States of Assam, Meghalaya, Tripura and Mizoram)

ii. Sixth Schedule: for the administration of Tribal Areas in the States of Assam, Meghalya, Tripura and Mizoram.

The Schedule-V areas covering nine states are characterized by poverty, illiteracy, weak infrastructure and deprivations in general. Given the vulnerability of the people, Schedule-V of the Constitution makes special provisions such as: (a) Report by Governor to the President regarding the administration of these areas, (b) Tribes Advisory Council to advise Governor on matters pertaining to the welfare and advancement of the STs, (c) Direction by Governor through public notification that any particular act of parliament or of the state legislature shall or shall not apply to a Scheduled Area or any part thereof, (d) Governor to make regulations for the peace and good government, (e) Union Government to give direction to the State as to the administration of these areas.

Novelity in Fifth Schedule to the Constitution

The main features of the Fifth Schedule include:

- Governor's Report to the President.
- Tribes Advisory Council.
- Special Legislative Powers of the Governor.
- President's Power to declare and redefine the Scheduled Areas

Fifth Schedule (Cl. 3) of the Constitution provides that the Governor of each state having Scheduled Areas should annually or whenever required so by the President make a report to the President, to keep the Union Government informed of the administration in Scheduled Areas. On the basis of this Report, the Union Government is to issue directives to the respective state governments for better administration of the Scheduled Areas.

As learnt from the information gathered from Ministry of Tribal Affairs, GoI in response to an RTI application by Mr.Venkatesh Nayak of CHRI, New Delhi, the Governors of the concerned states including Odisha have been sending annual reports to the President on administration of Scheduled Areas, if not on a regular basis. But hardly the members of public are in the know of the contents of such reports, and conversely, the Union Government also hardly took any action on such reports.

The Fifth Schedule under Article-244(1) of Constitution defines "Scheduled Areas" as such areas as the President may by order declare to be scheduled areas after consultation with the Governor of that State. The criteria for declaring any area as a "Scheduled Area" under the Fifth Schedule are:

(i) Preponderance of tribal population,

(ii) Compactness and reasonable size of the area,

(iii) A viable administrative entity such as a district, block or taluk, and, Economic backwardness of the area as compared to neighbouring areas.

The purpose and advantages of an area being declared as Scheduled Areas are as follows:

- The Governor of a State, which has Scheduled Areas, is empowered to make regulations in respect of the following:
  i. Prohibit or restrict transfer of land from tribals;
  ii. Regulate the business of money lending to the members of Scheduled Tribes in making any such regulation, the Governor may repeal or amend any Act of parliament or of the Legislature of the State, which is applicable to the area in question.
- The Governor may, by public notification, direct that any particular Act of Parliament or of the Legislature of the state shall not apply to a Scheduled Area or any part thereof in the state or shall apply to such area subject to such exceptions and modifications as he may specify.
- The Governor of a state having Scheduled Areas therein, shall annually, or whenever so required by the President of India, make a report to the President regarding the administration of the Scheduled Areas in that state and the executive power of the Union shall extend to the giving of directions to the State as to the administration of the said area.
- Tribes Advisory Council (TAC) shall be established in states having Scheduled Areas. The TAC may also be established in any state having Scheduled Tribes but not Scheduled Areas on the direction of the President of India. The TAC consists of not more than twenty members of whom, as nearly as may be, three fourth are from the representatives of Scheduled Tribes in the Legislative Assembly of the state. The role of TAC is to advise the state government on matters pertaining to the welfare and advancement of the Scheduled Tribes in the state as may be referred to it by the Governor.
- The provisions of the Panchayats (Extension to Scheduled Areas) Act, 1996, vide which the provisions of Panchayats, contained in

Part-IX of the Constitution, were extended to Scheduled Areas also contains special provisions for the benefit of Scheduled Tribes.

In contrast, the Sixth Schedule has always given the tribes considerable autonomy. This Schedule divides the tribal areas in India's north-eastern states into "autonomous" regions, each allocated to a particular tribe. The elected councils in the Sixth Schedule areas are vested with administrative authority, make laws with respect to a variety of subjects and even exercise judicial authority through traditional legal systems embedded with certain features of federal law. The councils are also financially independent and do not labour under the executive authority of the states. Though the Sixth Schedule's scheme renders all exercise of executive and legislative authority by the councils subject to the approval of the provincial Governor, the superior courts have interpreted the Governor's authority to be considerably restricted.

Gram Sabha and Gram Panchayat under the PESA

There are three partners in governance in the Scheduled Ares, namely, the community in the form of Gram Sabha, Panchayats and the State. While Panchayats are formal entities created by the State, the Gram Sabha in the Scheduled Areas as envisaged in PESA is basically a self-created, self-defined and self-managing institution with minimal formal provisions to accord it a legal identity. In this frame, therefore, the position of Gram Sabha is unique and supreme.

The community at the village level in the form of Gram Sabha in the Scheduled Areas is fundamental in the governance at that level under the Constitution. Therefore, all institutions including Panchayats and the State itself are expected to assist the Gram Sabha. This would require fine-tuning between the powers and jurisdiction of different authorities. For example, PESA envisages that the powers in respect of vital matters like prevention of alienation of land and restoration of unlawfully alienated land, control over money-lending and enforcement of prohibition shall be assigned to Panchayats at the appropriate level and the Gram Sabha. The conjunctive use of the two terms in this provision, however, cannot be deemed to place Panchayats and Gram Sabha at the same pedestal. Similarly, Section-4(i) envisages that 'the Gram Sabha or Panchayat at the appropriate level shall be consulted before making the acquisition of land in the Scheduled Areas…' The use of term 'or' in this clause cannot affect the inclusive character of the jurisdiction of the Gram Sabha. In this situation, therefore, if a State decides to exclude the concerned Gram Sabhas from the consultation process before acquisition of land by taking advantage of the term 'or' in the clause, it will go against the spirit of PESA in general. Moreover, such a step in particular will destroy the harmonious construct of PESA by ignoring the superseding provision about 'competence' of the Gram Sabha as a self-governing body as envisaged in Section-4(d).

It may be noted at this stage that extra caution has been exercised in PESA itself under Section-4 (n) to avoid any confusion. It envisages that the State Legislature, while 'endowing' powers on the Panchayats, has to ensure that 'Panchayats at the higher level do not assume the powers and authority of any Panchayats at the lower level or the Gram Sabha'. The powers of Gram Sabha are plenary and inclusive. Therefore, the powers that Panchayat at any level, be it village, intermediate or district, may be endowed with, cannot be inconsistent with that basic premise. They must be so construed so as to be supportive to the role of Gram Sabha. Once all partners in governance are clear about the basic objective of PESA and are imbued with its spirit, the differences in their perception about their respective roles will wear out.

Powers of Gram Sabha/Panchayats at appropriate level under PESA Act

India adopted the path of planned economic development in the frame of a mixed economy with the State as the senior partner enjoying in addition the authority to direct. The State was charged with a special responsibility for the Scheduled Tribes and the Scheduled Areas. Even though the general frame of planned economic development has been miserably destabilized in the wake of globalization and liberalization, the State's role in respect of the Scheduled Tribes and the Scheduled Areas has become still more tedious in the face of natural market forces let loose in the national economy. PESA attempted to vest legislative powers in the Gram Sabha, specifically in matters relating to development planning, management of natural resources and negotiation of disputes in accordance with prevalent traditions and customs. This significant legislation is expected to have far reaching consequences in the social, economic and cultural life of tribal people in scheduled areas. The Gram Sabha has been made the soul of PESA

The Gram Sabhas under PESA are deemed to be 'competent' to safeguard and preserve the traditions of their people, community resources and customary mode of dispute resolution. The Gram Sabhas further have:

- Right to mandatory consultation in land acquisition, resettlement and rehabilitation of displaced persons
- Planning and management of minor water bodies
- Mandatory recommendations for prospective licenses/lease for mines and concession for the exploitation of minor minerals
- Regulate sale/consumption of intoxicants
- Ownership of Minor Forest Produces
- Prevent land alienation and restore alienated land
- Manage village markets
- Control over money lending to STs
- Control over institutions and functionaries in social sector, local plans including tribal sub plans and resources

Administrative Management in Scheduled Areas

Article-339 of the Constitution relates to control of the Union over the administration of Scheduled Areas and the welfare of Scheduled Tribes. This Article provides that:

- The President may at any time and shall, at the expiration of ten years from the commencement of this Constitution by order appoint a Commission to report on the administration of the Scheduled Areas and the welfare of the Scheduled Tribes in the states. The order may define the composition, powers and procedure of the commission and may contain such incidental or ancillary provisions, as the President may consider necessary or desirable.
- The executive power of the Union shall extend to the giving of directions to a state as to the drawing up and execution of schemes specified in the direction to be essential for the welfare of the Scheduled Tribes in the state. In pursuance of the provisions of this Article, the first Scheduled Areas and Scheduled Tribes Commission were set up in 1960 under the Chairmanship of Shri U.N. Dhebar. The second such Commission was set up vide order dated 18th July, 2002 under the Chairmanship of Shri Dileep Singh Bhuria, Ex-MP (with ten other Members) (popularly known as Bhuria Commission) with a view to give a further thrust to the welfare and development of Scheduled Tribes. The Commission submitted its report to the President on 16 July, 2004.

Democratic Governance and PESA

PESA is constructed around the Gandhian concept of Gram Swaraj, the governance frame for the village republics. Gandhi's dream was included in the Constitution as Article-40, which came alive only when PESA was adopted. While the 73rd Amendment, which inserted Article-243, made the terms Gram (village) and Gram Sabha (village assembly) a part of the Constitution for the first time, PESA gave shape to the concept of self governance through empowerment of the Gram Sabha by constitutional recognition.

PESA is based on the cardinal principle of governance that human communities are the best agency to handle most of their survival challenges, manage their affairs and progress towards growing emancipation through the instrumentality of participatory deliberative democracy. Hence the first substantive section of PESA begins with the legal presumption that the 'Gram Sabha' is 'competent' and calls upon the state governments to ensure legal, procedural and administrative empowerment as a means of deepening democracy. The cardinal principal that underlies PESA has two corollaries in relation to development namely a) any community can best decipher advancement and modernity when it is grounded in the strength of its own culture and way of life and b) can negotiate both advancement and modernity only when it is founded on the bedrock of its own culture and way of life. PESA therefore seeks to restore to tribal communities the right of self governance (swaraj); what they had fought for in pre independence period, looked forward to as unfolding of independence (azadi) and believed was restored to them when the first Prime Minister of independent India declared the Panchsheel Policy for the development of the tribal people.

PESA is built around six facets of democratization as the means to rebuild swaraj the tribal areas. The first facet is self determination by a community of its human and administrative boundaries. 4(b) makes the first departure from a colonial administrative frame where the state authorities determined the locus and boundaries of a village, by providing that the 'village' is a habitation or a group of habitation or a hamlet or a group of hamlets comprising a community and managing its affairs in accordance with traditions and customs. A 'pre-existing' self governing community determines the character of a 'village' while 4(b) provides legal status. 4(b) therefore predicates a procedural and administrative departure from the frame of Panchayati Raj laws, a departure in some respects reflective of the progression from representative to participatory democracy.

The second facet of swaraj is the competency of the Gram Sabha to take safeguard and care for the interests of its members, preserve its natural and human resources, its material and non material culture and ensure peace and well being, expressed in 4(d) of PESA is founded on deliberative consensus based decision making by the people functioning through the village assembly. This aspect, however, predicates a face to face community provided for in 4(b) and a tradition of consensus based self governing institution, the stronger the institution the greater its reach and efficacy.

The third facet is the legal enablement of the community to negotiate development and modernity founded on the basis of appreciation of its own culture and traditions. This facet articulated in 4(e) makes the community the deliberative and deciding agency in determining plans, programs, selecting beneficiaries and monitoring resources 4(m)(vii) while the PRIs are its executive agency. In making the PRIs its executive agency, PESA ensures democracy at the grassroots as the PRIs remain accountable to the people as a condition of deepening democracy.

The fourth facet is the obligation on the state to recognize the competence of the community to takes steps to remedy its own ills and curb its own exploitation as required by 4(m) and ensure legal and procedural instrumentalities for the Gram Sabha to take efficacious measures to control alcohol, restore alienated lands, control money lending and curb market exploitation.

The fifth facet is the accountability of the executive to the legislative or deciding body-the Gram Sabha. PESA provides for the accountability of PRI members and functionaries for execution of plans and implementation of programs determined by the Gram Sabha 4(e) or for monies utilized 4(f) or the various personnel charged with the duty of ensuring the welfare of the people 4(m)(vi).

The sixth and significant facet is the guarantee of 'supremacy' of the Gram Sabha in the exercise of its powers as provided in 4(n) which stipulates the fundamental principle of administration in a democratic frame, but which was bypassed through the Westminster pattern of democracy. In a nutshell; accountability is to the people and not to the superior official. The facet is the recognition of the fundamentals of democracy – that is power inheres in the people and any power exercised by a 'superior' authority is the power granted by the people and no superior body can assume the powers of the people unless they have been conferred specifically by the people. PESA sought to pave the way for a vibrant and mature democracy.

PESA and Mungekar Committee

Mungekar Committee, a standing committee on inter-sectoral issues relating to tribal development on raising standards of administration in tribal areas.The most sensitive aspect of tribal life is self-governance. Even the British were forced to recognise and reconcile themselves to this fact. That is why they resorted to the creation of 'excluded areas'. They however succeeded in penetrating some tribal areas secretly by entering into some agreements with them and extending the British-made laws to these areas. These areas came to be known as the 'Partially excluded areas'. In 1950, with the adoption of the Constitution, all laws of the centre and concerned states got extended to the 'Scheduled Areas' (Partially Excluded Areas) in routine. This was a qualitative change in the legal regime in the tribal areas which happened after India attained independence. However, according to the committee, several fallouts occurring in a reverse direction were noticed across the country, such as -

- There was no place in the new Indian legal regime for the tribal community and the system of self-governance according its customs and traditions.
- The traditional frame of 'community ownership and individual use' went into the oblivion. The community resources were transformed into state resource with some concessions, or at best right to use, albeit at the will of the state;thus, the tribal got stripped of his/her protective shield of community, the very essence of his/her 'being'. He/She was obliged to face the unknown world all alone;
- The claim of the people over land and other resources got confined to what were acknowledged by the state in the form of pattas in favour of individuals, severally or collectively, in respect of specific areas.
- Even the actual possession of land had to be ratified by a prescribed procedure failing which the concerned person would be deemed as an encroacher;
- The symbiotic relationship between the people and their habitat including land, water and forest was disrupted;

- The extensive resources in the traditional territorial expanse of the tribal people including some of those in their possession and in active use for sustenance, thus, came under public domain that could be dealt with by the state or even other interested parties using the provisions of relevant laws, or even otherwise, depending on the situation in each case;
- All practices sanctified by the ancient tradition, which formed the basis of the tribal system of self-governance, were transformed into acts of 'violation of the law of the land' rendering the people vulnerable and virtually defenseless;
- It rendered tribal people resource-less, vulnerable and virtually defenseless;
- In the face of other legal claims it resulted in 'criminalisation' of the tribal community' and also to the de jure 'loss of command' over their resources for the tribal communities.
- Unfortunately all concerned, including the Governors, having full powers to adapt laws, remained virtually unaware about this tragic transformation;
- In sum the simple tribal was obliged under the law to approach some authority or other out somewhere there in the unknown wide world beyond. The situation has been worsening incessantly.

Dealing with the background to enactment of PESA, the Mungekar Committee observed that the Directive Principles of State Policy (Article-40 of the Constitution) envisaged organisation of 'Village Panchayats' as virtual 'Village Republics' through 'Panchayati Raj'. However, it was forgotten by the administrators and law makers that the tribal people had a strong functioning system of self-governance. This was so notwithstanding its non-recognition under the formal system. This omission has had adverse and devastating consequences. The community was greatly handicapped in facing the new situation that had resulted in serious unrest through out tribal India. The idea of 'Panchayati Raj' was resurrected in 1980s in search of an alternative for the dysfunctional politico-administrative system that has been incessantly running down. In the debate that followed about the structure of Panchayati Raj it was realised that any attempt to superimpose a formal system of Panchayats on tribals would lead to further accentuation of the confrontation. Accordingly a historic decision was taken by the

Government of India in 1988 not to extend the general scheme of Panchayats to the Scheduled Areas (SA).

PESA and Central Government

The Union Government took an impressive lead in attending the crucial issue of administration of SA in 1990s. Ministry of Rural Development dealing with tribal affairs has remained totally silent about PESA, for the simple reason that it was not an item in its duty-chart. The Ministry of Home Affairs that deals with SA, according to the Rules of Business, has no concern on this legal front. Even the formation of a separate ministry for the charge of Panchayats has made no difference even though PESA looms large in its agenda. The incongruity is that the ministry is still battling with the legal status of PESA and its real scope. The fact is that PESA confers specific powers upon GS in SA has been virtually ignored.

Only two ministries cared to issue guidelines to the states in 1997 with regard to two items in PESA. One was about the role of GS in land acquisition by the Ministry of Rural Development and the other related to its role before granting of leases for minor minerals by the Ministry of Mining and Minerals. There has been total silence ever since about the holistic frame of PESA in the entire establishment. There is hardly any realisation in the Union Government that implementation of PESA has to be a collaborative effort of almost all central ministries, in keeping with the policy that had been formally adopted in early 1970s in the Tribal Sub-Plan Strategy.

The Ramchandran Committee (Planning at the grass root Level: March, 2006, New Delhi) laid stress on the duties of the central government to ensure that PESA is effectively and correctively implemented in the fifth scheduled areas. PESA casts direct responsibility on the state legislature but being a central legislation and logical extension of the fifth schedule, a duty is cast on the central government to see that the provisions are strictly implemented. A critical issue in the implementation of PESA is to harmonize its provisions with those of the central legislations concerned and also recast relevant policies and schemes of central ministries/departments. According to available information, no integrative exercise has yet taken place to examine the relevance of different central laws to Schedule-V areas and to harmonize them with the aims and objectives of the PESA. The Land Acquisition Act, 1894, Mines and Minerals (Development and Regulation) Act, 1957, The Forest Act, 1927, The Forest Conservation

Act, 1980 and The Indian Registration Act are among the laws which warrant particular attention in this context. Besides, The National Policy on Resettlement and Rehabilitation of Project Affected Persons, 2007, National Water Policy, 2002, National Minerals Policy, 2008, and National Forest Policy, 2004 would require detailed examination from the viewpoint of ensuring compliance to the provisions of PESA.

PESA and Panchayats

The provisions about Panchayats, especially the district panchayat in the SA of Part-IX read with PESA are transitory. PESA places special responsibility on the SL with regard to redefining the role of panchayats at the district level, drawing upon the provisions of the sixth schedule in that regard. Section-4(o) of PESA envisages that: "The state legislature shall endeavour to maintain the pattern of the sixth schedule to the constitution while designing the administrative arrangements in the panchayats at the district level in the scheduled areas". Accordingly the roles and responsibilities of Panchayats, even at the intermediate level may undergo qualitative change. It may be mentioned here that demand for converting Fifth Schedule Areas into Sixth Schedule Areas has been raised far and wide.

The basic objective of the special provision in PESA about adopting the pattern of the Sixth Schedule at the district (level quoted) above is to facilitate structural transformation in higher-level panchayats, once the foundation has been laid at the village level. There is no point in going into detailed consideration of this provision because the associated structural change at the district level, as envisaged in Section-4(o), in the real sense can be planned on the firm foundation of the system of 'PESA Governance' at the village level. Any attempt to create a superstructure without laying the foundation can prove to be dysfunctional.

PESA and the Community

The community at the village level was excluded from the general legal framework adopted by the British in India beginning with 1860s. The objective was clear, viz., 'Break the community so that the authority of the imperial regime remains unchallenged.' The tribal tradition of self-governance during this period, however, remained largely undisturbed in the face of their persistent resistance against the intruders. This continued till the adoption of the Indian Constitution. The colonial legal frame got inadvertently superimposed, as it was, on the tribal people living in hitherto excluded areas. This unintentional action of the state has rendered the tribal people totally helpless in dealing with the outside world. This paradigm of governance would have been totally transformed into a non-centralised frame if PESA had been honestly implemented. The Act begins with redefining the village in terms of habitations that comprise a 'community' and accepting 'the competence of the community' to manage its affairs .

According to Section 4(b) of PESA: 'a village shall ordinarily consist of a habitation or a group of habitations or a hamlet or a group of hamlets comprising a community and managing its affairs in accordance with traditions and customs.' Thus, PESA accepts that the 'village' essentially comprises a functioning 'community'. The members of this community at the village level, albeit 'whose names are included in the electoral rolls'; together constitute the formal legal entity 'Gram Sabha'. Thus, in the new frame of governance the formal 'village' of PESA and the organic 'community' comprising the village become congruous. Thus Gram Sabha (GS) in a village in general areas comprises merely individuals whose names are recorded in the voter list of the concerned Panchayat. There is no mention about the community, if any.

There is a basic difference between the Gram Sabha (GS) as specified in PESA for the SA and 'Gram Sabha' in general areas. The provisions in Articles-40 and 243G concerning panchayats or even in Article-243A in the case of GS in general areas envisage 'endowment of powers as may be necessary to enable them to function as institutions of self-government'. There is a paradigm shift in Section-4(d) of PESA. It does not envisage 'endowment of powers' as in general areas, but simply acknowledges the 'competence' of the GS to manage all its affairs in accordance with its customs and traditions. Thus: 'Every Gram Sabha shall be competent to safeguard and preserve the traditions and the customs of the people, their cultural identity, community, resources and the customary mode of dispute resolution.'

PESA and Extremism

The Schedule-V areas to which PESA extends are characterized by a high degree of poverty, lack of infrastructure, illiteracy, exploitation and marginalization. Out of 94 PESA districts, 32 are also Extremist Affected Districts (EADs). The major causes of extremism in these areas are indifference to the needs of the people in governance, distress caused by land alienation and displacement (loss of land, livelihood, collective identity, culture) and lack of control over local resources. People- centric governance and people centric planning & implementation in these areas is essential for containing Left Wing Extremism, and can be brought about through the implementation of PESA in letter and spirit. This point has been emphasized in the seventh report of the Second Administrative Reforms Commission, 'Capacity Building for Conflict Resolution', the report of the expert group constituted by the Planning Commission on 'Development Challenges in Extremist Affected Areas' and the Standing Committee on inter-sectoral issues relating to tribal development on raising standards of administration in tribal areas (known as Mungekar Committee)".

PESA and the Minor Forest Products (MFPs)

India, for its wide ranging environmental regime and diverse biological communities, has been recognised as one of the world's top twelve 'megadiversity' nations. India's forest extend over 22.73 per cent of the total geographical area measuring 0.75 million sq.km. Of the nearly 425 families of flowering plants in the world, 328 families with 21000 species occur in India. From this varied emporium, over 3000 species of tress and plants common in India provide a range of useful commodities other than timber and fuelwood. These commodities have been traditionally referred to as Minor Forest Products (MFPs).

The Section-4(m-ii) of PESA Act 1996 has enjoined upon the State legislature to entrust both Grama Sabha and Panchayat at appropriate level with the ownership of minor forest produce. Though various state governments paid insincerity to this mandate through their respective compliance amendments, the situation at grassroots level has registered no improvement favouring the communities in PESA areas. The MoEF constituted an expert committee to define ownership, which recommended that "ownership means revenue from sale of usufructory rights, i.e. the right to net revenue after retaining the administrative expenses of the department and not right to control." The case of Andhra Pradesh is even more interesting. It gave ownership rights to the Van Suraksha Samitis (VSS, forest protection committees) with respect to all Non-Wood Forest Products (NWFPs) for which Girijan Cooperative Corporation (GCC) did not hold the monopoly rights. Similarly, there is no clarity on the issue of "community resource." The states have their own interpretations and legislations. While Odisha and Andhra Pradesh are silent about what constitutes community resource, Madhya Pradesh has defined it as land, water, and forest. This implies that the powers given by PESA to exercise rights over community resources are almost nonexistent in many states.

The Gujarat Act has vested in the Village Panchayat minor forest produce found (except found in the areas of National Parks or Sanctuaries) in such area of a forest as is situated in the jurisdiction of that village. This essentially means that while the ownership rights have been granted but the area on which such resources exist is exempt. The Himachal Pradesh Act provides that the 'Gram Panchayat or as the case may be Gram Sabha' shall have the ownership of minor forest produce within the local area of the Gram Sabha. Again which tier has been granted the ownership is not clear and what constitutes local area is ambiguous.

The Maharashtra Act, empowers the Gram Sabha in the Scheduled Areas to issue direction to the Panchayat with regard to the exploitation and regulation of trading of minor forest produce, subject to provisions of the Maharashtra Transfer of Ownership of Minor Forest Produce in the Scheduled Areas and the Maharashtra Minor Forest Produce (Regulation of Trade) (Amendment) Act, 1997. However, it does not transfer ownership. In 2012, it has come out with the instruction for stopping Maharahstra Forest Development Corporation from procuring MFP in scheduled areas.Although the central act leaves no room for doubt that reserve forests should be considered community resources under the purview of PESA; the official assumption is that reserve forests are out of the PESA domain. For instance, the NTFP Policy of 2000 in Odisha restricts the Panchayat's control over minor forest produce in reserve forests.

It says that the Gram Panchayats shall not have any control over minor forest produce collected from the reserve forests whereas the PESA, in its spirit, sought to extend ownership of forests to any forest located in the vicinity of the village that the people had been traditionally accessing. The policy-makers knew very well that it would be foolish to create such a distinction because it was almost impossible to differentiate between produce collected from reserve forests and that from others. Nevertheless, they went ahead with putting in place the proviso that reserve forests cannot come under the purview of PESA because the relevant laws laid down that no rights can exist in the reserve forest area.

The Standing Committee on Social Justice and Empowerment (2005-2006) constituted to look into the grants in aid to State Development

Cooperative Corporations for Minor Forest Produce noted that there is no uniformity in fixing the price of MFPs amongst the states. Generally, the district authorities fix the price of the MFPs through their Price Fixation Committees in consultation with the relevant bodies, including the representative from the STDCCs/FDCs, etc. However, the details of the price fixation committees are not available with eh ministry as well as TRIFED. The committee desired that members of tribal community should also be represented in the Price Fixation Committees proportionately and the state should adopt (as far as possible) common minimum prices for the minor forest produce of the trials and urge the ministry to pursue the matter with the states so that the issue is resolved and implanted at the earliest.

The Committee expressed serious concern over the fact that minimum support price is not available for the MFPs of the tribals as is available for other commodities in the agriculture sector through agriculture Price Commission. TRIFED has taken up the issue with the Ministry of Agriculture as well but they are yet to respond to the proposal. The committee feels that there is an urgent need to bring the minor forest produce under the ambit of minimum support price as they are the main source of livelihood and income for a majority of the tribal people. The committee, therefore, urge the ministry to earnestly pursue the nodal ministry, i.e. Ministry of Environment and Forests and also the Ministry of Agriculture to fix minimum support prices for the MFPs of the tribals, in consultation with concerned state governments so that the tribals could get proper value for the forest produce collected by them.

Shri A K Sharma Committee report on issues relating to Minor Forest Procuce in PESA states admitted that though most of PESA States have made the compliance amendment to the concerned laws and regulations in respect of minor forest produce, however at ground level the Grama Sabhas didn't enjoy real power over minor forest produce nor did the net benefits of MFP trade flow to the tribal and forest dwelling communities in the Scheduled Areas.

Gram Sabha and MFP

- One or more additional Gram Sabhas, in consultation with the forest department may decide the minimum purchase price for the minor forest produces or exchange rates for other commodities such as chiraunji and salt.

- Gram Sabha may determine the royalty payable by the collector/ trader on minor forest produce. This amount will be deposited in Gram Sabha Kosh.
- It will be mandatory to give details to Gram Sabha before taking any minor forest produce outside the area of the Gram Sabha collected by any department or institution on the basis of any act, rule or administrative instructions and obtain clearance from it for the same.
- For meeting the requirements of the villages such as grazing, fuel wood, making houses and ploughs, Gram Sabha will chalk out a minor forest scheme for the use of forest resources used traditionally by the people in consultation with the concerned forest officers. Under this scheme every person will be able to use the resources after getting permission letter from the RPMC.
- Gram Sabha may make rules to ensure that the interest of the poor persons for picking up the fuel wood and livelihood are protected.
- Gram Sabha may chalk out suitable programmes to conserve the forest, improve the environment and enhance employment at local level in their respective areas.
- Gram Sabha is competent to make enquiries, despite the departmental permit, about the wood or the forest produce passing through their areas.
- If there is a doubt of illegal operations on enquiry, Gram Sabha is competent to stop it on the spot.
- If the state government organizes the trade of any minor forest produce in order to protect tribal interests, that trade will be treated as trade carried out on behalf of people.
- But prior approval of the Gram Sabha will be needed for the proposed arrangement. On the basis of suggestions of the Gram Sabha, necessary changes may be carried out.
- In the above trade, Gram Sabha and the collectors will have complete right over net profit.

The Ministry of Panchayati Raj, Govt. of India, set up a committee to make recommendations on the ownership, price fixation, value addition and marketing of the MFP. The committee made the following recommendations. The report, which was submitted on 11th May 2011, has suggested that a Central Price Fixation Commission be set up to set Minimum Support Prices (MSP) for 14 economically important minor forest produce. It also makes recommendations concerning the transformation of minor forest produce trade in order to induce fair pricing mechanisms and suggests ways and measures for making state agencies more viable. These recommendations are particularly important because the revenue potential of minor forest produce is much higher than timber, especially in states like Odisha, Chhattisgarh, Jharkhand and Andhra Pradesh, which, together with Madhya Pradesh, account for nearly 90 per cent of its production and sale, most of which was done to large industry through a multi-layered trading system. In 2010, such produce was estimated to be supporting at least 275 million people, of which more than 80 per cent were tribal people.

Fixation of Minimum Support Price (MSP) of MFP

The Committee recommends that a Minimum Support Price (MSP) be provided to gatherers by government agencies. In general, while government agencies would be obliged to buy MFP at the designated MSP, gatherers of MFP would be free to sell the same elsewhere if they get better prices. This would ensure a basic minimum income for MFP gatherers and would minimize trader exploitation. In particular, the MSP would provide critical support to gatherers living in areas with poor access, as it is in these areas that trader exploitation is most rampant. These are also areas where livelihood opportunities are limited and consequently the dependence on MFP is the greatest.

The MSP for major MFPs would have to be fixed at the national level. The Committee has considered the possibility of fixing of MSP by state level agencies. The argument in favour of state level agencies fixing MSP has been that the MSP can be fixed depending on local factors such as quality of produce. However, the committee is of the opinion that if the MSP varies from state to state, there would be a great deal of cross state movement of MFPs in order to get better prices, and this would be counter-productive. Notably, in case of agricultural produce too, the quality varies, but a central MSP is determined which can be varied taking into account the variations in quality. The committee therefore recommends that the MSP for major MFPs be fixed centrally. As there are a very large number of MFPs in existence, the MSP may initially be fixed for the 14 most important MFPs in terms of livelihoods and value, namely bamboo, tendu leaf, tamarind, mahuwa flower, mahuwa seed, sal seed, myrobalan, chironji, lac, gum karaya, honey and seeds of karnaja, neem and puwad. As soon as possible, MSP may also be fixed for other MFPs.

Agency for Fixing MSP of MFP

- A National agency i.e. a Central Price Fixation Commission would have to be set up or designated to fix MSP for important MFPs with TRIFED functioning as its technical support wing. The commission should comprise one chairperson who will be an expert in the field of tribal and rural development and three other members having experience in the relevant field. The broad functions of the commission would be the following:
    - Fixation of Minimum Support Price as bench-mark and setting quality standards.
    - Formulation of broad guidelines for effective implementation of the MSP scheme.
    - Monitoring and evaluation of the aforementioned scheme; suggesting corrective measures from time to time.
- While fixing MSP for each crop season, the commission shall have in-depth consultations with the Ministry of Tribal Affairs (MoTA), Ministry of Panchayati Raj, Ministry of Environment & Forests, Department of AYUSH, tribal leaders from all the concerned regions, representatives of national level merchant/trade and industry associations dealing with MFP and state level agencies like the GCC, GFDC, MP MFP Federation, MSCTDC, etc. The administrative Ministry for the Commission will be MoTA.
- TRIFED can work as a technical support unit of the Central Price Fixation Commission and assist the commission by providing relevant information like estimated production potential, crop seasons, list of haats where tribals bring the MFP for sale, trend in prices (haats, terminal/retail market of MFP items) etc., providing quality standards/specifications of designated MFPs and formulating guidelines for procurement, storage and disposal, and other forms of technical support.

PESA and Water Resources Management

Sub-section 4(k) of PESA envisages that 'planning and management of minor water bodies shall be entrusted to Panchayats at the appropriate level'.This provision, however, does not affect the plenary powers of Gram Sabha concerning community resources which include water in its totality. While specific provisions may be made for 'minor water bodies, the larger water bodies must be managed in keeping with the plenary powers of Gram Sabha. As per the central PESA, the power to plan and manage 'minor water bodies' exclusively vested with the Panchayat at Appropriate Level (PAL), which in other words means that the central law gives a discretion to the states to assign to any tier of the local self government such power in the best interest of the community. However, the first obstacle is the definition itself. No legal definition of minor water bodies exists in the statute books. There is a high degree of variation in its operationalisation in states such as Gujarat, Himachal Pradesh and Maharashtra. This ambiguous power devolution becomes critical as there are a number of externally aided projects on water sheds and water users. The Participatory Irrigation Management laws enacted in states such as Rajasthan and Maharashtra, for instance, where Water Users Associations have been created, and Water Shed Committees that have been created in states such as Madhya Pradesh and Andhra Pradesh, have no linkage with the local self government units and more so in scheduled areas or tribal dominated areas. This in reality dilutes the powers of PESA. The ideal situation should be as follows.

- The management and use of water resources will be such that these are kept intact for future generations, and all the villagers have equal rights over this resource.
- Water bodies within a Gram Panchayat will be managed by the Gram Panchayat, those extending to more than one Gram Panchayat by the Block Panchayat and those extending to more than one Block Panchayat by Zilla Panchayat.
- The Gram Panchayat or the Block or District Panchayat as the case may be, after consulting the Gram Sabha, keeping in view its traditions and the spirit of prevalent laws, will regulate the use of available water in the village for various purposes and also decide about the priority of use.
- It will be mandatory for panchayats at all levels to consult the RPMC or the Gram consensus before taking any decision regarding water body.

PESA provides that local communities in Scheduled Areas should be entitled to manage minor water bodies a statutorily undefined term. While states would typically follow administrative guidelines setting out the rules for managing such water bodies, the difficulty is that the directives identify a "minor water body based on acreage rather th an territorial jurisdiction and traditional use patterns of the tribal communities.

The problems are compounded when some states either devolve management responsibilities without ascertaining community needs or neglect to pass new laws. The contrasting actions taken by the states of Madhya Pradesh and Maharashtra are noteworthy; while the state of Madhya Pradesh in central India swiftly and properly delineated rules for the use of minor water bodies in Scheduled Areas. The Maharashtra legislature entrusted management of minor water bodies to local governments, but left the actual determination of authority amongst the tiers of local government to the absolute discretion of the state executive.

PESA and Mining Lease for Minor Minerals

The Gram Sabha must be convened or the full body of the Panchayat and the compensation, resettlement and rehabilitation package discussed, delineated and chalked out to the mutual satisfaction of all parties under the supervision of the representatives of the District Collector and the commissioner Tribal Development.

Under the Section-4(i) PESA Act, it is mandatory to have recommendation of Gram Sabha and Panchayat at appropriate level prior to grant of prospecting licence or mining lease for minor minerals and for grant of concession for the exploitation of minor minerals by auction in the Scheduled Areas. Consultation should be interpreted as mandatory consultation. Full facts about the proposed activity, its zone of influence, its economic, social and environmental impact, rehabilitation and sustainable livelihood plans must be placed before the Gram Sabha. If at any point of time it is found that the information provided by the concerned authority is false or kept hidden, the Gram Sabha shall have the right to withdraw the recommendation. Authority must report the progress of the project for which it has obtained recommendation of the Gram Sabha. State PESA Rules will further detail out this provision of the PESA Act. This recommendation is required for obtaining a prospective lease, mining lease or a concession for exploitation of the mineral by auction. Thus a large amount of control on the minor mineral is devolved to the Gram Sabha. However, the act does not provide any rights of consultations with regards to the major minerals. Most land acquisition in the scheduled areas takes place for exploitation of major minerals. Sub-sections 4(k) and 4(l) envisage prior consultation with Gram Sabha before grant of leases etc, of minor minerals.In this case the following things should be kept in mind;

- Gram Sabha is competent to plan and control the excavation and use of all the minor minerals including soil, stones, sands, etc to be found in its area.
- The RPMC shall discharge this responsibility.
- The villagers may use minor minerals for their individual needs as per the traditional practice.
- The permission of Gram Sabha will be compulsory for use of minerals.
- Gram Sabha may decide the extent of use of the local material such as stone, sand, etc for making Pukka houses different from the traditional dwellings and may also impose royalty.
- The Gram Sabha may fix the responsibilities such as filling up pits, planting trees, constructing ponds etc. by persons undertaking excavation to compensate for the general or special ill effects of excavation.

It would be sufficient to take the views of the Gram Sabhas or the Gram Panchayat but that their advice need not be made binding and mandatory on the government before granting of prospecting licences. In Maharashtra before grant of prospecting licenses the survey is conducted by the Ground Surveyor and Development Authority (GSDA) and based on their recommendation decisions are taken after considering the environmental aspects.

- The Panchayat or the government department concerned may award mining lease for minor minerals only in consultation with Gram Sabha.
- Gram Sabha may impose conditions for protecting the environment, employment, etc in the leases of minor minerals.

For example, Rajasthan PESA Rules empowers Gram Sabha in case of mines falling in one Gram Panchayat area, Panchayat Samiti in case of mines falling in more than one Gram Panchayat area and Zila Parishad in case of mines falling in more than one Panchayat Samiti area for recommending grant of concession for the exploitation of minor minerals.

Mines department will issue orders to Mining Engineers to necessarily obtain recommendations from the concerned Gram Sabha before renewing mining lease of minor minerals.

In Maharashtra and Himachal Pradesh, the Gram Sabha is competent enough to plan and control the excavation and use of all the minor minerals including soil, stones, sands, etc., which are to be found in its area.The villagers may use minor minerals for their individual needs as per the traditional practice with the permission of the Gram Sabha. If any permission is given by any government department for the exploitation of minor minerals, it shall be mandatory for the said government department to obtain necessary consensus of the Gram Sabha.

In Andhra Pradesh and Telangana, only individual local members of ST or societies comprising of exclusively local ST members shall be entitled for grant of prospecting license or mining lease for minor minerals and grant of concession for exploitation of minor minerals by auction.

Role of Gram Sabhas in Regulating Mining

Gram Sabha has a role in recommending quarry lease which is mining lease for minor minerals or quarry permit under which mineral has to be extracted in certain time i.e. auction. Prospecting licence (PL) is a stage where the miner will ascertain economic value of mineral and some physical works will be involved. So, prior information on PL will give an indication that mining may take place in future, so the Gram Sabha can be involved from this stage. Where PL is not needed i.e. where there are good prospects, quarry lease or permit is applied for, where Gram Sabha can put conditions, revenue sharing as per MMCR rules etc. A brief is provided below;

- Prior Information to take decisions: To make any consultation fruitful, prior information is essential. Information about mining in the respective village to be notified on the information board of the respective local authorities. The state mining department issues notification of areas for which auction is invited, in such cases; there may be different policy directions at the state level which may have a royalty sharing provisions, like the case of Madhya Pradesh, Chhattisgarh etc.
- Environment Protection: Mine Closure Plans or the Sustainable Development Framework (SDF) so reached at should be complied with to which the Gram Sabha can play a monitoring and

compliance role to decide about the future land use so desired and needed after the mine is closed. This is also for environmental protection of areas where mining is proposed. Similarly, Gram Sabha level FRC have to be formed and there is compatibility with FRA

- Checking illegal mining as well as compliance to the conditions under which the mining lease / quarry licence has been approved. Most of the states are framing rules for curbing illegal mining and transportation, the powers to issue notice and penalties are with the state and district machinery but considering this as a breach of conditions to which the miner agreed with the Gram Sabha, it is well within the domain of Gram Sabha to notify or take action with consensus and knowledge of other line departments.

Additional Facts on PESA

Important Powers provided to Gram Sabha under PESA

- Safeguard and preserve the–
    - Traditions and customs of the people, and their cultural identity,
    - Community resources, and
    - Customary mode of dispute resolution
- Carry out executive functions to
    - Approve plans, programmes and projects for social and economic development;
    - identify persons as beneficiaries under the poverty alleviation and other programmes; and
    - Issue a certificate of utilisation of funds by the panchayat for the plans; programmes and projects

Quorum of the Gram Sabha in PESA Area

- A Gram Sabha may constitute its committee(s) to carry out functions like maintaining peace and law and order, management of minor forest produce, village markets, sale or consumption of intoxicants, control over money lending and management of water bodies, etc. The duties assigned to the committees can be modified at any time by passing a resolution by the Gram Sabha. The standing committees should act in accordance with the instructions of Gram Sabha. A joint committee representing two or more PESA villages may be constituted with the consent of concerned Gram Sabhas.

- Quorum of the Gram Sabha will be as per the State PESA Rules, State Panchayati Raj Acts and State Panchayati Raj Rules. For example, in Rajasthan quorum is 10% of total members of Gram Sabha. In Andhra Pradesh, the quorum is not less than 1/3rd of members of Gram Sabha of whom at least 50% shall be ST members. In Maharashtra, the quorum is twenty-five per cent of the total members or one hundred, whichever is lower.
- Number of mandatory meetings of the Gram Sabha will be as per State PESA Rules, State Panchayati Raj Acts and State Panchayati Raj Rules. Many states have prescribed a minimum of four mandatory meetings of Gram Sabha in a year.
- For taking decisions on a project or proposal having impact on more than one village and requiring opinion of more than one Gram Sabha, a joint meeting of two or more Gram Sabhas may be called.

Provisions for resolution of dispute under PESA

Gram Sabha is competent to safeguard and preserve customary modes of dispute resolution. As per PESA Act, dispute resolution is in the domain of village community. These disputes may include minor disputes of any description, including those relating to property, land, sharing of crops, land boundary, inheritance, easement rights, use of community resources, issues involving customary practices and usages, cases involving galaxy of beliefs including magic, sorcery, etc., and also disputes vis-à-vis individuals, institutions and the state concerning credits of all descriptions, molestation, fake caste certification cases and the like. For example, Rajasthan PESA Rules, 2011 provide for constitution of a Peace Committee for dispute resolution and maintenance of law and order. On the direction of Gram Sabha, the Peace Committee tries to resolve the dispute and report to Gram Sabha or with approval of Gram Sabha report to designated Magistrate. Such dispute resolution will be as per customs and traditions and through open hearings. All decisions on the proposals to the Peace Committee will be taken by Gram Sabha on the basis of majority. In case of any threat of contravene of peace or law and order in the village, local police will report to Gram Sabha or Peace Committee except where immediate action is necessary. Police will register FIR only in case of a serious crime (with provision of punishment more than two years under IPC, 1860) and send a copy to Gram Sabha/Peace Committee. Gram Sabha will try to resolve the conflict in its next or special meeting.

Responsibility of Gram Sabha in Land Acquisition

PESA Act provides that the Gram Sabha or the Panchayat at appropriate level shall be consulted before making the acquisition of land for development projects or before resettling or rehabilitating persons affected by such projects in the Scheduled Areas. The concerned project authorities shall place all the relevant written information before the Gram Sabha along with the proposal which would include:

- Complete outline of the proposed project including the possible impact of the project;
- Proposed land acquisition;
- The new people likely to settle in the village and possible impact on the area and society; and
- Proposed participation, amount of compensation and job opportunities, for the people of the village.

The Gram Sabha after considering all the facts shall make a recommendation regarding the proposed land acquisition, rehabilitation and resettlement plan of persons who are affected or displaced. In case the Land Acquisition Officer is not in agreement with the recommendations of the Gram Sabha, she/he will send the matter again to the Gram Sabha for its reconsideration and decision. The Land Acquisition Officer or the project authorities may pass an order against the recommendations of the Gram Sabha, if aggrieved, after recording the reasons for doing so and same shall be communicated to Gram Sabha. In case of industrial projects, all the Gram Sabhas that are impacted by such projects shall be consulted before commencing any activity. State Revenue Department may issue instructions to all District Collectors to necessarily consult the concerned Gram Sabha before land acquisition.

Prevention of Tribal's Land Alienation by Gram Sabha

PESA Act empowers Gram Sabha to prevent alienation of land in the Scheduled Areas and take appropriate action to restore unlawfully alienated land of a scheduled tribe. The Gram Sabha must ensure that no land belonging to scheduled tribes is transferred to non- ST persons. If the Gram Sabha is of the opinion that attempts are being made to alienate land belonging to STs, it may go into details of such cases and pass resolution as to how such attempts should be tackled. If Gram Sabha finds that a non-ST is in unlawful occupation of any land belonging to ST member, it shall restore the possession of such land to the original owner as per laid down procedure. The Gram Sabha adopts traditional dispute resolution method while adjudicating land conflicts. Concerned department officials shall make available land records for taking correct decision by the Gram Sabha.

State government has to provide detailed procedures about how alienated land will be restored to the original landowners. For example, as per Rajasthan PESA Rules, 2011, to remove possession of unlawfully alienated tribal land, Panchayat Samiti will use powers of Tahsildar under the provisions of Rajasthan LandRevenue Act, 1956 (Section-15). Under the Himachal Pradesh PESA Rules 2011, if the Gram Sabha finds that a non-ST is in unlawful possession of any land owned by an ST, it can take up the matter with the concerned authority of the Revenue Departmentthrough the Pradhan of the Gram Panchayat, for restoration of possession of such land to that person to whom it originally belonged.

Provisions under PESA Act to control Money Lending

PESA mandates the state legislature to empower Gram Sabha to exercise control over money lending transactions. Money lending transactions include loan, etc., extended by the government, co-operatives, money lenders, banks and other institutions. Gram Sabha may constitute a Debt Relief Committee to deal with money lending transactions and its related issues in relation to STs. A borrower can bring to the notice of Gram Sabha if he or she is harassed by a money lender or by a lending institution and is being charged exorbitant rates of interests, etc. Gram Sabha can authorise the Debt Relief Committee to conduct an enquiry into such complaints with the support of Gram Sabha/Community Mobilizer and place a report before Gram Sabha for its decision. Gram Sabha, especially in the case of the tribals, may instruct a bank, society or any individual money lender that loans be disbursed or repayments made after informing the lending details to the Gram Sabha. It should also inform the government of any cases of exploitation, so that the concerned Department of Revenue, Banking, and Cooperatives can also take corrective action. Gram Sabha is competent to review agreements of all kinds of labourers in the village and ensure that there is no forced labour in lieu of money borrowed from the lender. However, the concerned state government is required to make rules in this regard. In Rajasthan, Gram Panchayats have been assigned the powers of Assistant Registrar and Panchayat Samiti has been given powers of Registrar under Rajasthan Moneylending Act, 1963.

Powers of Gram Sabha under PESA Act to Control, Sale and Consumption of Intoxicants

Gram Sabha is endowed with the power to enforce prohibition or regulate or restrict the sale or consumption of any intoxicant. Gram Sabha shall carry out the following functions:

- Impose restrictions on usage or ban the preparation or sale or consumption of any intoxicant.
- Impose restrictions on transport of any type of intoxicant or storage, etc.
- Prohibit the sale of mahua, jaggery or any other material which is used in making liquor in the village or sale in the market.

The Gram Sabha may constitute an Intoxicant Control Committee to inquire into complaints related to intoxicants. State governments shall formulate rules and detail out procedures in this regard. For example, in Andhra Pradesh and Telangana, the Gram Sabha shall be consulted before the grant of any license to open liquor shop in the village. Gram Sabha will convey its opinion in the form of resolution within four weeks, which shall be binding on the state government. The license shall be granted to local ST only. The Gram Sabha shall determine the quantity of traditional liquor that may be brewed/produced by the STs living in a village for their personal consumption but not for sale. In Himachal Pradesh and Maharashtra, the Gram Sabha shall be competent to enforce prohibition or regulation or restriction on sale and consumption of any intoxicant within its limits. Gram Sabha may constitute an Intoxication Control Committee, with at least 50 percent women members, to inquire into matters and complaints relating to intoxicants and to make suitable suggestions regarding the control of intoxicants for the benefit of the Sabha members. In Rajasthan, Gram Sabha can act against persons involved in illicit trade of intoxicants, promote prohibition and pass resolutions for change of locations of liquor vends. Certified copy of Gram Sabha resolutions with regard to prohibition will be sent to Collector and Excise Commissioner. Collector will depute an officer not below the rank of Tahsildar to verify the situation, which will then be sent to Excise Commissioner who will initiate action on the resolution of Gram Sabha. On special occasions such as birth, marriage, etc., Gram Sabha may issue date wise permit to keep limited quantity of local liquor. While considering proposal on regulation of sale and intoxicants, views of women will be significant. Gram Sabha can also impose penalty in case of consumption of intoxicants in public places and domestic violence after consumption of intoxicants.

Provisions to manage Village Markets by Gram Sabha under the PESA Act

Gram Sabha is competent to control and manage the village markets. Gram Sabha may carry out different activities for management of village markets, including the following:

- Gram Sabha can constitute a village market committee to carry out the functions assigned to it by Gram Sabha.
- Make available water, sheds and other physical facilities to the shopkeepers and the consumers in the market.
- Prohibit the inflow and sale of harmful objects in the market.
- Ensure that the weight, measurement and the transactions are fair.
- Obtain and share information about the prices of various items being charged.
- Prohibit all unfair practices, including cheating or misinformation regarding prices or exploitation.
- Prohibit gambling, betting, testing luck, cock-fighting, etc., in the market or its surrounding areas.
- May impose fee on the shopkeepers of the market.
- Gram Sabhas of two or more villages can organise a common market by constituting a Joint Market Committee to manage such market
- Market Committees shall be accountable for its activities in relation to the management of the market. The decision of Gram Sabha shall be final in case of any market related dispute arising from trade, etc.

Conclusion and Recommendations

PESA is a most powerful legislation which can play an instrumental role in recognizing the rights of the tribal population in Scheduled areas over natural resources thus transforming their quality of life. PESA posed a totally new set of challenges before the members of PRIs, a few of which had not been contemplated before. Here the Gram Sabha is designed to be a new center of power to deliberate, decide and monitor the development. It is almost true that due to lack of political will, their rights have been disregarded strategically. Though central government has taken several measures to implement the act in letter and spirit, lack of initiative from concerned state government is quite evident. PESA has great potential in harnessing the human and social capital of the tribal people to address the problems faced by them in some of the most remote areas. Central government should take appropriate action to eliminate the loopholes in the central legislation followed by a strong direction to abide by the constitutional mandate. State governments should follow the guideline issued by the central government to incorporate changes in the state acts and take appropriate measures to amend state laws which are in conflict with the provisions of PESA. Moreover, it may take appropriate initiatives to enhance the capacity of government machinery and stakeholders who play vital role in actual implementation of the act at the ground level. For the improvisation in the implementation of the act the following things may be taken into account;

- The implementation of PESA has not been seriously attempted by the state governments. They still want to govern the PESA areas through the centralized administration and laws that actually weaken what PESA provisions offer the tribal community.
- There are some legal as well as political difficulties in implementing the PESA Act in schedule areas. The Legal difficulties like definition of village, gaps and inconsistencies between the Central and the State Acts, clash between PESA and pre-existing laws, lack of clarity about customary practices and cultural identity etc. Similarly, the political difficulties like lack of political will, ignorance about PESA, fragmentation of well-knit tribal society because of electoral competition etc. Therefore, a multipronged approach needs to be adopted by the government to overcome those difficulties in all respect.
- The Central Government should direct the states to gear up the process of amendments to existing laws so that it follows the provisions of PESA in letter and spirit.

- A High Power Committee at the central level may be formed to oversee the progress of the concerned states regarding implementation of PESA. This committee can play advisory role with concrete suggestions to restrict deviations by the states.
- Though there is provision for taking annual reports from Governors on regular basis but it is not given due importance. The process should be taken up seriously. The report should be made available to the public by uploading it in the website in a time bound manner.
- Traditional tribal councils are dominated by male by and large in all respective states. Hence, in order to ensure active participation of women in tribal governance, special attention should be given. Appropriate measure should be taken to ensure at least one third participation of women in all meetings at the Gram Sabha level.
- As per the available information, no integrative exercise has yet taken place to examine the relevance of different Central Laws to Schedule-V Areas and to harmonize them with the aims and objectives of the PESA. The Land Acquisition Act-1894, Mines and Minerals (Development and Regulation) Act-1957, the Forest Act-1927, the Forest Conservation Act-1980 and the Indian Registration Act are among the laws which call for particular attention in this context. Besides, the National Policy on Resettlement and Rehabilitation of Project Affected Persons-2007, National Water Policy-2002, National Minerals Policy-2008 and National Forest Policy-2004 would require detailed assessment from the standpoint of ensuring compliance to the provisions of PESA. There is also an urgent need to verify these acts and policies and made it need based, area specific and PESA compliant.
- There is no provision for appeal against the decision of the Gram Sabha, which is not in conformity with the democratic process and introduces an element of absolute power, rather than checks and balances on power of institutions. It should be taken care of in priority basis.
- Many state governments have passed laws not fully in conformity with the central law. The implementation of the law has been severely hampered by the reluctance of most state governments to make laws and rules that conform to the spirit of the law.

- The power envisaged for Gram Sabha in respect of 'prevention of land alienation as also restoration of illegally alienated land' is unequivocal. But suitable provisions in the Panchayati Raj Acts or the relevant Land Regulations have not been properly made in all states.

It is important to emphasize that profit and commercial exploitation of MFP are not the core issues. The key concern is instead, protecting and enhancing the livelihoods of people who depend on MFP, as these are among the poorest in the country. Further, though programmes such as MGNREGA offer new livelihood opportunities, income from MFP remains especially important for women and the less able bodied. The government would need to take measures to develop markets, strengthen the bargaining position of gatherers, enable Gram Sabhas to exercise ownership rights and to enhance livelihoods of gatherers.

MFP markets are poorly developed, with buyers having the upper hand. The high degree of exploitation of gatherers by traders has been noted. In the short and medium term, and at least over the next 5-7 years, government intervention in MFP trade is essential. Such intervention would ultimately lead to the development of markets. However, government Corporations and Federations need to shift from playing a controlling role to a supportive and facilitative one.

It would be obligatory for state governments to ensure payment of MSP through their agencies. Currently, most PESA and other States with significant forest area have designated some public sector Corporations or Co-operative Federations to fix Statutory Minimum Price for MFPs that are brought to the purchase centers of the designated agencies. While these agencies should continue to trade in MFPs, the centrally fixed MSP should be the bottom line to be offered to the gatherers, although the designated agencies can offer a higher price if they find it feasible and profitable to do so. In this context, all such government supported procurement agencies should function autonomously in a professional manner.

Transparency and accountability of corporations/federations can be enhanced by mechanisms such as placing of accounts in the Gram Sabha, information sharing & social audit. As Corporations/Federations expand MSP support to a larger number of MFPs, simple 'profitability' will not be an adequate measure of performance. Instead, a range of parameters such as percentage of administrative costs in relation to the total turnover, the number of MFPs for which MSP is provided, improvements in sale prices, regeneration and value addition activities promoted and outreach to inaccessible areas should be adopted:

Moreover, the basic infrastructure (storage facilities) and manpower support along with training and capacity building of the staff engaged in the tasks of procurement and disposal in these agencies have to be provided by the state government, with adequate central assistance.

Market information system will be needed for proper planning of the procurement, value addition and marketing of MFP by the stake-holders. The existence and dissemination of complete and accurate market information is the key to achieve both operational and pricing efficiency. Therefore, it is necessary to develop advanced information and communication technology based schemes, which may be called MFPNET, or any other nomenclature with the basic objectives to establish nationwide information network for speedy collection and dissemination of market information and data for its efficient and timely utilization. Building marketing intelligence would also enable these procurement agencies to dispose the procured MFPs at competitive market rates and not suffer losses due to lack of information.

7

Capacity Building of PRI-Members

"Panchayats should be given greater powers, for we want the villagers to have a greater measure of Swaraj (Self-Government) in their own villages."

— ***Pt. Jawaharlal Nehru***

Introduction

The capacity building of PRIs and their members is very much indispensable to accelerate the pace of democratic decentralisation. A 'capacity' is the ability or skill that exists in present scenario, whereas, the 'capability' refers to the higher level of ability that could be manifested under the right conditions as per the inevitability. Similarly, an 'ability' is the skill or competency to perform a task whether it is physical or mental and It is intrinsic that depends on the genetic structure of a person. So, the capability is a feature, ability or process that can be developed or improved. A capability is a collaborative process that can be deployed and through which individual competencies and abilities can be applied and exploited. In other words, the capability can refer to an ability that exists in an individual but can be improved upon. Moreover, the 'empowerment' is the process of enhancing the capacity of individuals or groups to make choices and to transform those choices into desired actions and outcomes. Capacity, then, is a finite resource but is renewable under certain deliberate conditions. Capacity building (or capacity development) is the process by which individuals and organizations acquire, improve and retain the skills, knowledge, tools, equipment and other resources needed to do their jobs competently or to a greater capacity with a larger scale and larger impact. Capacity building and capacity development are often used interchangeably.

Strengthening the Panchayati Raj system across the country is a key objective of the Ministry of Panchayati Raj. The Rajiv Gandhi Panchayat Sashaktikaran Abhiyan (RGPSA) launched in March 2013, seeks to enhance the capabilities and effectiveness of Panchayats and the Gram Sabhas to function in a democratic fashion. Article-243D of the Constitution mandates reservation for women, Schedule Castes (SCs) and Schedule Tribes (STs) at all three tiers of PRIs. In Panchayats across the country, Elected Women Representatives (EWRs) constitute 42.3 per cent, SCs-13.7 per cent while STs constitute 14.6 per cent of all ERs. Further, among the EWRs, almost one-third belong to the deprived sections i.e. SCs and STs. Thus a large number of women ERs face multiple deprivations of caste, class and gender. The practical impact of this revolutionary constitutional provision would only be evident when these EWRs and SC and ST ERs, are fully empowered and made aware of their rights and duties. Thus, capacity building of these historically marginalized ERs is extremely essential, so as to help realize the constitutional vision of inclusive and participatory democratic governance at the grassroots. The revised National Capability Building Framework (NCBF) 2014 complements the initiatives taken under RGPSA. It is expected that as more funds become available under RGPSA for capacity building, its outreach and quality will be enhanced.The capability building & training (CB&T) is a provision of appropriate training to Elected Representatives (ERs) and functionaries at all levels of Panchayats or Panchayati Raj Institutions (PRIs), especially ensuring the inclusion of the cutting-edge level ERs and functionaries. Expanding the outreach of training also entails ensuring coverage of the diverse groups of stakeholders in Panchayats. For CB&T for Panchayats, the challenge is to, on the one hand, cover very large numbers of ERs of the three tiers of Panchayats, as well as the core officials functioning at all these levels, and on the other hand, undertake appropriate capacity building of various stakeholders such as Gram Sabhas, departmental functionaries and even experts, media and other groups. Comprehensive outreach ultimately also implies reaching out to heterogeneous groups in terms of gender, age-group, socio-economic background, geographical location, educational profile as well as addressing a comprehensive range of subjects, while maintaining the quality of training.

CB & T of PRIs involves huge numbers PRI members, government officials, line department officers and other stakeholders. Further, soon after Panchayat elections, the need to reach out to large numbers becomes vital, as several new ERs have to start functioning and many of them work in a public institution for the first time. It is necessary to train this target group within the first six months of Panchayat elections. Further, as ERs change every five years, new ERs are to be trained with every electoral cycle. Apart from ERs, there are several other stakeholders who must be trained to ensure that Panchayats perform optimally. These include Core Panchayat functionaries, who perform the basic functions of Panchayats, such as Panchayat secretaries, accountants, Panchayat Development Officers, technical staff such as watermen, cleaners etc. Departmental functionaries, especially of departments devolved to Panchayats, who need to understand the Panchayati Raj system, as well as their role in it. Departmental functionaries need to be trained to plan in their sector in the local area and support the Panchayats in preparing and implementing various projects. Several other stakeholders that function as support groups to Panchayats, such as management committees, standing committees, working groups and Community Based Organisations (CBOs) that have a critical role in the formulation and implementation of local development plans especially in states such as Kerala where the level of devolution is high. As states strengthen their Panchayati Raj systems, and establish committees, working groups, etc., for planning and implementation, it is likely that the need for the capacity building of such bodies will grow. While reaching out to a large number of stakeholders, it is necessary to ensure that the quality of the training programme is maintained, and the needs of people with diverse backgrounds are addressed.

Capacity Building Framework for GPDP

Formulation of a comprehensive and holistic GPDP necessarily requires intense participation of people, understanding of the process by various stakeholders, visioning, situation analysis to identify the problems and the priority areas, projectisation, implementation etc. Capacity Building & Training (CB&T) including facilitation, is a pre-requisite as well as one of the important means to enable this process. To enhance professional knowledge and skills of the members of GPPFTs including the elected representatives, functionaries of GPs, community leaders and employees of the line departments operating at the GP level for better planning, implementation and monitoring of GPDP, each state has to develop an appropriate strategy and action plan for organizing action-oriented training and learning by field-based practice. National Institute of Rural Development and Panchayati Raj (NIRD&PR), Hyderabad should take lead and organize training for national resource persons for two types of trainings one each for training of Panchayat leader & SHG women and facilitator (CRPs/Rojgar Sahayak) for GPDP.

The focus of training should be on "igniting the vision of the local Panchayat leadership" for strengthening the GP as an institution of local government as envisaged in the Constitution without restricting their thinking to the available resource envelope and limiting plan activities to creating some infrastructure. Improved institutional capacity of the GPs to carry out the planning exercise on the strength of their own rather than depending much on external support should be the outcome of such training plans. A GP can plan, implement and monitor only if and when it becomes institutionally strong. So focus of CB&T interventions must be on an intertwined effort for institutional strengthening of GP and strengthening of processes and systems for GPDP.

Objectives of the Capacity Building Framework

This capacity building framework is intended to serve as a model to the state Panchayati Raj departments, SIRDs and other support organizations to design and implement proper action plans for enabling the GPs to prepare a comprehensive GPDP.

The key objectives of GPDP CB&T framework are as follows:

- Form and develop strong teams of trainers at State, District/Block, GP and community levels to develop capacities of the major stakeholders at various levels to launch and implement the GPDP initiative effectively and efficiently;
- Build the confidence of the Panchayats leadership to prepare effective GPDPs;
- Raise awareness of communities about the importance of GPDP and inspire them towards participatory planning;
- Create a vision for the GP, enable to explore opportunities for additional resource mobilization beyond the budgeted allocations under the government schemes including unconventional sources;
- Localize SDGs with GPDP by identifying the priority areas of interventions for achieving socio-economic goals;
- Enable the GP to congregate leadership to enable partnership with line departments so that all the functionaries of the line departments can implement the departmental schemes and programme from out of the GPDP components with full involvement and support of the GP;
- Emphasize social development parameters which can be addressed mostly with no cost and low cost interventions;

- Bring about attitudinal development in all concerned including the ERs, functionaries of GPs, employees of the line departments and community leadership to strive for better service delivery through GPDP;
- Enable GPs to come out as strong institutions of local government with all round development of their people and to empower them to address the new challenges/issues of climate change, social development, human resource development etc.

Institutional Support

In the context of substantial devolution of funds to GPs, operationalization of GPDP framework and achievement of the SDGs by 2030, all concerned elected representatives and functionaries of GPs, Government officials and other stakeholders need to attain adequate capabilities for planning and implementation of schemes. Capabilities of the stakeholders can be developed through a combined effect of adequate training and non-training interventions in addition to the required interventions for organizational and institutional development. Therefore, it is necessary to focus training in an 'institutional mode' through which the GPs should take the ownership of preparing GPDP on the strength of their own institutional capacity through appropriate action-oriented training and field- based practice. For more effective CB&T of Panchayats across the states, the institutional structures required at National, State, District and Block Panchayat .

National Nodal Institution for Capacity Building

The National Institute of Rural Development and Panchayati Raj (NIRD&PR), Hyderabad is the apex organization for designing the capacity building of Panchayati Raj functionaries and all other stakeholders on GPDP at national, state and district level with the assistance of State Institutes of Rural Development & Panchayati Raj (SIRD&PRs) or any other state level institution as may be determined by the states which are to function as state nodal agencies. The responsibilities of the national nodal agency would be as follows:

- Focus on democratic decentralization process, policies and programmes of centre and state governments that benefit the rural poor,
- Examine and analyze all the factors contributing to the improved planning process on economic and social well-being of people in

rural areas on a sustainable basis through training, workshops, seminars and documentation etc.

- Organise orientation programmes for national level resource persons from each state, heads of the SIRD&PRs and state nodal officers for GPDP on formulation of strategy for CB&T and grounding GPDP based on the revised guidelines;
- Impart training as ToT programmes for master resource persons for GPDP;
- Guide the SIRDs/State Nodal Institution for GPDP/ other state institutions for implementing training programmes for GPDP based on sound training needs analysis;
- Review and research on the progress and quality of implementation of CB&T programmes conducted at state and district level from time to time;
- Facilitate the process of creation of some Beacon GPDPs as islands of success on cluster approach across the country on action research mode;
- Revitalize the existing mechanism for CB&T in order to make it more relevant for achieving better outcomes from rural development programmes through grassroots level planning process.

State Nodal Institutions

The State Institute of Rural Development & Panchayati Raj (SIRD& PR) or designated state nodal institution for GPDP is to function as the apex institute for training and capacity building of Panchayat Raj and Rural Development functionaries at state level for GPDP. The main objective of the state nodal institutes is to enhance knowledge base, develop managerial skills, organizational abilities, leadership qualities and decision making skills among different categories of the elected representatives and Panchayat Raj & Rural Development functionaries and other stakeholders including CRP of SHG of women and representatives of NGO/CBO/CSR who are engaged in GPDP activities in the state. The state nodal institutions would be supported/guided by the national nodal agency in all aspects of PRI CB&T.

To ensure uniformity of inputs of knowledge, skills and attitudinal orientation of the members of GPPFT including Sarpanch and Panchayat

Secretary, one senior officer/senior faculty form NIRD&PR will be nominated as State Link Officer (SLO) for each state, who will assist and coordinate with SIRD & PRs for implementation and monitoring of training programmes. While the SIRD & PR could continue to be the nodal agency for training and the overall coordination, other institutions like academic institutions and partnering institutions will also play critical role in the training process.

Panchayat Resource Centres

To reach out to large numbers, particularly grassroots level functionaries and to help deliver on the CB&T challenges, there is a need for dedicated training institutions in the districts. The following resource centres are available in some places:

i. State Panchayat Resource Centre (SPRC)

ii. District Panchayat Resource Centre (DPRC)

The State Nodal Agencies will support the efforts of these resource centres at strategic level to plan and deliver CB&T programmes besides providing policy, programme and other support. The State may develop a vision of setting up at least one DPRC, especially in those districts where there is no Extension Training Centres (ETC) or Panchayat Training Centre (PTC), for the purpose of residential training of the facilitator, elected representatives and functionaries of three-tier Panchayats, particularly GPs in the context of GPDP.

Local Level Training Institutions for GPDP

The states may also find viable alternatives for organizing training at local levels. For example, the meeting halls of the GPs (wherever available) and the meeting halls of the Intermediate Panchayats may be upgraded, with minor addition/alteration, into meeting- cum-training halls for non-residential training. Collaboration with NGOs, universities, colleges etc. may also be ventured to augment the scope of training using their infrastructure.

Empanelment of National/State Resource Institutions

Capacity development of Panchayat functionaries under GPDP encompass various aspects of planning and managing wide range of programmes for economic development and social justice to public service delivery. The

Ministry of Panchayati Raj (MoPR), in association with NIRD&PR/ SIRD&PRs/States has been working for CB&T of elected representatives and functionaries of Panchayati Raj Institutions across the states in a comprehensive manner. In order to further strengthen GP capabilities in the planning process, the NIRD&PR will identify and empanel the renowned national/state resource institutions from both government and non-government sectors having first-hand experience in decentralized participatory planning to help SIRD&PRs and States. They will be thoroughly oriented through a national workshop for common understanding of the GPDP process. Their services can be utilized by NIRD&PR/ SIRD&PRs to provide support to the state government, SIRD&PR and the state resource teams as per demand expressed by the States or as may be considered necessary by the NIRD&PR and MoPR.

Trainers/Resource Persons for Capacity Building

Addressing the challenges of training a huge number of Panchayat functionaries in the country without dilution of quality, requires quality trainers at all levels. A multi-layered resource team structure for Capacity Building & Training for GPDP may be set up as proposed below.

State Level Master Trainers' Team

A State Level Master Trainers' Team (SLMTT) needs to be constituted with (RPs) committed officers/Panchayat leaders having knack for training in order to train and guide the members of the District Resource Groups. Faculty members of SIRD, ETCs, DTCs, PTCs, other State level or regional level training institutions and officials of the State Nodal Institutions for GPDP/ State Programme Management Unit (SPMU) for RGSA may be made members of SLMTT. The SIRD or the State Nodal Institutions for GPDP/ State Programme Management Unit (SPMU) for RGSA may be authorized by the State Government to be in charge of steering and coordinating the SLMTT for GPDP.

District Resource Group (DRG) for GPDP

A District Resource Group (DRG) for GPDP may be constituted in each district with CRPs/committed officers/Panchayat leaders selected from district administration/District Panchayat level and Block/Intermediate Panchayat level. Committed and capable officials from line departments and representatives from NGO/CSR/Academic Institutions may be made members of the DRG. The selection of resource persons from the line departments, Universities, former ERs, NGOs, social activists and other partner institutions should be well planned and systematic. However, the functions of any member of the DRG will be (i) to develop capacity of the GPs through iterative training and non-training interventions; (ii) to provide continuous handholding support to the GPs, singly in case of big GPs and on cluster basis in case of small GPs, and facilitate all the stages of preparation of GPDP; (iii) to supervise and monitor the entire process; and (iv) to function as Facilitator as well as Charge Officers for GPDP in respect of one or two big GPs or a cluster of small GPs. The members of the DRG will have to discharge such functions over a maximum of 10 to 12 working days in a year in addition to their own duties. Since most of the members of the DRG are likely to come from a number of line departments, it would be helpful if an executive order is issued under signature of the chief secretary to the effect that it is obligatory on the part of any member of the DRG to function as Trainer-cum-Hand-holding Support Provider-cum-Charge Officer for GPDP and that discharge of such responsibility should be treated to be 'on duty' for official work. One deputy to the chief executive officer of the Intermediate Panchayat or the district officer looking after Panchayati Raj affairs may be authorized by the state government to be in charge of steering and coordinating the DRG.

Approaches to CB&T for GPDP

Since GPDP is not only to be understood conceptually but to be physically prepared through several steps of action at the GP level for actual implementation, there needs to be a shift in approach from the popular 'conventional classroom-based training' to 'action-oriented field work based training'. Conventional classroom-based training generally caters to the cognitive aspects of capacity building that helps in enhancing mainly 'knowledge' about any subject or task, ignoring or attaching little importance to 'skill development' that becomes possible through 'learning by doing'. Hence, there needs to be a combined effort of the following training and non-training interventions for effective CB&T for GPDP:

I. Training Interventions may include:

- Institution-based face-to-face training
- Facilitation and hand-holding support at the level of GP or cluster of GPs

- Sensitization camps for awareness generation at various levels including community level
- Distance learning/E-learning etc.

II. Non-training Interventions may include:

- Policy support on statutory issues and corrective measures
- Application of IEC tools
- Exposure visits
- Appraisal interactions
- Participation in the process of GPDP in Beacon Panchayats
- Writeshops/mock planning exercises
- Helpline

Plan of Action for CB&T for GPDP

Based on the above-mentioned principles, a concrete plan of action for all the components for training and non-training interventions along with a district-wise calendar of training programmes for GPDP needs to be prepared every year by the state government with support from the SLMTT and the DRGs.

A wide range of training methods need to be adopted to build the institutional capacity of the GPs on GPDP. While the "classroom-based training" has its own significance for theoretical orientation on "Plan Cycle" , "Focus Areas" and 'What' and 'Why' aspects of GPDP, there should be more emphasis on the 'How' aspect of planning. For this purpose frequent 'action-oriented field work based training programmes on the practical aspects GPDP at the GP level or at the level of cluster of GPs, after an institution-based face-to-face training will be more useful for effective implementation of the GPDP initiative. The classroom training may include Brainstorming, Interactive Lecture, Participatory Reading and Learning, Group Work, Case Study, Role Play, Screening of Video Films and Quiz etc. The practical training may include practical hands on exercises relating to participatory tools and techniques. Community based interactions, Transect Walk, Focus Group Discussion, Social Mapping, Natural Resource Mapping etc.

Information, Education and Communication (IEC) is an extremely important component to trigger the participation of all the villagers in the

GPDP exercise. Effective materials are important tools to reach out to all the stakeholders in the villages and to motivate them to identify their financial and non-financial needs in formulation and implementation of GPDP. IEC strategy should be a compulsory part of the State's CB&T strategy which may include the following:

- Structured learning material mostly in FAQ form
- Develop Charts, Posters, Wall writing/painting
- Create a 'material bank' at the state/district level for wide coverage of content
- Prepare small documentaries/video clips/snippets on the critical aspects of the GPDP and its implementation using real life experiences and dramatics/narration.
- Popularize success stories/case studies from the same state to learn about best practices
- Undertake strategic campaign with use of print/social media/folk media

Monitoring of CB&T interventions of GPDP

It is necessary to develop a strong mechanism through IT application for quantitative and qualitative monitoring of the CB&T interventions of GPDP. The scope of monitoring should not be confined to the level of data collection and online uploading of plans. The monitoring at district, state and national level should also capture the progress of CB&T programmes and their impact on the field.

(A) Overview of Outreach Methods

(i) *Reaching out to Large Numbers*

State Institutes of Rural Development (SIRDs) along with resource institutions, NGOs and other support training institutes have dealt with the issue of capacity building of a large number of persons in several ways. The main strategies include the cascade model of training, distance education, expansion of the number of institutes to decentralized levels and networking and collaboration with NGOs.

(a) Cascade Mode: The cascade mode of training enables decentralization of training to many locations, such as the district and block level, so that many training programmes can be conducted simultaneously, thereby enabling face-to-face training of large numbers. For this type of training, there is need to ensure that an adequate number of trainers is available, as well as appropriate locations. Usually, the trainers too have to be trained. Training through the cascade mode may be done institutionally, with the help of NGOs and district and block Panchayats. Considerable amount of organization and planning is required in preparing training modules and materials, monitoring, addressing emerging problems, etc. It is important to maintain quality in the cascade mode through rigorous monitoring.

(b) Distance Learning through SATCOM: In order to ensure wider coverage of stakeholders spread out in different locations, appropriate distance learning systems have been used. SATCOM training, used successfully by many SIRDs, is based on satellite communication through a central studio relay centre and decentralised Satellite Interactive Terminals (SITs). It allows outreach to a large number of trainees from a central location. The SATCOM strategy has been effectively used in several SIRDs,

(c) Establishing Training Institutes at Decentralized Levels: The availability of training institutes at decentralized levels also enables training of large numbers. At present, the availability of training institutes is highly variable across states. While some states, such as UP and Maharashtra, have a large number of district level institutes, in other states, few exist - such as Rajasthan, which is a huge state of 33 districts, but has only three functioning Extension Training Centres (ETCs). Similarly, another huge state, Madhya Pradesh, has only five ETCs. Even these minimal ETCs do not have adequate human resource and appropriate training infrastructure. Under the Rajiv Gandhi Panchayat Sashaktikaran Abhiyan (RGPSA), states can access funds to establish District Panchayat Resource Centres (DPRCs) and also Block Resource Centres (BRCs). The establishment of such centres will enhance the capacity to outreach to a large number of ERs and functionaries.

(d) Collaboration with NGOs and Academic Institutes to Expand Outreach: Several states that lack an adequate number of training centres at decentralized levels have collaborated with NGOs to organize multiple training programmes. This involves selecting good NGOs and then training trainers to undertake capacity building in a cascade mode. The selection of NGOs and rigorous monitoring are key aspects of this exercise. SIRDs of Rajasthan, Andhra Pradesh, Chhattisgarh, Jharkhand, Odisha, Kerala Institute of Local Administration (KILA) in Kerala are capitalising on partnering with NGOs and academic institutes to expand the outreach for CB&T initiatives.

(ii) Reaching out to a range of Stakeholders

As stated earlier, CB&T of Panchayats involves training of several stakeholders. Strategies regarding addressing these stakeholders are discussed below.

(a) Elected Representatives: The training of ERs has been the core of CB &T efforts. Though all States have organized training of ERs, the extent to which SIRDs are able to outreach training to ERs varies. While some SIRDs are barely able to reach out to all ERs in one complete election cycle, others are able to cover all ERs several times in an election cycle. Ideally, all ERs should get CB&T inputs three times in an election cycle. Especially in reaching out the newly elected ERs within the first six months after elections Induction-cum-GPDP as a prime CB&T programme has been doing by all SIRDs,ETCs and other training institutes like KILA, Kerala and the like.

(b) Core Panchayat Functionaries: While training of ERs is the central concern of CB &T, the training of core Panchayat functionaries, who perform the day to day functions of Panchayats is also very important. Only when Panchayats are assisted by well trained staff, will their performance be optimal. This issue becomes especially important as new staff is being hired under RGPSA at the Gram Panchayat level. Some SIRDs have become aware of the importance of training core Panchayat staffs.

(c) Gram Sabhas: For strengthening grassroots democracy, efforts have to be made to sensitize the village community at large, i.e. the Gram Sabha members – who are mandated to prepare local development plans and review the working of the Gram Panchayat through social audit and other means.

(d) Departmental Functionaries: The training of departmental functionaries can be undertaken in two forms. Firstly, SIRDs may try to train them through their own training mechanisms. This is a demanding task, as the number of departments aligned with which Panchayats are large and the capacity of various SIRDs to train departmental functionaries is highly variable. Where there are a large number of decentralized training institutes and good facilities for distance education, SIRDs can reach out to at least some departmental functionaries.

(e) Functional Committees and CBOs Associated with Panchayats: As stated above, as the Panchayat system is strengthened, it becomes more complex. While in States such as Kerala, Panchayats set up their own functional committees to advise on various issues, in all States, there exist various CBOs related to health, education, women and child welfare etc. The need to make CBOs accountable to Panchayats has been stressed by MoPR, and several Central Government departments as well as State Governments are taking steps in this direction. As the interface of CBOs with Panchayats grows, it will be necessary to ensure that they are adequately trained to perform their role in collaboration with Panchayats. As in the case of departmental officials, it would be important to form networks with departmental training institutes, as well as NGOs.

(f) Other Stakeholders that support Panchayats: The support of policy makers, especially Members of Legislative Assemblies (MLAs) and Members of Parliament (MPs), activists as well as of the media can be obtained by sensitizing them to Panchayats. Such programmes need not be very formal, but can be in the form of workshops, discussions, as is being done by KILA-Kerala, by way of 'Interface Programme' with the MLAs, leaders of political parties and the media, to sensitise them for empowerment of PRIs.

(B) Modes of Training

The strategies to reach out to large numbers have also been delineating. The different modes of training, i.e. the cascade mode, distance education and so on may be adopted as per the number of persons that can be reached through the training. Similarly, different modes of training have varying potential for ensuring quality, reaching out to marginalized groups, etc.

Primary Issues and Challenges

The primary issues and challenges while considering various modes of training are:

(i) Elected Representatives differ in age, experience, educational status, income group, caste, ethnicity, and gender. Modes of training have to be selected to cater to the different needs of different groups. For example, if women ERs find it difficult to leave their homes for a length of time, various distance education modes, or on-site training, may be better suited to them. The needs of trainees have to be kept in mind while selecting a mode of training.

(ii) The mode of training has to be suited to the number of persons to be trained. While distance education may be suitable to train a large number of people, institution based training may be more desirable when a small number is to be trained.

(iii) The quality of training also has to be kept in view while choosing an appropriate mode of training. Quality can be improved in all modes of training, but is harder to maintain in some modes of training. While institution-based training is inadequate for delivering fast track training to all ERs and officials because of their huge numbers and short tenures, the cascade training mode poses the problem of ensuring quality, in view of possible transmission losses in content and methodology. Modes of training can affect quality in the following ways:

- The extent of interaction between the trainer and trainee is different in various modes of training. While in distance modes it is less, in face to face modes it is much more.
- A common abstain expressed by ERs and officials, especially in case of experienced persons, when they come for training, is that class room learning is 'theory' while the practical reality is different. Therefore, training modes have to be devised to address the need for a practical approach.
- The level of participation needed also has to be kept in view while selecting a mode of training. In general, greater participation of trainees in training programmes is desirable. But with some groups, participation becomes critical, and the training has to take this into account.
- Training modes can also make a topic more or less interesting for the trainee. Several participants may find classroom training dull, while enjoy lively media based training.
- Different subjects are also better or worse addressed in different modes of training. For example, training in accounts through mass media is difficult.

(iv) Different modes of training also vary in cost, which has to be kept in mind while selecting a particular mode of training

(v) Institutional capacity is a key issue. If specialised manpower and infrastructure for a particular mode of training is simply not available, it is not a suitable mode of training in that particular context.

Various Modes of Training

In approaching the challenging task of capacity building of Elected Representatives, officials and other stakeholders of Panchayats, SIRDs and other resource institutes have been using a range of approaches/methods for training of PRIs, described below.

(a) Institution-based Training: As validated from the experience of SIRDs and NGOs in the country, institution-based training is critical; as such training allows participants to interact with a wide range of subject experts, in an atmosphere that is conducive to learning and spot-problem solving.

(b) Cascade Decentralized Mode Training: The cascade Mode of Training is in fact a top-down approach to deliver training, while it is also considered as a method to transfer or diffuse knowledge/training in an organization. It is a mechanism of delivering training messages from trainers at the central level to trainees at the local level through several layers quickly and economically. The cascade mode involves the delivery of training through layers of trainers until it reaches the final target group.

Since the Panchayat functionaries and other stakeholders to be capacitated are large in numbers, the target audience can be reached out only in a cascading mode. For organizing the cascading trainings, without dilution of quality, it requires quality resource persons. The certified national/state level Master Resource Persons (MRPs) already created by NIRD&PR need to be actively involved by the SIRDs/State nodel agency for GPDP to conduct CB&T programmes for GPDP. The MRPs will deliver trainings based on a common training design, content and methodology with the help of training modules and learning materials created by NIRD&PR/SIRDs. To ensure uniformity of inputs of knowledge, skills and attitudinal orientation on GPDP, one senior officer form State Panchayati Raj department should be nominated as "Nodal Officer" for each state, who along with SIRD/Nodal agency for GPDP will be responsible for implementation and monitoring of training programmes and aim for the end result of improved institutional capacity of GPs as well as GPDP.

Looking to the huge numbers of ERs and officials to be trained in every state, even institutional training has to be decentralized at multiple locations, e.g.– Zilla Parishad (ZP) Chairpersons, Vice-Chairpersons & Chief Executive Officers (CEOs), Additional Chief Executive Officers (ACEOs) can be trained at the SIRD/State level. Block Chairpersons, Vice-Chairpersons and BDOs can be trained at divisional headquarters. Zila Parishad members & district level officers can be trained at all Zila Parishads simultaneously. Similarly, two types of training can be decentralized simultaneously at the block level, i.e.training for intermediate panchayat members and block level officers. Training of Sarpanches & Gram Sevaks-cum-secretaries and training of ward members can be further decentralized at sub-block levels-at a cluster of 10 to 15 Gram Panchayats. This decentralized training system enables training for ERs which is more accessible-near their locations, affordable- minimizing travel costs, time saving, reducing travel time and is more user friendly- enabling inclusive training for all- including women- who are more than 50 per cent in PRIs and cannot easily leave their homes, on account of continuing gender roles in the family. Thus, the decentralized approach of PRI training at multiple locations helps to ensure higher participation rates, gender-inclusion and fast tracks the training delivery to all PRIs within a reasonable time frame.

(c) Online (ICT) Mode Training: Web and computer-based self-learning modules can be created and made available online, for easy, cost-free access of all PRI-ERs & officials. This mode of training holds immense potential for promoting self-learning at the learner's own pace, time and space. However, presently, it is constrained by the fact that e-literacy among ERs is very limited. Also, there is a paucity of self-learning ICT applications available online for capacity building of ERs & officials. This mode can be channelized through outsourcing to ICT professionals, creation of online self-learning ICT Modules relevant for PRIs, and promoting e-literacy among elected representatives and officials of PRIs. Initiative has to be taken by SIRDs to encourage the creation of more user-friendly learning materials for PRIs in online/ICT applications, with the support of professional agencies, in Hindi and other regional languages, which after creation, has to be made available on websites/online.

(d) Mass Media-Based Training: Various forms of mass media can be very effectively utilized for raising awareness on Panchayati Raj & Rural Development issues, not only among PRI-ERs & officials, but also among Gram Sabha members, to play an effective and informed role. The various channels that can be tapped for mass communication with people at large and PRI stakeholders in particular, include–

(i) **All India Radio**-Radio serials can be promoted covering Panchayati Raj & Rural Development related issues, for building sustained awareness among people & PRIs. These experiences can be up-scaled and promoted both in countrywide initiatives of radio programmes as well as State level radio serials.

(ii) **FM Radio**-Similar use for promoting PR&RD related awareness can be made through FM radio, which is accessible on public transport, buses and also on mobile phones and thus, can reach individuals in the rural community who are now frequent users of mobile phones.

(iii) **Community Radio**-This can also be gainfully used as a powerful communication tool for reaching out to rural audiences, such as Gram Sabha members, Self Help Groups (SHGs), village Panchayats-where rural people can listen in groups. Hence, community radio, which has been successfully tried by NGOs-as in Mewat Region of Haryana by Institute of Rural Research & Development (IRRAD), Unnati Sanstha in Jodhpur- Rajasthan and others, can be replicated

(iv) **Doordarshan and other TV Channels**- Success stories of Elected Representatives and officials of PRIs can be serialized in institutionalized channels of TV, including Doordarshan-for which documented stories of good performing Panchayats-who have won National Awards such as the Panchayat Sashaktikaran Puraskar, Nirmal Gram awards or any other National or State awards can be televised as documentaries for TV relay, for inspiring other elected leaders and officials of PRIs.

(v) **Print Media**-National and Regional Newspapers- Print media such as National & regional newspapers and magazines can also be motivated to serialize positive stories of Panchayats who have performed well and can become role-models for inspiring other PRIs. The newspaper dailies/magazines may be asked to dedicate a weekly space or column on Panchayats-success stories/challenges faced and overcome and even question & answer columns/weekly quiz on Panchayati Raj.

(vi) **Newsletters-** The Ministries of Panchayati Raj and Rural Development bring out periodic newsletters. Similarly, State departments of Panchayati Raj and Rural Development also publish their magazines, along with some SIRDs and NIRD & PR also publishing newsletters. The Institute of Social Sciences, New Delhi has sustained a newsletter for Panchayats, since over 20 years,

(e) Traditional and Folk Media: For training of Gram Sabha members, Mahila Sabha members, Ward-Panches of Panchayats, Sarpanches and Gram Sevaks, use of traditional or folk media can be explored as a creative means of 'Infotainment' i.e. audio-visual folk-media can be successfully deployed for providing information along with entertainment on Panchayati Raj & Rural Development issues, for rural semi-literate/non-literate audiences Folk and traditional media which are popular with rural audiences can include: (i) Inspirational Songs and Slogans, (ii) Skits and Street Plays, (iii) Puppet Shows, Folk Dances, Local Traditional Dance-Drama , and (iv) Village Contact Drives

(f) Exposure Visits to Good Performing Panchayats/NGOs/ Projects: It is seen that if GP leaders visit another GP where things have worked better in terms of effective mobilization of the community either for the Gram Sabha or for the preparation of GPDP, there will be a fair chance of adoption of best practices by such leaders. GPDP CB&T should also include field visits for Sarpanch and Standing Committee members to the successful GPs for experiential learning and exposure visit.

(g) Distance Learning: Many institutions like National Institute of Rural Development & Panchayati Raj (NIRD & PR), Indira Gandhi National Open University (IGNOU) and regional/State specific open universities are already running distance education courses-by way of post graduate diploma, certificate courses on Panchayati Raj, rural development, tribal development etc.

(h) SATCOM Training: As already discussed, SATCOM training is also an effective mode of training. However, to increase the effectiveness of the SATCOM mode of training, a two way audio & video connectivity system has to be installed at all SATCOM centers. SATCOM training is recommended to be used for problem-solving, follow-up training and experience sharing after basic training, and is not a substitute for direct training.

(i) Quiz-Contest Based Learning Events: This mode of capability building has been effectively used by SIRD Chattisgarh in an innovative manner. Quiz-contest based learning events for capacity building of PRIs are especially useful in years 4 and 5 of the electoral cycle of PRI-ERs, who through exposure to training opportunities in previous 3 years. Quiz contests at State and National levels can be promoted on Doordarshan-TV Network, on Panchayati Raj issues, on the lines of-'Kaun Banega Crorepati'–with Bollywood anchors being the hosts of the quiz programme. Such programmes can help generate public consciousness on Panchayati Raj issues, across all sections of the population in the country at large.

(j) Information, Education & Communication (IEC): Events other than quiz contests like debate contests, essay writing, poster-making, photography, mock Panchayats and mock Gram Sabhas can be undertake to increase community awareness. Similarly, Mobile Training Vans and IEC Chetna Trains can also be deployed. Moreover, Chetna Shivirs (Awareness Camps)- holding awareness camps amongst the disadvantaged sections of society viz.-tribals, dalits, rural women, minorities living in rural areas and facing exclusion in community decision making platforms like ward & Gram Sabhas, can foster their inclusion and participation.

(k) Peer-Education Mode of Training: This mode of training entails involvement of Elected Representatives as trainers. ERs that have gained hands-on experience and have emerged as good performing leaders during their tenure and effective PRI officials are inducted as trainers in state/ district/block training teams. The advantage of involving experienced and effective ERs and officials as trainers is not only in their becoming inspiring role-models for newly elected PRI-representatives, but also of increased receptivity and acceptability of their own peer group among newly elected representatives.

(l) Experiential Learning Mode: 'Learning by doing' or 'On the job training' have been established modes of learning one's job by practice. In this approach, priority-based dedicated efforts are made by Panchayat functionaries to learn all about the chosen sector, ensure its quality implementation in their area and improve their knowledge and skills in relation to the sector under focus, thereby, learning on the job, through immersion in grappling with emerging challenges.

(m) Help Desk/Help-Line: For providing hand-holding support to PRIs beyond training, the system of Help Desk/Help-Line can be established, for enabling problem- solving in the day-to-day field reality and actual job performance. Help Desk/Help-Line system can be established at state and district levels. This can act as a forum for bringing together experts and advocates of decentralization, including, experts drawn from several departments/sectors devolved to PRIs like education, health, women and child, agriculture and social justice and empowerment etc. for addressing queries received from various districts from PRIs or citizens The district level Help Desk can comprise of 5-10 subject experts drawn from the officials and NGOs of the district. SIRD may be the secretariat of this district level Help Desk. One faculty member could be made in charge of the same. A booklet containing the names and phone numbers of these Help Desk members in different districts of the State, could be prepared , published and circulated among all PRIs.

(n) Model Learning Outreach Centres: For showcasing good practices in decentralised planning, governance, effective public grievance redressal, as well as in sectoral interventions like agriculture, watershed, health, education, water and sanitation, women empowerment etc., model learning centres can be established at different Panchayats, with support of SIRDs and ETCs. These beacon Panchayats can then become learning centres for promoting peer learning through exposure visits. Some good examples of beacon Panchayats that have provided good learning exposure to PRIs in the country are : Hiware Bazar Gram Panchayat in Ahmednagar district , Maharashtra, Pipalantri Gram Panchayat in Rajsamand and Bardod GP in Alwar district, Rajasthan, Adat GP in Thrissur, Kerala, Gangadevapalli GP in Warangal and Ramchadrapuram GP in Karim Nagar district in Andhra Pradesh.

(o) Video-Conferencing: This is a very effective approach for face to face interactive problem-solving, programme monitoring, sharing of feedback of field problems and impact of training and development initiatives. For training, this technique has been used by MANAGE, Hyderabad for outreaching exchange of knowledge with regional centres, equipped with video conferencing facilities.

(p) Social Media: Increasingly, social media and networking can be included as one of the tools of training. Face book pages/You Tube videos of best practices can be promoted.

Selection of the Appropriate Mode of Training

While several tried and tested modes of training by various SIRDs and NGOs have been delineated, the essence of arriving at an appropriate combination of different modes of training varies from time to time and place to place. The number of people to be trained, quality control, special problems of trainees, costs and institutional capacities has to be kept in view while selecting the appropriate mode of training. It may also be necessary to combine various modes of training to optimise learning. For example, institution based training, combined with exposure visits can be extremely effective. It is also necessary to assess the impact of various modes of training to improve and supplement them from time to time. There cannot be a 'one size fits all' formula for choosing effective modes of capacity building of PRIs. Each SIRD or other training institute has to explore best options for increasing user-friendly, participatory, demand-driven modes of learning, thereby, maximizing outputs of capability building of ERs and officials of PRIs. Designing demand-driven, user-friendly, customized training interventions is an iterative process-where past experiences and experiments become guiding lamp-posts to move on to new horizons.

Building Institutional Capacity for Several Modes of Training

Too often, a particular mode of training is used simply because institutional capacity exists only for that particular mode. For example, an institution comfortable with cascade based training may continue to use only that, simply because it has trained manpower and infrastructure to undertake such type of training. To have a genuine choice regarding the mode of training, institutions must develop capacities for various modes of training. It is incumbent on each SIRD to review whether it has the capacity to use the large range of options regarding modes of training and develop the expertise and infrastructure to work with various modes.

(C) Areas of Training

Areas or subjects of training have to be defined in the context of different types of training programmes designed for various stakeholders of Panchayats. The subjects of training would obviously differ for different clientele groups.

Key Issues and Challenges in Areas of Training

The key issues and challenges while identifying appropriate areas of training for the various stakeholders of Panchayats are:

- While a basic training is provided by most SIRDs, Panchayat ERs and functionaries are not provided adequate concurrent knowledge and skill-building support, in continuation of basic training exposure, by all SIRDs.

- Most states lack a perspective plan or framework for CB&T specifically customized for Panchayats, in tandem with their electoral cycle of five years to ensure that all the relevant subjects are covered.
- Gender is not integrated as a cross-cutting issue in the major training courses for PRIs.
- The focus of the training content is largely on the information and knowledge part, with the result that skill development and attitudinal change is not significantly impacted.
- New policy measures, legislations, new schemes and guidelines and field-based success stories of good initiatives are not quickly disseminated to PRIs.
- There is lack of a common level of understanding among ERs and officials, with regard to desired service delivery standards in implementation of devolved subjects and schemes, operational procedures of government functioning, and relevant Acts and Rules.
- There is lack of capacity of SIRDs to take up training in devolved subjects like agriculture, health and promotion of IT-skills like computer training, mobile applications online self-learning modules etc. , which includes:
    (a) Inadequate availability of sector subject experts as master trainers.
    (b) Lack of networking with sectoral training institutes to undertake sectoral training in a synergistic mode.
- Training needs of multi-termers are not properly addressed, as they are exposed to the same training as first time elects – leading to their alienation from training.

Approaches to incorporate Appropriate Subjects

The key strategies to ensure that CB&T across all relevant subjects are:

(i) *Range of Subjects*

The areas or subjects in which training needs to be provided to ERs and other stakeholders largely depend upon the existing status of devolution in different States, in respect of the 3Fs viz.: Funds, Functions and Functionaries. Key areas to be included in the training also need to be spelt out based on the target groups to be trained. In India, there is an increasing policy pressure for accelerating decentralisation through devolution of more and more subjects – as suggested in the 11th schedule of the Constitution – to the Panchayats by state governments. Further, the role of Panchayats in Centrally Sponsored Schemes (CSSs) is also increasing. As a result, new stakeholders (departmental functionaries and CBOs) are continuously being added to the training ambit. New training areas also emerge with every additional sector devolved to Panchayats. Moreover, new concerns of human rights, environmental issues such as global warming, climate change, disasters, changing demographic profile etc. are also important local governance issues. Depending on the clientele to be addressed, the range of subjects to be addressed in CB&T include the functioning of Panchayats, such as accounts and management, sectors in which Panchayats have to work such as drinking water, sanitation, education, livelihoods etc. as well as issues relate to social justice and marginalized groups.

(ii) *Core and State Specific curriculum*

The subjects that need to be addressed while imparting training to ERs and Panchayat functionaries may vary from state to state, corresponding to the extent of devolution, as well as the socio-economic context. Therefore, it is not meaningful to design and implement a uniform training framework for the country as a whole. The training curricula and modules can be categorized under the following two broad headings:

1. Core curriculum, consisting of 'Fundamentals of Panchayati Raj' - that are common and need to be addressed by all states, with reference to 73rd and 74th Constitutional Amendments, the National Policy Framework, and core issues related to Panchayats such as functioning of Panchayats, provision of civic services etc. Even in the core curriculum, state specificity is important.
2. State specific curriculum, as per the identified CB & T needs of the target groups in line with the extent of powers devolved to PRIs and the socio-economic context.

(iii) *Mandatory and Optional Training*

The CB&T strategy for Panchayats may be planned to offer five types of training courses under two broad categories: i.Mandatory courses, which are non-negotiable for ensuring effective functioning of PRIs and, ii.

Optional courses of two types, which should be demand and need-based, to be planned for state-specific needs. Some training institutes may be able to go beyond this also.

There can be three 'Mandatory Courses' for Panchayats, namely:

- Basic Orientation-Foundation Course, which can be given to all stakeholders of Panchayats, though in different modes.
- Theme-Sector- specific Course, which may be provided as relevant to various stakeholders. For ERs, several themes would need to be addressed, while for functionaries dealing with various sectors, the focus would be on the specific sectors.
- Refresher Course, which can touch upon key issues, problems faced etc.

'Optional Courses' could be of following two types viz.:

- Special Courses for ERs of special categories or Panchayat employees working in a particular sector such as accounts
- Advanced Thematic Focused Courses

The Foundation Course should have all the basic contents related to Panchayati Raj and the day to day functioning of Panchayats. The Thematic-Sector- specific Course and the Refresher Course should further update the Panchayat stakeholders with knowledge and skill inputs for handling sector-specific responsibilities with regard to devolved subjects and coping with challenges of disaster management, conflict resolution, inter-sectoral coordination, effective monitoring and supervision, leadership and team building etc. for promoting convergence across transferred subjects. This may be the supply-driven part of training, but designed in response to emerging training needs, based on Training Needs Assessment (TNA). With regard to the design of the demand-driven training interventions, in response to new articulated needs of Panchayat, which may vary from state to state, special courses and thematic focussed courses, may be designed. The course content and material for such demand-driven courses should be prepared based on the needs articulated by the ERs and officials.

The duration of Panchayat training can vary from 1 to 6 days, depending upon the training delivery strategy adopted by states and the profile of participants and their entry behaviour i.e. first termer/multi-termer, educated/non-literate etc.

Suggested content areas for different types of training courses

(i) *Basic Orientation - Foundation Course*

The Foundation Course is a mandatory course designed to orient all the new ERs, as well as core Panchayat functionaries such as Panchayat secretaries, with the fundamental concepts related to Panchayati Raj. This should be conducted within six months of every fresh PRI election. The desired duration may be three days, in a face-to-face, direct interactive mode.

The suggested course content for Basic Orientation – Foundation Course is as follows:

(a) Common Core Content:

- ❒ Concept of democracy and people's participation in development
- ❒ Meaning of local self-government
- ❒ Overview of Panchayati Raj in India
- ❒ 73rd and 74th Constitutional Amendments
- ❒ Gram Sabha and participatory development
- ❒ Human development, gender equality, social justice and women empowerment
- ❒ E-Governance and e-Panchayats
- ❒ Good governance
- ❒ Quality-assured service delivery of all development programmes

(b) State-Specific Content:

- ❒ Overview of State Panchayati Raj Act and Rules
- ❒ Roles and Responsibilities of Panchayats – at all three levels
- ❒ Devolution of '3Fs' with respect to XI-Schedule-29 Subjects
- ❒ Activity-Mapping for 3 tiers of Panchayats actually devolved by respective state governments
- ❒ Relevant issues related to Scheduled-V Areas- such as PESA
- ❒ Participatory and Decentralised Planning
- ❒ District Planning Committee
- ❒ Conduct of mandatory meetings by Panchayats – General Body and Standing Committees

- Office management of Panchayats
- Maintenance of registers and records
- Transparency & accountability mechanisms: RTI and Social Audit
- Financial management: budgeting and accounting systems, including Panchayat data base of funds received, expenditure incurred and own income
- Revenue matters related to Panchayats – Collection of taxes/fees/ penalties; Removal of encroachments from Panchayat lands and common property resources; Issue of housing Pattas and land records and mutation.
- Registration of births, marriages and deaths
- Flagship programmes of devolved subjects (e.g. agriculture, health, education, women and child development etc.)
- National flagship programmes - including MGNREGS, NHM, NBA, SSA, Mid-Day Meal etc.
- Team building (coordination and convergence)
- Inclusive development planning, with focus on disadvantaged communities, viz. – SCs, STs, minorities, women, senior citizens, children, differently abled

(ii) *Thematic Sector-specific Course*

A detailed thematic sector-specific training course could be planned for ERs and officials or for standing committees, in a direct interactive face to face mode. The duration could be 2-3 days for these thematic courses, which should be planned during the second year after election. The sector-specific training can emphasize on service delivery, infrastructure and governance aspects in the given sector. This can be delivered through a series of interactive exercises, presentations of live cases that can guide the Panchayat functionaries on different modalities of planning, implementation and concurrent review of sector-specific initiatives. The broad themes for the sector-specific training could be decided by each state based on the extent of devolution. The suggested list is as follows:

- Provision of civic services
- Health
- Water and sanitation

- Education
- Women and child development
- Social justice and empowerment
- Natural Resource Management/Agriculture

The topics and discussion can centre on the following:

(a) Overview and status of the concerned sector

(b) Core issues to be addressed

(c) Decentralized planning process in each sector

(d) Role of PRIs related to planning, supervision and coordination of devolved subjects

(e) Management of flagship programmes under each sector

(iii) *Refresher Courses*

The Mandatory Refresher Course may be of 2 to 3 days' duration. This should be designed for reinforcement of knowledge generated in the Foundation Course in the first year of the electoral cycle and could ideally be during second or third year after election. The Refresher Course should be organized after the basic orientation and thematic sector specific courses have been considered. The content of the Refresher Course should be developed based on the TNA conducted with the ERs and officials of Panchayats

The Refresher Training Course may be in the face to face or distance mode of training, supported by documentary films, e-learning tools, video-conferencing, newsletters, etc. to refresh the members with the latest information and to relate their learning to real life examples and coping with field-based challenges

(iv) *Special Courses*

(a) Special Courses for Marginalized Groups

Special attention needs to be given to SC, ST and Elected Women Representatives (EWRs) to enhance their involvement in decision making, institutional management and team building, so that they can emerge as assertive local leaders. This course may ideally be designed for 2 to 3 days, and be conducted within six months to one year of PRI election.

(b) Special Courses for Panchayat Functionaries

Similarly, specifically designed courses may be organized for the Panchayat officials, taking into account their designated tasks/job profile.

(c) Leadership Courses

Leadership courses can help ERs in playing the leadership role that is expected of them. The suggested topics of Leadership Training could be as below:

- Leadership and motivation
- Communication/public speaking
- Meeting management
- Office management
- Conflict management
- Inter-personal relationships
- Coordination and convergence
- Public speaking
- Time management
- Stress management
- Management of assets of PRIs
- Participatory decision making

(d) Thematic Focussed Courses

Thematic focussed courses are optional courses designed to provide detailed exposure to Elected Representatives, based on their indicated interests and preferences to pursue further learning. These may be planned as short-term courses of individual modules ranging from 3 to 5 days in a direct interaction mode. Such courses may be planned in the third year after election. These courses may be especially relevant to the needs of experienced, multi-termer ERs, who understand the basic functioning of Panchayats and need to move ahead.

The suggested themes for special courses are given below:

- Participatory inclusive planning

- Water conservation, harvesting, water audit etc.
- Food security and public distribution system
- Rural housing
- Waste management
- Tapping non-conventional sources of energy
- Environmental management
- Livelihoods (agriculture, horticulture, animal husbandry, fisheries, dairy etc.)
- Micro-enterprise management
- Education, health, nutrition etc.

(e) Training in IT and Computer Literacy

ERs and Panchayat functionaries also need to be supported in becoming computer literate, so that they can manage their work efficiently. The SIRD, Tripura has successfully tried out computer trainings for ERs and officials of Panchayats, by networking with expert private partners MoPR also provides computer literacy support in collaboration with the National Institute of Electronics and Information Technology (NIELIT), which states can access. Equally important is training on the Panchayat Enterprise Suite (PES) applications. The MoPR has trained master trainers in states. Each of the PES applications also includes computer based tutorial and application specific presentations that users can engage for self-learning. Use of these may also be encouraged.

The Geographic Information System (GIS) may be promoted in decentralised planning and training programmes on this aspect may be included.

(f) Special Training for Sectoral Functionaries

In addition to the thematic focused training of ERs and officials of Panchayats, special trainings may be planned for other sectoral functionaries assisting the Panchayats. An interesting effort has been made by SIRD, Karnataka for outreaching training to watermen (hand pump mechanics) – responsible for the maintenance of hand pumps in rural areas, under the supervision of GPs.

(D) Quality of Training

The impact of CB&T depends on its quality. Poor quality CB &T can be meaningless, while high quality CB & T can be inspiring and invigorating, and build skills of the trainees to perform their roles. Therefore, it is important to strive towards high quality CB&T.

Key Issues and Challenges

The following are the key issues and challenges regarding the quality of training:

- Given the large number of ERs who have to be trained, the emphasis on training largely tends to be on quantitative coverage of ERs and officials.
- Training outcomes are not properly defined, nor systematically measured.
- There is a shortage of competent trainers, and in the wake of high attrition rates of trainers, retraining new trainers is a continuous challenge.
- There is a paucity of good quality training modules and learning materials, especially in regional languages.
- Monitoring and supervision mechanisms for ensuring training quality during implementation are not well developed.
- PRIs are not supported with continuous hand-holding beyond training, for day to day mentoring and problem solving.
- The challenge of concurrent/regular impact assessment of training of PRIs not adequately addressed by most SIRDs.

Strategies to Address Training Quality

SIRDs and other resource institutions have come up with different strategies for improving training quality. Some have consciously followed the Systematic Approach to Training - SAT Cycle.

(i) *Training Needs Assessment (TNA)*

This stage entails the conduct of an investigative exercise of identifying the training needs as perceived by ERs & officials at the three levels, i.e. Zila Panchayats, Block Panchayats & Gram Panchayats. This can be done through facilitating multi-stakeholder workshops at decentralized locations of divisional/district headquarters. In these workshops, different stakeholders can be invited for interaction on different days, viz. – on day one – ZP level ERs & officials, on day two block level ERs & officials, on day three- GP level ERs & officials and on day four-Gram Sabha members can be consulted. The TNA tools can include interactive methods like; brainstorming on key questions in plenary sessions through participatory methods, eliciting responses to the questions raised, focus group discussions-with homogenous small groups of 10 to 15 members, viz.-general category ERs, SC-ERs, ST-ERs, women-ERs and officials. In-depth interview-with key informants, opinion poll-by show of hands and expressing group's choice through strength of numbers. The training needs emerging from each TNA round can be shared, discussed and prioritized at the state level experience sharing of TNA.

(ii) *Training Material Development (TMD)*

Based on the training needs prioritization after TNA, need-based training modules and learning materials have to be developed, in a user-friendly and easy to understand language. The training modules comprise of a compendium of a design briefs of the training plan and session-wise programme schedule. Training modules for different levels of Panchayats entail spelling out of programme objectives, profile and number of participants with their entry-behaviour, profile of trainers, key content areas to be covered, training methodology to be used, training media to be used viz.-flipcharts, flash cards, audio-visual aids, training films, LCD projector, marker pens, games-kits etc., training outputs and outcomes expected and the session plan-from the start of training to close of training. The accompanying learning materials may include; reference booklets for building clarity of knowledge, PPTs-for AV aids, flipcharts on specific themes, training films, Frequently Asked Questions (FAQs) with answers etc.

Standard training materials should be designed for training. Toolkits, handbooks and manuals for training should be prepared for each category of functionaries, as per needs, keeping in view the diverse characteristics of Panchayats in each state. The training manuals should contain Must Know, Should Know and Could Know aspects. These manuals/materials should be field- tested and modified accordingly. The line departments should also be involved in developing sector-specific training module and reading material. A specific training module may be prepared for PESA region ERs and officials. Likewise separate modules may also be designed for EWRs, SC and ST- ERs. ICT-based interactive learning materials need to be developed, including video-films on best practices of beacon Panchayats.

(iii) ***Training of Trainers (ToT)***

Addressing the challenge of training a huge number of Panchayat ERs and functionaries, without dilution of quality, requires identification and training of quality trainers. The more efficient way of outreaching trainings all stakeholders of Panchayats is the decentralized training mode in which trainings for Panchayats are held at multiple locations, viz.-state, division, district, block, sub-block/cluster of Gram Panchayats etc., thereby ensuring universal and speedy coverage. An essential pre-condition for holding decentralized trainings at multiple locations is creating a strong cadre of trainers.

(iv) ***Training of PRIs***

For delivering high quality inclusive training for Panchayats, the decentralized training system, held at multiple locations simultaneously Each training round should be designed on the needs emerging from TNA and implemented with the help of trained trainers.

(v) ***Training Impact Assessment (TIA)***

After completion of each Panchayat training campaign, with a due gap of about 6 months, Training Impact Assessment (TIA) also needs to be conducted, either through multi-stakeholder workshops to take feedback or through field-based sample research study, among Panchayat-stakeholders. TIA helps to validate as to how and to what extent training has proved beneficial for improving the effectiveness of performance of roles and responsibilities by PRI-ERs & officials. This stage of the SAT-cycle also reveals insights regarding the extent to which transfer of learning has taken place, in terms of updating knowledge, improving skills and re-orienting towards desired attitudinal attributes among PRI-ERs & officials. Further, it can also help evaluate the quality of training

(E) ER of SC, ST and Women

Article-243D of the Constitution mandates reservation for women, Schedule Castes (SCs) and Schedule Tribes (STs) at all tiers of PRIs. In Panchayats across the country, Elected Women Representatives (EWRs) constitute 42.3 per cent, SCs-13.7 per cent while STs constitute 14.6 per cent of all ERs. Further, among the EWRs, almost one-third belong to the deprived sections i.e. SCs and STs. Thus a large number of women ERs face multiple deprivations of caste, class and gender. The practical impact of this revolutionary constitutional provision would only be evident when these EWRs and SC and ST ERs, are fully empowered and made aware of their rights and duties. Thus, capacity building of these historically marginalized ERs is extremely essential, so as to help realize the constitutional vision of inclusive and participatory democratic governance at the grassroots.

Key Issues and Challenges

The key issues and challenges to be addressed regarding CB&T of women SCs and STs are:

- These ERs face socio-cultural exclusion and discrimination and therefore, have greater difficulty in performing their roles.
- Often, ERs from marginalized groups have low self-esteem and confidence level.
- ERs from marginalized groups tend to be inexperienced and often have no previous exposure to political and administrative functioning
- Women ERs are bogged down because of the triple burden of roles and responsibilities viz., - house-work role, rural economy role and their public elected representative role
- Many EWRs are often not able to travel for training and exposure.
- ERs from marginalized groups often lack exposure to formal education, legal literacy and general awareness
- The proxy participation syndrome is still continuing, whereby these ERs are forced to continue to function as dummy candidates, due to pressures of prevailing dominant role players
- These ERs experience lack of freedom in participating fully in opportunities of training, exposure visits, Panchayat meetings – where powerful groups may dominate.
- These marginalized section of ERs are also victims of oppression; violence-verbal, non-verbal, physical, emotional and even sexual abuse; continuing exclusion even in the public domain of

Panchayats – exemplified in instances of being stopped from hoisting the national flag, being stopped from occupying the chairperson's seat, being offered tea/water in different utensils, being hushed into silence when they try to make a point in Panchayat meetings, not being allowed to conduct the Gram Sabha, suggestions being made by them not recorded in meeting resolutions, inequity in fund allocation to Panchayats headed by these sections.

- There is a lack of specifically designed focused training campaigns and lack of hand-holding support beyond training for the marginalized categories of ERs in the early part of their tenure.
- There is a lack of support services for EWRs. Although many states have increased reservation of seats for women to 50 percent in PRIs, setting up of child care centres and the Grievance Redressal Committee for lodging complaints of sexual harassment (as per Supreme Court guidelines) lag behind.
- In the Schedule-V areas, Gram Sabhas have been given special powers through the Panchayats Extension Scheduled Areas Act 1996. The ERs and Gram Sabhas of this region need to be enabled to undertake this task.

(F) Capacity Building and Training Strategies for ERs of Marginalized Sections

(i) *Need for a Special Strategy*

It is essential to have a specialized strategy for CB&T of women, SC and ST ERs and ERs in PESA regions. As these ERs continue to face many socio-cultural barriers to their effective participation in public life, one uniform basic orientation training for all ERs is not adequate. These categories would often require special training, in addition to the common training programme with other ERs.

SIRD Jharkhand has created a special Women's Resource Centre for capacity building of EWRs. Special courses on leadership can also be designed. For example, KILA, Kerala has initiated training of Elected Women Standing Committee Chairpersons on leadership. The steps that may guide the designing of special focused trainings for elected women/ SC/ST representatives, which can be taken up by SIRDs for effective outreach of CB&T.

(ii) *Focussed Training Needs Assessment (TNA)*

A high degree of sensitivity is required for facilitating TNA for women/SC/ST ERs, wherein apart from ensuring stakeholder participation in terms of numbers, special efforts have to be made to draw them out to articulate their problems, concerns and aspirations. Special TNA exercises can be undertaken to identify the training needs of women/SC/ST ERs by conducting focussed TNA workshops for these sections. TNA tools like brainstorming sessions, focus group discussions, in depth interviews with select key informants from each category may be used for culling out their training needs. These TNA workshops could be conducted regionally, with compilation of training needs for each category undertaken with the technical support of SIRDs.

(iii) *Training Modules and Material Development*

Based on the emerging training needs for EWRs, SC & ST ERs, identified through TNA, special modules and materials sensitive to their needs have to be created, preferably in pictorial illustrated format, with the use of simple language, thought-provoking exercises for learning by doing, spaces for listing out problems faced in relation to each topic of study, area specific issues and action planning for problem solving. The print materials should be accompanied by enabling self-learning audio-visual e-materials, for enabling learning at their own pace, beyond training.

(iv) *Training of Trainers*

Special attention has to be paid to the proper selection of trainers. The additional attributes desired in trainers responsible for training for EWRs and SC, ST-ERs are:

- Gender sensitivity and sensitivity to concerns of SCs and STs
- Vision of Inclusive Development
- Effective communication skills to draw out participation of relatively inhibited/hesitant people
- Experienced trainers, especially those who have had hands-on experience as elected leaders, civil society members/activists or as Panchayat functionaries, who have closely interacted with these marginalized groups and are committed to empower them.
- Competent women trainers, SC and ST trainers, who have proven credentials as PRI trainers, from the point of view of social inclusion.

- Felicity in the use of local dialects and participatory training methods relevant for these categories.

(v) *Special ToTs for Sensitizing Trainers*

In addition to the ToTs conducted by SIRDs for PRI training in general, special ToTs by way of sensitization of specially selected trainers for training of marginalized section ERs have to be arranged. Such ToTs should be arranged under SIRD technical support and supervision, at the state and regional levels, for enabling communications skills of delivering effective training for these categories, based on the special modules and learning materials designed for them. Also, role-reflection exercises for continuing the hand-holding support by trainers as mentors to the marginalized section-ERs have to be specially integrated in these ToTs.

(vi) *Focused Training Campaign*

A specially designed and targeted training campaign for the reserved categories has to be conducted in the first year after PRI elections – either before or soon after the common basic foundation course for all ERs and officials.

(vii) *Mainstreaming concerns of ERs of Marginalized Sections in Common Training Campaigns for PRIs*

While a special focused training campaign for the ERs of marginalized groups is needed to empower them for effective participation, simultaneously, it is also desirable to sensitize all ERs and officials in the common PRI training campaigns, to the concerns, problems and aspirations of these historically excluded categories. There is a strong need to integrate at least two special thematic sessions – (i) on gender issues in development planning and local governance and (ii) on social inclusion and elimination of all forms of discrimination against the disadvantaged categories, in every type of training i.e., Foundation Course, Thematic Sectoral Training and refresher courses, for bringing the desired attitudinal change among PRIs. Spouses of EWRs may also need to be sensitized.

(G) Separate Training in PESA Region for ERs and Officials of PRIs

Ten states in the country have areas which come under Schedule-V of the Constitution, which have predominant population of Scheduled Tribes.

Panchayats have been extended in Scheduled Areas through the Panchayat Extension to Scheduled Areas (PESA) Act 1996. PESA confers special powers to Gram Sabhas for self-governance. Therefore, it is important to undertake special CB&T measures in Schedule-V areas to ensure that ERs and officials are aware of the special powers of Gram Sabha under PESA and ensure compliance of the same. PESA provides for special powers for Gram Sabha with respect to land acquisition, control of minor water bodies, and issue of licence and permits for mining of minor minerals, management of minor forest produce, control of intoxicants and liquor, control of money lending, along with natural resource management, local dispute resolution, development planning and social audit etc. This poses special problems for designing appropriate CB&T for PESA areas, because when provisions of PESA are explained to trainees they point out the discrepancies with state laws as well as actual practice. PESA training therefore has to be undertaken with special care, interweaving in the design as well as implementation; training of ERs and officials along with the concerned subject specific departmental officials like Forests, Mines, Excise, Revenue, Water Resources, Police, Cooperatives etc. The National Institute of Rural Development and Panchayati Raj (NIRD & PR) was entrusted by MoPR with the task of preparing a special training manual for training of ERs and officials of PESA states. Under this initiative, NIRD & PR partnered with SIRDs of PESA states to first undertake TNA of PESA region ERs and officials of respective states. Based on the TNA, a comprehensive training manual for training of trainers was created by NIRD & PR with support and inputs of linked SIRDs. States have been asked to adapt and customise this NIRD & PR PESA training manual as per their needs.

(H) Institutional Structures and Processes

To deliver high quality CB &T to a large number of trainees in varied subjects, a high order of institutional capacity is needed. Given the large number of trainees, institutional capacity is required not just at the state level, but at decentralized levels too.

As per the Ministry of Rural Development (MoRD), GoI mandate, most states have established State Institutes of Rural Development (SIRDs), which are state level apex organizations for conducting training and research in Rural Development and Panchayati Raj. The SIRDs in different states have developed at different paces, presenting a varied growth pattern and engagement with training and capability building activities. Extension

Training Centres (ETCs) below the state level have also been supported by MoRD, and some states have their own sub-state level Panchayat Raj training institutes.

Key Issues and Challenges regarding Institutional Capacity

The key issues and challenges with respect to institutional capacity are:

- The SIRDs are yet to develop a long term human resource policy, including a career advancement scheme for the faculty members and other support staff. There is no logical, planned, area-specific expertise based faculty recruitment and development policy.
- The placement of personnel in SIRDs tends to be ad hoc, deputation-based (borrowed human resource from different departments) whereby often people seeking deputation at SIRD are basically looking for parking slots for personal reasons, which is detrimental to quality and institutional growth.
- Hardly any SIRD is truly autonomous and several SIRDs are under the direct control of the concerned departments, which hampers their day to day functioning. At times, SIRDs face inordinate delays in receiving funds from the state governments, which impedes their planned training activities.
- States vary a great deal in the institutional structure that exists below the state level. Several districts in the country have no training institute that caters to the needs of Panchayats.
- The ETCs suffer from lack of a clear policy on administrative control of the ETCs by the SIRDs, instead of departmental control. Therefore, there is no organizational linkage between SIRDs and ETCs.
- The training infrastructure and human resource quality available in ETCs and at other institutes at district/block level, is highly inadequate.
- There is a lack of institutionalized networking of NIRD & PR, SIRDs and ETCs-as linked specialized academic institutions for CB&T of PRIs.
- There is also no parity in terms of sanctioned fund-flow, faculty strength, parity of pay-structures, recruitment and promotion policies, infrastructure, etc. among these institutions.

Key Strategies for Development of Institutional Structure

There is an urgent need to strengthen and synchronize the institutional structure for capability building of PRIs at the national, state, district and sub-district levels. The key suggested strategies are detailed ahead.

(i) *Establishment and Development of State Panchayat Resource Centre (SPRC)*

The RGPSA scheme of MoPR, GoI provides for the establishment of State Panchayat Resource Centres (SPRCs) in SIRDs or any other state nodal institute, to focus exclusively on Panchayati Raj – CB&T and in case of PESA states, focus also on PESA region CB&T.

Role of SPRCs: The SPRC has to be created to accelerate the capability building of Panchayats, develop and disseminate knowledge about Panchayati Raj across the state and function as a think-tank on Panchayati Raj for the state government. The specific responsibilities of the SPRCs may be as follows:

- Formulation of a strategy for capability building of Panchayats.
- Development of appropriate training modules and materials
- Support to district and block resource centers in conducting training at decentralized levels
- Development of technical master trainers and resource persons for training of Panchayat representatives and functionaries.
- Establishment of linkages and coordination with specialist institutes to provide training in various subjects such as education, health, sanitation, women and child, agriculture, etc.
- Networking with NGOs and other resource institutes to share experiences, mutual learning and sharing of training material
- Conduct of training, seminars, conferences and workshops in the broad field of Panchayati Raj, decentralized planning, decentralized development and other emerging needs of topical relevance.
- Promotion and coordination of research work on its own and also in association with universities, specialized research institutes etc. on Panchayati Raj, decentralized development and other related contemporary issues.
- Analysis of specific problems of PRIs and formulation of strategies for problem solving.

- Act as a resource house for all the literature relating to Panchayati Raj system, decentralized development and other allied matters. The resource centre will also be the store house of all relevant information, baseline data relating to various developmental aspects of the state to facilitate planning process in the rural areas.
- Prepare, print and publish papers, periodicals, books relating to various subjects in the field of Panchayati Raj and decentralized development.
- Provision of guidance for or conduct of monitoring and evaluation on various aspects relating to Panchayati Raj system in the state.

(ii) *District Panchayat Resource Centres*

RGPSA provides funds for staffing and infrastructure for District Panchayat Resource Centres (DPRCs). DPRCs can be established by strengthening existing institutions such as ETCs or other Panchayat training institutions or, where no Panchayat training institutions exist, by establishing new institutions.

Role of DPRCs: The role of DRPCs would include the following:

- Better outreach to cater to the training needs of increasing number of ERs and other functionaries of PRIs, as well as a more diverse set of stakeholders.
- Networking with local NGOs working in Panchayati Raj and associated fields for training and knowledge dissemination
- Handholding/on the job training programmes.
- Coordination & convergence of different sectors at the grassroots.
- Wider dissemination of knowledge.
- Adaptation of state level training programmes as per local needs.
- Promotion of networking among the ERs at the grassroots.

(iii) *Block Resource Centres (BRCs)*

Block level satellite resource centres need to be established, to facilitate satellite based and other training programmes. In fact, there is an increasing realization that strong block level facilities are needed, as non residential training programmes can be organized at the block level. Such centres should be attached to the intermediate level Panchayats.

Role of BRCs: The role of BRCs would include the following:

- Be critical nodal points for satellite-based and distance mode training.
- Conduct decentralized training programmes, which reduce costs and allow ERs to access training easily.
- Facilitate Panchayat members for congregating at these resource centres for smaller meetings, mutual consultation and networking.

(iv) ***Network of Training Institutes***

CB & T can be enriched vastly with collaboration among institutes and experts. Each state needs to develop a network of training institutes and resource centres to support Panchayats.

(a) Linkages among Core Training Institutes: The core institutes needed have been described above. It is important to ensure that these are well linked together. SPRCs should provide support and have administrative control over the DPRCs and BRCs. DPRCs would assist the SPRCs to regularly supervise and monitor the BRCs

(b) Partnerships with other Specialist Institutions: Given the very wide range of topics on which CB & T is required for the Panchayat system, SIRDs would need to develop very strong partnerships with other government and non government resource institutions, especially to provide CB &T in various sectors such as education, health, drinking water etc. In some sectors, such as education, there is a strong network of government resource institutions such as State Council of Educational Research and Training (SCERTs) and District Institutes of Educational Training (DIETs) as well as numerous NGOs. In other sectors, such as drinking water, there may be few government specialist institutes. Each SIRD needs to survey the resource institutes available in the state and form a partnership to ensure appropriate sector based training.

(c) Empanelment and Training of Resource Persons: Given the vast and varied CB &T required for Panchayats, active collaboration with a range of resource persons is required. A panel of resource persons may be developed for quality training in a decentralized mode can be developed at the state, district and sub district level. The number of resource persons needed at different levels will depend on the total number of courses to be covered per year, total number of participants at different levels, number of subjects to be handled by resource persons at different levels etc. A process for the selection and certification of trainers may be devised. Such trainers may be identified by SIRDs, or reputed learning and development institutions may be assigned the task of selecting and certifying the trainers. A directory of resource persons (generalists and specialists) can be prepared and published by SIRD.

The broad categories of resource persons to be empanelled at various levels are suggested below:

- Academicians/professors of colleges and institutes- committed to CB&T of PRIs-and knowledgeable in desired fields.
- Retired professors committed to support PRI training in related fields.
- Eminent bureaucrats and technocrats-having experience in RD&PR sector.
- Retired officials having good track record in RD&PR sector.
- Eminent social workers, social activists in relevant subjects.
- Sectoral officials belonging to different line departments.
- ERs of Panchayats who have performed well in more than one tenure at different tiers of Panchayats.

The primary criteria for selecting the RPs/Master Trainers must be their competence. The RPs/Master Trainers should be competent in the subject matter and skilled in the training methods being used. Trainers may also be involved in assessment activities, either to provide informative feedback to the trainees or to assess competence of trainees.

The important criteria for selection of RPs/Master Trainers are:

- Effective communicator with the trainees.
- Range of experience and competence in the desired subjects.
- Availability and commitment for decentralized training.
- Skill in participatory training methods.
- Gender sensitivity.
- Experience of RD&PR sector related work.
- Pro poor, pro-rural & pro-disadvantaged orientation

The broad areas in which Resource Persons/Master Trainers are required include:

- General Orientation on Panchayati Raj System, Decentralized Development including 73rd Amendment, Gram Sabhas, etc.
- Management of Panchayati Raj Institutions.
- Roles and responsibilities of ERs and officials of PRIs
- Interpersonal, motivational, leadership and soft-skills.
- Planning & management of RD & sectoral programmes.
- Decentralized/micro planning.
- Flagship programmes of GoI
- Livelihood promotion.
- Resource mobilization, management and budgeting.
- Maintenance of accounts, record keeping & audit compliances
- Social development and human development.
- Social justice and women empowerment.
- Participatory development and monitoring.
- Social audit, grievance redressal, transparency, RTI etc.
- Disaster management and environmental issues.
- Land and water resource management.
- IT related training programmes.

Conclusion and Recommendations

The capacity building and training of different stakeholders of Panchayati Raj system must need some improvisation in the following field;

In the domain of Modes of Training these are the things that may be taken care of;

- Modes of training have to address the large numbers required to be trained, as well as maintain and upgrade the quality of training programmes. Needs of special groups also have to be kept in mind. Therefore, the mode of training to be used should be considered with care when deciding on a training plan.
- While the cascade mode of training and distance education, along with the use of media, can form the bedrock for training all ERs, there is also need to continue diverse training methods such as

hand-holding through Help Desk/Help Line, peer-interaction, quiz contests, experimental learning etc. to meet the diverse needs.

- Mass-media, i.e., radio, community radio, television, print media folk-media etc. need to be used effectively, as these can enable training at lower costs and can also generate interest. Mass media based orientation can complement regular training programmes.
- E-Modules and distance learning material can be designed and disseminated to supplement direct training.
- Innovative modes of training, such as quiz contest based training, the experiential learning mode etc. should be attempted, especially with ERs who have experienced other modes of training.
- For optimal learning, various modes of training should be combined to expose the trainee to theoretical and practical understanding, greater interaction with trainers or peers etc.
- SIRDs and other training institutes need to review training modes for various training programmes and select the most suitable ones.
- Institutional capacities need to be built to undertake training in various modes. Each SIRD can increase its range continuously to use various modes of training for effective delivery.

In the domain of Areas of Training these are the things that may be taken care of;

- SIRDs need to plan for mandatory basic courses and specialized thematic courses for Panchayats along their five yearly performance cycle – with a basic foundation course in year one, soon after elections, subsequent thematic refresher/specialized courses in second and third years.
- A five year Capacity Building Strategic Framework (Perspective Plan) may be evolved for each state, based on TNA of PRI stakeholders.
- SIRDs need to take up and sustain subject-specific specialized training, related to the devolved subjects. For this SIRDs may develop expertise in devolved–sectoral areas like agriculture, health, water and sanitation, maintenance of assets etc. by setting up specialized centers and appointing desired subject-specific expert faculty.

- SIRDs may identify and network with sectoral training institutes to undertake in-depth sectoral trainings.
- Sectoral experts may be developed as master trainers with the help of sectoral training institutes and also be exposed to basic understanding of PRIs.
- Training for various functionaries should match the skills they need. In particular, training modules for core Panchayat functionaries such as secretaries, accountants, Panchayat Development Officers should be developed.
- All SIRDs need to develop context specific training modules for mandatory and optional training courses for various stakeholders, especially:
    - Special courses for marginalized groups.
    - Special courses for Panchayat functionaries
    - Leadership training
    - Thematic focused courses
    - IT and computer literacy
    - Special training for sector functionaries

Moreover, in the field of Quality of Training these are the things that might be taken care of;

- The Systematic Approach to Training Cycle(SAT-Cycle) should be followed by all SIRDs to ensure quality of training of PRIs. This entails Training Needs Assessment, Training Material Development, Training of Trainers, followed by actual training and Training Impact Assessment. The quality of each of these processes needs to be continuously improved.
- SIRDs need to focus on training design to maintain quality. New methods and materials should be used to enhance the quality of training.
- Creation of need - based training modules, work-books and learning materials has to precede each PRI training campaign/round for ensuring quality and uniformity of training across the state.
- Training of an adequate number of competent trainers, committed to deliver training to PRIs at decentralized locations, is of prime

importance for ensuring high quality and high speed training in decentralized mode. SIRDs should develop certificate courses for trainers to ensure quality.

- Good organization is vital for high quality training. Regular feed-back should be taken to ensure that no lacunae remain. Further, state level observers/monitors may be deployed.
- Convergence with other sectors such as agriculture, education, health etc. can enrich training.

Similarly, under Institutional Structures and Processes of Training the following things that may be taken care of;

- States need to create a sound institutional and human resource policy for sustained and systematic arrangement for CB&T of PRIs.
- RGPSA/RGSA guidelines and funding provisions may be used optimally for creation of SPRCs, DPRCs and BRCs-for developing a logically spread-out training institutional at various decentralized locations.
- The human resources in training institutions need to be carefully selected and also trained and encouraged for professional growth.
- Adequate infrastructure in training institutes at various levels needs to be ensured.
- Networking of training institutions across national, state, district and block levels needs to be promoted and given mentoring support for facilitating best utilization of infrastructural and human resources available in them.
- PRI CB&T requires creation and sustenance of strong trainers and resource persons at decentralized locations for faster and wider outreach.
- Synergy has to be encouraged across PRI & RD related training institutions, with sectoral and other resource institutions, for widening the exchange of RPs, knowledge products and training materials.
- Autonomy of SIRDs needs to be promoted and their exposure to National/International institutes of excellence has to be institutionalized for building their potential to themselves become centers of excellence for PR & RD sector.

Appendices

APPENDIX-I

FAQs on Gram Panchayat Development Plan (GPDP) and Mission Antyodaya

Gram Panchayats have been mandated for the preparation of Gram Panchayat Development Plan (GPDP) for economic development and social justice utilizing the resources available to them. The GPDP planning process has to be comprehensive and based on participatory process which involves the full convergence with Schemes of all related Central Ministries / Line Departments related to 29 subjects enlisted in the Eleventh Schedule of the Constitution. Panchayats have a significant role to play in the effective and efficient implementation of flagship schemes on subjects of National Importance for transformation of rural India. The People's Plan Campaign initiated under "Sabki Yojana Sabka Vikas" will be an intensive and structured exercise for planning at Gram Sabha through convergence between Panchayati Raj Institutions (PRIs) and concerned Line Departments of the State

Q. What is GPDP?

Ans. Gram Panchayats have been mandated for the preparation of Gram Panchayat Development Plan (GPDP) for economic development and social justice utilizing the resources available to them. The GPDP planning process has to be comprehensive and based on participatory process which involves the full convergence with Schemes of all related Central Ministries / Line Departments related to 29 subjects enlisted in the Eleventh Schedule of the Constitution. Panchayats have a significant role to play in the effective and efficient implementation of flagship schemes on subjects of National Importance for transformation of rural India. The People's Plan Campaign will commence from 2ndOctober to 31st December 2018 for preparing GPDP for 2019-20. The campaign initiated under "Sabki Yojana Sabka Vikas" will be an intensive and structured exercise for planning at Gram Sabha through convergence between Panchayati Raj Institutions (PRIs) and concerned Line Departments of the State.

Q. Types of users in GPDP?

Ans. Following types of users will exist in the system:

- State Nodal User
- State Department users
- District Panchayat (DP)/ District level users
- Intermediate Panchayat/ Block level users
- Facilitators at the GP level

Q. What are the helpline details of GPDP?

Ans. For any assistance, contact us on: 011-23753821, 011-23355373, 011-23356128 between 9 AM – 6PM (Monday to Saturday), or gpdp[dot]mopr[at]nic[dot]in

Q. I am not able to login in the GPDP Portal

Ans. In case you are not able to login in the system, try resetting your password using **Forgot Password** option. In case the message populates, "Invalid Mobile Number", Kindly contact your State/District/Block level nodal officer and get yourself registered in the system. The list of State/ District Nodal officers for GPDP can also be seen at https://gpdp.nic.in/nodalOfficerReport.html?OWASP_CSRFTOKEN=W7JZ-RTK1-Q8AC-PUYF-NLSE-55IG-2N7I-93GR

Q. How to retrieve the lost/ forgotten Password?

Ans.
- Open **gpdp.nic.in** website and click on **Login** Icon.
- On the login page, there will be a link "**Forgot Password**". Click on Forgot Password and enter the registered Mobile number.
- Click on **GET OTP** button. One Time Password (OPT) is sent on the registered Mobile Number as an SMS and Email.
- Enter the OTP; enter new Password and confirm Password and click on Submit button.

- The new Password entered should be 8-12 characters with one upper case, 1 lower case, 1 number and 1
- The new Password will be setup and the user can login with the new Password.

Q. I have not received the OTP on submitting request using Forgot Password option.

Ans. There could be some network congestion due to which the SMS is not received. Wait for some time. If the SMS is still not received, report the issue to helpdesk on **011-23753821, 011-23355373, 011-23356128, Monday- Saturday between 9 AM – 6PM.**

Q. Website is not working.

Ans. There may be some intermittent changes going on in the website. If at all, when you access the website, the portal happens to be in non-working state, Kindly wait and check back again after some time. If the issue persists for a long time, report the issue to helpdesk on **011-23753821, 011-23355373, 011-23356128, Monday to Saturday between 9 AM – 6 PM. Issue can also be reported at gpdp[dot]mopr[at]nic[dot]in**

Q. Not able to operate the portal.

Ans. There is a user manual on how to operate the GPDP portal with proper screenshot for easy navigation. Click on Downloads tab, and under "About GPDP Portal", user manual has been placed with the name GPDP user Manual v1.3.

Q. How to register the State level user?

Ans. Central level NIC officials will register the state nodal officers. Full Name, Designation, Mobile number and email id will be captured for the State User (Nodal officer). Mobile number should be unique as mobile number is the login id of user. State Nodal Officers username and password will be generated at the central level.

Q. Privileges/roles of State Nodal officer?

Ans.
- To create all department nodal officers on state level

- To create user for District/Block or ZP/BP and facilitator
- Reset its own password

Q. How to register the District/District Panchayat level user?

Ans.
- State level Nodal user will register the District/District Panchayat level user.
- The State Nodal user will decide whether to create users using the District hierarchy or District Panchayat hierarchy. At any point of time, the state level user can create user using either of the hierarchy.
- Full Name, Designation, Mobile number and email id will be captured for the District User.
- Mobile number should be unique as mobile number is the login id of user.
- On registering the user, the user will receive an SMS with the User ID and Password.

NB: In case a user has multiple mobile number, he/she should ensure that the same number is used at all times.

Q. Privileges/roles of District Nodal officer?

Ans.
- Create users at the Block/ Block Panchayat Level.
- Create users for the GP level facilitators.
- Map Facilitators to GPs.
- Add Frontline workers at District and Block level.
- Map Frontline workers to GPs.
- Reset its own password
- View Facilitator Report GP wise.
- Schedule Gram Sabha for each Gram Panchayat.

Q. How to register the Block/Block Panchayat level user?

Ans.
- District level user will register the Block/Block Panchayat level user.
- If the District user is created by the State Admin, then user can create only Block user. Whereas, if the District panchayat user is

created, then Block Panchayat user may further be created in the hierarchy.

- Full Name, Designation, Mobile number and email id will be captured for the Block
- User. Mobile number should be unique as mobile number is the login id of user.
- On registering the user, the user will receive an SMS with the User ID and Password.

Q. Privileges/roles of Block/Block Panchayat Nodal officer?

Ans.
- Create users for the GP level facilitators.
- Map Facilitators to GPs.
- Add Frontline workers at Block level.
- Map Frontline workers to GPs.
- Reset its own password.
- View Facilitator Report GP wise.
- Schedule Gram Sabha for each Gram Panchayat.

Q. Role of a Facilitator?

Ans. Facilitator user for each gram panchayat will be appointed by the District/Block level user. State may consider appropriate persons (including officials, CRPs, GRS, etc.) for nominations.

Roles of a facilitator are:

- Have a sound understanding of the concept of GPDP
- Facilitate the special Gram Sabha for GPDP on the designated day.
- Submit the report regarding the conduct of the Gram Sabha on the portal.
- Upload Gram Sabha images.
- Coordinating with frontline staff of participating ministries/ departments.

- Supporting preparation of GPDP
- Upload GPDP on PlanPlus.

Q. Role of a Frontline worker?

Ans. State level, District Level, Block level users are responsible for appointing and uploading the names of frontline workers to be deputed for Gram Sabha meetings on the designated days. The frontline workers will give a brief structured presentation regarding the activities of the department. Multiple frontline workers can be created at a single time for a department. A Facilitator can also be assigned for multiple GPs, if the ground situation so demands.

Q. What are the things that need to be kept in mind while scheduling Gram Sabha?

Ans. Gram Sabha wise calendar for holding of Gram Sabha's will be finalized at State /district/Block level and the same will be uploaded on the portal. While scheduling the calendar of events of the Gram Sabha, States/Block/Block may take care that within a block no two Gram Sabha meetings are scheduled on the same date so as to ensure presence of frontline workers of all line Departments. However, States/Block/Facilitator may schedule more than one Gram Sabha meetings in a block on the same date if they can ensure the presence of frontline workers from the line department in all Gram Sabha meetings.

For scheduling Gram Sabha of a GP, user need to select the GP, Date of Gram Sabha, facilitator who will be facilitating the Gram Sabha and Department wise frontline worker.

Q. How many Gram Sabhas could be scheduled for a GP?

Ans. The State has a provision to schedule only 1 special Gram Sabha for a GP in the portal. However, the state has the liberty to hold more than 1 Gram Sabha in the campaign period. The details of the special Gram Sabha that is held to discuss on GPDP should be entered on the portal.

Q. Till when can the Facilitator submit the Facilitator Report?

Ans. The Facilitator can submit the report any time after the Gram Sabha has been held.

Q. What if the GP is showing in LGD and GPDP portal but not in MA?

Ans. Please reach out to the MA team at Delhi (**nictech-ma@gov.in**) and the **Helpdesk (011-23074309) between 9 AM – 6PM (Monday to Friday)** to get this resolved.

Q. What all information should the Resource Envelope include and from where to get the data?

Ans. Details of all funds available to GP for the following year should be included in the GPDP. For this, the functionaries of line departments should be reached out to know the quantum of funds / activities to be undertaken in the GP during next year. Activities for which funds would not be going to the GP directly, but are some social goal (e.g. zero school dropout) should also be included in the Resource Envelope.

Q. Do we need to create users separately on GPDP portal and also on MA portal?

Ans. Yes, users will need to separately register on both GPDP & MA portal

Q. What to do, if a GP is not visible in the reports under their parental District or Block Panchayat?

Ans. All the reports developed in GPDP portal are based on the District Panchayat/Block Panchayat hierarchy. As per the Land Region hierarchy, a respective GP can come under different District Panchayat/ Block Panchayat. User should check the GP in LGD application for the correct hierarchy.

Q. Count of Frontline worker/Facilitator is not matching with the GP count?

Ans. A facilitator/frontline worker can be mapped to multiple GPs and 1 facilitator/frontline worker can be mapped to many GPs.

Q. Who can unfreeze, the scheduled Special Gram Sabha meeting?

Ans. State Nodal Officer can unfreeze the special gram Sabha meeting, on receiving the request and should also record reason. Also, the attachment needs to be uploaded in the portal.

Q. How a user can be registered again with the already registered mobile number in GPDP portal.

Ans. A user /person with same mobile number can be registered only once. If the user has to register at any other entity, then that existing user should be deactivated first and then can assign at any other entity.

Q. How a user can reset the password of GPDP Portal?

Ans. User can reset password by clicking on the Forgot Password Link (https://gpdp.nic.in/forgotPassword.html?). Registered user should enter mobile number and click on the get OTP button. User need to enter the received OTP and captcha and then can change his password.

Q. How a user can create district/block nodal officer for a participating line department?

Ans. State nodal officer is having the privilege to create the state nodal officer of a respective line department. The state nodal officer of line department can further register the district and block nodal officer of the line departments using their credential. Similarly, the district/block nodal officers can create and map the frontline workers to their districts/block's GPs.

Q. How can a user/citizen track the progress made by the GPs in GPDP Portal?

Ans. On the home page of GPDP Portal, under statistical reports section, there are various reports (drill down till GP) are available to track the progress made by the GPs. It is also possible to view the GPs where no progress have been made in GPDP portal.

Q. How the Gram Sabha meeting proceeding/ PIB images uploaded by a citizen/ Registered user is available on the GPDP portal?

Ans. Registered User/ Citizen can upload a geo-tagged photograph from the GPDP Facilitator Report Mobile App. If the photo uploaded by a citizen (without login) will be visible on the GPDP portal, if it is approved/moderated either by the State Nodal officer or by the district nodal officer.

Q. Facilitator is not able to see the GP while filling the facilitator feedback form?

Ans. The Facilitator registered with mobile number is allowed to fill the facilitator feedback form in respect to assigned GP only. The Gram Sabha meeting schedule should be freezed before filling of facilitator feedback form. The facilitator can fill the feedback on the date or after the date of special Gram Sabha meeting. Facilitator must have to check the all the discussion points before filling the facilitator feedback form.

Q. How can a facilitator feedback form be updated once it is filled?

Ans. The Facilitator has to fill the facilitator feedback form using Facilitator Report mobile app. If some updation is required after submitting the form, the facilitator can make the changes from the web portal only using the same credentials.

Q. What is Mission Antyodaya ?

Ans. Mission Antyodaya is an accountability and convergence framework for transforming lives and livelihoods on measurable outcomes.

Q. What is the main focus area of Mission Antyodaya?

Ans. Mission Antyodaya focus on most backward districts.

Q. Why this application has been developed?

Ans. Ministries has been consistently been adopting new methodologies and technologies to enhance its service delivery capacity. The main advantage of this application is convergence of data from Gram Panchayat Level.

Q. User name and password are mandatory fields.

Ans. User name and password are mandatory fields.

Q. How Mission Antyodaya is related to Digital India?

Ans. The convergence of multiple schemes under a single scheme could enable the government to migrate all these to the digital Aadhar-enabled platform thereby contributing further to the Digital India mission aims.

Q. Is a Internet Data Connection mandatory?

Ans. Yes.

Q. What are the charges for downloading and using Mission Antyodaya App?

Ans. Ministry of Rural Development offers mobile app free of Charge to public. You can download and use this application as and when needed without any charge. Your Mobile operator will levy charges for GPRS/3G. Please check with your operator for details.

Q. What are the charges for downloading and using Mission Antyodaya App?

Ans. You don't need to login into the application. You have to take the following steps to register: Download the application on your device from Google Play Store Register on the application by giving User name and Password and press Submit button. Click "Register" button.

Q. Which Ministries are involved in Mission Antyodaya Project?

Ans. Over 25 Ministries/ Departments through specific programs

- Department of Rural Development
- Ministry of Panchayati Raj
- Ministry of Health and Family Welfare
- Ministry of Drinking Water & Sanitation
- Ministry of Women and Child Development
- Ministry of Agriculture Cooperation & Farmers Welfare
- Ministry of Social Justice & Empowerment
- Ministry of Finance
- Ministry of Micro Small and Medium Enterprises
- Ministry of New and Renewable Energy
- Ministry of Petroleum & Natural Gas
- Ministry of Power Ministry of Water Resources
- Ministry of Textiles Ministry of Culture
- Ministry of Tourism

- Ministry of Tribal Affairs
- Ministry of Electronics & Information Technology
- Ministry of Skill Development & Entrepreneurship.

Q. Who are eligible to enter data in Mission Antyodaya System?

Ans. State, Development Block, District and Gram Panchayat users are eligible to enter data in Mission Antyodaya system.

Q. Is this system integrated with Aadhar card authentication?

Ans. Not now, but we are in the process of integration.

Q. What types of reports are available in Mission Antyodaya?

Ans. Various types of reports are available in Mission Antyodaya: MIS Reports, Reports on Infrastructure, Ranking Report, Score card Report, Clean Energy Reports.

Q. Can a normal user view and download the report?

Ans. Yes, users can view and download the reports

Q. What is new with Mission Antyodaya?

Ans. Response to multi-dimensional nature of poverty under leadership of State Convergence from Central ministries to gram panchayat level.

APPENDIX-II

FAQs on Finance Commission

Q. What is the Finance Commission?

Ans. The Finance Commission is constituted by the President under Article 280 of the Constitution, mainly to give its recommendations on distribution of tax revenues between the Union and the States and amongst the States themselves. Two distinctive features of the Commission's work involve redressing the vertical imbalances between the taxation powers and expenditure responsibilities of the centre and the States respectively and equalization of all public services across the States.

Q. Why need Finance Commission?

Ans. The following are the reasons for need of Finance Commission in India

- The framers of the Constitution were seeking to address the vertical imbalance between the taxation powers and expenditure and responsibilities of the federal government and the states, and the horizontal imbalance, or inequality, between states that were at different stages of development.
- Ensuring inclusiveness is, therefore, a key mandate of the Finance Commission.
- That means assigning weights to things like population, the fiscal distance between the top ranked states and the others, etc.
- It is not that the best-performing state will be allocated the highest share — even if delivery execution and governance are better — rather, the effort will be to narrow the development gap between states.

Q. What are the functions of the Finance Commission?

Ans. It is the duty of the Commission to make recommendations to the President as to—

- the distribution between the Union and the States of the net proceeds of taxes which are to be, or may be, divided between them and the allocation between the States of the respective shares of such proceeds;
- the principles which should govern the grants-in-aid of the revenues of the States out of the Consolidated Fund of India;
- the measures needed to augment the Consolidated Fund of a State to supplement the resources of the Panchayats in the State on the basis of the recommendations made by the Finance Commission of the State;
- the measures needed to augment the Consolidated Fund of a State to supplement the resources of the Municipalities in the State on the basis of the recommendations made by the Finance Commission of the State;
- any other matter referred to the Commission by the President in the interests of sound finance.

The Commission determines its procedure and have such powers in the performance of their functions as Parliament may by law confer on them.

Q. Who appoints the Finance Commission and what are the qualifications for Members?

Ans. The Finance Commission is appointed by the President under Article 280 of the Constitution. As per the provisions contained in the Finance Commission [Miscellaneous Provisions] Act, 1951 and **The Finance Commission (Salaries & Allowances) Rules, 1951,** the Chairman of the Commission is selected from among persons who have had experience in public affairs, and the four other members are selected from among persons who—

(a) are, or have been, or are qualified to be appointed as Judges of a High Court; or

(b) have special knowledge of the finances and accounts of Government; or

(c) have had wide experience in financial matters and in administration; or

(d) have special knowledge of economics

Q. How are the recommendations of Finance Commission implemented?

Ans. The recommendations of the Finance Commission are implemented as under:-

Those to be implemented by an order of the President:

- The recommendations relating to distribution of Union Taxes and Duties and Grants-in-aid fall in this category.

Those to be implemented by executive orders:

- Other recommendations to be made by the Finance Commission, as per its Terms of Reference

Q. When was the first Commission Constituted and how many Commissions have been Constituted so far?

Ans. The First Finance Commission was constituted vide Presidential Order dated 22.11.1951 under the chairmanship of Shri K.C. Neogy on 6th April, 1952. Fifteenth Finance Commissions have been Constituted so far at intervals of every five years.

Q. Is the Finance Commission unique to India?

Ans. Most federal systems resolve the vertical and horizontal imbalances through mechanisms similar to the Finance Commission. For example Australia and Canada.

APPENDIX-III

FAQs on Panchayats (Extension to the Scheduled Areas) Act (PESA)

Q. What is PESA?

Ans. This is a legislation which extends the provisions of Panchayats to the Fifth Schedule Areas. These areas have preponderance of tribal population. This Act is called "The Provisions of the Panchayats (Extension to the Scheduled Areas) Act, 1996". In short form this is popular as"'PESA".

Q. How many States with Fifth Schedule Areas are covered under PESA?

Ans. Total ten States are covered under PESA. These States are: Andhra Pradesh, Chhattisgarh, Gujarat, Himachal Pradesh, Jharkhand, Madhya Pradesh, Maharashtra, Odisha, Rajasthan and Telangana.

Q. Which community has the right to contest elections for the post of Chairperson of Panchayati Raj Institutions (PRIs)?

Ans. All posts of Chairpersons of PRIs in the areas covered under PESA are reserved for tribal community and only persons belonging to tribal community can contest for these posts.

Q. What are the important powers provided to Gram Sabha under PESA?

Ans. Following three types of powers have been given to a Gram Sabha under PESA:

(i) **Developmental**: consultation before land acquisition, prevent land alienation, power to enforce prohibition, prior approval of all developmental projects and control over tribal sub-plan, power to issue utilization certificate for developmental expenditure, selection of beneficiaries of poverty alleviation and other schemes of individual benefits, control over institutions and functionaries of social sectors.

(ii) **Dispute resolution as per traditional laws and customs:** collective resolution of disputes on the basis of customs, traditional laws and religious beliefs of tribal areas.

(iii) **Ownership and management of natural resources**: maintaining ownership of local tribal community over water resources, common lands, minor forest produce, minor minerals, etc. as well as effective implementation and monitoring of related laws.

Q. What are the powers given to Gram Sabha/ PRIs under PESA Act?

Ans. Following legal powers have been given to Gram Sabha/PRIs under PESA Act:

i. Safeguard and preserve the traditions and customs of the people, their cultural identity, community resources and the customary mode of dispute resolution.

ii. Approve plans, programmes and projects for social and economic development before such plans, programmes and projects are taken up for implementation by the Panchayat at the village level.

iii. Identification or selection of persons as beneficiaries under the poverty alleviation and other programmes.

iv. Certification of utilisation of funds by the Panchayat for the plans, programmes and projects for identification or selection of persons as beneficiaries under the poverty alleviation and other programmes.

v. Right to be consulted before making acquisition of land in the Scheduled Areas for development projects and before re-settling or rehabilitating persons affected by such projects in the Scheduled Areas.

vi. Right to plan and manage minor water bodies in the Scheduled Areas.

vii. Recommendations prior to grant of prospecting licence or mining lease for minor minerals and for grant of concession for the exploitation of minor minerals by auction in the Scheduled Areas.

viii. Power to enforce prohibition or to regulate or restrict the sale and consumption of any intoxicant.

ix. Ownership of minor forest produce.

x. Power to prevent alienation of land in the Scheduled Areas and to restore any unlawfully alienated land of a Scheduled Tribe.

xi. Power to manage village markets.

xii. Power to exercise control over money lending to the Scheduled Tribes.

xiii. Power to exercise control over institutions and functionaries in all social sectors.

xiv. Power to control over local plans and resources for such plans including tribal sub-plans.

Q. Which forest produces are termed as Minor Forest Produce?

Ans. "Minor Forest Produce" has been defined in "The Scheduled Tribes and Other Traditional Forest Dwellers (Recognition of Forest Rights) Act, 2006" which includes all non-timber forest produce of plant origin, including bamboo, brush wood, stumps, cane, tussar, cocoons, honey-wax, lac, tendu leaves, medicinal plants, herbs, roots, tubers, etc.

Q. Who are members of Gram Sabha?

Ans. All registered voters in the electoral roll of the Panchayat in the village are members of Gram Sabha.

Q. How is a village constituted under PESA?

Ans. A Village shall ordinarily consist of a habitation or a group of habitations or a hamlet or a group of hamlets.

Q. How is Gram Sabha constituted under PESA?

Ans. As per PESA, every village shall have a Gram Sabha consisting of persons whose names are included in the rolls for the Panchayat at the village level.

Q. Who is the Secretary of the Gram Sabha?

Ans. Secretary of the Gram Panchayat is also the Secretary of the Gram Sabha.

Q. What will be the quorum of the Gram Sabha?

Ans. Quorum of the Gram Sabha will be as per State PESA Rules, State Panchayati Raj Acts and State Panchayati Raj Rules. For example, in Rajasthan quorum is 10% of total members of Gram Sabha. In Andhra Pradesh, the quorum is not less than 1/3" of members of Gram Sabha of whom at least 50% shall be ST members. In Maharashtra, the quorum is twenty-five per cent of the total members or one hundred, whichever is lower.

Q. How many meetings of Gram Sabha are mandatory in a year?

Ans. Number of mandatory meetings of the Gram Sabha will be as per State PESA Rules, State Panchayati Raj Acts and State Panchayati Raj Rules. Many States have a minimum number of 4 mandatory meetings of Gram Sabha in a year.

Q. When can a special meeting of Gram Sabha be called?

Ans. Other than the mandatory meetings of Gram Sabha, special meetings may also be convened as per the provisions of State PESA Rules, State Panchayati Raj Acts and State Panchayati Raj Rules. It is normally convened when in the general meeting of a Gram Sabha, a decision is taken in this regard or when the Gram Panchayat receives a proposal on which opinion of Gram Sabha is necessary or when a certain percentage or number of members of Gram Sabha submit a written demand to the Secretary for a special meeting.

Q. When can a joint meeting of two or more Gram Sabhas be called?

Ans. For taking decisions on a project or proposal having impact on more than one village and requiring opinion of more than one Gram Sabha, a joint meeting of two or more Gram Sabhas may be called.

Q. Can Gram Sabha constitute its committee/s?

Ans. Gram Sabha may constitute Committee/s to carry out its functions like maintaining peace and order, management of minor forest produce, village markets, sale or consumption of intoxicants, control over money lending and management of water bodies, etc. The duties assigned to the Committees may be withdrawn or modified at any time by passing a resolution by the Gram Sabha. The Standing Committees should act in accordance with the instructions of Gram Sabha. A joint committee representing two or more PESA villages may be constituted with the consent of concerned Gram Sabhas.

Q. What is a Gram Sabha Kosh (fund)?

Ans. Gram Sabha can maintain a corpus fund (e.g. Gram Sabha Kosh) which will be required for carrying out several management functions assigned to Gram Sabha. The corpus fund may be raised through taking contributions either in the form of cash, or goods, either from Government or non- Government organisations or in the term of value of labour in villages.

Q. What are the provisions of dispute resolution under PESA?

Ans. Gram Sabha is competent to safeguard and preserve customary modes of dispute resolution. As per PESA Act, dispute resolution is in the domain of village community. These disputes may include minor disputes of any description, including those relating to property, land, sharing of crops, land boundary disputes, inheritance, easement rights, use of community resources, issues involving customary practices and usages, cases involving galaxy of beliefs including magic, sorcery, etc. and also disputes vis-a-vis individuals, concerning credit of all descriptions, molestation, fake caste certification cases and such like. Rajasthan PESA Rules 2011 provide for constitution of a Peace Committee for dispute resolution and maintenance of law and order. On the direction of Gram Sabha, the Peace Committee tries to resolve the dispute and report to Gram Sabha or with approval of Gram Sabha report to designated Magistrate. Such dispute resolution will be as per customs and traditions and through open hearings. All decisions on the proposal of Peace Committee will be taken by Gram Sabha on the basis of majority. In case of any threat of breach of peace or law & order in the village, local Police will report to Gram Sabha or Peace Committee except where immediate action is necessary. Police will register FIR only in case of serious crime (with provision of punishment more than 2 years under IPC, 1860) and send a copy to Gram Sabha/ Peace Committee. Gram Sabha will try to resolve the conflict in its next or special meeting.

Q. What are the responsibilities of Gram Sabha in management of Common Property Resources?

Ans. Gram Sabha has following responsibilities in the management of community resources:

(i) Conservation and management of all community resources in the village such as water, common land, community forest, pasture land, minor minerals, etc. as per local traditions and customs.

(ii) Gram Sabha will ensure that community resources are utilised in a manner that there is improvement in means of livelihood and equality among people.

Q. What is the responsibility of Gram Sabha in land acquisition?

Ans. PESA Act provides that the Gram Sabha or the Panchayats at appropriate level shall be consulted before making the acquisition of land for development projects or before resettling or rehabilitating persons affected by such projects in the Scheduled Areas. The concerned project authorities shall place all the relevant written information along with the proposal which would include:

(i) complete outline of the proposed project including the possible impact of the project;

(ii) proposed land acquisition;

(iii) the new people likely to settle in the village and possible impact on the area and society; and

(iv) proposed participation, amount of compensation and job opportunities, for the people of the village.

The Gram Sabha after considering all the facts, shall make a recommendation regarding the proposed land acquisition and rehabilitation and resettlement plan of persons who are affected or displaced. In case the Land Acquisition Officer is not in agreement with the recommendations of the Gram Sabha, she/he will send the matter again to the Gram Sabha for its reconsideration and decision. The Land Acquisition Officer or the Project Authorities may pass an order against the recommendations of the Gram Sabha, if aggrieved, after recording the reasons for doing so and same shall be communicated to Gram Sabha. In case of industrial projects, all the Gram Sabhas that are influenced by such projects shall be consulted before commencing any activity.

State Revenue Department may issue instructions to all District Collectors to necessarily consult the concerned Gram Sabha before land acquisition.

Q. What can Gram Sabha do to prevent other forms of tribal land alienation?

Ans. PESA empowers Gram Sabha to prevent alienation of land in the Scheduled Areas and take appropriate action to restore unlawfully alienated land of a Scheduled Tribe. The Gram Sabha must ensure that no land belonging to Scheduled Tribes is transferred to non- ST persons. If the Gram Sabha is of the opinion that attempts are being made to alienate land belonging to STs, it may go into details of such cases and pass resolution as to how such attempts should be tackled. If Gram Sabha finds that a non-ST is in unlawful occupation of any land belonging to ST member, it shall restore the possession of such land to the original owner as per laid down procedure. The Gram Sabha adopts traditional dispute resolution method while adjudicating land conflicts. Concerned department officials shall make available land records for taking correct decision by Gram Sabha.

State Government has to provide detailed procedures about how alienated land will be restored to the original landowners. For example, as per Rajasthan PESA Rules, 2011, to remove possession of unlawfully alienated tribal land, Panchayat Samiti will use powers of Tahsildar under the provisions of Rajasthan Land-Revenue Act, 1956 (Section-15). Under the Himachal Pradesh PESA Rules 2011, if Gram Sabha finds that a non-ST is in possession of any land owned by an ST, it can take up the matter with the concerned authority of the Revenue Department through the Pradhan of the Gram Panchayat, for restoration of possession of such land to that person to whom it originally belonged.

Q. What are the provisions under PESA Act to control money lending?

Ans. PESA mandates the State Legislatures to empower Gram Sabha to exercise control over money lending transactions. Money lending transactions include loan, etc. extended by Government, Co-operatives, money lenders, banks and other institutions. Gram Sabha may constitute a Debt Relief Committee to deal with money lending transactions and its related issues in relation to STs. A borrower can bring to the notice of

Gram Sabha if he or she is harassed by a money lender or by a lending institution and is being charged exorbitant rates of interests, etc. Gram Sabha can authorise the Debt Relief Committee to conduct an enquiry into such complaints with the support of Gram Sabha/ Community Mobilizer and place a report before Gram Sabhas for its decision. Gram Sabha, especially in the case of the tribals, may instruct a bank, society or any individual money lender that loans be disbursed or repayments made after informing the lending details to the Gram Sabha. It should also inform the Government of any cases of exploitation, so that the concerned Department of Revenue, Banking, and Cooperatives can also take corrective action. Gram Sabha is competent to review agreements of all kinds of labourers in the village and ensure that there is no forced labour in lieu of money borrowed from the lender. However, the concerned State Government is required to make Rules in this regard. In Rajasthan, Gram Panchayats have been assigned the powers of Assistant Registrar and Panchayat Samiti has been given powers of Registrar under Rajasthan Moneylending Act, 1963.

Q. What are the provisions under PESA for the Gram Sabha's ownership of Minor Forest Produce?

Ans. Under PESA Act, Gram Sabha is endowed with ownership of Minor Forest Produce (MFP). Gram Sabha is competent to ensure protection of trees or plants which yield minor forest produce and also take steps for protection of endangered plant species and impose restrictions on collection or extraction of plant material or products. The State Government is required to make rules in this regard. One or more Gram Sabhas together, in consultation with the Forest Department or State Co-operative or any other State owned agencies involved in MFP trade, may decide the minimum support price for the collection of Minor Forest Produce or exchange rates for other commodities. Gram Sabha may determine the royalty payable by the collector or the trader on Minor Forest Produce. This amount generated from such methods shall be deposited in Gram Sabha Kosh. Permission is required from the Gram Sabha to collect or transport any item of Minor Forest Produce by any department or institution or individual who is not a member of the Gram Sabha. Prior approval of the Gram Sabha is required for organising trade of any Minor Forest Produce by the State Agencies. The Gram Sabha and the collectors will have right over net profit arising from such trade. Gram Sabha can adjudicate the disputes among the members of MFP collection groups.

Q. What powers Gram Sabha/ PRIs have been given under PESA with regard to control over minor minerals?

Ans. Under PESA Act, it is mandatory to have recommendation of Gram Sabha and Panchayats at appropriate level prior to grant of prospecting licence or mining lease for minor minerals and for grant of concession for the exploitation of minor minerals by auction in the Scheduled Areas. Consultation should be interpreted as mandatory consultation. Full facts about the proposed activity, its zone of influence, its economic, social and environmental impact, rehabilitation and sustainable livelihood plans must be placed before the Gram Sabha. If at any point of time it is found that the information provided by the authority concerned is false or information has been kept hidden, the Gram Sabha shall have the right to withdraw the recommendation. Authority concerned must report the progress of the project for which it has obtained recommendation of Gram Sabha. State PESA Rules will further detail out this provision of PESA Act.

For example, Rajasthan PESA Rules empowers Gram Sabha in case of mines falling in one Gram Panchayat area, Panchayat Samiti in case of mines falling in more than one Gram Panchayat area and Zila Parishad in case of mines falling in more than one Panchayat Samiti area for recommending grant of concession for the exploitation of minor minerals. Mines Department will issue orders to Mining Engineers to necessarily obtain recommendations from the concerned Gram Sabha before renewing mining lease of minor minerals.

In Maharashtra and Himachal Pradesh, the Gram Sabha is competent to plan and control the excavation and use of all the minor minerals including soil, stones, sands, etc., which is to be found in its area. The villagers may use minor minerals for their individual needs as per the traditional practice with permission of the Gram Sabha. If any permission is given by any Government Department for the exploitation of minor minerals, it shall be mandatory for the said Government Department to obtain the necessary concurrence from the Gram Sabha.

In Andhra Pradesh and Telangana, only individual local members of ST or societies comprising of exclusively local ST members shall be entitled for grant of prospecting license or mining lease for minor minerals and grant of concession for exploitation of minor minerals by auction.

APPENDIX-IV

FAQs on Mahatma Gandhi NREGA

Q. What is the Mandate of Mahatma Gandhi National Rural Employment Guarantee Act (MGNREGA)?

Ans. The mandate of the MGNREGA is to provide at least 100 days of guaranteed wage employment in a financial year to every rural household whose adult members volunteer to do unskilled manual work.

Q. What are the core objectives of the Mahatma Gandhi National Rural Employment Guarantee Scheme (MGNREGS)?

Ans. The core objectives of the MGNREGS are:

a) Providing not less than one hundred days of unskilled manual work as a guaranteed employment in a financial year to every household in rural areas as per demand, resulting in creation of productive assets of prescribed quality and durability;

b) Strengthening the livelihood resource base of the poor;

c) Proactively ensuring social inclusion and

d) Strengthening Panchayati Raj Institutions.

Q. What are the Goals of MGNREGA?

Ans. The goals are:

a) Social protection for the most vulnerable people living in rural India by guaranteeing wage employment opportunities.

b) Enhance livelihood security of the rural poor through generation of wage employment opportunities in works leading to creation of durable assets.

c) Rejuvenate natural resource base of rural areas.

d) Create a durable and productive rural asset base.

e) Empowerment of the socially disadvantaged, especially, women, Scheduled Castes (SCs) and Scheduled Tribes (STs), through the processes of a rights-based legislation.

f) Strengthen decentralised, participatory planning through convergence of various anti-poverty and livelihoods initiatives.

g) Deepen democracy at the grassroots by strengthening Panchayati Raj Institutions.

Q. When was Mahatma Gandhi National Rural Employment Guarantee Act passed by the Indian Parliament?

Ans. The Indian Parliament passed the Mahatma Gandhi National Rural Employment Guarantee Act on 23rd August 2005.

Q. When was the Mahatma Gandhi National Rural Employment Guarantee Act Notified?

Ans. The Mahatma Gandhi National Rural Employment Guarantee Act was notified through the Gazette of India (Extraordinary) Notification dated September 7, 2005; it came into force on February 2, 2006 in 200 backward districts.

Q. When and what amendment was made to change the nomenclature of the Act from NREGA to MGNREGA?

Ans. On 2nd October 2009 an amendment was made in the National Rural Employment Guarantee Act 2005, to change the nomenclature of the Act from NREGA to MGNREGA. The Section 1 (1) was amended by renaming the National Rural Employment Guarantee Act with the words the Mahatma Gandhi National Rural Employment Guarantee Act (The Gazette of India Extraordinary Notification dated 2nd October 2009, No. 53).

Q. Is the Employment Guarantee Act restricted to particular States or districts?

Ans. No, it is implemented in all rural districts of the country.

MGNREGA was implemented in 200 districts in the first phase with effect from February 2006 and extended subsequently, to additional 113 and 17 districts with effect from April 1st 2007 and May 15th 2007, respectively. The remaining districts were included under the Act with effect from April 1st, 2008. Currently, the Act is under implementation in 644 districts of the country with substantial rural population.

Q. What is the relationship between the Mahatma Gandhi National Rural Employment Guarantee Act (Mahatma Gandhi NREGA) and the Mahatma Gandhi National Rural Employment Guarantee Scheme (Mahatma Gandhi NREGS)?

Mahatma Gandhi NREGA	Mahatma Gandhi NREGS
The Mahatma Gandhi National Rural Employment Guarantee Act (Mahatma Gandhi NREGA) is the foundation for the Mahatma Gandhi National Rural Employment Guarantee Scheme Mahatma Gandhi NREGS) and provides guaranteed employment	The Mahatma Gandhi National Rural Employment Guarantee Scheme (Mahatma Gandhi NREGS), created as directed in Mahatma Gandhi NREGA and the means to implement the Act so that the guarantee comes into effect
The Central Government specified the features and conditions for guaranteed employment in Mahatma Gandhi NREGA 2005	The State Governments have to incorporate all features of Mahatma Gandhi NREGA in the State Mahatma Gandhi NREGS as mentioned in Schedule –I and condition of employment as mentioned in Schedule-II of Mahatma Gandhi NREGA
The Central Government has powers to make rules and to amend Mahatma Gandhi NREGA	The State Governments have powers to make rules and amend the concerned State scheme
Mahatma Gandhi NREGA has been notified through the Gazette of India Extraordinary notification and is National legislation	Mahatma Gandhi NREGS of a State has been notified through the Official Gazette of concerned State
Mahatma Gandhi NREGA was notified on 7th September 05	Different States have notified Mahatma Gandhi NREGS on different dates but within a year of Mahatma Gandhi NREGA notification

Q. How an amendment can be made to the schedules of Mahatma Gandhi NREGA 2005?

Ans. If the Central Government is satisfied that it is necessary or expedient to do so, it may, by notification, amend Schedule I or Schedule II and thereupon Schedule I or Schedule II, as the case may be, shall be deemed to have been amended (Section 29, of the Act).

Q. Whether State Government is having any powers to make rules for effective implementation of Mahatma Gandhi NREGS?

Ans. Yes, the State Government may by notification make rules to carry out the provisions of Act subject to the conditions of consistency with Mahatma Gandhi NREGA and rules made by the Central Government [(Section 32(1)].

Q. Can the Central and State Governments delegate the powers of implementation?

Ans. Yes, the Central Government may delegate powers (excluding the power to make rules) to State Governments or subordinate officer by a notification and State Governments can delegate the powers to subordinates (Section 26).

Q. In what way paradigm shift has taken place with the implementation of MGNREGA?

Ans. MGNREGA is demand driven wage employment programme and resource transfer from Centre to States is based on the demand for employment in each State. MGNREGA is bottom-up, people- centred, demand-driven, self-selecting and rights-based programme. It provides a legal guarantee for wage employment by providing allowances and compensation both in cases of failure to provide work on demand and delays in payment of wages for work undertaken. Plans and decisions regarding the nature and choice of works to be undertaken, the order in which each worksite selection etc., are all to be made in open assemblies of the Gram Sabha (GS) and ratified by the GP. Social audit is a new feature, which creates accountability of performance, especially towards immediate stakeholders. Thus MGNREGA also marks a break from the relief programmes of the past towards an integrated natural resource management and livelihoods generation perspective.

Q. Who are the key stakeholders of MGNREGS?

Ans. The key stakeholders are:

1. Wage Seekers
2. Gram Sabha (GS)
3. Three-tier Panchayati Raj Institutions (PRIs)
4. Programme Officer at the Block level
5. District Programme Coordinator (DPC)
6. State Government
7. Ministry of Rural Development (MoRD)
8. Civil Society
9. Other stakeholders [viz. line departments, convergence departments, Self-Help Groups (SHGs), etc.]

Q. What are the Rights and Entitlements of wage- seekers in MGNREGS?

Ans. Rights and Entitlements of wage- seekers in MGNREGS :

a) Application for registration
b) Obtaining a Job Card (JC)
c) Application for work and to obtain a dated receipt for the application made
d) Choice of time and duration of the work applied for
e) Getting work within fifteen days of application or from the date when work is sought in the case of an advance application, whichever is later
f) Facilities of crèche, drinking water, first aid etc., on the worksite.
g) Right to get 10 per cent extra wage in case of employment provided beyond 5 km of radius
h) Right to check their Muster Rolls (MRs) and to get all the information regarding their employment entered in their JCs.
i) According to Section 3(3) of MGNREGA, workers are entitled to payment on a weekly basis, and in any case within a fortnight of the date on which work was done.

j) Right to get unemployment allowance; in case employment is not provided within fifteen days of submitting the application or from the date when work is sought in the case of an advance application, whichever is later.

k) Right to receive payment of compensation for the delay, at the rate of 0.05 per cent of the unpaid wages per day beyond the sixteenth day of closure of muster roll.

l) Medical treatment in case of injury in the course of employment including cost of hospitalisation if required and ex gratia payment in case of disability or death in the course of employment

Q. What is the role of Gram Sabha in MGNREGS?

Ans. The Gram Sabha (GS) has the following rights and responsibilities under the Act:

a) It determines the order of priority of works in the meetings of the Gram Sabha keeping in view potential of the local area, its needs, local resources (Para 4 (2), Schedule I)

b) Monitor the execution of works within the GP.

c) It is the primary forum for conduct of social audits. It provides a platform to all residents to seek and obtain all relevant information from all the Implementing Agencies including GP in relation to MGNREGA works implemented in the GP area.

Q. What are the Roles of Gram Panchayat in MGNREGS?

Ans. The Gram Panchayat (GP) is responsible for the following activities:

a) Receiving applications for registration

b) Verifying registration applications

c) Registering households

d) Issuing Job Cards(JCs)

e) Receiving applications for work

f) Issuing dated receipts for these applications for work

g) Allotting work within fifteen days of submitting the application or from the date when work is sought in the case of an advance application, whichever is later, irrespective of the implementing agency

h) Conducting periodical surveys to assess demand for work

i) Identification and planning of works, developing shelf of projects including determination of the order of their priority. Forward the list of works to Programme Officer for scrutiny and preliminary approval

j) Executing works that shall meet the required technical standards and measurements

k) Maintaining records as specified in the MGNREGA Operational Guidelines, 2013

l) Maintaining accounts and providing utilisation certificates in formats prescribed by Central/ State Government.

m) Prepare annually a report containing the facts and figures and achievements relating to the implementation of the Scheme within its jurisdiction and, copy of the same to be made available to the public on demand and on payment of such fee as may be specified in the Scheme

n) Awareness generation and social mobilisation.

o) Convening the GS for planning and social audit

p) Make available all relevant documents including the Muster Rolls, bills, vouchers, measurement books, copies of sanction orders and other connected books of account and papers to the GS for the purpose of conducting the social audit

q) Monitoring implementation at the village level

r) Pro-actively disclosing -Details of works both completed and on-going (including wages paid and material component) at worksites and names of persons (with JC numbers) who have worked, days worked for and wages paid, quantity and price of materials purchased for each project along with name of agency supplying the material at GP offices and other prominent public places

s) Providing all information specified in Audit of Schemes Rules to the Social Audit Unit.

t) Organise Rozgar Diwas at every ward and Gram Panchayat level at least once a month.

Q. What are the Roles and Responsibilities of PO in MGNREGS?

Ans. The PO acts as a coordinator for Mahatma Gandhi NREGS (MGNREGS) at the Block level. The primary responsibility of the PO is to ensure that anyone who applies for work gets employment within 15 days. Other important functions of the PO are:

a) Consolidating, after scrutiny, all project proposals received from GPs into the Block Plan and submitting it to the District Panchayat for scrutiny and consolidation

b) Matching employment opportunities arising from works within the Block Plan with the demand for work at each GP in the Block

c) Ensuring baseline surveys to assess work demand

d) Monitoring and supervising implementation of works taken up by GPs and other implementing agencies within the Block

e) Ensuring prompt and fair payment of wages to all labourers and payment of unemployment allowance in case employment is not provided on time

f) Maintaining proper accounts of the resources received, released and utilised

g) Redressing grievances within the Block. The PO shall enter every complaint in a complaint register and issue dated and numbered acknowledgement. Complaints that fall within the jurisdiction of the PO, including any complaints concerning the implementation of the Act by a GP shall be disposed of by the PO within 7 days, as prescribed under Section 23(6) of the Act. In case a complaint relates to a matter to be resolved by any other authority, the PO shall conduct a preliminary enquiry and refer the matter to such authority within seven days under intimation to the complainant

h) Ensuring conduct of social audits and following up on required actions

i) Ensuring all the required information and records of all implementing agencies such as JC register, employment register, work register, GS resolution, copies of the sanctions (administrative or technical or financial), work estimates, work commencement order, Muster Roll issue and receipt register, Muster Rolls, wage payment acquaintance, materials – bills and vouchers (for each work), measurement books (for each work), asset register, action taken report on previous social audits, grievance or complaints register

j) Ensuring any other documents that the Social Audit Unit (SAU) requires to conduct the social audit processes are properly collated in the requisite formats; and provided along with photocopies to the SAU for facilitating conduct of social audit at least fifteen days in advance of the scheduled date of meeting of the GS

k) Setting up Cluster-Level Facilitation Teams (CFTs) to provide technical support to GPs within each Cluster of GPs where the CFTs are not established in convergence with National Rural Livelihood Mission (NRLM) as per the convergence project of MGNREGA with NRLM

l) Facilitating technical support to Gram Panchayats by CFTs

m) Liaison with banks and post offices in opening up of new accounts and making regular and timely payments to labour. Liaison between GPs and block as also between block and district for all correspondence and communication

n) Organise formal monthly meetings with civil society organisations (CSOs) involved in facilitating MGNREGS implementation in the block

Q. What are the functions of Intermediate Panchayat in MGNREGS?

Ans. The function of the Panchayat at intermediate level shall be, to:

a) Approve the works with the expected outcomes to be executed by Intermediate Panchayat;

b) Approve the block level plan for forwarding it to the district Panchayat at the district level for final approval;

c) Supervise and monitor the projects taken up at the Gram Panchayat and block level;

d) Carry out such other functions as may be assigned to it by the State Council, from time to time;

e) Where Part IX of the Constitution does not apply, local councils/ authorities as mandated by the State concerned, will be vested with these responsibilities.

Q. Who is DPC in MGNREGS?

Ans. The State Government designates a DPC, who can be either the Chief Executive Officer of the District Panchayat (DP), or the District Collector (DC), or any other district level officer of appropriate rank. The DPC is responsible for the implementation of the scheme in the district, in accordance with the provisions made in the MGNREGA 2005 and rules and guidelines made thereunder.

Q. What are the functions of DPC in MGNREGS?

Ans. The DPC shall:

a) Assist the DP in discharging its functions

b) Receive the Block Panchayat plans and consolidate them along with project proposals received from other implementing agencies for inclusion in the District Plan for approval by the DPs

c) Accord timely sanction to shelf of projects

d) Ensure that any new projects added at block and district level are presented again for ratification and fixing priority by concerned GS(s) before administrative sanction is accorded to them.

e) Ensure timely release and utilisation of funds

f) Ensure that wage-seekers are provided with work as per their entitlements under this Act.

g) Review, monitor and supervise the performance of the POs and all implementing agencies in relation to MGNREGA works

h) Conduct and cause to be conducted periodic inspection of the works in progress and verification of Muster Rolls

i) Ensure that First Information Report (FIR) is filed in every case in which there is *prima facie*, evidence of misutilisation of funds

j) Appoint Project Implementation Agencies (PIAs) throughout the district, keeping in mind that for at least 50 per cent of value of works, the PIAs need to be GPs

k) Coordinate an Information Education and Communication (IEC) campaign for MGNREGA within the district

l) Develop annual plans for training and capacity building of various stakeholders within the district

m) Submit periodic progress and updates to the State Government

n) Ensure that social audits are conducted in all GPs once in six months and ensure follow-up action on social audit reports

o) Ensure that all transactions including issue of JCs, recording of applications for work, allocation of work, generation of wage slips and Fund Transfer Orders (FTOs), entries relating to work performed, delayed payment of wages, and unemployment allowance are made through NREGASoft only

p) Ensure that all entries relating to works such as details of the shelf of works, GPS coordinates, status of implementation, photographs of works at three different stages are entered in NREGASoft at every required stage. Information regarding completion of work should be entered in as soon as possible but in any case no later than two months from the time of physical completion

q) Ensure that all funds received by Implementing Agencies and district level authorities including Panchayats are posted in NREGASoft no later than two days of receipt of such funds

r) Ensure that all required entries in NREGASoft are made by all concerned officials including the line departments, in the district

Q. What are the responsibilities of District Panchayat under MGNREGA?

Ans. District Panchayats (DPs) are responsible for:

a) Approving the works with the expected outcomes to be executed by District Panchayat.

b) Consolidation of Annual Block Plans (within the district) into a District Plan

c) Monitoring and supervision of the MGNREG Scheme in the district

d) Carry out such other functions as may be assigned to it by the State Council, from time to time.

Q. What are the Roles of State Employment Guarantee Council (SEGC)?

Ans. The SEGC has the following roles and responsibilities:

a) Advise the State Government on the implementation of the Scheme

b) Review the monitoring and redressal mechanisms and suggest improvements

c) Evaluate and monitor the Scheme within the State

d) Recommend the proposals of works to be submitted to the Central Government under para 4(IV)(ix), Schedule I of the Act

e) Promote widest possible dissemination of information about this Act and the Schemes therein

f) Prepare the annual report to be laid before the State Legislature by the State Governments

Q. What are the responsibilities of State Government in MGNREGS?

Ans. The responsibilities of the State Government are following:

a) Frame Rules on matters pertaining to State responsibilities under Section 32 of the Act

b) Develop and notify the Rural Employment Guarantee Scheme for the State

c) Set up the SEGC

d) Set up a State level MGNREGS implementation agency/ mission with adequate number of high calibre professionals

e) Set up a State level MGNREGS social audit agency/directorate with adequate number of people with knowledge on MGNREGA processes and demonstrated commitment to social audit

f) Establish and operate a State Employment Guarantee Fund (SEGF)

g) Ensure that the State share of the MGNREGS budget is provisioned for and released into the SEGF in the beginning of the financial year so that it can be used as a revolving fund

h) Ensure that full time dedicated personnel, wherever required, are in place for implementing MGNREGA, specially the Employment Guarantee Assistant (Gram Rozgar Sahayak), the PO and the staff at State, district, cluster and GP level

i) Delegate financial and administrative powers to the DPC and the Programme Officer, as is deemed necessary for the effective implementation of the Scheme

j) Establish a network of professional agencies for training, technical support and for quality- control measures

k) Regular review, research, monitoring and evaluation of MGNREGS processes and outcomes

l) Ensure accountability and transparency in the Scheme at all levels

m) Generate widest possible awareness about MGNREGA across the State

n) Ensure that civil society organisations involved in mobilising MGNREGA workers are able to formally meet State, district and block level officials in a formal setting at least once a month

o) Ensure compliance with all processes laid down in Act, Rules and guidelines.

Q. What are the roles and responsibilities of Central Employment Guarantee Council (CEGC)?

Ans. The roles and responsibilities of the CEGC, as per the Act, are to:

a) Establish a central evaluation and monitoring system

b) Advise the Central Government on all matters concerning the implementation of the Act

c) Review the monitoring and redressal mechanism from time to time and recommend improvements required

d) Promote the widest possible dissemination of information about the Schemes

e) Monitoring the implementation of this Act

f) Preparation of annual reports to be laid before Parliament by the Central Government on the implementation of this Act.

Q. What are the Roles & Responsibilities of the Ministry of Rural Development (MoRD)?

Ans. The roles and responsibilities of the MoRD are:

a) Frame Rules under the Act

b) Issue Operational Guidelines for the effective implementation of the Act

c) Review list of permissible works under MGNREGA in response to demands of State Governments

d) Constitute the CEGC and organise meetings of the council.

e) Set up and operate National Employment Guarantee Fund

f) Set up National Management Team (NMT) within the Department of Rural Development to perform the national level functions under MGNREGA

g) Make budgetary allocation and ensure timely release of Central share

h) Maintain and operate the MIS to capture and track data on critical aspects of implementation, and assess the utilisation of resources through a set of performance indicators

i) Support and facilitate use of Information Technology (IT) to increase the efficiency and transparency in implementation of the Act

j) Facilitate technical support and capacity building to improve outcomes

k) Support innovations that help in improving processes towards the achievement of the objectives of the Act

l) Monitor, evaluate and conduct research on the performance of MGNREGA

m) Empanel agencies that can be used by State Governments as PIAs for implementation of MGNREGA works and determine the percentage value of funding that can be given to them to meet their administrative costs.

Q. What roles can Civil Society Organisations (CSOs) and Self-Help Groups (SHGs) play in MGNREGS?

Ans. The CSOs working at the grassroots can play a very significant role in awareness generation among wage-seekers and in supporting and building capacities of GPs and State Governments in planning, implementation and social audit of MGNREGA. The SHGs can play a direct role in spreading awareness, organising work, accessing entitlements, assistance in door to door survey and ensuring social accountability. The MGNREGA Operational Guidelines provide the framework for engagement of CSOs, support in the operationalisation of CFT project in convergence with NRLM.

Q. Who are the other stakeholders in MGNREGS?

Ans. Other important stakeholders include: Members of Social Audit Unit, Vigilance and Monitoring Committees, Technical Staff of implementing agencies, Departments with whom MoU has been signed for convergence with MGNREGA, viz, Ministry of Agriculture, Ministry of Forest & Environment, Ministry of Water Resources, Department of Rural Development, Department of Land Resources and Ministry of Drinking Water and Sanitation and Departments which stand to benefit from MGNREGA like Agriculture, Water Resources/Irrigation, Forest etc.

Q. What is a Job Card?

Ans. Job Card is a key document that records workers' entitlements under MGNREGA. It legally empowers the registered households to apply for work, ensures transparency and protects workers against fraud.

Q. What is the procedure to register oneself for employment?

Ans. Household having adult members desirous of seeking unskilled wage employment in MGNREGA may apply for registration. The application for registration may be given on prescribed form or plain paper to the local Gram Panchayat. To allow maximum opportunities to families that may migrate, registration shall also be opened throughout the year at the GP office.

Q. How is Household defined in MGNREGA?

Ans. "Household" means the members of a family related to each other by blood, marriage or adoption and normally residing together and sharing meals or holding a common ration card.

Q. What is the significance of door to door survey in identification of eligible household under MGNREGA?

Ans. Door to door survey helps to identify eligible households who have been missed out and wish to be registered under the Act. It should be undertaken by each GP every year and need to be ensured that this survey is held at that time of the year when people have not migrated to other areas in search of employment or for other reasons.

Q. Who can apply for Job Card Registration?

Ans. A household having adult members desirous of seeking unskilled employment in MGNREGA may apply for registration.

Q. What is the frequency of Job Card registration?

Ans. Throughout the Year

Q. Who should apply for Job Card on behalf of a Household?

Ans. Any adult member can apply on behalf of Household.

Q. What is the definition of an adult in a household?

Ans. Adult means a person who has completed 18 years of age.

Q. Can all adult members of a household register for Job Card?

Ans. Adult members of a household willing to do unskilled manual work can register themselves to obtain a job card under MGNREGA.

Q. Is there any pre-printed form for providing details while registering for Job Card?

Ans. The State Government may make a printed form available as per format prescribed in the relavant Annexures of the MGNREGA Operational Guidelines 2013. However, a printed form should not be insisted upon.

Q. What are the issues the Gram Panchayat need to verify when application was made for Job Card?

Ans. The Gram Panchayat need to verify:

- Whether the household is really an entity as stated in the application
- Applicant households are local residents in the GP concerned
- Applicants are adult members of the household

The process of verification shall be completed not later than a fortnight after the receipt of the application.

Q. For how many years is the registration for Job Card valid?

Ans. The registration is valid for five years and may be renewed/re-validated following process prescribed for renewal/revalidation as and when required.

Q. If the information contained in the application found to be incorrect, what is the process to be adopted?

Ans. The Gram Panchayat will refer the application to PO. The PO, after independent verification of facts and giving the person concerned an opportunity to be heard, may direct the GP to either (i) Register the household or (ii) Reject the application or (iii) Secure the particulars correct and re-process the application.

Q. What is the time limit for issuing Job Cards (JC) if the application made is correct?

Ans. Within a fortnight after due verification is completed on finding out eligibility of a household, the job cards should be issued to all such eligible households

Q. Can the Job Card be handed over to any member of the household?

Ans. Yes, it can be handed over to any adult member of the applicant's household in the presence of a few other residents of the GP.

Q. Should the cost towards Job Card (including the photograph affixed on it) be borne by the applicant?

Ans. No, the cost of the Job Cards, including that of the photographs affixed on it, are covered under the administrative expenses and borne as a part of the programme cost.

Q. If a person has grievance against the non-issuance of a Job Card, then to whom s/he has to represent the matter?

Ans. The matter can be brought to the notice of PO. If the grievance is against the PO, then the matter can be brought to the notice of DPC or the designated grievance-redressal authority at the block or district level.

Q. Is there any time-limit to address the grievances in regard to non-issuance of Job Card?

Ans. Yes, all such complaints shall be disposed off within 15 days.

Q. Is there any provision to provide duplicate Job Card for a lost one?

Ans. Yes, a Job Cardholder may apply for a duplicate Job Card, if the original is lost or damaged. The application will be given to the GP and shall be processed in the manner of a new application, with the difference being that the particulars may also be verified using the duplicate copy of the JC maintained by the Panchayat.

Q. Who is the custodian of Job Card?

Ans. It must be ensured that the JC is always in the custody of the household to whom it is issued. If for any reason i.e., updation of record, it is taken by implementing agencies it should be returned on the same day after the updates. ***JCs found in the possession of any Panchayat or MGNREGA functionary, without a valid reason, will be considered as an offence punishable under Section 25 of the Act.***

Q. Can any adult member of household seek wage employment?

Ans. Every adult member of a registered household whose name appears in the JC shall be entitled to apply for unskilled manual work.

Q. Is there any duration limit fixed for seeking work by adult individuals registered in the JC?

Ans. Yes, as per Para 11, Schedule II normally, applications for work must be for at least fourteen days of continuous work, other than the works relating to access to sanitation facilities, for which application for work shall be for atleast six days of continuous work. As per Para 10, Schedule II there shall be no limit on the number of days of employment for which a person may apply, or on the number of days of employment actually provided subject to the aggregate entitlement of the household.

Q. Can a job card be cancelled?

Ans. No, as per Para 4, Schedule II no job card can be cancelled except where it is found to be a duplicate, or if the entire household has permanently migrated to a place outside the Gram Panchayat and no longer lives in the village.

Q. When is an applicant eligible for Unemployment allowance?

Ans. If an applicant is not provided employment within fifteen days of receipt of his/her application seeking employment, in all cases of advance application, employment should be provided from the date that employment has been sought, or within 15 days of the date of application, whichever is later. Else, unemployment allowance becomes due. It will be calculated automatically by the computer system or the Management Information System (MIS).

Q. Who is responsible for the payment of Unemployment allowance?

Ans. As per Section 7(3) of MGNREGA, State Government is liable to pay unemployment allowance to the household concerned. State Government shall:

- Specify the rate of unemployment allowance payable [Section 7 (2) of Act]
- Frame Rules governing the procedure for payment of unemployment allowance and
- Make necessary budgetary provision for payment of unemployment allowance.

Q. When does the liability of State Government cease in regard to payment of unemployment allowance?

Ans. The liability of the State Government to pay unemployment allowance to a household during any financial year shall cease as soon as:

a) The applicant is directed by the GP or the PO to report for work either by himself or depute at least one adult member of his household; or

b) The period for which employment is sought comes to an end and no member of the household of the applicant had turned up for employment; or

c) The adult members of the household of the applicant have received in total at least one hundred days of work within the financial year; or

d) The household of the applicant has earned as much from the wages and unemployment allowance taken together which is equal to the wages for one hundred days of work during the financial year.

e) An applicant who:-

   - Does not accept the employment provided to his/her household; or

- Does not report for work within fifteen days of being notified by the Programme Officer or the implementing agency to report for the work; or
- Continuously remains absent from work, without obtaining permission from the concerned implementing agency for a period of more than one week or remains absent for a total period of more than one week in any month.

Q. Who are the key functionaries at GP level?

Ans. *Gram Rozgar Sahayak* or Employment Guarantee Assistant and Mates or worksite supervisors are the key functionaries at GP level.

Q. What are the responsibilities of Gram Rozgar Sahayak?

Ans. The responsibilities of the GRS are as follows:

a) Overseeing the process of registration, distribution of job cards, provision of dated receipts against job applications, allocation of work to applicants etc.;

b) Facilitating Gram Sabha meetings, social audits and Rozgar Diwas;

c) Recording attendance of labour every day either himself/ herself or through the mate in the prescribed muster rolls at the worksite;

d) Ensuring that group mark-outs are given at worksite for every group of labourers, so that the workers know the output required to be given to earn wage rate every day;

e) Ensuring that all mates attend worksites on time and take roll calls/ attendance in prescribed muster roll at worksite only;

f) Ensuring worksite facilities [as defined in the Operational Guidelines] and updating job cards of the workers regularly;

g) Maintaining all MGNREGS-related registers at the Gram Panchayat level, assist the Panchayat Secretary or any other official responsible for maintenance of MGNREGA accounts; and ensuring that these documents are conveniently available for public scrutiny.

Q. Who is Mate under MGNREGS?

Ans. A mate is a worksite supervisor. At least one mate should be present for every 100 workers. A person working as a mate should not be a worker on the same MGNREGS worksite at the same point of time.

Q. What are the responsibilities of a Mate?

Ans. The responsibilities of a Mate are:

a) Supervise worksites.

b) Record daily attendance in muster roll.

c) Give mark-outs at the worksite before beginning the work.

d) Take measurement at the end of the day.

e) Update entries in the job cards.

f) Facilitate applications for job cards and submit them to the GP.

g) Facilitate demand for work from individual workers or groups of labourers, submit them to GP and obtain dated receipt as acknowledgement.

h) Facilitate participatory identification of works in the GP.

i) Ensure there is no free-riding within his/her group of workers.

j) Submit filled-in muster rolls to GRS.

k) Ensure that the first aid box with adequate material for emergency treatment for minor injuries and other health hazards connected with the work being executed are available at the worksite.

l) Help illiterate labourers in his/her group to learn to sign and to calculate wages earned.

m) Create awareness about rights and entitlements under the MGNREGA.

Q. Who are the key functionaries at cluster of GPs/sub- district/ block level?

Ans. Human resources at cluster of GPs/sub- district/block level are the (i) Programme Officer, (ii) Technical Assistant, (iii) Computer Operator-cum-Accounts Clerk, (iv) Voluntary Technical Corps and the (v) Cluster Facilitation Team.

Q. Who is Programme Officer and what are his responsibilities?

Ans. The PO is the overall in-charge of all MGNREGS works in the block and is not below the rank of a Block Development Officer (BDO). The Programme Officer reports to DPC and Additional DPC of the district.

Q. What are the roles and responsibilities of PO?

Ans. The responsibilities of the PO are as follows:

a) Consolidating, after scrutiny, all project proposals received from GPs into the Block Plan and submitting it to the District Panchayat for scrutiny and consolidation

b) Matching employment opportunities arising from works within the Block Plan with the demand for work at each GP in the block

c) Ensuring baseline surveys to assess work demand

d) Monitoring and supervising implementation of works taken up by GPs and other implementing agencies within the block

e) Ensuring prompt and fair payment of wages to all labourers and payment of unemployment allowance in case employment is not provided on time

f) Maintaining proper accounts of the resources received, released and utilised

g) Redressing grievances in the block within 7 days, as prescribed under Section 23(6) of the Act. In case a complaint relates to a matter to be resolved by any other authority, the PO shall conduct a preliminary enquiry and refer the matter to such authority within seven days under intimation to the complainant

h) Ensuring conduct of social audits and following up on required actions

i) Ensuring availability of all the required information and records of all implementing agencies (JC register, employment register, work register, GS resolution, copies of the sanctions (administrative or technical or financial), work estimates, work commencement order, Muster Roll issue and receipt register, Muster Rolls, wage payment acquaintance, materials – bills and vouchers (for each work), measurement books (for each work), asset register, action taken report on previous social audits, grievance or complaints register)

j) Ensuring availability of any other documents that the Social Audit Unit (SAU) requires to conduct the social audit processes are properly collated in the requisite formats; and provided along with photocopies to the SAU for facilitating conduct of social audit at least fifteen days in advance of the scheduled date of meeting of the GS

k) Facilitating technical support to Gram Panchayats by CFTs

l) Liaison with banks and post offices in opening up of new accounts and making regular and timely payments to labour. Liaison between GPs and block as also between block and district for all correspondence and communication

m) Organise formal monthly meetings with civil society organisations (CSOs) involved in facilitating MGNREGS implementation in the block

Q. What is a State Employment Guarantee Mission and who are on Management Team?

Ans. State Employment Guarantee Mission (SEGM) is headed by a senior officer (Secretary/Commissioner MGNREGS), who is designated as Chief Executive Officer (CEO) of the Mission. SEGM will also have a Chief Operating Officer (COO). The following is an indicative list of fields where thematic experts may be required.

a) Rights and entitlements;

b) Participatory planning process for livelihoods and convergence;

c) Natural Resource Management (NRM), livelihoods, Quality Standardisation and Assurance;

d) Technical Works & Measurement;

e) Wage payment;

f) Information and Communication Technology (ICT);

g) MIS;

h) Strategy & Planning;

i) Monitoring & Evaluation;

j) Social Inclusion;

k) Capacity building – Training of field staff at the block, cluster and GP;

l) Human resource management – Developing a sensitive human resource management policy for contract staff and/or permanent staff;

m) Social audit and grievance redress mechanism;

n) Vigilance;

o) Knowledge Management and learning including research;

p) External communication.

Q. What is a Gram Panchayat Development Plan under MGNREGA?

Ans. Section 16 (3) & (4) of the Act states that every Gram Panchayat shall prepare a Development Plan and maintain a shelf of works to meet the employment demand. A development plan is an annual work plan that comprises shelf of projects for each village with administrative and technical approvals.

The development plan is a rolling plan, since the approved shelf of projects may carry over one financial year to the next depending upon this lifespan of the projects.

Q. What is a District Perspective Plan under MGNREGA?

Ans. District Perspective Plan is prepared for five years, which identifies the needs and gap in the districts in all the sectors. The district perspective plan is a multi-year plan for different departmental projects. The district perspective plans should be prepared in such a manner that it can be breakable into various annual plans.

Q. List out the Components of Development Plan?

Ans. Components of Development Plan :

a) Assessment of labour demand

b) Identification of works- to meet estimated labour demand

c) Estimated cost of works and wages

d) Benefits expected in terms of employment generated and physical improvements. (Water conservation and Land productivity).

Q. List out the guiding principle for preparing the Development Plan?

Ans. There are five guiding principles to be followed while preparing the development plan:

a) The number of works in the shelf of projects in a village should be much more than the estimated demand.

b) The plot numbers of the sites where works are to be executed should be mentioned, so that each work has a unique location code.

c) Outcomes expected from the works should be stated in terms of :

   i. Estimated benefits in terms of employment generated measurable in persondays

   ii. Physical improvement envisaged measurable in specific units

   iii. Benefits to the community

d) List of approved works with technical estimates should be displayed in the gram panchayat in simple local language

e) Pre-Mid-Post Project condition of works to be recorded with photographs

f) Each work taken up with unique number (irrespective of the implementing agency) has to be recorded in the works register to be maintained at GP to enable verification and prevent duplication

Q. Timeline for planning and labour budget preparation

Date	Action to be taken
15th August	Gram Sabha to approve GP Annual Plan and submit to PO
15th September	PO submits consolidated GP Plans to Block Panchayat
2nd October	Block Panchayat to approve the Block Annual Plan and submit to DPC
15th November	DPC to present District Annual Plan and LB to District Panchayat
1st December	District Panchayat to approve District Annual Plan
15th December	DPC to ensure that shelf of projects for each GP is ready after approval of labour budget and list of works of the respective GP should be entered in MIS before 15th December of each year (as mentioned below)
31st December	Labour Budget is submitted to Central Government
January	Ministry scrutinises the Labour Budget and requests for compliance for deficiencies, if any

February	Meetings of Empowered Committee are held and LB finalised
February, March	Agreed to LB communicated to States. States to feed data of month-wise and district-wise break-up of "Agreed to" LB in MIS and communicate the same to districts/ blocks/ GPs
Before 7th April	States to communicate Opening Balance (OB), Centre to release upfront/ 1st Tranche.

Q. What types of works are taken up under Mahatma Gandhi NREGS?

Ans. Para 4(1), Schedule I provides provision for the following works under MGNREGA:

I. Category: A: Public Works Relating to Natural Resources Management -

i) Water conservation and water harvesting structures to augment and improve groundwater like underground dykes, earthen dams, stop dams, check dams with special focus on recharging groundwater including drinking water sources;

ii) Watershed management works such as contour trenches, terracing, contour bunds, boulder checks, gabion structures and springshed development resulting in a comprehensive treatment of a watershed;

iii) Micro and minor irrigation works and creation, renovation and maintenance of irrigation canals and drains;

iv) Renovation of traditional water bodies including desilting of irrigation tanks and other water bodies;

v) Afforestation, tree plantation and horticulture in common and forest lands, road margins, canal bunds, tank foreshores and coastal belts duly providing right to usufruct to the households covered in Paragraph 5; and

vi) Land development works in common land.

II. Category B : Individual Assets for Vulnerable Sections (Only for Households in Paragraph 5 of Schedule I)

i) Improving productivity of lands of households specified in Paragraph5 through land development and by providing suitable infrastructure for irrigation including dug wells, farm ponds and other water harvesting structures;

ii) Improving livelihoods through horticulture, sericulture, plantation, and farm forestry;

iii) Development of fallow or wastelands of households defined in Paragraph 5 of the Schedule I to bring it under cultivation;

iv) Unskilled wage component in construction of houses sanctioned under the Indira Awaas Yojana or such other State or Central Government Scheme;

v) Creating infrastructure for promotion of livestock such as, poultry shelter, goat shelter, piggery shelter, cattle shelter and fodder troughs for cattle; and

vi) Creating infrastructure for promotion of fisheries such as, fish drying yards, storage facilities, and promotion of fisheries in seasonal water bodies on public land;

III. Category C: Common Infrastructure for NRLM Compliant Self-Help Groups

i) Works for promoting agricultural productivity by creating durable infrastructure required for bio-fertilisers and post-harvest facilities including pucca storage facilities for agricultural produce; and

ii) Common worksheds for livelihood activities of self-help groups.

IV. Category D: Rural Infrastructure

i) Rural sanitation related works, such as, individual household latrines, school toilet units, Anganwadi toilets either independently or in convergence with schemes of other Government Departments to achieve 'open defecation free' status. and solid and liquid waste management as per prescribed norms;

ii) Providing all-weather rural road connectivity to unconnected villages and to connect identified rural production centres to the existing pucca road network; and construction of pucca internal roads or streets including side drains and culverts within a village;

iii) Construction of play fields;

iv) Works for improving disaster preparedness or restoration of roads or restoration of other essential public infrastructure including flood control and protection works, providing drainage in water-logged areas, deepening and repairing of flood channels, chaur renovation, construction of storm water drains for coastal protection;

v) Construction of buildings for Gram Panchayats, women self-help groups' federations, cyclone shelters, anganwadi centres, village haats and crematoria at the village or block level;

vi) Construction of Food Grain Storage Structures for implementing the provisions of The National Food Security Act 2013 (20 of 2013);

vii) Production of building material required for construction works under the Act.

viii) Maintenance of rural public assets created under the Act; and

ix) Any other work which may be notified by the Central Government in consultation with the State Government in this regard.

Q. What are the conditions for development of individual farmer's land under Mahatma Gandhi NREGA?

Ans. Individual farmer's land that is to be developed under Mahatma Gandhi NREGA should be treated as a project with the following conditions.

- The individual land owner shall be a job card holder and also work in the project and the proposed activity should be part of annual shelf of projects.
- All projects to be executed under MGNREGA have to be approved by Gram Sabha.
- No contractor shall be involved in the execution of work.
- No labour displacing machinery shall be used in the execution of work.
- No labour displacing machinery shall be purchased / hired.

Q. Define negative works under MGNREGS?

Ans. The works which are not included in the list of permissible works and works which are non-tangible, not measurable, non-quantifiable, repetitive such as removing grass, pebbles, agricultural operation are not permitted.

Q. List out the Negative Works?

Ans. Negative Works:

a) Works which are non-tangible, not measurable, non-quantifible repetitive such as, removing grass, pebbles, agricultural operations, shall not be taken up.

b) Works like boulder pebble or shrub removal silt application and similar activities are not as a stand-alone activities. However, these can be a part of tasks in projects for converting uncultivable/barren/fallow lands into cultivable lands through one time land development activities.

c) Agriculture inputs and agriculture operations are not allowed. Removal of weeds and watering may be considered only for forestry plantation and horticulture limited for a duration of 2-3 years. This shold also be a part of the consolidated project to be assisted under MGNREGA.

d) Expenditure incurred to finance non-permissible activities will be recovered from the person responsible for such expenses.

e) Execution of pilot activity under MGNREGA is discouraged. However, pilots using MGNREGA funds, involving only a few Panchayats could be taken up only upon approval of the Ministry.

f) MGNREGS funds cannot be used for land acquisition.

g) Specified criteria to be followed while executing dug wells under MGNREGA.

Q. Besides worksite facilities what are the other entitlements to Mahatma Gandhi NREGS workers?

Ans. As per Schedule II of Mahatma Gandhi NREGA the other entitlements to Mahatma Gandhi NREGS workers are:

- If any personal injury is caused to any person employed under the Scheme by any accident arising out of and in the course of his employment, he shall be entitled to such medical treatment as required, free of cost. (Para 25, Schedule II)
- Where hospitalisation of the injured worker is necessary, the State Government shall arrange for such hospitalisation including accommodation, treatment, medicines and payment of daily allowance which is not less than half of the wage rate. (Para 26, Schedule II)
- If a person employed under the Scheme meets with death or becomes permanently disabled by accident arising out of and in the course of employment, he or his legal heirs, as the case may be, shall be paid by the implementing agency an *ex gratia* as per entitlements under the Aam Aadmi BimaYojana or as may be notified by the Central Government. (Para 27, Schedule II)
- If any personal injury is caused by accident to a child accompanying a person who is employed under the Scheme, such person shall be entitled to medical treatment free of cost; and in case of death or disablement of the child due to the said accident, *ex gratia* shall be paid to the legal guardians as determined by the State Government. (Para 27, Schedule II)

Q. Are the Mahatma Gandhi NREGS labourers entitled to any specific facilities at worksite?

Ans. Yes. Worksite facilities include safe drinking water, shade for children and periods of rest, first aid box with adequate material for emergency treatment for minor injuries and other health hazards connected with the work being performed (Para 23, schedule II). In case the number of children below the age of five years accompanying the women working at any site is five or more, provisions should be made to depute one of such women workers to look after such children. The most marginalised women in the locality, women in exploitative conditions or bonded labour or those vulnerable to being trafficked or liberated manual scavengers should be employed for providing child care services (Para 24, Schedule II).

Q. Who issues the muster rolls (MR) and how are they maintained at worksite?

Ans. As per Schedule I, Para 15, the muster rolls are to be maintained as given below:

- Every muster roll shall be signed by the authorised person of the Gram Panchayat or by the Programme Officer; and shall contain such mandatory information as may be specified by the Central Government;
- Each muster roll shall be in English or local language and have a unique identity number electronically generated by the computer system (e-Muster) along with the list of workers applied for work;
- Muster rolls shall be maintained at the worksite by marking attendance daily by a person authorised under the Scheme, details of which shall be made available in public view on a daily basis using the computer system;
- The muster roll shall be periodically checked by officials in the manner prescribed in the Scheme;
- The muster roll shall be closed on the last given day, countersigned by every worker who has worked, and shall be handed over to the technical personnel for measurement;
- A detailed record of muster rolls shall be maintained in the registers as specified from time to time;
- When a work is in progress, the workers engaged in that work may select from amongst themselves not less than five workers on a weekly rotational basis to verify and certify all the bills or vouchers of their worksite at least once in a week;
- Any person shall have access to muster rolls on the worksite on demand all days during all working hours.

Q. Who constitutes Special Category of Workers (Vulnerable Groups) under MGNREGA?

Ans. The special category of workers are from:

a) Persons with disabilities

b) Primitive Tribal Groups

c) Nomadic Tribal Groups

d) De-notified Tribes

e) Women in special circumstances
f) Senior citizens above 65 years of age
g) HIV positive persons
h) Internally displaced persons
i) Rehabilitated bonded labour

Q. List the different registers to be maintained under MGNREGA and at what level they need to be maintained?

Ans. Different Registers to be maintained under MGNREGA

S.No.	Name of Register	Level at which Register is to be maintained
1	Tender/Contract Register	Gram Panchayat/ Block/District
2	Material Procurement Register	Gram Panchayat/ Block/District
3	Muster Roll Issue Register	Block
4	Muster Roll Receipt Register	Gram Panchayat/ Other implementing agencies
5	Job Card Application Register	Gram Panchayat/ Block
6	Job Card Register	Gram Panchayat/ Block
7	Employment Register	Gram Panchayat/ Block/other implementing agencies
8	Works Register	Gram Panchayat/ Block/other implementing agencies
9	Assets Register	Gram Panchayat/ Block/other implementing agencies
10	Complaint Register	Gram Panchayats/ Block/District / other Implementing agencies
11	Monthly Allotment and Utilisation Certificate Watch Register	Gram Panchayat/ Block/District/other implementing agencies
12	Financial Records	Gram Panchayat/ Block/District/other implementing agencies

APPENDIX-V

The Mahatma Gandhi National Rural Employment Guarantee Act, 2005

Act No. 42 of 2005 **[5th September, 2005.]**

An Act to provide for the enhancement of livelihood security of the households in rural areas of the country by providing at least one hundred days of guaranteed wage employment in every financial year to every household whose adult members volunteer to do unskilled manual work and for matters connected therewith or incidental thereto.

BE it enacted by Parliament in the Fifty-sixth Year of the Republic of India as follows:—

Chapter-I : Preliminary

1. Short title, extent and commencement.—

1) This Act may be called [1][theMahatma Gandhi National Rural Employment Guarantee Act], 2005.
2) It extends to the whole of India except the State of Jammu and Kashmir*.
3) It shall come into force on such date[2] as the Central Government may, by notification in the Official Gazette, appoint; and different dates may be appointed for different States or for different areas in a State and any reference in any such provision to the commencement of this Act shall be construed as a reference to the coming into force of that provision in such State or, as the case may be, in such area:

Provided that this Act shall be applicable to the whole of the territory to which it extends within a period of five years from the date of enactment of this Act.

2. Definitions.—In this Act, unless the context otherwise requires,—

(a) "adult" means a person who has completed his eighteenth years of age;

(b) "applicant" means the head of a household or any of its other adult members who has applied for employment under the Scheme;

(c) "Block" means a community development area within a district comprising a group of Gram Panchayats;

(d) "Central Council" means the Central Employment Guarantee Council constituted under sub-section (*1*) of section 10;

(e) "District Programme Coordinator" means an officer of the State Government designated as such under sub-section (*1*) of section 14 for implementation of the Scheme in a district;

(f) "household" means the members of a family related to each other by blood, marriage or adoption and normally residing together and sharing meals or holding a common ration card;

(g) "implementing agency" includes any department of the Central Government or a State Government, a Zila Parishad, Panchayat at intermediate level, Gram Panchayat or any local authority or Government undertaking or non-governmental organisation authorised by the Central Government or the State Government to undertake the implementation of any work taken up under a Scheme;

(h) "minimum wage", in relation to any area, means the minimum wage fixed by the State Government under section 3 of the Minimum Wages Act, 1948 (11 of 1948) for agricultural labourers as applicable in that area;

(i) "National Fund" means the National Employment Guarantee Fund established under sub- section (*1*) of section 20;

(j) "notification" means a notification published in the Official Gazette;

(k) "preferred work" means any work which is taken up for implementation on a priority basis under a Scheme;

(l) "prescribed" means prescribed by rules made under this Act;

(m) "Programme Officer" means an officer appointed under sub-section (*1*) of section 15 for implementing the Scheme;

(n) "project" means any work taken up under a Scheme for the purpose of providing employment to the applicants;

(o) "rural area" means any area in a State except those areas covered by any urban local body or a Cantonment Board established or constituted under any law for the time being in force;

(p) "Scheme" means a Scheme notified by the State Government under sub-section (*1*) of section4;

(q) "State Council" means the State Employment Guarantee Council constituted under sub- section (*1*) of section 12;

(r) "unskilled manual work" means any physical work which any adult person is capable of doing without any skill or special training;

(s) "wage rate" means the wage rate referred to in section 6.

Chapter-II : Guarantee of Employment in Rural Areas

3. Guarantee of rural employment to households.—

1) Save as otherwise provided, the State Government shall, in such rural area in the State as may be notified by the Central Government, provide to every household whose adult members volunteer to do unskilled manual work not less than one hundred days of such work in a financial year in accordance with the Scheme made under this Act.

---

1. Subs. by Act 46 of 2009, s. 2, for "the National Rural Employment Guarantee Act" (w.e.f. 2-10-2009).
2. 2nd February, 2006, *vide* notification No. S.O. 87(E), dated 24th January, 2006, *see* Gazette of India, Extraordinary, Part II sec.3(*ii*).

* *Vide* notification No. S.O. 3912(E), dated 30th October, 2019, this Act is made applicable to the Union territory of Jammu and Kashmir and the Union territory of Ladakh.

2) Every person who has done the work given to him under the Scheme shall be entitled to receive wages at the wage rate for each day of work.

3) Save as otherwise provided in this Act, the disbursement of daily wages shall be made on a weekly basis or in any case not later than a fortnight after the date on which such work was done.

4) The Central Government or the State Government may, within the limits of its economic capacity and development, make provisions for securing work to every adult member of a household under a Scheme for any period beyond the period guaranteed under sub-section (*1*), as may be expedient.

Chapter-III : Employment Guarantee Schemes and Unemployment Allowance

4. Employment Guarantee Schemes for Rural Areas.—

1) For the purposes of giving effect to the provisions of section 3, every State Government shall, within six months from the date of commencement of this Act, by notification, make a Scheme, for providing not less than one hundred days of guaranteed employment in a financial year to every household in the rural areas covered under the Scheme and whose adult members, by application, volunteer to do unskilled manual work subject to the conditions laid down by or under this Act and in the Scheme:

   Provided that until any such Scheme is notified by the State Government, the Annual Action Plan or Perspective Plan for the *Sampoorna Grameen Rozgar Yojana* (SGRY) or the National Food for Work Programme (NFFWP) whichever is in force in the concerned area immediately before such notification shall be deemed to be the action plan for the Scheme for the purposes of this Act.

2) The State Government shall publish a summary of the Scheme made by it in at least two local newspapers, one of which shall be in a vernacular language circulating in the area or areas to which such Scheme shall apply.

3) The Scheme made under sub-section (*1*) shall provide for the minimum features specified in Schedule I.

5. Conditions for providing guaranteed employment.—

1) The State Government may, without prejudice to the conditions specified in Schedule II, specify in the Scheme the conditions for providing guaranteed employment under this Act.

2) The persons employed under any Scheme made under this Act shall be entitled to such facilities not less than the minimum facilities specified in Schedule II.

6. Wage rate.—

1) Notwithstanding anything contained in the Minimum Wages Act, 1948 (11 of 1948), the Central Government may, by notification, specify the wage rate for the purposes of this Act:

Provided that different rates of wages may be specified for different areas:

Provided further that the wage rate specified from time to time under any such notification shall not be at a rate less than sixty rupees per day.

2) Until such time as a wage rate is fixed by the Central Government in respect of any area in a State, the minimum wage fixed by the State Government under section 3 of the Minimum Wages Act, 1948 (11 of 1948) for agricultural labourers, shall be considered as the wage rate applicable to that area.

7. Payment of Unemployment Allowance.—

1) If an applicant for employment under the Scheme is not provided such employment within fifteen days of receipt of his application seeking employment or from the date on which the employment has been sought in the case of an advance application, whichever is later, he shall be entitled to a daily unemployment allowance in accordance with this section.

2) Subject to such terms and conditions of eligibility as may be prescribed by the State Government and subject to the provisions of this Act and the Schemes and the economic capacity of the State Government, the unemployment allowance payable under sub-section (*1*) shall be paid to the applicants of a household subject to the entitlement of the household at such rate as may be specified by the State Government, by notification, in consultation with the State Council:

Provided that no such rate shall be less than one-fourth of the wage rate for the first thirty days during the financial year and not less than one-half of the wage rate for the remaining period of the financial year.

3) The liability of the State Government to pay unemployment allowance to a household during any financial year shall cease as soon as—

(a) the applicant is directed by the Gram Panchayat or the Programme Officer to report for work either by himself or depute at least one adult member of his household; or

(b) the period for which employment is sought comes to an end and no member of the household of the applicant had turned up for employment; or

(c) the adult members of the household of the applicant have received in total at least one hundred days of work within the financial year; or

(d) the household of the applicant has earned as much from the wages and unemployment allowance taken together which is equal to the wages for one hundred days of work during the financial year.

4) The unemployment allowance payable to the household of an applicant jointly shall be sanctioned and disbursed by the Programme Officer or such local authority (including the Panchayats at the district, intermediate or village level) as the State Government may, by notification, authorise in this behalf.

5) Every payment of unemployment allowance under sub-section (*1*) shall be made or offered not later than fifteen days from the date on which it became due for payment.

6) The State Government may prescribe the procedure for payment of unemployment allowance under this Act.

8. Non-disbursement of unemployment allowance in certain circumstances.—

1) If the Programme Officer is not in a position to disburse the unemployment allowance in time or at all for any reason beyond his control, he shall report the matter to the District Programme Coordinator and announce such reasons in a notice to be displayed

on his notice board and the notice board of the Gram Panchayat and such other conspicuous places as he may deem necessary.

2) Every case of non-payment or delayed payment of unemployment allowance shall be reported in the annual report submitted by the District Programme Coordinator to the State Government along with the reasons for such non-payment or delayed payment.

3) The State Government shall take all measures to make the payment of unemployment allowance reported under sub-section (*1*) to the concerned household as expeditiously as possible.

9. Disentitlement to receive unemployment allowance in certain circumstances.—An applicant who—

(a) does not accept the employment provided to his household under a Scheme; or

(b) does not report for work within fifteen days of being notified by the Programme Officer or the implementing agency to report for the work; or

(c) continuously remains absent from work, without obtaining a permission from the concerned implementing agency for a period of more than one week or remains absent for a total period of more than one week in any month, shall not be eligible to claim the unemployment allowance payable under this Act for a period of three months but shall be eligible to seek employment under the Scheme at any time.

Chapter-IV : Implementing and Monitoring Authorities

10. Central Employment Guarantee Council.—

1) With effect from such date as the Central Government may, by notification specify, there shall be constituted a Council to be called the Central Employment Guarantee Council to discharge the functions, and perform the duties, assigned to it by or under this Act.

2) The headquarters of the Central Council shall be at Delhi.

3) The Central Council shall consist of the following members to be appointed by the Central Government, namely:—

(a) a Chairperson;

(b) not more than such number of representatives of the Central Ministries including the Planning Commission not below the rank of Joint Secretary to the Government of India as may be determined by the Central Government;

(c) not more than such number of representatives of the State Governments as may be determined by the Central Government;

(d) not more than fifteen non-official members representing Panchayati Raj Institutions, organisations of workers and disadvantaged groups:

Provided that such non-official members shall include two chairpersons of District Panchayats nominated by the Central Government by rotation for a period of one year at a time:

Provided further that not less than one-third of the non-official members nominated under this clause shall be women:

Provided also that not less than one-third of the non-official members shall be belonging to the Scheduled Castes, the Scheduled Tribes, the Other Backward Classes and Minorities;

(e) such number of representatives of the States as the Central Government may, by rules, determine in this behalf;

(f) a Member-Secretary not below the rank of Joint Secretary to the Government of India.

4) The terms and conditions subject to which the Chairperson and other members of the Central Council may be appointed and the time, place and procedure of the meetings (including the quorum at such meetings) of the Central Council shall be such as may be prescribed by the Central Government.

11. Functions and Duties of Central Council.—

1) The Central Council shall perform and discharge the following functions and duties, namely:—

(a) establish a central evaluation and monitoring system;

(b) advise the Central Government on all matters concerning the implementation of this Act;

(c) review the monitoring and redressal mechanism from time to time and recommend improvements required;

(d) promote the widest possible dissemination of information about the Schemes made under this Act;

(e) monitoring the implementation of this Act;

(f) preparation of annual reports to be laid before Parliament by the Central Government on the implementation of this Act;

(g) any other duty or function as may be assigned to it by the Central Government.

2) The Central Council shall have the power to undertake evaluation of the various Schemes made under this Act and for that purpose collect or cause to be collected statistics pertaining to the rural economy and the implementation of the Schemes.

12. State Employment Guarantee Council.—

1) For the purposes of regular monitoring and reviewing the implementation of this Act at the State level, every State Government shall constitute a State Council to be known as the .... (name of the State) State Employment Guarantee Council with a Chairperson and such number of official members as may be determined by the State Government and not more than fifteen non-official members nominated by the State Government from Panchayati Raj institutions, organisations of workers and disadvantaged groups:

Provided that not less than one-third of the non-official members nominated under this clause shall be women:

Provided further that not less than one third of the non-official members shall be belonging to the Scheduled Castes, the Scheduled Tribes, the Other Backward Classes and Minorities.

2) The terms and conditions subject to which the Chairperson and members of the State Council may be appointed and the time, place and procedure of the meetings (including the quorum at such meetings) of the State Council shall be such as may be prescribed by the State Government.

3) The duties and functions of the State Council shall include—

(a) advising the State Government on all matters concerning the Scheme and its implementation in the State;

(b) determining the preferred works;

(c) reviewing the monitoring and redressal mechanisms from time to time and recommending improvements;

(d) promoting the widest possible dissemination of information about this Act and the Schemes under it;

(e) monitoring the implementation of this Act and the Schemes in the State and coordinating such implementation with the Central Council;

(f) preparing the annual report to be laid before the State Legislature by the State Government;

(g) any other duty or function as may be assigned to it by the Central Council or the State Government.

3) The State Council shall have the power to undertake an evaluation of the Schemes operating in the State and for that purpose to collect or cause to be collected statistics pertaining to the rural economy and the implementation of the Schemes and Programmes in the State.

13. Principal authorities for planning and implementation of Schemes.—

1) The Panchayats at district, intermediate and village levels shall be the principal authorities for planning and implementation of the Schemes made under this Act.

2) The functions of the Panchayats at the district level shall be—

(a) to finalise and approve block wise shelf of projects to be taken up under a programme under the Scheme;

(b) to supervise and monitor the projects taken up at the Block level and district level; and

(c) to carry out such other functions as may be assigned to it by the State Council, from time to time.

3) The functions of the Panchayat at intermediate level shall be—

(a) to approve the Block level Plan for forwarding it to the district Panchayat at the district level for final approval;

(b) to supervise and monitor the projects taken up at the Gram Panchayat and Block level; and

(c) to carry out such other functions as may be assigned to it by the State Council, from time to time.

4) The District Programme Coordinator shall assist the Panchayat at the district level in discharging its functions under this Act and any Scheme made thereunder.

14. District Programme Coordinator.—

1) The Chief Executive Officer of the District Panchayat or the Collector of the district or any other district level officer of appropriate rank as the State Government may decide shall be designated as the District Programme Coordinator for the implementation of the Scheme in the district.

2) The District Programme Coordinator shall be responsible for the implementation of the Scheme in the district in accordance with the provisions of this Act and the rules made thereunder.

3) The functions of the District Programme Coordinator shall be—

(a) to assist the district Panchayat in discharging its functions under this Act and any scheme made thereunder;

(b) to consolidate the plans prepared by the Blocks and project proposals received from other implementing agencies for inclusion in the shelf of projects to be approved by the Panchayat at district level;

(c) to accord necessary sanction and administrative clearance, wherever necessary;

(d) to coordinate with the Programme Officers functioning within his jurisdiction and the implementing agencies to ensure that the applicants are provided employment as per their entitlements under this Act;

(e) to review, monitor and supervise the performance of the Programme Officers;

(f) to conduct periodic inspection of the works in progress; and

(g) to redress the grievances of the applicants.

4) The State Government shall delegate such administrative and financial powers to the District Programme Coordinator as may be required to enable him to carry out his functions under this Act.

5) The Programme Officer appointed under sub-section (*1*) of section 15 and all other officers of the State Government and local authorities and bodies functioning within the district shall be responsible to assist the District Programme Coordinator in carrying out his functions under this Act and the Schemes made thereunder.

6) The District Programme Coordinator shall prepare in the month of December every year a labour budget for the next financial year containing the details of anticipated demand for unskilled manual work in the district and the plan for engagement of labourers in the works covered under the Scheme and submit it to the district panchayat.

15. Programme Officer.—

1) At every Panchayat at intermediate level, the State Government shall appoint a person who is not below the rank of Block Development Officer with such qualifications and experience as may be determined by the State Government as Programme Officer at the Panchayat at intermediate level.

2) The Programme Officer shall assist the Panchayat at intermediate level in discharging its functions under this Act and any Scheme made thereunder.

3) The Programme Officer shall be responsible for matching the demand for employment with the employment opportunities arising from projects in the area under his jurisdiction.

4) The Programme Officer shall prepare a plan for the Block under his jurisdiction by consolidating the project proposals prepared by the Gram Panchayats and the proposals received from intermediate panchayats.

5) The functions of the Programme Officer shall include—

    (a) monitoring of projects taken up by the Gram Panchayats and other implementing agencies within the Block;

(b) sanctioning and ensuring payment of unemployment allowance to the eligible households;

(c) ensuring prompt and fair payment of wages to all labourers employed under a programme of the Scheme within the Block;

(d) ensuring that regular social audits of all works within the jurisdiction of the Gram Panchayat are carried out by the Gram Sabha and that prompt action is taken on the objections raised in the social audit;

(e) dealing promptly with all complaints that may arise in connection with the implementation of the Scheme within the Block; and

(f) any other work as may be assigned to him by the District Programme Coordinator or the State Government.

6) The Programme Officers shall function under the direction, control and superintendence of the District Programme Coordinator.

7) The State Government may, by order, direct that all or any of the functions of a Programme Officer shall be discharged by the Gram Panchayat or a local authority.

16. Responsibilities of the Gram Panchayats.—

1) The Gram Panchayat shall be responsible for identification of the projects in the Gram Panchayat area to be taken up under a Scheme as per the recommendations of the Gram Sabha and the Ward Sabhas and for executing and supervising such works.

2) A Gram Panchayat may take up any project under a Scheme within the area of the Gram Panchayat as may be sanctioned by the Programme Officer.

3) Every Gram Panchayat shall, after considering the recommendations of the Gram Sabha and the Ward Sabhas, prepare a development plan and maintain a shelf of possible works to be taken up under the Scheme as and when demand for work arises.

4) The Gram Panchayat shall forward its proposals for the development projects including the order of priority between different works to the Programme Officer for scrutiny and preliminary approval prior to the commencement of the year in which it is proposed to be executed.

5) The Programme Officer shall allot at least fifty per cent. of the works in terms of its cost under a Scheme to be implemented through the Gram Panchayats.

6) The Programme Officer shall supply each Gram Panchayat with—

   (a) the muster rolls for the works sanctioned to be executed by it; and

   (b) a list of employment opportunities available elsewhere to the residents of the Gram Panchayat.

7) The Gram Panchayat shall allocate employment opportunities among the applicants and ask them to report for work.

8) The works taken up by a Gram Panchayat under a Scheme shall meet the required technical standards and measurements.

17. Social Audit of work by Gram Sabha.—

1) The Gram Sabha shall monitor the execution of works within the Gram Panchayat.

2) The Gram Sabha shall conduct regular social audits of all the projects under the Scheme taken up within the Gram Panchayat.

3) The Gram Panchayat shall make available all relevant documents including the muster rolls, bills, vouchers, measurement books, copies of sanction orders and other connected books of account and papers to the Gram Sabha for the purpose of conducting the social audit.

18. Responsibilities of State Government in implementing Scheme.— The State Government shall make available to the District Programme Coordinator and the Programme Officers necessary staff and technical support as may be necessary for the effective implementation of the Scheme.

19. Grievance Redressal Mechanism.—The State Government shall, by rules, determine appropriate grievance redressal mechanisms at the Block level and the district level for dealing with any complaint by any person in respect of implementation of the Scheme and lay down the procedure for disposal of such complaints.

Chapter-V : Establishment of National and State Employment Guarantee Funds and Audit

20. National Employment Guarantee Fund.—

1) The Central Government shall, by notification, establish a fund to be called the National Employment Guarantee Fund for the purposes of this Act.

2) The Central Government may, after due appropriation made by Parliament by law in this behalf, credit by way of grants or loans such sums of money as the Central Government may consider necessary to the National Fund.

3) The amount standing to the credit of the National Fund shall be utilised in such manner and subject to such conditions and limitations as may be prescribed by the Central Government.

21. State Employment Guarantee Fund.—

1) The State Government may, by notification, establish a fund to be called the State Employment Guarantee Fund for the purposes of implementation of the Scheme.

2) The amount standing to the credit of the State Fund shall be expended in such manner and subject to such conditions and limitations as may be prescribed by the State Government for the purposes of implementation of this Act and the Schemes made thereunder and for meeting the administrative expenses in connection with the implementation of this Act.

3) The State Fund shall be held and administered on behalf of the State Government in such manner and by such authority as may be prescribed by the State Government.

22. Funding Pattern.—

1) Subject to the rules as may be made by the Central Government in this behalf, the Central Government shall meet the cost of the following, namely: —

   (a) the amount required for payment of wages for unskilled manual work under the Scheme;

   (b) up to three-fourths of the material cost of the Scheme including payment of wages to skilled and semi-skilled workers subject to the provisions of Schedule II;

   (c) such percentage of the total cost of the Scheme as may be determined by the Central Government towards the administrative expenses, which may include the salary and allowances of the Programme Officers and his supporting staff, the administrative expenses of the Central Council, facilities to be provided under Schedule II and such other item as may be decided by the Central Government.

2) The State Government shall meet the cost of the following, namely:—

(a) the cost of unemployment allowance payable under the Scheme;

(b) one-fourth of the material cost of the Scheme including payment of wages to skilled and semi- skilled workers subject to the provisions of Schedule II;

(c) the administrative expenses of the State Council.

23. Transparency and Accountability.—

1) The District Programme Coordinator and all implementing agencies in the District shall be responsible for the proper utilisation and management of the funds placed at their disposal for the purpose of implementing a Scheme.

2) The State Government may prescribe the manner of maintaining proper books and accounts of employment of labourers and the expenditure incurred in connection with the implementation of the provisions of this Act and the Schemes made thereunder.

3) The State Government may, by rules, determine the arrangements to be made for the proper execution of Schemes and programmes under the Schemes and to ensure transparency and accountability at all levels in the implementation of the Schemes.

4) All payments of wages in cash and unemployment allowances shall be made directly to the person concerned and in the presence of independent persons of the community on pre-announced dates.

5) If any dispute or complaint arises concerning the implementation of a Scheme by the Gram Panchayat, the matter shall be referred to the Programme Officer.

6) The Programme Officer shall enter every complaint in a complaint register maintained by him and shall dispose of the disputes and

complaints within seven days of its receipt and in case it relates to a matter to be resolved by any other authority it shall be forwarded to such authority under intimation to the complainant.

24. Audit of accounts.—

1) The Central Government may, in consultation with the Comptroller and Auditor General of India, prescribe appropriate arrangements for audits of the accounts of the Schemes at all levels.

2) The accounts of the Scheme shall be maintained in such form and in such manner as may be prescribed by the State Government.

Chapter-VI : Miscellaneous

25. Penalty for non-compliance.—Whoever contravenes the provisions of this Act shall on conviction be liable to a fine which may extend to one thousand rupees.

26. Power to delegate.—

1) The Central Government may, by notification, direct that the powers exercisable by it (excluding the power to make rules) may, in such circumstances and subject to such conditions and limitations, be exercisable also by the State Government or such officer subordinate to the Central Government or the State Government as it may specify in such notification.

2) The State Government may, by notification, direct that the powers exercisable by it (excluding the power to make rules and Schemes) may, in such circumstances and subject to such conditions and limitations, be exercisable also by such officer subordinate to it as it may specify in such notification.

27. Power of Central Government to give directions.—

1) The Central Government may give such directions as it may consider necessary to the State Government for the effective implementation of the provisions of this Act.

2) Without prejudice to the provisions of sub-section (1), the Central Government may, on receipt of any complaint regarding the issue or improper utilisation of funds granted under this Act in respect of any Scheme if *prima facie* satisfied that there is a case, cause an investigation into the complaint made by any agency designated

by it and if necessary, order stoppage of release of funds to the Scheme and institute appropriate remedial measures for its proper implementation within a reasonable period of time.

28. Act to have overriding effect.—The provisions of this Act or the Schemes made thereunder shall have effect notwithstanding anything inconsistent therewith contained in any other law for the time being in force or in any instrument having effect by virtue of such law:

Provided that where a State enactment exists or is enacted to provide employment guarantee for unskilled manual work to rural households consistent with the provisions of this Act under which the entitlement of the households is not less than and the conditions of employment are not inferior to what is guaranteed under this Act, the State Government shall have the option of implementing its own enactment:

Provided further that in such cases the financial assistance shall be paid to the concerned State Government in such manner as shall be determined by the Central Government, which shall not exceed what the State would have been entitled to receive under this Act had a Scheme made under this Act had to be implemented.

29. Power to amend Schedules.—

1) If the Central Government is satisfied that it is necessary or expedient so to do, it may, by notification, amend Schedule I or Schedule II and thereupon Schedule I or Schedule II, as the case may be, shall be deemed to have been amended accordingly.
2) A copy of every notification made under sub-section (*1*) shall be laid before each House of Parliament as soon as may be after it is made.

30. Protection of action taken in good faith.—No suit, prosecution or other legal proceedings shall lie against the District Programme Coordinator, Programme Officer or any other person who is, or who is deemed to be, a public servant within the meaning of section 21 of the Indian Penal Code (45 of 1860) in respect of anything which is in good faith done or intended to be done under this Act or the rules or Schemes made thereunder.

31. Power of Central Government to make rules.—

1) The Central Government may, by notification, and subject to the

condition of previous publication, make rules to carry out the provisions of this Act.

2) In particular, and without the prejudice of the foregoing power, such rules may provide for all or any of the following matters, namely:—

(a) the number of representatives of the State Governments under clause (*e*) of sub-section (*3*) of section 10;

(b) the terms and conditions subject to which the Chairman and other members of the Central Council may be appointed, and the time, place and procedure of the meetings (including the quorum at such meetings) of the Central Council, under sub-section (*4*) of section 10;

(c) the manner in which and the conditions and limitations subject to which the National Fund shall be utilised under sub-section (*3*) of section 20;

(d) the rules relating to funding pattern to meet the cost of certain items under sub-section (*1*) of section 22;

(e) any other matter which is to be, or may be, prescribed or in respect of which provision is to be made by the Central Government by rules.

32. Power of State Government to make rules.—

1) The State Government may, by notification, and subject to the condition of previous publication, and consistent with this Act and the rules made by the Central Government, make rules to carry out the provisions of this Act.

2) In particular, and without prejudice to the generality of the foregoing power, such rules may provide for all or any of the following matters, namely:—

(a) the terms and conditions upon which eligibility for unemployment allowance may be determined under sub-section (2) of section 7;

(b) the procedure for payment of unemployment allowance under sub-section (6) of section 7;

(c) the terms and conditions subject to which the Chairperson and members of the State Council may be appointed, and the time, place and procedure of the meetings (including the quorum at such meetings) of their appointment to the State Council, under sub-section (2) of section 12;

(d) the grievance redressal mechanism at the Block level and the District level and the procedure to be followed in such matter under section 19;

(e) the manner in which and the conditions and limitations subject to which the State Fund shall be utilised under sub-section (2) of section 21;

(f) the authority who may administer and the manner in which he may hold the State Fund under sub-section (3) of section 21;

(g) the manner of maintaining books of account of employment of labourers and the expenditure under sub-section (2) of section 23;

(h) the arrangements required for proper execution of Schemes under sub-section (3) of section 23;

(i) the form and manner in which the accounts of the Scheme shall be maintained under sub-section (2) of section 24;

(j) any other matter which is to be, or may be, prescribed or in respect of which provision is to be made by the State Government by rules.

33. Laying of Rules and Schemes.—

1) Every rule made by the Central Government under this Act shall be laid, as soon as may be after it is made, before each House of Parliament, while it is in session, for a total period of thirty days which may be comprised in one session or in two or more successive sessions, and if, before the expiry of the session immediately following the session or the successive sessions aforesaid, both Houses agree in making any modification in the rule or both the Houses agree that the rule should not be made, the rule shall have thereafter have effect only in such modified form or be of no effect, as the case may be; so, however, that any such

modification or annulment shall be without prejudice to the validity of anything previously done under that rule.

2) Every rule or Scheme made by the State Government under this Act shall, as soon as may be after it is made, be laid before each House of the State Legislature where there are two Houses, and where there is one House of the State Legislature, before that House.

34. Power to remove difficulties.—

1) If any difficulty arises in giving effect to the provisions of this Act, the Central Government may, by order published in the Official Gazette, make such provisions, not inconsistent with the provisions of this Act, as appear to it to be necessary or expedient for removing the difficulty:

Provided that no order shall be made under this section after the expiry of three years from the commencement of this Act.

2) Every order made under this section shall be laid, as soon as may be after it is made, before each House of Parliament.

Schedule-I [*See* section 4(*3*)]

Minimum Features of a Rural Employment Guarantee Scheme

1. The focus of the Scheme shall be on the following works in their order of priority:—

   a) water conservation and water harvesting;

   b) drought proofing (including afforestation and tree plantation);

   c) irrigation canals including micro and minor irrigation works;

   d) provision of irrigation facility to land owned by households belonging to the Scheduled Castes and Scheduled Tribes or to land of beneficiaries of land reforms or that of the beneficiaries under the Indira Awas Yojana of the Government of India;

   e) renovation of traditional water bodies including desilting of tanks;

   f) land development;

   g) flood control and protection works including drainage in water logged areas;

h) rural connectivity to provide all-weather access; and

i) any other work which may be notified by the Central Government in consultation with the State Government.

2. Creation of durable assets and strengthening the livelihood resource base of the rural poor shall be an important objective of the Scheme.

3. The works taken up under the scheme shall be in rural areas.

4. (1) The focus of the Scheme shall be on the following works as categorised below:

I. Category-A: Public Works Relating to Natural Resources Management-

[3](*i*) Water conservation and water harvesting structures to augment and improve ground water like underground dykes, earthen dams, stop dams, check dams and rooftop rain water harvesting structures in Government or Panchayat buildings with special focus on recharging ground water including drinking water sources.

(ii) Watershed management works such as contour trenches, terracing, contour bunds, boulder checks, gabion structures and spring shed development resulting in a comprehensive treatment of a watershed;

(iii) Micro and minor irrigation works and creation, renovation and maintenance of irrigation canals and drains;

(iv) Renovation of traditional water bodies including desilting of irrigation tanks and other water bodies;

(v) Afforestation, tree plantation and horticulture in common and forest lands, road margins, canal bunds, tank foreshores and coastal belts duly providing right to usufruct to the households covered in Paragraph 5; and

(vi) Land development works in common land.

II. Category-B: [4][Community Assets or Individual Assets] For Vulnerable Sections (Only for Households in Paragraph 5)

(i) Improving productivity of lands of households specified in Paragraph 5 through land development and by providing suitable infrastructure for irrigation including dug wells, farm ponds and other water harvesting structures;

(ii) Improving livelihoods through horticulture, sericulture, plantation, and farm forestry;

(iii) Development of fallow or waste lands of households defined in Paragraph 5 to bring it under cultivation;

[5](*iv*) Unskilled wage component in construction of houses sanctioned under the Pradhan Mantri Awaas Yojana-Gramin or such other State or Central Government Scheme;

(v) Creating infrastructure for promotion of livestock such as, poultry shelter, goat shelter, piggery shelter, cattle shelter and fodder troughs for cattle; and

(vi) Creating infrastructure for promotion of fisheries such as, fish drying yards, storage facilities, and promotion of fisheries in seasonal water bodies on public land;

III. Category-C: Common Infrastructure [6][Including for NRLM] Compliant Self Help Groups

(i) Works for promoting agricultural productivity by creating durable infrastructure required for bio-fertilizers and post-harvest facilities including pucca storage facilities for agricultural produce; and

(ii) Common work-sheds for livelihood activities of self-help groups.

IV. Category-D: Rural Infrastructure:

[7](*i*) Rural sanitation related works, such as, individual household latrines, School toilet units, Anganwadi toilets either independently or in convergence with schemes of other Government Departments **and unskilled wage component for construction of Community Sanitary Complexes in convergence with Swachh Bharat Mission (Grameen)** to achieve 'open defecation free' status, and solid and liquid waste management as per prescribed norms;

(ii) Providing all-weather rural road connectivity to unconnected villages and to connect identified rural production centers to the existing pucca road network; and construction of pucca internal roads or streets including side drains and culverts within a village;

---

3. Subs. by Notification No. S.O. 4274(E), for "(*i*) Water conservation and water harvesting structures to augment and improve groundwater like underground dykes, earthen dams, stop dams, check dams with special focus on recharging ground water including drinking water sources;" (dated 27-11-2019).

(iii) Construction of play fields;

(iv) Works for improving disaster preparedness or restoration of roads or restoration of other essential public infrastructure including flood control and protection works, providing drainage in water logged areas, deepening and repairing of flood channels, chaur renovation, construction of storm water drains for coastal protection;

(v) Construction of buildings for Gram Panchayats, women self-help groups' federations, cyclone shelters, Anganwadi centers, village haats and crematoria at the village or block level.

(vi) Construction of Food Grain Storage Structures for implementing the provisions of The National Food Security Act 2013 (20 of 2013);

(vii) Production of building material required for construction works under the Act as a part of the estimate of such construction works.

(viii) Maintenance of rural public assets created under the Act; and

(ix) any other work which may be notified by the Central Government in consultation with the State Government in this regard.

(2) The order of priority of works shall be determined by each Gram Panchayat in the meetings of the Gram Sabha keeping in view potential of the local area, its needs, local resources and in accordance with the provisions of Paragraph 9.

[8][Provided that the District Programme Coordinator shall ensure that at least 60% of the works to be taken up in a district in terms of cost shall be for creation of productive assets directly linked to agriculture and allied activities through development of land, water and trees.]

(3) Works which are non-tangible, not measurable, repetitive such as, removing grass, pebbles, agricultural operations, shall not be taken up.]

5. The Scheme shall be subject to appropriate arrangements as may

---

4. Subs by the Notification No. S.O. 1888(E), for "INDIVIDUAL ASSETS" (dated 21-07-2014).

5. Subs. by the Notification No. S.O. 403(E), for "(*iv*) Unskilled wage component in construction of houses sanctioned under the Indira Awaas Yojana or such other State or Central Government Scheme;" (dated 25-01-2018).

be laid down by the State Government under the rules issued by it for proper maintenance of the public assets created under the Scheme.

6. Under no circumstances shall the labourers be paid less than the wage rate.
7. When wages are directly linked with the quantity of work, the wages shall be paid according to the schedule of rates fixed by the State Government for different types of work every year, in consultation with the State Council.
8. The schedule of rates of wages for unskilled labourers shall be so fixed that a person working for seven hours would normally earn a wage equal to the wage rate.
9. The cost of material component of projects including the wages of the skilled and semi-skilled workers taken up under the Scheme shall not exceed forty per cent. of the total project costs.
10. It shall be open to the Programme Officer and Gram Panchayat to direct any person who applied for employment under the Scheme to do work of any type permissible under it.
11. The Scheme shall not permit engaging any contractor for implementation of the projects under it.
12. As far as practicable, a task funded under the Scheme shall be performed by using manual labour and not machines.
13. Every Scheme shall contain adequate provisions for ensuring transparency and accountability at all level of implementation.
14. Provisions for regular inspection and supervision of works taken up under the Scheme shall be made to ensure proper quality of work as well as to ensure that the total wages paid for the completion of the work is commensurate with the quality and quantity of work done.

---

6. Subs. by the Notification No. S.O. 1888(E), for "FOR NRLM" (dated 21-07-2014).
7. Subs. by Notification No. S.O. 2198(E), for "(*i*) Rural sanitation related works, such as, individual household latrines, school toilet units, Anganwadi toilets either independently or in convergence with schemes of other Government Departments to achieve 'open defecation free' status and solid and liquid waste management as per prescribed norms" (dated 02-07-2020).

15. The District Programme Coordinator, the Programme Officer and the Gram Panchayat implementing the Scheme shall prepare annually a report containing the facts and figures and achievements relating to the implementation of the Scheme within his or its jurisdiction and a copy of the same shall be made available to the public on demand and on payment of such fee as may be specified in the Scheme.
16. All accounts and records relating to the Scheme shall be made available for public scrutiny and any person desirous of obtaining a copy or relevant extracts therefrom may be provided such copies or extracts on demand and after paying such fee as may be specified in the Scheme.
17. A copy of the muster rolls of each Scheme or project under a Scheme shall be made available in the offices of the Gram Panchayat and the Programme Officer for inspection by any person interested after paying such fee as may be specified in the Scheme.

Schedule-II (*See* section 5)

Conditions For Guaranteed Rural Employmentunder A Scheme And Minimum Entitlements Of Labourers

1. The adult members of every household who—
   (i) reside in any rural areas; and
   (ii) are willing to do unskilled manual work, may submit their names, age and the address of the household to the Gram Panchayat at the village level (hereafter in this Schedule referred to as the Gram Panchayat) in the jurisdiction of which they reside for registration of their household for issuance of a job card.
2. It shall be the duty of the Gram Panchayat to register the household, after making such enquiry as it deems fit and issue a job card containing such details of adult members of the household affixing their photographs, as may be specified by the State Government in the Scheme.
3. The registration made under paragraph 2 shall be for such period

8. Ins. by the Notification No. S.O.1888 (E) (dated 21-07-2014).

as may be laid in the Scheme, but in any case not less than five years, and may be renewed from time to time.

4. Every adult member of a registered household whose name appears in the job card shall be entitled to apply for unskilled manual work under the Scheme.

5. All registered persons belonging to a household shall be entitled to employment in accordance with the Scheme made under the provisions of this Act, for as many days as each applicant may request, subject to a maximum of one hundred days per household in a given financial year.

6. The Programme Officer shall ensure that every applicant referred to in paragraph 5 shall be provided unskilled manual work in accordance with the provisions of the Scheme within fifteen days of receipt of an application or from the date he seeks work in case of advance application, whichever is later:

   Provided that priority shall be given to women in such a way that at least one-third of the beneficiaries shall be women who have registered and requested for work under this Act.

7. Applications for work must be for at least fourteen days of continuous work.

8. There shall be no limit on the number of days of employment for which a person may apply, or on the number of days of employment actually provided to him subject to the aggregate entitlement of the household.

9. Applications for work may be submitted in writing either to the Gram Panchayat or to the Programme Officer, as may be specified in the Scheme.

10. The Gram Panchayat and Programme Officer, as the case may be, shall be bound to accept valid applications and to issue a dated receipt to the applicant. Group applications may also be submitted.

11. Applicants who are provided with work shall be so intimated in writing, by means of a letter sent to him at the address given in the job card and by a public notice displayed at the office of the Panchayats at the district, intermediate or village level.

12. As far as possible, employment shall be provided within a radius

of five kilometres of the village where the applicant resides at the time of applying.

13. A new work under the Scheme shall be commenced only if—

    (a) at least fifty labourers become available for such work; and

    (b) the labourers cannot be absorbed in the ongoing works:

    Provided that this condition shall not be applicable for new works, as determined by the State Government, in hilly areas and in respect of aforestation.

14. In cases the employment is provided outside such radius, it must be provided within the Block, and the labourers shall be paid ten per cent. of the wage rate as extra wages to meet additional transportation and living expenses.

15. A period of employment shall ordinarily be at least fourteen days continuously with not more than six days in a week.

16. In all cases where unemployment allowance is paid, or due to be paid, the Programme Officer shall inform the District Programme Coordinator in writing the reasons why it was not possible for him to provide employment or cause to provide employment to the applicants.

17. The District Programme Coordinator shall, in his Annual Report to the State Council, explain as to why employment could not be provided in cases where payment of unemployment allowance is involved.

18. Provision shall be made in the Scheme for advance applications, that is, applications which may be submitted in advance of the date from which employment is sought.

19. Provision shall be made in the Scheme for submission of multiple applications by the same person provided that the corresponding periods for which employment is sought do not overlap.

20. The Gram Panchayat shall prepare and maintain or cause to be prepared and maintained such registers, vouchers and other documents in such form and in such manner as may be specified in the Scheme containing particulars of job cards and passbooks issued, name, age and address of the head of the household and the adult members of the household registered with the Gram Panchayat.

21. The Gram Panchayat shall send such list or lists of the names and addresses of households and their adult members registered with it and supply such other information to the concerned Programme Officer at such periods and in such form as may be specified in the Scheme.

22. A list of persons who are provided with the work shall be displayed on the notice board of the Gram Panchayat and at the office of the Programme Officer and at such other places as the Programme Officer may deem necessary and the list shall be open for inspection by the State Government and any person interested.

23. If the Gram Panchayat is satisfied at any time that a person has registered with it by furnishing false information, it may direct the Programme Officer to direct his name to be struck off from the register and direct the applicant to return the job card:

    Provided that no such action under this paragraph shall be directed unless the applicant has been given an opportunity of being heard in the presence of two independent persons.

24. If any personal injury is caused to any person employed under the Scheme by accident arising out of and in the course of his employment, he shall be entitled to, free of charge, such medical treatment as is admissible under the Scheme.

25. Where hospitalisation of the injured worker is necessary, the State Government shall arrange for such hospitalisation including accommodation, treatment, medicines and payment of daily allowance not less than half of the wage rate required to be paid had the injured been engaged in the work.

26. If a person employed under a Scheme dies or becomes permanently disabled by accident arising out of and in the course of employment, he shall be paid by the implementing agency an *ex gratia* payment at the rate of twenty-five thousand rupees or such amount as may be notified by the Central Government, and the amount shall be paid to the legal heirs of the deceased or the disabled, as the case may be.

[9][27. If a person employed under the Scheme meets with death or becomes permanently disabled by accident arising out of and in the course of employment, he or his legal heirs, as the case may

be, shall be paid by the implementing agency an *ex-gratia* as per entitlement under the *Pradhan Mantri Suraksha Bima Yojana* or as may be notified by the Central Government.]

28. In case the number of children below the age of six years accompanying the women working at any site are five or more, provisions shall be made to depute one of such women worker to look after such children.

29. The person deputed under paragraph 28 shall be paid wage rate.

30. In case the payment of wages is not made within the period specified under the Scheme, the labourers shall be entitled to receive payment of compensation as per the provisions of the Payment of Wages Act, 1936 (4 of 1936).

31. The wages under a Scheme may be paid either wholly in cash or in cash and kind provided that at least one-fourth of the wages shall be paid in cash only.

32. The State Government may prescribe that a portion of the wages in cash may be paid to the labourers on a daily basis during the period of employment.

33. If any personal injury is caused by accident to a child accompanying any person who is employed under a Scheme, such person shall be entitled to, free of charge, such medical treatment for the child as may be specified in the Scheme and in case of death or disablement, through an *ex gratia* payment as may be determined by the State Government.

34. In case of every employment under the Scheme, there shall be no discrimination solely on the ground of gender and the provisions of the Equal Remuneration Act, 1976 (25 of 1976), shall be complied with.

APPENDIX-VI

The Finance Commission (Miscellaneous Provisions) Act, 1951

Act No. 33 of 1951 **[16th May, 1951]**

An Act to determine the qualifications requisite for appointment as members of the Finance Commission and the manner in which they shall be selected, and to prescribe their powers.

BE it enacted by Parliament as follows:—

1. **Short title.**—This Act may be called the Finance Commission (Miscellaneous Provisions) Act, 1951.
2. **Definition.**—In this Act, "the Commission" means the Finance Commission constituted by the President pursuant to clause (1) of Article 280 of the Constitution.
3. **Qualifications for appointment as, and the manner of selection of, members of the Commission.**—The Chairman of the Commission shall be selected from among persons who have had experience in public affairs, and the four other members shall be selected from among persons who—

   (a) are, or have been, or are qualified to be appointed as Judges of a High Court; or

   (b) have special knowledge of the finances and accounts of Government; or

   (c) have had wide experience in financial matters and in administration; or

9. Subs. by *vide* notification No. S.O. 2309(E), for paragraph 27 (dated 13-7-2020).

(d) have special knowledge of economies.

4. **Personal interest to disqualify members.**—Before appointing a person to be a member of the Commission, the President shall satisfy himself that that person will have no such financial or other interest as is likely to affect prejudicially his functions as a member of the Commission; and the President shall also satisfy himself from time to time with respect to every member of the Commission that he has no such interest and any person who is, or whom the President proposes to appoint to be, a member of the Commission shall, whenever required by the President so to do, furnish to him such information as the President considers necessary for the performance by him of his duties under this section.

5. **Disqualifications for being a member of the Commission.**—A person shall be disqualified for being appointed as, or for being, a member of the Commission,—

(a) if he is of unsound mind;

(b) if he is an undischarged insolvent;

(c) if he has been convicted of an offence involving moral turpitude;

(d) if he has such financial or other interest as is likely to affect prejudicially his functions as a member of the Commission.

6. **Term of office of members and eligibility for reappointment.**—Every member of the Commission shall hold office for such period as may be specified in the order of the President appointing him, but shall be eligible for reappointment:

Provided that he may, by letter addressed to the President, resign his office.

7. **Conditions of service and salaries and allowances of members.**—

[1](1) The members of the Commission shall render wholetime or part-time service to the Commission as the President may in each case specify, and there shall be paid to the members of the Commission such fees or salaries and such allowances as the Central Government may, by rules made [1][by notification in the official Gazette] in this behalf, determine.

[2](2) Every rule made under this section shall be laid, as soon as may be after it is made, before each House of Parliament, while it is in session, for a total period of thirty days which may be comprised in one session or in two or more successive sessions and if, before the expiry of the session immediately following the session or the successive sessions aforesaid, both Houses agree in making any modification in the rule or both houses agree that the rule should not be made, the rule shall thereafter have effect only in such modified form or be of no effect, as the case may be; so, however, that any such modification or annulment shall be without prejudice to the validity of anything previously done under that rule.]

8. Procedure and powers of the Commission.—

(1) The Commission shall determine their procedure and in the performance of their functions shall have all the powers of a civil court under the Code of Civil Procedure, 1908 (5 of 1908), while trying a suit in respect of the following matters, namely:—

(a) summoning and enforcing the attendance of witnesses;

(b) requiring the production of any document;

(c) requisitioning any public record from any court or office.

(2) The Commission shall have power to require any person to furnish information on such points or matters as in the opinion of the Commission may be useful for, or relevant to, any matter under the consideration of the Commission [2][and any person so required shall, notwithstanding anything contained in sub-section (*2*) of section 54 of the Indian Income Tax Act, 1922 or in any other law for the time being in force, be deemed to be legally bound to furnish such information within the meaning of section 176 of the Indian Penal Code (45 of 1860).]

(3) The Commission shall be deemed to be a civil court for the purposes of sections 480 and 482 of the Code of Criminal Procedure, 1898 (5 of 1898).

Explanation.—For the purposes of enforcing the attendance of witnesses, the local limits of the Commission's jurisdiction shall be the limits of the territory of India.

APPENDIX-VII

The Provisions of the Panchayats (Extension to the Scheduled Areas) Act, 1996

Act No. 40 of 1996 **[24th December, 1996]**

An Act to provide for the extension of the provisions of Part IX of the Constitution relating to the Panchayats to the Scheduled Areas.

BE it enacted by Parliament in the Forty-seventh Year of the Republic of India as follows:—

1. **Short title.**—This Act may be called the Provisions of the Panchayats (Extension to the Scheduled Areas) Act, 1996.
2. **Definition.**—In this Act, unless the context otherwise requires, "Scheduled Areas" means the Scheduled Areas as referred to in clause (1) of Article 244 of the Constitution.
3. **Extension of Part IX of the Constitution.**—The provisions of Part IX of the Constitution relating to Panchayats are hereby extended to the Scheduled Areas subject to such exceptions and modifications as are provided in section 4.
4. **Exceptions and modifications to Part IX of the Constitution.**—Notwithstanding anything contained under Part IX of the Constitution, the Legislature of a State shall not make any law under that Part which is inconsistent with any of the following features, namely:—

1. Ins. by Act 4 of 1986, s. 2 and the Schedule (w.e.f. 15-5-1986).

(a) State legislation on the Panchayats that may be made shall be in consonance with the customary law, social and religious practices and traditional management practices of community resources;

(b) Village shall ordinarily consist of a habitation or a group of habitations or a hamlet or a group of hamlets comprising a community and managing its affairs in accordance with traditions and customs;

(c) every village shall have a Gram Sabha consisting of persons whose names are included in the electoral rolls for the Panchayat at the village level;

(d) every Gram Sabha shall be competent to safeguard and preserve the traditions and customs of the people, their cultural identity, community resources and the customary mode of dispute resolution;

(e) every Gram Sabha shall—

(i) approve the plans, programmes and projects for social and economic development before such plans, programmes and projects are taken up for implementation by the Panchayat at the village level;

(ii) be responsible for the identification or selection of persons as beneficiaries under the poverty alleviation and other programmes;

(f) every Panchayat at the village level shall be required to obtain from the Gram Sabha a certification of utilisation of funds by that Panchayat for the plans, programmes and projects referred to in clause(*e*);

(g) the reservation of seats in the Scheduled Areas at every Panchayat shall be in proportion to the population of the communities in that Panchayat for whom reservation is sought to be given under Part IX of the Constitution:

Provided that the reservation for the Scheduled Tribes shall not be less than one-half of the total number of seats:

Provided further that all seats of Chairpersons of Panchayats at all levels shall be reserved for the Scheduled Tribes;

---

2. Added by Act 13 of 1955, s. 2.

(h) the State Government may nominate persons belonging to such Scheduled Tribes as have no representation in the Panchayat at the intermediate level or the Panchayat at the district level:

Provided that such nomination shall not exceed one-tenth of the total members to be elected in that Panchayat;

(i) the Gram Sabha or the Panchayats at the appropriate level shall be consulted before making the acquisition of land in the Scheduled Areas for development projects and before re-settling or rehabilitating persons affected by such projects in the Scheduled Areas; the actual planning and implementation of the projects in the Scheduled Areas shall be coordinated at the State level;

(j) planning and management of minor water bodies in the Scheduled Areas shall be entrusted to Panchayats at the appropriate level;

(k) the recommendations of the Gram Sabha or the Panchayats at the appropriate level shall be made mandatory prior to grant of prospecting licence or mining lease for minor minerals in the Scheduled Areas;

(l) the prior recommendation of the Gram Sabha or the Panchayats at the appropriate level shall be made mandatory for grant of concession for the exploitation of minor minerals by auction;

(m) while endowing Panchayats in the Scheduled Areas with such powers and authority as may be necessary to enable them to function as institutions of self-government, a State Legislature shall ensure that the Panchayats at the appropriate level and the Gram Sabha are endowed specifically with—

i) the power to enforce prohibition or to regulate or restrict the sale and consumption of any intoxicant;

ii) the ownership of minor forest produce;

iii) the power to prevent alienation of land in the Scheduled Areas and to take appropriate action to restore any unlawfully alienated land of a Scheduled Tribe;

iv) the power to manage village markets by whatever name called;

v) the power to exercise control over money lending to the Scheduled Tribes;

vi) the power to exercise control over institutions and functionaries in all social sectors;

vii) the power to control over local plans and resources for such plans including tribal sub- plans;

(n) the State legislations that may endow Panchayats with powers and authority as may be necessary to enable them to function as institutions of self-government shall contain safeguards to ensure that Panchayats at the higher level do not assume the powers and authority of any Panchayat at the lower level or of the Gram Sabha;

(o) the State Legislature shall endeavour to follow the pattern of the Sixth Schedule to the Constitution while designing the administrative arrangements in the Panchayats at district levels in the Scheduled Areas.

5. **Continuance of existing laws and Panchayats.** — Notwithstanding anything in Part IX of the Constitution with exceptions and modifications made by this Act, any provision of any law relating to Panchayats in force in the Scheduled Areas immediately before the date on which this Act receives the assent of the President which is inconsistent with the provisions of Part IX with such exceptions and modifications shall continue to be in force until amended or repealed by a competent Legislature or other competent authority or until the expiration of one year from the date on which this Act receives the assent of the President:

Provided that all the Panchayats existing immediately before such date shall continue till the expiration of their duration unless sooner dissolved by a resolution passed to that effect by the Legislative Assembly of that State or, in the case of a State having Legislative Council, by each House of the Legislature of that State.

APPENDIX-VIII

The Constitution (Seventy-third Amendment) Act, 1992

Statement of Objects and Reasons appended to the Constitution (Seventy-second Amendment) Bill, 1991 which was enacted as the Constitution (Seventy-third Amendment) Act, 1992

Statement of Objects and Reasons

1. Though the Panchayati Raj Institutions have been in existence for a long time, it has been observed that these institutions have not been able to acquire the status and dignity of viable and responsive people's bodies due to a number of reasons including absence of regular elections, prolonged supersession, insufficient representation of weaker sections like Scheduled Castes, Scheduled Tribes and women, inadequate devolution of powers and lack of financial resources.

2. Article 40 of the Constitution which enshrines one of the Directive Principles of State Policy lays down that the State shall take steps to organise village panchayats and endow them with such powers and authority as may be necessary to enable them to function as units of self-government. In the light of the experience in the last forty years and in view of the short-comings which have been observed, it is considered that there is an imperative need to enshrine in the Constitution certain basic and essential features of Panchayati Raj Institutions to impart certainty, continuity and strength to them.

3. Accordingly, it is proposed to add a new Part relating to Panchayats in the Constitution to provide for among other things, Gram Sabha in a village or group of villages; constitution of Panchayats at village and other level or levels; direct elections to all seats in Panchayats at the village and intermediate level, if any, and to the offices of Chairpersons of Panchayats at such levels; reservation of seats for the Scheduled Castes and Scheduled Tribes in proportion to their population for membership of Panchayats and office of Chairpersons in Panchayats at each level; reservation of not less than one-third of the seats for women; fixing tenure of 5 years for Panchayats and holding elections within a period of 6 months in the event of supersession of any Panchayat; disqualifications for membership of Panchayats; devolution by the State Legislature of powers and responsibilities upon the Panchayats with respect to the preparation of plans for economic developments and social justice and for the implementation of development schemes; sound finance of the Panchayats by securing authorisation from State Legislatures for grants-in-aid to the Panchayats from the Consolidated Fund of the State, as also assignment to, or appropriation by, the Panchayats of the revenues of designated taxes, duties, tolls and fees; setting up of a Finance Commission within one year of the proposed amendment and thereafter every 5 years to review the financial position of Panchayats; auditing of accounts of the Panchayats; powers of State Legislatures to make provisions with respect to elections to Panchayats under the superintendence, direction and control of the chief electoral officer of the State; application of the provisions of the said Part to Union territories; excluding certain States and areas from the application of the provisions of the said Part; continuance of existing laws and Panchayats until one year from the commencement of the proposed amendment and barring interference by courts in electoral matters relating to Panchayats.
4. The Bill seeks to achieve the aforesaid objectives.

The Constitution (Seventy-third Amendment) Act, 1992 [20th April, 1993.]

An Act further to amend the Constitution of India.

BE it enacted by Parliament in the Forty-third Year of the Republic of India as follows:-

1. Short title and commencement.-

(1) This Act may be called the Constitution (Seventy-third Amendment) Act, 1992.

(2) It shall come into force on such date_680 as the Central Government may, by notification in the Official Gazette, appoint.

2. Insertion of new Part IX.- After Part VIII of the Constitution, the following Part shall be inserted, namely:-

'Part-IX : The Panchayats

243. Definitions.- In this Part, unless the context otherwise requires,-

(a) "district" means a district in a State;

(b) "Gram Sabha" means a body consisting of persons registered in the electoral rolls relating to a village comprised within the area of Panchayat at the village level;

(c) "Intermediate level" means a level between the village and district levels specified by the Governor of a State by public notification to be the intermediate level for the purposes of this Part;

(d) "Panchayat" means an institution (by whatever name called) of self-government constituted under Article 243B, for the rural areas;

(e) "Panchayat area" means the territorial area of a Panchayat;

(f) "population" means the population as ascertained at the last preceding census of which the relevant figures have been published;

(g) "village" means a village specified by the Governor by public notification to be a village for the purposes of this Part and includes a group of villages so specified.

243A. Gram Sabha.- A Gram Sabha may exercise such powers and perform such functions at the village level as the Legislature of a State may, by law, provide.

243B. Constitution of Panchayats.-

(1) There shall be constituted in every State, Panchayats at the village, intermediate and district levels in accordance with the provisions of this Part.

(2) Notwithstanding anything in clause (1), Panchayats at the intermediate level may not be constituted in a State having a population not exceeding twenty lakhs.

243C. Composition of Panchayats.-

(1) Subject to the provisions of this Part, the Legislature of a State may, by law, make provisions with respect to the composition of Pancayats:

Provided that the ratio between the population of the territorial area of a Panchayat at any level and the number of seats in such Panchayat to be filled by election shall, so far as practicable, be the same throughout the State.

(2) All the seats in a Panchayat shall be filled by persons chosen by direct election from territorial constituencies in the Panchayat area and; for this purpose, each Panchayat area shall be divided into territorial constituencies in such manner that the ratio between the population of each constituency and the number of seats allotted to it shall, so far as practicable, be the same throughout the Panchayat area.

(3) The Legislature of a State may, by law, provide for the representation-

(a) of the Chairpersons of the Panchayats at the village level, in the Panchayats at the intermediate level or, in the case of a State not having Panchayats at the intermediate level, in the Pancayats at the district level;

(b) of the Chairpersons of the Panchayats at the intermediate level, in the Panchayats at the district level;

(c) of the members of the House of the People and the members of the Legislative Assembly of the State representing constituencies which comprise wholly or partly a Panchayat area at a level other than the village level, in such Panchayat;

(d) of the members of the Council of States and the members of the Legislative Council of the State, where they are registered as electors within-

(i) a Panchayat area at the intermediate level, in Panchayat at the intermediate level;

(ii) a Panchayat area at the district level, in Panchayat at the district level.

(4) The Chairperson of a Panchayat and other members of a Panchayat whether or not chosen by direct election from territorial constituencies in the Panchayat area shall have the right to vote in the meetings of the Panchayats.

(5) The Chairperson of -

(a) a Panchayat at the village level shall be elected in such manner as the Legislature of a State may, by law, provide; and

(b) a Panchayat at the intermediate level or district level shall be elected by, and from amongst, the elected members thereof.

243D. Reservation of seats.-

(1) Seats shall be reserved for-

(a) the Scheduled Castes; and

(b) the Scheduled Tribes, in every Panchayat and the number of seats of reserved shall bear, as nearly as may be, the same proportion to the total number of seats to be filled by direct election in that Panchayat as the population of the Scheduled Castes in that Panchayat area or of the Scheduled Tribes in that Panchayat area bears to the total population of that area and such seats may be allotted by rotation to different constituencies in a Panchayat.

(2) Not less than one-third of the total number of seats reserved under clause (1) shall be reserved for women belonging to the Scheduled Castes or, as the case may be, the Scheduled Tribes.

(3) Not less than one-third (including the number of seats reserved for women belonging to the Scheduled Castes and the Scheduled Tribes) of the total number of seats to be filled by direct election in every Panchayat shall be reserved for women and such seats may be allotted by rotation to different constituencies in a Panchayat.

(4) The offices of the Chairpersons in the Panchayats at the village or any other level shall be reserved for the Scheduled Castes, the Scheduled Tribes and women in such manner as the Legislature of a State may, by law, provide:

Provided that the number of offices of Chairpersons reserved for the Scheduled Castes and the Scheduled Tribes in the Panchayats at each level in any State shall bear, as nearly as may be, the same proportion to the total number of such offices in the Panchayats at each level as the population of the Scheduled Castes in the State or of the Scheduled Tribes in the State bears to the total population of the State:

Provided further that not less than one-third of the total number of offices of Chairpersons in the Panchayats at each level shall be reserved for women:

Provided also that the number of offices reserved under this clause shall be allotted by rotation to different Panchayats at each level.

(5) The reservation of seats under clauses (1) and (2) and the reservation of offices of Chairpersons (other than the reservation for women) under clause (4) shall cease to have effect on the expiration of the period specified in Article 334.

(6) Nothing in this Part shall prevent the Legislature of a State from making any provision for reservation of seats in any Panchayat or offices of Chairpersons in the Panchayats at any level in favour of backward class of citizens.

243E. Duration of Panchayats, etc.-

(1) Every Panchayat, unless sooner dissolved under any law for the time being in force, shall continue for five years from the date appointed for its first meeting and no longer.

(2) No amendment of any law for the time being in force shall have the effect of causing dissolution of a Panchayat at any level, which is functioning immediately before such amendment, till the expiration of its duration specified in clause (1).

(3) An election to constitute a Panchayat shall be completed-

(a) before the expiry of its duration specified in clause (1);

(b) before the expiration of a period of six months from the date of its dissolution:

Provided that where the remainder of the period for which the dissolved Panchayat would have continued is less than six months, it shall not be necessary to hold any election under this clause for constituting the Panchayat for such period.

(4) A Panchayat constituted upon the dissolution of a Panchayat before the expiration of its duration shall continue only for the remainder of the period for which the dissolved Panchayat would have continued under clause (1) had it not been so dissolved.

243F. Disqualifications for membership.-

(1) A person shall be disqualified for being chosen as, and for being, a member of a Panchayat-

(a) if he is so disqualified by or under any law for the time being in force for the purposes of elections to the Legislature of the State concerned:

Provided that no person shall be disqualified on the ground that he is less than twenty-five years of age, if he has attained the age of twenty-one years;

(b) if he is so disqualified by or under any law made by the Legislature of the State.

(2) If any question arises as to whether a member of a Panchayat has become subject to any of the disqualifications mentioned in clause (1), the question shall be referred for the decision of such authority and in such manner as the Legislature of a State may, by law, provide.

243G. Powers, authority and responsibilities of Panchayats.- Subject to the provisions of this Constitution, the Legislature of a State may, by law, endow the Panchayats with such powers and authority as may be necessary to enable them to function as institutions of self-government and such law may contain provisions for the devolution of powers and responsibilities upon Panchayats at the appropriate level, subject to such conditions as may be specified therein, with respect to-

(a) the preparation of plans for economic development and social justice;

(b) the implementation of schemes for economic development and social justice as may be entrusted to them including those in relation to the matters listed in the Eleventh Schedule.

243H. Powers to impose taxes by, and Funds of, the Panchayats.-The Legislature of a State may, by law,-

(a) authorise a Panchayat to levy, collect and appropriate such taxes, duties, tolls and fees in accordance with such procedure and subject to such limits;

(b) assign to a Panchayat such taxes, duties, tolls and fees levied and collected by the State Government for such purposes and subject to such conditions and limits;

(c) provide for making such grants-in-aid to the Panchayats from the Consolidated Fund of the State; and

(d) provide for Constitution of such Funds for crediting all moneys received, respectively, by or on behalf of the Panchayats and also for the withdrawal of such moneys therefrom, as may be specified in the law.

243-I. Constitution of Finance Commission to review financial position.-

(1) The Governor of a State shall, as soon as may be within one year from the commencement of the Constitution (Seventy-third Amendment) Act, 1992, and thereafter at the expiration of every fifth year, constitute a Finance Commission to review the financial position of the Panchayats and to make recommendations to the Governor as to-

(a) the principles which should govern-

(i) the distribution between the State and the Panchayats of the net proceeds of the taxes, duties, tolls and fees leviable by the State, which may be divided between them under this Part and the allocation between the Panchayats at all levels of their respective shares of such proceeds;

(ii) the determination of the taxes, duties, tolls and fees which may be assigned to, or appropriated by, the Panchayat;

(iii) the grants-in-aid to the Panchayats from the Consolidated Fund of the State;

(b) the measures needed to improve the financial position of the Panchayats;

(c) any other matter referred to the Finance Commission by the Governor in the interests of sound finance of the Panchayats.

(2) The Legislature of a State may, by law, provide for the composition of the commission, the qualifications which shall be requisite for appointment as members thereof and the manner in which they shall be selected.

(3) The Commission shall determine their procedure and shall have such powers in the performance of their functions as the Legislature of the State may, by law, confer on them.

(4) The Governor shall cause every recommendation made by the Commission under this Article together with an explanatory memorandum as to the action taken thereon to be laid before the Legislature of the State.

243J. Audit of accounts of Panchayats.- The Legislature of a State may, by law, make provisions with respect to the maintenance of accounts by the Panchayats and the auditing of such accounts.

243K. Elections to the Panchayats.-

(1) The superintendence, direction and control of the preparation of electoral rolls for, and the conduct of, all elections to the Panchayats shall be vested in a State Election Commission consisting of a State Election Commissioner to be appointed by the Governor.

(2) Subject to the provisions of any law made by the Legislature of a State, the conditions of service and tenure of office of the State Election Commissioner shall be such as the Governor may by rule determine:

Provided that the State Election Commissioner shall not be removed from his office except in like manner and on the like grounds as a Judge of a High Court and the conditions of service of the State Election Commissioner shall not be varied to his disadvantage after his appointment.

(3) The Governor of a State shall, when so requested by the State Election Commission, make available to the State Election Commission such staff as may be necessary for the discharge of the functions conferred on the State Election Commission by clause (1).

(4) Subject to the provisions of this Constitution, the Legislature of a State may, by law, make provision with respect to all matters relating to, or in connection with, elections to the Panchayats.

243L. Application to Union territories.-The provisions of this Part shall apply to the Union territories and shall, in their application to a Union territory, have effect as if the references to the Governor of a State were references to the Administrator of the Union territory appointed under Article 239 and references to the Legislature or the Legislative Assembly of a State were references, in relation to a Union territory having a Legislative Assembly, to that Legislative Assembly:

Provided that the President may, by public notification, direct that the provisions of this Part shall apply to any Union territory or part thereof subject to such exceptions and modifications as he may specify in the notification.

243M. Part not to apply to certain areas.-

(1) Nothing in this Part shall apply to the Scheduled Areas referred to in clause (1), and the tribal areas referred to in clause (2), of Article 244.

(2) Nothing in this Part shall apply to-

(a) the States of Nagaland, Meghalaya and Mizoram;

(b) the Hill Areas in the State of Manipur for which District Councils exist under any law for the time being in force.

(3) Nothing in this Part-

(a) relating to Panchayats at the district level shall apply to the hill areas of the District of Darjeeling in the State of West Bengal for which Darjeeling Gorkha Hill Council exists under any law for the time being in force;

(b) shall be construed to affect the functions and powers of the Darjeeling Gorkha Hill Council constituted under such law.

(4) Notwithstanding anything in this Constitution,-

(a) the Legislature of a State referred to in sub-clause (a) of clause (2) may, by law, extend this Part to that State, except the areas, if any, referred to in clause (1), if the Legislative Assembly of that State passes a resolution to that effect by a majority of the total membership of that House and by a majority of not less than two-thirds of the members of that House present and voting;

(b) Parliament may, by law, extend the provisions of this Part to the Scheduled Areas and the tribal areas referred to in clause (1) subject to such exceptions and modifications as may be specified in such law, and no such law shall be deemed to be an amendment of this Constitution for the purposes of Article 368.

243N. Continuance of existing laws and Panchayats.-Notwithstanding anything in this Part, any provision of any law relating to Panchayats in force in a State immediately before the commencement of the Constitution (Seventy-third Amendment) Act, 1992, which is inconsistent with the provisions of this Part, shall continue to be in force until amended or repealed by a competent Legislature or other competent authority or until the expiration of one year from such commencement, whichever is earlier:

Provided that all the Panchayats existing immediately before such commencement shall continue till the expiration of their duration, unless sooner dissolved by a resolution passed to that effect by the Legislative Assembly of that State or, in the case of a State having a Legislative Council, by each House of the Legislature of that State.

243-O. Bar to interference by courts in electoral matters.- Notwithstanding anything in this Constitution,-

(a) the validity of any law relating to the delimitation of constituencies or the allotment of seats to such constituencies, made or purporting to be made under Article 243K, shall not be called in question in any court;

(b) no election to any Panchayat shall be called in question except by an election petition presented to such authority and in such manner as is provided for by or under any law made by the Legislature of a State.'.

Constitution, after sub-clause (b), the following sub-clause shall be inserted, namely:-

"(bb) the measures needed to augment the Consolidated Fund of a State to supplement the resources of the Panchayats in the State on the basis of the recommendations made by the Finance Commission of the State;".

Constitution, the following Schedule shall be added, namely:-

"Eleventh Schedule (Article 243G)

1. Agriculture, including agricultural extension.
2. Land improvement, implementation of land reforms, land consolidation and soil conservation.
3. Minor irrigation, water management and watershed development.
4. Animal husbandry, dairying and poultry.
5. Fisheries.
6. Social forestry and farm forestry.
7. Minor forest produce.
8. Small scale industries, including food processing industries.
9. Khadi, village and cottage industries.
10. Rural housing.
11. Drinking water.
12. Fuel and fodder.
13. Roads, culverts, bridges, ferries, waterways and other means of communication.
14. Rural electrification, including distribution of electricity.
15. Non-conventional energy sources.
16. Poverty alleviation programme.
17. Education, including primary and secondary schools.
18. Technical training and vocational education.
19. Adult and non-formal education.
20. Libraries.
21. Cultural activities.
22. Markets and fairs.
23. Health and sanitation, including hospitals, primary health centres and dispensaries.
24. Family welfare.
25. Women and child development.
26. Social welfare, including welfare of the handicapped and mentally retarded.

27. Welfare of the weaker sections, and in particular, of the Scheduled Castes and the Scheduled Tribes.
28. Public distribution system.
29. Maintenance of community assets."

Bibliography

Andhra Pradesh Panchayat Samitis and Zila Samitis Act, 1959

Aparna Mitra (2007); The Status of Women among the Scheduled Tribes in India. The Journal of Socio-economics. 2007. p.1-16.

Arnab Sen and Esther Lalhrietpui (2006); Scheduled Tribes (Recognition of Forest Rights) Bill: A View from Anthropology and Call for Dialogue. Economic & Political Weekly. September 30, 2006. p.4205-4210.

Article - 244 V and VI Schedule

Aslam, M (2007); Panchayati Raj in India, National Book Trust.

Aslam, M. (2011); Article on "Empowering Gram Sabha: Heart and Soul of Panchayati Raj System in India" (The Grassroots Governance Journal, Vol. IX No-2 July-December 2011, Published by Academy of Grassroots Studies and Research of India, Tirupati, Andhra Pradesh,

Asrani, Shalini and Kaushik, Sushma (2011); Problems Perceived by Scheduled Caste Women in Haryana. Studies of Tribes and Tribal's. Vol. 9. No. 1. 2011. p.29-36.

Aureliano Fernandes (2003); 'Aggrandiser Government and Local Governance'. Economic and Political Weekly, July 5, p.2873.

Axel Hadenius (2003); Decentralisation and Democratic Governance: Experiences from India, Bolivia and South Africa, Elanders Gotab, Stockholm.

Bakshi, P.M. (2007); Constitution of India, Universal Law company, New Delhi

Balakrishnan, P (2010); Economic Growth in India. History and Prospect. Oxford University Press.

Baldev Singh (1996); "Decentralization : Panchayati Raj and District Planning", New Delhi, Atlantic Publishers, p.25

Banerjee, Rahul (2013); 'What Ails Panchayati Raj?'; Economic and Political Weekly, Volume XLVIII, No. 30 (Jul. 27), p.173.

Bardhan, P. and Dilip Mookherjee (2006); 'The Rise of Local Governments: An Overview', in: Pranab Bardhan and Dilip Mookherjee (eds.) Decentralization and Local Governance in Developing Countries, (London: The MIT Press)

Barthakur, R. and I. Khurana (eds) (2015); Reflections on Managing Water: Earth's Greatest Natural Resource. Balipara Foundation.

Bhasin, Veena (2007); Status of Tribal Women in India. Studies on Home and Community Science. Vol. 1. No. 1. 2007. p.1-16.

Bijoy, C.R. (2012); Policy brief on Panchayat Raj (Extension to Scheduled Areas) Act of 1996. Delhi: UNDP

Billava, Narayan; Nayak, Nayanatara (2016); "Empowerment of Women Representatives in Panchayat Raj Institutions: A Thematic Review". Journal of Politics and Governance, 5(4).

Bose, N. K. (1996); The Structure of Hindu Society, Orient Longman Limited, New Delhi.

Buse, K. and S. Hawkes(2015); "Health in the Sustainable Development Goals: Ready for a Paradigm Shift?" Globalization and Health, p.11-13.

Chakravarty, S. (1991); "Development Planning: A Reappraisal," Cambridge Journal of Economics.

Chandrasekhar, K. M. (30th October 2017); "Agenda for 15th Finance Commission". Business Standard.

Chatterjee, Biswajit (1988); Decentralized Planning in India-Conceptual Issues and Policy Options, IEA Conference Volume 1988, Calcutta.

Chaudhuri, Shubham(2006); 'What Difference Does a Constitutional Amendment Make? The 1994 Panchayati Raj Act and the Attempt to Revitalize Rural Local Government in India', in Pranab Bardhan and Dilip Mookherjee (eds.) Decentralization and Local Governance in Developing Countries, (London: The MIT Press)

Choubey, K.N. (2014); The Forest Rights Act and the politics of marginal society. NMML Occasional Paper: Perspectives in Indian Development, New Series 31, Nehru Memorial Museum and Library

Choubey, K.N. (2015); Enhancing PESA: The unfinished agenda. Economic and Political Weekly, 50(8), p.21-23

Choudhary, R.C. & Jain, S.P. (1999); Strengthening Village Democracy (Proceedings of National Conference on Gram Sabha). Hyderabad, National Institute of Rural Development.

Constitution of India (4th Ed.) (2008); Allahabad: Central Law Publications

Cottrell, Allin; Cockshott, W. Paul (1993); Towards a New Socialism (Nottingham, England: Spokesman.

Crook, Richard and James Manor (1995); 'Democratic Decentralization and Institutional Performance: Four Asian and African Experiences Compared', Journal of Commonwealth & Comparative Politics, Volume 33, No. 3, p.309-334 (Frank Cass: London).

Dandekar, A., Choudhury, C. (2010); PESA, Left-wing extremism and governance concerns and challenges in India's tribal districts; Institute of Rural Management Anand.

Das, Sanjay Kanti (2012); An Analysis of Constraints in Women Empowerment in Tribal Area: Evidences from Assam. Asian Journal of Research in Social Sciences and Humanities. Vol. 2. No. 4. April 2012. p.61-74.

Dasgupta, P., and R. Dasgupta (2015); "Immunization Coverage in India: An Urban Conundrum" in Economic and Political Weekly, May 23, Vol. I. No. 21.

Dash, S.N. (2001); A study of the Problem of Land Alienation in Tribal Areas with Special Reference to the District of Koraput, Utkal University, Bhubaneswar.

Debjani Roy (2012); Socio-economic Status of Scheduled Tribes in Jharkhand. Indian Journal of Spatial Science. Vol. 3. No. 2. Winter 2012. p.26-34.

Development Alternatives (2016); Tracking the Global Goals in India.

Dwivedi, R. & Poddar, K.M. (2013); Functioning of Panchayati Raj Institutions in India: A Journal of Management Sciences. 3(2), 1-21.

Dwivedi, Ritesh; Poddar, Krishna (1st December 2013); "Functioning of Panchayati Raj Institutions in India: A Status Paper". Adhyayan. 3 (2).

Effective Gram Sabha implementation Guidelines- MoPR

FAO (2014); The State of Food Security in the World. Food and Agriculture Organization of the United Nations (FAO), Rome.

Freenstra R.C and G.Hanson(1997); "Foreign Direct Investment and Relative Wages: Evidence from Mexico's Maquiladoras." Journal of International Economics, 42(3-4): p, 371-393.

Galor, O. and J. Zeira (1993); "Income Distribution and Macroeconomics." Review of Economic Studies, 60(1): p, 35- 52.

Gannon, C. and Z. Liu (1997); "Poverty and Transport." Mimeo, The World Bank.

Geeta and Sanjay Misra (2016); Panchayat Raj Institution in India: Prospects and Retrospections, published on March.

Gershberg, Alec Ian (1998); "Decentralisation, Recentralisation and Performance Accountability: Building an Operationally Useful Framework for Analysis", Development Policy Review, 16 (4): p.405-431.

Ghodase, Sanjay B (2013); Women Development in Geographical Perspective: A Case Study of Tribal Women in Dhule Tehsil (Dist: Dhule, Maharashtra). Golden Research Thoughts. Vol. 2. No. 7. January 2013.

Ghosh, Ratna and Alok, Kumar, Pramanik(2007); Panchayat System in India. New Delhi, Kanishka Publishers.

Goals (SDGS). Journal of Rural Development Review, 2(2).

GOI, Planning Commission (1986); Report of the Study Group on Land Holding Systems in Tribal Areas. New Delhi, Planning Commission

Government of India (1985); Report of the Committee to Review the Existing Administrative Arrangements for Rural Development and Poverty Alleviation Programmes (CAARD) Department of Rural Development, New Delhi, p.17.

Government of India (2015); Millennium Development Goals: India Country Report.

Government of India (2015); Post-2015 Development Agenda; National Consultation Report.

Government of India (GoI) . (1996); The provisions of Panchayats (Extension to the Scheduled Areas) Act, 1996, No 40 of 1996. Delhi: Ministry of Rural Development.

Government of India (GoI). (2007); Scheduled Tribes and Other Traditional Forest Dwellers (Recognition of Forest Rights) Act 2006. New Delhi: Ministry of Law and Justice.

Government of India, Ministry of Health and Family Welfare (2016); National Family Health Survey-4, 2015 -16.

Government of India, Ministry of Home Afairs.(1961); Report of the Commission on Scheduled Areas and Scheduled Tribes, New Delhi.

Government of India. "Energy Statistics-2014"; Ministry of Statistics and Programme Implementation.

Greenwood, J. and B. Jovanovich (1990); "Financial Development, Growth, and the Distribution of Income." Journal of Political Economy, 98(5), 1076-1107.

Hanson, E. Mark (1998); Strategies of Educational Decentralization: Key Questions and Core Issues. Journal of Educational Administration, 36 (2): p.111-128.

Hanson, G.H (2003); "What Has Happened to Wages in Mexico since NAFTA? Implications for Hemispheric Free Trade." NBER Working Paper No. 9563.

Hardgrave, Robert L. & Kochanek, Stanley A. (2008); India: Government and Politics in a Developing Nation (seventh ed.). Boston, Massachusetts

Hazarika, Sujata D (2006); 'Political Participation of Women and the Dilectics of 73rd Amendment'. The Indian Journal of Political Science, Vol. 67, No.2 (April- June), p.245-260.

Higgins, M. and J.G. Williamson (1999); "Explaining Inequality the World Round: Cohort Size, Kuznets Curves, and Openness." NBER Working Paper No. 7224.

Hooda, Shailender Kumar (2015); "Determinants of Public Expenditure on Health in India: The Panel Data Estimates." Working Paper 177. Institute for Studies in Industrial Development.

James, K. S., A. Pandey, D. W. Bansod and L. Subaiya (eds) (2010); Population, Gender and Health in India. New Delhi: Academic Foundation.

Jean-Paul Faguet (2012); Decentralization and Popular Democracy: Governance from Below in Bolivia, University of Michigan Press.

Joseph, T.M. (2007); Local Governance in India, ideas challenges and Strategies, Concept Publishing company, New Delhi,.

Joshi, R. P. (1998); Constitutionalization of Panchayati Raj- A Reassessment. Jaipur and New Delhi, Rawat Publications..

Joshi, R.P. and Narwani, G.S. (2002); Panchayat Raj in India - Emerging Trends across States. Jaipur and New Delhi, Rawat Publications..

Joumard, I and A. Kumar (2015); "Improving Health Outcomes and Health Care on India." Economics Department Working Papers No. 1184, OECD.

Kalam, APJ and S. P. Singh (2015); Advantage India from Challenge to Opportunity. Harper Collins Publishers India.

Kar, S. (2017); Grama Panchayats and Sustainable Development

Karat, P. (2010, January-March); On democratic. The Marxist, 26(1), 3-20.

Kumar, D & Singh, B. K. (2018); Training needs assessment of Gram Panchayat mukhiya regarding health and family welfare programmes in Bihar state. International Journal for Advance Research and Development, 3(7), 9-16.

Kumar, U. and A. Subramanian (2011); "India's Economic Growth in the 2000s: Four Facts", Working Paper, November. Pietersen Institute for International Economics.

Kuznets, S (1955); "Economic Growth and Income Inequality." American Economic Review, 45(1), p, 1-28.

Kuznets, S. (1963) "Quantitative Aspects of the Economic Growth of Nations: VIII. Distribution of Income by Size." Economic Development and Cultural Change, 11 (2), p, 1-80.

Lele, M. K. (2001, December 22-28); Local Government: Conflicts of interests and issues of legitimization; Economic & Political Weekly, 36(51), 4702-4704.

Mahipal (2008); Decentralized Planning and Development in India", New Delhi, Mittal Publications, p.16-17.

Mathew, G. (2013); Status of Panchayati Raj in the states and union territories of India. (p.4). New Delhi: Institute of Social Sciences and Concept Publishing Company.

Mathur, K. (2013); Panchayati Raj (p.4). New Delhi: Oxford University Press

Mathur, P.C., Rakesh Hooja(1996);"Projects, Planning and Development Administration, Jaipur, Rawat Publications, p.108-109.

Mazumdar, I. and N. Neetha (2011); "Gender Dimensions: Employment Trends in India, 1993-94 to 2009-10". Economic and Political Weekly, Vol. 46, No. 43, 22nd October.

Mearns, Robin and Saurav Sinha. (1998); Social Exclusion and Land Administration in Odisha, India. Washington, World Bank

Mehrotra, S. and E. Delamonica(2007); Eliminating Human Poverty. Macro-economic and Social Policies for Equitable Growth. London: Zed Press

Meshram, Mahendrakumar and Nandapurkar, VJ (2012); Educational Development of Scheduled Caste and Scheduled Tribe. Indian Streams Research Journal. Vol. 2. No. 6.

Ministry of Law and Justice, Government of India(December ,2007), The Constitution of India,

Ministry of P R, Government of India (2018); Guidelines for preparation of GPDP-2018.

Ministry of Panchayati Raj, Government of India(2017);Report of the NITI Aayog to Restructure the Existing Scheme of the Ministry of Panchayati Raj as Rashtriya Gram Swaraj Abhiyan,.

Ministry of Panchayati Raj, Government of India, (October, 2014); Governance in GPs, Active Panchayat Book-III.

Ministry of Panchayati Raj, Government of India, Annual Report 2009-10, 2010-11 and State of Panchayati Raj Report, 2006-07, 2007-08 (2010)

Ministry of Panchayati Raj, Government of India, B.N. Yugandhar Committee Report (2003)

Ministry of Panchayati Raj, Government of India, Report of the B.D. Sharma Sub-Committee (2006)

Ministry of Panchayati Raj, Government of India,(2014); National Capability Building Framework,.

Mitra, Subrata K (2001); "Making Local Government Work: Local elites, Panchayati raj and governance in India", Cambridge University Press.

Mitra, Subrata K.; Singh, V.B. (1999); Democracy and Social Change in India: A Cross-Sectional Analysis of the National Electorate. New Delhi: Sage Publications.

Mondal, Ajit and Mete, Jayanta (2012); Tribal Development in India: Educational Perspective. Indian Streams Research Journal. Vol. 2. No. 11. December 2012.

MoPR Amendments in the Sixth Schedule

MoPR Amendments to Article-243 of the Constitution for Strengthening the Local Governance

MoPR Amendments to PESA

MoPR Model Rules for PESA

MoPR PESA Guidelines 21st May 2010

Naganahalli, Vidyadhar S (2013); Tribal Women in India. Indian Streams Research Journal. Vol. 3. No. 1. February 2013.

Niju, P (2013); Land Alienation: Challenges before Kerala Tribal's. Golden Research Thoughts. Vol. 3. No. 1. July 2013.

Nonkynrih, AK (2010); Scheduled Tribes and the Census: A Sociological Inquiry. Economic & Political Weekly. Vol. 45. No. 9. May 8, 2010. p.43-47.

Nzouankeu (1994); Discussion on "The relationship between Decentralization and Democracy".

Pal, M. (2004, January 10-16); Panchayati Raj and rural governance: Experiences of a decade. Economic & Political Weekly, 39(2), p.139.

Palanithurai, Ganapathi (ed.) (2002) Dynamics of New Panchayati Raj System in India: Concept Publishing Company, New Delhi, volumes, volume-1.

Panda, G.R. and N. Jena (2012); "Evaluating the Performance of the National Clean Energy Fund." Economic and Political Weekly, 47 (37), p, 18-21.

Pandey, B.(1998); Depriving the underprivileged for development, 1st Edn. Institute for Socio-Economic Development, Bhubaneswar.

Pandey, J.N (2013); The Constitution of India, Central Law Agency, 50th Edition.

Pargal, S. and S.G. Banerjee (2014); "More Power to India: The challenges of Electricity Distribution." Directions in Development, Energy and Mining, World Bank.

Pathania, Raj, et al. (2007); Gender Differentials in Participation of Tribal Adolescents in Various Activities. Studies of Tribes and Tribal's. Vol. 5. No. 1. 2007. p.1-4.

Phansalkar, S J and Verma S (2004); Improving Water Control as a Strategy for Enhancing Tribal Livelihoods. Economic and Political Weekly. July 31, 2004

Planning Commission (2013); The Twelfth Five Year Plan: Towards Faster, Inclusive and More Sustainable Growth. New Delhi: Sage Publications.

Prakash Louis (2003); Scheduled Castes and Tribes: The Reservation Debate. Economic & Political Weekly. June 21, 2003. p.2475-2478.

Prasad, Nageshwar (1984); Decentralisation in Historical Perspective, Gandhian Institute of Studies, Varanasi.

Raju, M.R. (1998); Panchayati Raj in Kerala: problems and prospects. Kurukshetra, April, 70-71.

Rangarajan, C., Padma Iyer, and S. Kaul (2011); "Where is the Missing Labour Force". Economic and Political Weekly, Vol. 46, No. 39, p, 24-30 September.

Rao, Hanumantha C.H. (1989); Decentralised Planning: An overview of Experience and Prospects in India, Man and Development, Vol. XI, No. 3, p.17.

Rao,V.M (1991); 'Decentralised Planning: Priority Economic Issues', Deep & Deep Publication, New Delhi, p.21

Rastogi, Anupm (2008); "The Infrastructure Sector in India,2007", Oxford University Press, New Delhi

Raykar N., M. Majumder, R. Laxminarayan and P. Menon (2015); India Health Report: Nutrition 2015. Public Health Foundation of India, New Delhi.

Reddy, G. (2013); Status of decentralized bodies: Post-73rd Amendment scenario. Economic & Political Weekly, 38(12, 13).

Reddy, Nandana and Damodar Acharya (2007); 'Striking at the Roots of Democracy'. Economic and Political Weekly, 5th May , p.1601.

Robinson (2007); Definitions on decentralization, p.7.

Rondinelli, Dennis, et al (1983); 'Decentralization in Developing Countries'. World Bank Staff Working Papers Number 581, Management and Development Series Number 8 (World Bank: Washington).

Sanyal, B.M. (2001); "India : Decentralised Planning Themes and Issues", New Delhi, Concept Publishing, p.9-10.

Sapra, Ipsita (February 2013); "Living in the villages". Rural Democracy.

Sarma, A., & Chakravarty, D (2018); Two Decades of the Panchayati Raj. In Integrating the Third Tier in the Indian Federal System (p, 83-121). Palgrave Macmillan, Singapore

Seetharam, Mukkavilli (1st January 1990); Citizen Participation in Rural Development. Mittal Publications. p.34

Sen, Amartya (2000); Development as Freedom. Oxford University Press.

Sharma, A., & Chakravarty, D. (2018); Two Decades of the Panchayati Raj. In Integrating the Third Tier in the Indian Federal System (p.83-121). Palgrave Macmillan, Singapore.

Sharma, B.D. (2010); Unbroken history of broken promises: Indian state and the tribal people. New Delhi: Freedom Press and Sahyog Pustak Kuteer.

Shastry, V.N.V.K, et al. (1991);.Evolution of Scheduled areas and changes in Muttadari System in Andhra area (1724-1970). Tribal Welfare Department, Hyderabad.

Shinde, Jitendra Subhash (2012); Educational Situation of Tribal Community: A Study. Golden Research Thoughts. Vol. 2. No. 3. September 2012.

Singh, H (1994); Constitutional base for Panchayati Raj in India: The 73rd Amendment Act. Asian Survey, 34(9).

Singh, R. (2009); Unfinished agenda of Gandhi's Gram Swaraj: Fifty years of Panchayati Raj. Mainstream, 46(43).

Singh, Vijandra (2003); "Panchayati Raj and Gandhi". Panchayati Raj and Village Development: Volume 3: Sarup & Sons. p.84-90. .

Singhal, Vipin (2015); "Dynamics of Panchayati Raj Institutions - Problems and Prospects". Rochester, NY.

Sisodia, R. S (1971); "Gandhiji's Vision of Panchayati Raj". Panchayat aur Insan. 3 (2): 9-10.

Sisodia, Yatindra Singh (2005); Functioning of Panchayat Raj System. Jaipur, Rawat Publications.

Siva Subrahmanyam K & R.C. Chowdhury (2002); Functional and Financial Devolution on Panchayats in India, NIRD, Hyderabad.

Sivarama Krishna K.C (2003); Power to the People: The Politics and Progress of Decentralisation, Konark Publishers, New Delhi.

Sivaramakrishnan, Kallidaikurichi Chidambarakrishnan (2000); Power to the People: The politics and progress of decentralization; Konark Publishers, New Delhi.

Smith, B.C (1985); Decentralisation: the Territorial Dimension of the State; George Allen and Unwin: London.

Srinivas, V. (2018); "The challenges before 15th Finance Commission are many". The Economic Times. Indo-Asian News Service

Srivastava, K.K. (2011); "Decentralized Governance and Panchayati Raj", Delhi, Kalpaz Publications, p.58-59

Srivastava, T.N. (2002);"Local 'Self' Government and the Constitution", 'Economic and Political Weekly'

Stevens, P. and D. Chakraborty (2009); Towards a Healthy Future? Indian and Global Experiences; Book well, New Delhi

Sundar Ram, D (2007); Panchayat Raj Reforms in India: Power to the People at the Grassroots. Kanishka Publishers,.

Sundar Ram. D (2006); Decentralization and Rural Development in India: Empowerment, Strategies and Emerging Challenges, The Grassroots Governance Journal, Vol. IV, No. 1, June.

Sundaram, K., and S.D. Tendulkar (2003b) "Poverty in India in the 1990s: An Analysis of Changes in 15 Major States." Economic and Political Weekly, 38(14), p, 1385-1393.

Swaleha Sindhi (2012); Prospects and Challenges in Empowerment of Tribal Women. IOSR Journal of Humanities and Social Science. Vol. 6. No. 1. November-December 2012. p.46-54.

TERI (2015); TERI Energy and Environment Data Diary and Yearbook 2014-15, Chapter 14, TERI, New Delhi.

Thakur, BR and Sharma, DD (2012): Evaluation of Tribal Development Programmes with Special Reference to Bharmaur Region of Himachal Pradesh. Studies of Tribes and Tribal's. Vol. 10. No. 2. 2012. p.189-194.

The Finance (Miscellaneous Provisions) Act, 1951

The Gazette of India, The Provision of Panchayat (Extension to Scheduled Areas) Act, 1996.

Tiwari, Nupur (2013); "Two Decades of Panchayati Raj as Institutions of Local Self-Governments in India", The Grassroots Governance Journal p.62.

Tsai, P.L (1995); "Foreign Direct Investment and Income Inequality: Further Evidence." World Development, 23(3), p, 469-483.

Uma, S., V. Abraham and K. J. Joseph (2010); "Impact of Trade Liberalization on Employment: The Experience of India's Manufacturing Industries." Indian Journal of Labour Economics, Issue 4: 53(4) p, 587-605.

UN (2015); India and the MDGs: Towards a Sustainable Future for All.

UNDP (2002); Decentralization in India, Challenges and Opportunities, Discussion Paper Series - 1. New Delhi, Human Development Resource Centre,

United Nations (2015); Transforming Our World: The 2030 Agenda for Sustainable Development

Vayunandan E. and Dolly Mathew (ed) (2003) Good Governance: Initiatives in India, Prentice Hall of India Private Limited, New Delhi.

Venkatraman, A. (1989). Proposed constitutional amendment on Panchayati Raj-some reflections. The Indian Journal of Political Science, p.405-406.

Viegas, P. (1991); Encroached and enslaved: alienation of tribal lands and its dynamics, Indian Social Institute, New Delhi.

Water Aid (2013); Drinking Water Quality in Rural India: Issues and Approaches.

World Bank (2002); Overview of Rural Decentralization in India, India, 3 volumes. World Bank.

World Health Organization (2016); World Health Statistics 2016: Monitoring Health for the SDGs, Geneva.

Index